MIGRATION AND REMITTANCES FACTBOOK 2016

MIGRATION AND REMITTANCES

FACTBOOK 2016

3rd Edition

ISBN (paper): 978-1-4648-0319-2
ISBN (electronic): 978-1-4648-0320-8
DOI: 10.1596/978-1-4648-0319-2

Library of Congress Cataloging-in-Publication Data has been applied for.

This is product of the Global Knowledge Partnership on Migration and Development (KNOMAD). A global hub of knowledge and policy expertise on migration and development, KNOMAD aims to create and synthesize multidisciplinary knowledge and evidence; generate a menu of policy options for migration policy makers; and provide technical assistance and capacity building for pilot projects, evaluation of policies, and data collection.

KNOMAD is supported by a multidonor trust fund established by the World Bank. Germany's Federal Ministry of Economic Cooperation and Development (BMZ), Sweden's Ministry of Justice, Migration and Asylum Policy, and the Swiss Agency for Development and Cooperation (SDC) are the contributors to the trust fund.

Contents

List of Figures

Foreword

The number of migrants has risen rapidly in the past few years for various reasons: job opportunities, labor shortages resulting from falling birth rates, internal conflict and war, natural disasters, climate change, and improved access to information through phone and the Internet.

Migrants are now sending earnings back to their families in developing countries at levels above US$441 billion, a figure three times the volume of official aid flows. These inflows of cash constitute more than 10 percent of GDP in some 25 developing countries and lead to increased investments in health, education, and small businesses in various communities. The loss/benefit picture of this reality is twofold: while the migration of highly skilled people from small, poor countries can affect basic service delivery, it can generate numerous benefits, including increased trade, investment, knowledge, and technology transfers from diaspora contributions.

The *Migration and Remittances Factbook 2016* provides a comprehensive picture of emigration, immigration, and remittance flows for 214 countries and territories and 15 country groups, drawing on authoritative, publicly available data. The current edition of the Factbook updates the information in the 2011 edition with data collected from various sources, including national censuses, labor force surveys, and population registers. In addition, for each country and regional grouping from the World Bank's World Development Indicators (World Bank 2015), it provides selected socioeconomic characteristics such as population, labor force, age-dependency ratio, gross national income per capita, and poverty headcount.

More frequent and timely monitoring of migration and remittance trends can provide policy makers, researchers, and the development community with the tools needed to make informed decisions. The Factbook makes an important contribution to this effort by providing the latest available data and facts on migration and remittance trends worldwide in a comprehensive and readily accessible format.

The Factbook is part of a broader effort by the Global Knowledge Partnership on Migration and Development (KNOMAD) to fill the knowledge gaps for monitoring and analyzing migration and remittances from a development perspective.

At the end of the day, development is not just about facts, figures, and economic models. It is about human beings. This Factbook could not be more timely, coming as it does after the Sustainable Development Goals (SDGs) have been finalized. More and better data are needed. The World Bank will continue to work on collecting more data and evidence disaggregated by migratory status, and it will contribute its expertise on migration, remittances, and diaspora matters.

Augusto Lopez-Claros
Director, Development Indicators Group
The World Bank

Acknowledgments

Migration and Remittances Factbook 2016 was compiled by Dilip Ratha, Sonia Plaza, and Ervin Dervisevic. Special thanks to Seyed Reza Yousefi for updating the programs, country profiles, tables, and graphs, and to the research assistants Florencia Paz and Peter Vincze for collecting the data from the censuses and various country sources. The authors gratefully acknowledge the constructive comments and advice given at the various stages of writing this book from Bela Hovy and Pablo Lattes of the UN Population Division, and Supriyo De, Christian Eigen-Zucchi, Kirsten Schuettler, Hanspeter Wyss, and Soonhwa Yi of the World Bank. Neil Fantom, Rakesh Kochhar, and Susan Martin served as peer reviewers, and we thank Augusto Lopez-Claros for his guidance in the final stages of publication.

Production of this volume (including design, editing, and layout) was coordinated by Paola Scalabrin and Susan Graham of External and Corporate Relations, Publishing and Knowledge.

Highlights

Migration and Remittances Factbook 2016 presents numbers and facts behind the stories of international migration and remittances, drawing on authoritative, publicly available data. Some interesting facts:

- More than 247 million people, or 3.4 percent of the world population, live outside their countries of birth. Although the number of international migrants rose from 175 million in 2000 to more than 247 million in 2013 and will surpass 251 million in 2015, the share of migrants has remained just above 3 percent (of world population) for the last fifteen years.

- The top migrant destination country is the United States, followed by Saudi Arabia, Germany, the Russian Federation, the United Arab Emirates, the United Kingdom, France, Canada, Spain, and Australia. The top six immigration countries, relative to population, are outside the high-income OECD countries: Qatar (91 percent), United Arab Emirates (88 percent), Kuwait (72 percent), Jordan (56 percent), and Bahrain (54 percent).

- According to available official data, the Mexico–United States corridor is the largest migration corridor in the world, accounting for 13 million migrants in 2013. Russia–Ukraine is the second largest corridor, followed by Bangladesh–India, and Ukraine–Russia. For the former Soviet Union corridors, many natives became migrants without moving when new international boundaries were drawn.

- The volume of South-South migration stands at 38 percent of the total migrant stock. Migration between the "North" and the "South" follows the United Nations classification. South-South migration is larger than South-North migration, which is about 34 percent.

- Smaller countries tend to have higher rates of skilled emigration. Close to 93 percent of highly skilled persons born in Guyana lived outside that country, followed by Haiti (75.1 percent), Trinidad and Tobago (68.2 percent) and Barbados (66.2 percent).

- Excluding refugees from the West Bank and Gaza, the number of refugees in 2014 was 14.4 million, or 6 percent, of international migrants in 2013. About 86 percent of refugees are hosted by developing countries. Turkey, Pakistan, Lebanon, the Islamic Republic of Iran, Ethiopia, Jordan, Kenya, Chad, and Uganda are the largest host countries. The Syrian Arab Republic was the top source country of refugees in 2014. In Lebanon, refugees made up 35 percent of the population.

- In 2015, worldwide remittance flows are estimated to have exceeded $601 billion. Of that amount, developing countries are estimated to receive about $441 billion, nearly three times the amount of official development assistance. The true size of remittances, including unrecorded flows through formal and informal channels, is believed to be significantly larger.

- In 2015, the top recipient countries of recorded remittances were India, China, the Philippines, Mexico, and France. As a share of GDP, however, smaller countries such as Tajikistan (42 percent), the Kyrgyz Republic (30 percent), Nepal (29 percent), Tonga (28 percent), and Moldova (26 percent) were the largest recipients.

- High-income countries are the main source of remittances. The United States is by far the largest, with an estimated $56.3 billion in recorded outflows in 2014. Saudi Arabia ranks as the second largest, followed by Russia, Switzerland, Germany, the United Arab Emirates, and Kuwait. The six Gulf Cooperation Council countries accounted for $98 billion in outward remittance flows in 2014.

- Remittance flows at the regional level vary. Highlights for 2015 include: A sharp decline in remittances from Russia to the Commonwealth of Independent States, as a result of the economic slowdown in Russia and the depreciation of the ruble; a rebound in Latin America benefiting Mexico and Central America as the result of the U.S. economic recovery; continued growth in South Asia despite low oil prices in the Gulf Cooperation Council (GCC) countries; and stagnant growth in the Middle East and North Africa and in Sub-Saharan Africa regions. The Arab Republic of Egypt has become the top remittance receiver in the MENA region, with remittances of more than three times the revenue from the Suez Canal.

- The cost of remittances is the highest in Sub-Saharan Africa and in the Pacific Island countries (for example, it costs more than 20 percent to send $200 from Australia to Vanuatu, and 19 percent from South Africa to Zambia). As of the third quarter of 2015, the average cost worldwide remained close to 8 percent—far above the 3 percent target set in the Sustainable Development Goals.

Migration and Remittances Factbook 2016 is also available online at http://www.knomad.org and http://www.worldbank.org/prospects/migrationand remittances. The website provides updates of data and information on migration and remittances.

Data Notes

The data on migration, remittances, and other socioeconomic variables presented in the *Migration and Remittances Factbook 2016,* 3rd edition (Factbook 2016) are the latest available as of December 1, 2015. Given the availability of data, the report presents migrant stocks for 2013, refugee numbers for 2014, remittance outflows for 2014, and remittance inflows for 2015.

The World Bank classifications (World Bank 2015a) include all 188 World Bank member countries, plus 26 other economies with populations of more than 30,000, for which authorities report separate social and economic statistics. Two exceptions are Palau and Tuvalu, whose populations are less than 30,000 but appear in the classifications because they are World Bank member states. The term "country," used interchangeably with "economy," does not imply political independence; rather, it refers to any territory for which authorities report separate social or economic statistics. Residents of some of these countries and economies have access to citizenship rights of other entities (for example, Puerto Ricans are U.S. citizens). However, to maintain consistency with the World Bank's country classification, migrants between these entities are considered international migrants in this edition of the Factbook.

The reader should note the pitfalls of using the data on international migration and remittances; the data are often missing, lagging, or lacking in cross-country comparability owing to the use of different definitions and the lack of consistent collection. Capturing data on irregular flows of migrants and remittances remains a big challenge.

Changes to Country Classifications since the 2011 Edition of the Factbook

The aggregate data on migration and remittances for different regions and income groups have changed since the publication of *Migration and*

Table 1. Countries with Changes to Their Income Classification, Factbook 2011 to Factbook 2016

Country	Income group (Factbook 2011)	Income group (Factbook 2016)
Antigua and Barbuda	Middle	High
Argentina	Middle	High
Bangladesh	Low	Middle
Chile	Middle	High
Curaçao[a]	. .	High
Ghana	Low	Middle
Gibraltar	High	. .
Kenya	Low	Middle
Kyrgyz Republic	Low	Middle
Lao PDR	Low	Middle
Lithuania	Middle	High
Mauritania	Low	Middle
Mayotte	Middle	. .
Myanmar	Low	Middle
Netherlands Antilles[a]	High	. .
Paraguay		Upper
Russian Federation	Middle	High
Seychelles	Middle	High
Sint Maarten (Dutch part)[a]	. .	High
Solomon Islands	Low	Middle
South Sudan	. .	Low
St. Kitts and Nevis	Middle	High
St. Martin (French part)	. .	High
Tajikistan	Low	Middle
Tuvalu[b]	. .	Middle
Uruguay	Middle	High
Venezuela, RB	Middle	High
Zambia	Low	Middle

Source: World Bank country classifications (World Bank 2015a).

Note: . . indicates that these countries were not included in the World Bank's country classification.

a. The Netherlands Antilles is now dissolved, and Curaçao and Sint Maarten (Dutch part) were parts of it.

b. This economy was added to the World Bank's country classifications in July 2010, but it was not included in Factbook 2011 because very little data were available.

Remittances Factbook 2011, 2nd edition, because of changes in country classification (see table 1). Factbook 2016 uses the World Bank's 2016 fiscal year income classification. According to this classification, low-income economies are defined as those with a gross national income (GNI) per capita of $1,045 or less in 2014; middle-income economies are those with a GNI per capita of more than $1,045 but less than $12,736; high-income economies are those with a GNI per capita of $12,736 or more. Lower-middle-income and upper-middle-income economies are separated at a GNI per capita of $4,125. The countries that have changed income group status between the publication of Factbook 2011 and the current Factbook are listed in table 1.

Data on Migration

According to the "Recommendations on Statistics of International Migration" by the United Nations Statistics Division (1998), "long-term migrants" are persons who move to a country other than that of their usual residence for a period of at least one year, so that the country of destination effectively becomes their new country of usual residence. "Short-term migrants" are persons who move to a country other than that of their usual residence for a period of at least three months but less than one year, except in cases where the movement to that country is for purposes of recreation, holiday, visits to friends and relatives, business, medical treatment, or religious pilgrimage (UN 1998).

The duration threshold that identifies migrants, however, varies across countries (Lemaitre, Liebig, and Thoreau 2006). For example, under the United Nations (UN) definition, international students who study in the receiving country for more than one year would be considered migrants. The *International Migration Outlook* (OECD 2006) made a first attempt to characterize migrants by "reasons for movement" and to harmonize statistics among Organisation for Economic Co-operation and Development (OECD) countries.

The database of the UN Population Division is the most comprehensive source of information on international migrant stocks for the period 1960–2013. This dataset "Trend in International Migrant Stock: The 2013 Revision" contains estimates of the total number of international migrants for all 214 countries and territories by country or territory, by destination, and by origin.[1] Factbook 2016 extends this dataset using data from new censuses and country sources, including: (1) data from the 2010 round census that the UN Population Division did not include in the 2013 revision because the census data were released later; (2) new censuses from Sub-Saharan Africa and Latin America and the Caribbean that provided more disaggregated data by country; and (3) revised numbers for Oman, Qatar, Kuwait, Saudi Arabia, and the United Arab Emirates based on recent data from Gulf Labour Markets and Migration (GLMM), a joint program of the Gulf Research Center and the Migration Policy Centre of the European University Institute. The Factbook also includes more recent data on refugees (published by the UN High Commissioner for Refugees [UNHCR]).

As in the case of data on trade and investment flows, there were discrepancies in the reporting of migration data. For example, at times the number of immigrants from country A reported by country B is different from the number of emigrants to country B reported by country A. Such discrepancies arise because of differences in definition and reporting time. In constructing the bilateral migration matrix, the Factbook followed a convention to use data on immigration reported by the host country, since data on inflows are better measured than those on outflows.

Preliminary efforts to estimate bilateral migration data include data by Harrison, Britton, and Swanson (2004); the University of Sussex data originally constructed for the Global Trade Analysis Project trade modeling; and data by the Development Prospects Group of the World Bank used for estimating

---

[1] United Nations database POP/DB/MIG/Stock/Rev.2013.

South-South migration and remittance flows (Ratha and Shaw 2007). Parsons et al. (2007) have created a "composite" matrix that contains estimates of bilateral migrant stocks for 226 x 226 countries. Because these data were constructed for modeling purposes, Parsons et al. use a variety of assumptions to make total immigrant stock add up to total emigrant stock.[2]

Bilateral migration data for the following countries were updated using national censuses: Armenia, Serbia, Marshall Islands, Thailand, Malaysia, Australia, Czech Republic, Estonia, Lithuania, Latvia, New Zealand, Argentina, Bermuda, Bolivia, Cameroon, Kenya, Tanzania, and South Africa.

The latest immigration data for Denmark, Finland, Norway, and Sweden were obtained from the Central Person Register 2013. Available bilateral migration data for the United States from the 2010 census were complemented with the nationally representative American Community Survey for 2013 (U.S. Census Bureau 2013). Census data on immigrants in Argentina, Australia, Canada, Georgia, Lithuania, and Latvia were complemented with new data flows. For Switzerland, we used data from the 2013 Statistique de la population et des ménages (STATPOP); this is the continuous replacement for Census Statistics. Immigration data for the six Gulf Cooperation Council countries (Bahrain, Kuwait, Oman, Qatar, Saudi Arabia, and United Arab Emirates) were obtained from Gulf Labor Markets and Migration (GLMM cited above).[3]

Data for refugees have been compiled from the UN Relief and Works Agency (UNRWA) and from UNHCR's Global Trends Forced Displacement in 2014. Refugees from the West Bank and Gaza include those in Jordan, Lebanon, the Syrian Arab Republic, and the West Bank and Gaza obtained from UNRWA, and those Palestinian refugees in other countries reported by UNHCR.

Data on Second Generation Diaspora

Many people seem to underestimate the size of the diaspora including first, second, and third generations (Ratha and Plaza 2014). Factbook 2016 presents some basic data on the size of the world's diaspora living in Australia, the United States, and Western Europe. Data on "second generation diaspora" in countries other than those in Europe, the United States, and Australia are not available. Definitions on "second generation" also differ. For example, according to Eurostat (2011), "second-generation diaspora" refers to two different groups of immediate descendants of migrants. The first group, with a mixed background, is defined as "persons who are native born and who have one foreign-born parent and one native-born parent." The second group, with a foreign background, is defined as "persons who are native born with both parents foreign born." The OECD applies the first definition of second generation diaspora: native-born children aged 15 and over with at least one parent foreign-born living in an OECD country. In the United States, second generation refers to all persons born in the United States with one or both parents born outside the country.

Data for the second generation diaspora have been compiled from the OECD (2012), *Connecting with Emigrants: A Global Profile of Diasporas*; Pew

---

[2] The resulting final bilateral migrant stock matrix, according to Parsons et al. (2007), "though the fullest, is arguably the least accurate set of data."

[3] See: http://cadmus.eui.eu/bitstream/handle/1814/32151/GLMM%20ExpNote_01-2014. pdf?sequence=1&isAllowed=y.

Research Center (2013), *Second-Generation Americans: A Portrait of the Adult Children of Immigrants*; Commonwealth of Australia 2013, *Australia's Migration Trends 2011–12.*

Data on Remittances

A new notion of remittances introduced in the sixth edition of the *IMF Balance of Payments and International Investment Position Manual* (BPM6) is starting to be used by many countries (IMF 2010a). According to the new definition, personal remittances are the sum of two main components: "compensation of employees" and "personal transfers" (see the table below). Personal remittances also consist of a third item, "capital transfers between households," but data on this item are difficult to obtain and hence reported as missing for almost all countries.

Total remittances: a+b+c+d			
Personal remittances: a+b+c			
a	b	c	d
Personal transfers (standard component in BPM5)	Compensation of employees less taxes, social contributions, transport, and travel	Capital transfers between households	Social benefits

Source: International Transactions in Remittances: Guide for Compilers and Users, IMF 2009.

Compensation of employees, unchanged from BPM5, represents "remuneration in return for the labor input to the production process contributed by an individual in an employer-employee relationship with the enterprise." The definition of "personal transfers," however, is broader than the old "worker's remittances"—it comprises "all current transfers in cash or in kind made or received by resident households to or from nonresident households." Therefore, "personal transfers" include current transfers from migrants not only to family members but also to any recipient in their home country. If migrants live in a host country for one year or longer, they are considered residents, regardless of their immigration status. If the migrants have lived in the host country for less than one year, their entire income in the host country should be classified as compensation of employees.

Although the residence guideline in the IMF manual is clear, the rule is often not followed for various reasons. Many countries compile data based on the citizenship of the migrant worker rather than on their residency status. Further, data are shown entirely as either compensation of employees or personal transfers, although they should be split between the two categories if the guidelines were correctly followed.[4] The distinction between these two

---

[4] For example, India shows very little compensation of employees, but large personal transfers, although it is well known that India supplies a large number of temporary information technology workers to the United States and to European countries.

categories appears to be entirely arbitrary, depending on country preference, convenience, and tax laws or data availability.[5]

Some countries do not report data on remittances in the IMF Balance of Payments statistics. Several developing countries (for example, Cuba, Turkmenistan, Uzbekistan, and Zimbabwe) do not report remittance inflows data to the IMF, even though it is known that emigration from those countries has taken place. Some high-income countries (notably Singapore and the United Arab Emirates) do not report data on remittance outflows, even though they are important destinations for migrants.

A global survey of central banks conducted in 2010 revealed significant heterogeneity in the quality of remittance data compilation across countries (Irving, Mohapatra, and Ratha 2010). Some central banks use remittance data reported by commercial banks, but they do not adequately capture flows through money transfer operators, post offices, and emerging channels, such as mobile money transfers. Even when data are available and properly classified, the data are sometimes out of date. The methodologies used by countries for remittance data compilation are not always publicly available. It is hoped that increased awareness about the importance of remittances and the shortcomings in the data on both remittances and migrant workers will result in efforts to improve data collection.

Perhaps the most difficult aspect of tracking remittance data is estimating informal flows. One way to estimate the true size of remittances is to undertake surveys of remittance senders and recipients. Without new, adequately representative surveys of recipients and senders, evidence from existing household surveys will only be indicative rather than comprehensive.

Caveats on the Quality of Data

As discussed previously, Factbook 2016 builds on the two previous editions of Factbooks and it includes the latest data from various authoritative sources (see below). It has arguably the most comprehensive collection of data and facts on migration and remittances that are available. Validations on the data from the censuses and other sources have been conducted to obtain accurate data.

However, the reader should note the pitfalls of using currently available migration and remittance data. Remittance flows and the stock of migrants may be underestimated because of the use of informal remittance channels, irregular migration, and ambiguity in the definition of migrants (foreign born versus foreigner, seasonal versus permanent, foreign born versus citizen). This is especially true of the bilateral remittance flows pages: Because actual data are not available, estimates of bilateral remittances are presented using the Ratha and Shaw (2007) methodology. It will take a considerable effort to improve the quality of data, especially considering the global need for monitoring indicators on migration and remittances as part of the 2030 Sustainable Development Goals.

Sources of Data

Data on immigration and emigration, both totals and for women, are from the UN Population Division (2013) and from 2010 round censuses. Data on the

---

[5] Because of the difficulty in classification, countries have often classified personal transfers as either other current transfers or transfers from other sectors. In some countries, notably China, remittances may have been misclassified as foreign direct investment. In the case of India and many other countries, remittances may have been classified as nonresident deposits, especially those in local currency terms.

educational levels of immigrants in OECD countries are from OECD (2014). Data on remittances and on the components of remittances are from the IMF Balance of Payments Statistics database (2015) and World Bank data obtained from central banks and statistical offices websites (World Bank 2015c). Data on refugees are from UNHCR.

Data on the following variables are from the World Bank's World Development Indicators (World Bank 2015b): Population, population growth, population density, labor force, unemployment rate, urban population, surface area, GNI, GNI per capita, GDP growth, poverty headcount ratio at national poverty line, age dependency ratio, mobile cellular subscriptions, and Internet users. Data on accounts at a formal financial institution are from the Financial Inclusion Database—Findex (World Bank 2015d). Data on refugees are from the UNHCR (2015) and UNRWA (2014). The data were accessed in November 2015.

In the tables, we use "–" to indicate that the data are not available, and "2015e" indicates 2015 estimates.

Bibliography

Center for Global Development. 2009. *Migrants Count: Five Steps toward Better Migration Data*. Report of the Commission on International Migration Data for Development Research and Policy, Washington, DC: Center for Global Development.

De Bel-Air, Françoise. 2015. "Demography, Migration and Labour Market in Oman." Migration Policy Centre, GLMM: Explanatory note: 09/2015. http://hdl.handle.net/1814/37398.

GLMM (Gulf Labour Markets and Migration). 2014a. Demographic and Economic Module of the GLMM Database, Migration Policy Centre, European University Institute, Florence. http://gulfmigration.eu/glmm-database/demographic-and-economic-module/.

———. 2014b. "Demography, Migration and Labour Market in Saudi Arabia." Migration Policy Centre, GLMM: Explanatory note: 1/2014. http://cadmus.eui.eu/bitstream/handle/1814/32151/GLMM%20ExpNote_01-2014.pdf?sequence=1&isAllowed=y.

Harrison, Anne, Tolani Britton, and Annika Swanson. 2004. "Working Abroad: The Benefits Flowing from Nationals Working in Other Economies." Paper prepared for the Meeting of the Technical Subgroup for the Task Force on International Trade in Services, Movement of Natural Persons—Mode 4, Paris, September, 2004. Statistics Division, United Nations Department of Economic and Social Affairs.

IMF (International Monetary Fund). 2009. *International Transactions in Remittances: Guide for Compilers and Users*. Washington, DC: IMF.

———. 2010. *Balance of Payments Manual*. 6th ed. Washington, DC: IMF.

———. 2015. Balance of Payments Statistics Database. Washington, DC: IMF. http://www2.imfstatistics.org/BOP/.

Irving, Jacqueline, Sanket Mohapatra, and Dilip Ratha. 2010. "Migrant Remittance Flows: Findings from a Global Survey of Central Banks." Working Paper 94, World Bank, Washington, DC.

Lemaître, G., T. Liebig, and C. Thoreau. 2006. "Harmonised Statistics on Immigrant Inflows—Preliminary Results, Sources, And Methods." Paris, OECD.

OECD (Organisation for Economic Co-operation and Development). 2014. Database on Immigrants in OECD and Non-OECD Countries: DIOC 2010/11. Paris: OECD. http://www.oecd.org/els/mig/dioc.htm.

Parsons, Christopher R., Ronald Skeldon, Terrie L. Walmsley, and L. Alan Winters. 2007. "Quantifying International Migration: A Database of Bilateral Migrant Stocks." Policy Research Working Paper 4165, World Bank, Washington, DC.

Ratha, Dilip, and Sonia Plaza. 2014. "Diaspora and Development: Critical Issues." In *India Migration Report*, edited by S. Irudaya Rajan. London: Routledge.

Ratha, Dilip, and William Shaw. 2007. "South–South Migration and Remittances." Working Paper 102, World Bank, Washington, DC.

United Nations. 1998. "Recommendations on Statistics of International Migration." Revision 1, Statistical Papers, Series M, No. 58, United Nations, New York.

UN Population Division. 2013. "Trends in International Migrant Stock: The 2013 Revision." New York: UN Department of Economic and Social Affairs. http://www.un.org/en/development/desa/population/migration/data/index.shtml.

UNHCR (United Nations High Commissioner for Refugees). 2015. "Global Trends Forced Displacement in 2014." http://unhcr.org/556725e69.html.

UNRWA (United Nations Relief and Works Agency). 2014. http://www.unrwa.org/resources.

U.S. Census Bureau 2013. American Community Survey 2013. https://www.census.gov/programs-surveys/acs.

World Bank. 2015a. *World Bank Country Classifications*. Washington, DC: World Bank. http://data.worldbank.org/about/country-and-lending-groups.

———. 2015b. *World Development Indicators*. Washington, DC: World Bank. http://data.worldbank.org/products/wdi.

———. 2015c. *Monthly and Quarterly Remittances Flows to Selected Countries*. Washington, DC: World Bank. http://siteresources.worldbank.org/INTPROSPECTS/Resources/334934-1110315015165/Monthly_Remittances_Public.xlsx.

———. 2015d. The Global Findex Database. Washington, DC: World Bank. http://datatopics.worldbank.org/financialinclusion/.

Abbreviations

Bn	billion
FDI	foreign direct investment
GCC	Gulf Cooperation Council
GDP	gross domestic product
GLMM	Gulf Labor Markets and Migration
GNI	gross national income
IMF	International Monetary Fund
ODA	official development assistance
OECD	Organisation for Economic Co-operation and Development
UN	United Nations
UNDESA	United Nations Department of Economic and Social Affairs
UNHCR	United Nations High Commissioner for Refugees
UNRWA	UN Relief and Works Agency

Migration and Remittances: Top Countries

Top Immigration Countries[a], 2013

Stock of immigrants, millions

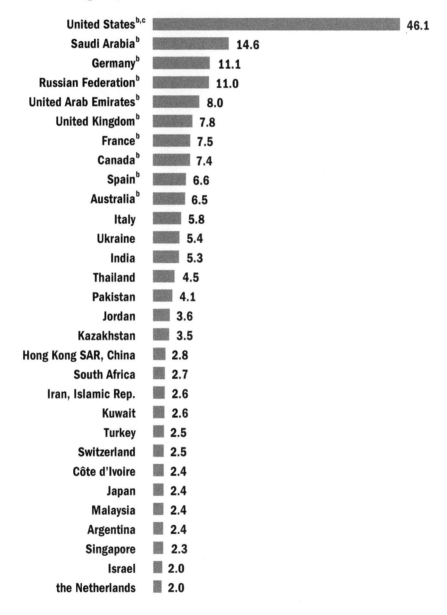

United States[b,c]	46.1
Saudi Arabia[b]	14.6
Germany[b]	11.1
Russian Federation[b]	11.0
United Arab Emirates[b]	8.0
United Kingdom[b]	7.8
France[b]	7.5
Canada[b]	7.4
Spain[b]	6.6
Australia[b]	6.5
Italy	5.8
Ukraine	5.4
India	5.3
Thailand	4.5
Pakistan	4.1
Jordan	3.6
Kazakhstan	3.5
Hong Kong SAR, China	2.8
South Africa	2.7
Iran, Islamic Rep.	2.6
Kuwait	2.6
Turkey	2.5
Switzerland	2.5
Côte d'Ivoire	2.4
Japan	2.4
Malaysia	2.4
Argentina	2.4
Singapore	2.3
Israel	2.0
the Netherlands	2.0

Sources: Development Prospects Group, World Bank; UN Population Division 2013; national censuses.
a. Includes countries and territories (see Data Notes).
b. Top 10 country.
c. Puerto Rico is treated as a separate country and, therefore, Puerto Ricans residing in the United States are considered foreign born.

Top Immigration Countries[a], 2013

Percentage of population

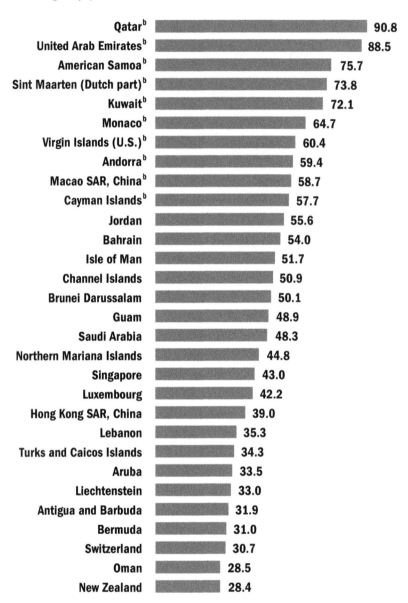

Qatar[b]	90.8
United Arab Emirates[b]	88.5
American Samoa[b]	75.7
Sint Maarten (Dutch part)[b]	73.8
Kuwait[b]	72.1
Monaco[b]	64.7
Virgin Islands (U.S.)[b]	60.4
Andorra[b]	59.4
Macao SAR, China[b]	58.7
Cayman Islands[b]	57.7
Jordan	55.6
Bahrain	54.0
Isle of Man	51.7
Channel Islands	50.9
Brunei Darussalam	50.1
Guam	48.9
Saudi Arabia	48.3
Northern Mariana Islands	44.8
Singapore	43.0
Luxembourg	42.2
Hong Kong SAR, China	39.0
Lebanon	35.3
Turks and Caicos Islands	34.3
Aruba	33.5
Liechtenstein	33.0
Antigua and Barbuda	31.9
Bermuda	31.0
Switzerland	30.7
Oman	28.5
New Zealand	28.4

Sources: Development Prospects Group, World Bank; UN Population Division 2013; national censuses.

a. Includes countries and territories (see Data Notes).

b. Top 10 country.

c. Puerto Rico is treated as a separate country and, therefore, Puerto Ricans residing in the United States are considered foreign born.

Migration and Remittances Factbook 2016

Top Emigration Countries[a], 2013

Number of emigrants, millions

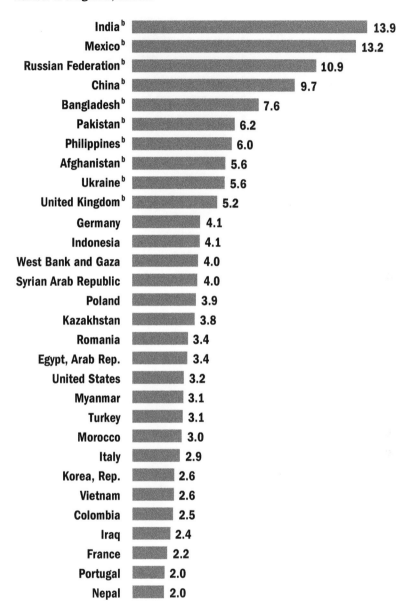

India[b]	13.9
Mexico[b]	13.2
Russian Federation[b]	10.9
China[b]	9.7
Bangladesh[b]	7.6
Pakistan[b]	6.2
Philippines[b]	6.0
Afghanistan[b]	5.6
Ukraine[b]	5.6
United Kingdom[b]	5.2
Germany	4.1
Indonesia	4.1
West Bank and Gaza	4.0
Syrian Arab Republic	4.0
Poland	3.9
Kazakhstan	3.8
Romania	3.4
Egypt, Arab Rep.	3.4
United States	3.2
Myanmar	3.1
Turkey	3.1
Morocco	3.0
Italy	2.9
Korea, Rep.	2.6
Vietnam	2.6
Colombia	2.5
Iraq	2.4
France	2.2
Portugal	2.0
Nepal	2.0

Sources: Development Prospects Group, World Bank; UN Population Division 2013; national censuses.

a. Includes countries and territories (see Data Notes).

b. Top 10 country.

c. Puerto Rico is treated as a separate country and, therefore, Puerto Ricans residing in the United States are considered foreign born.

Top Emigration Countries[a], 2013

Percentage of population

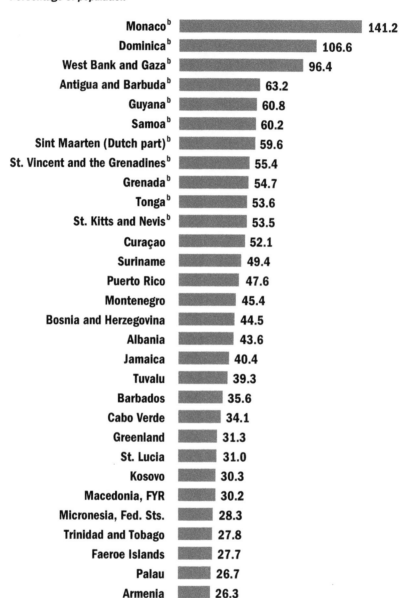

Monaco[b]	141.2
Dominica[b]	106.6
West Bank and Gaza[b]	96.4
Antigua and Barbuda[b]	63.2
Guyana[b]	60.8
Samoa[b]	60.2
Sint Maarten (Dutch part)[b]	59.6
St. Vincent and the Grenadines[b]	55.4
Grenada[b]	54.7
Tonga[b]	53.6
St. Kitts and Nevis[b]	53.5
Curaçao	52.1
Suriname	49.4
Puerto Rico	47.6
Montenegro	45.4
Bosnia and Herzegovina	44.5
Albania	43.6
Jamaica	40.4
Tuvalu	39.3
Barbados	35.6
Cabo Verde	34.1
Greenland	31.3
St. Lucia	31.0
Kosovo	30.3
Macedonia, FYR	30.2
Micronesia, Fed. Sts.	28.3
Trinidad and Tobago	27.8
Faeroe Islands	27.7
Palau	26.7
Armenia	26.3

Sources: Development Prospects Group, World Bank; UN Population Division 2013; national censuses.

a. Includes countries and territories (see Data Notes).

b. Top 10 country.

c. Puerto Rico is treated as a separate country and, therefore, Puerto Ricans residing in the United States are considered foreign born.

Top Migration Corridors, 2013
Stock of migrants, millions

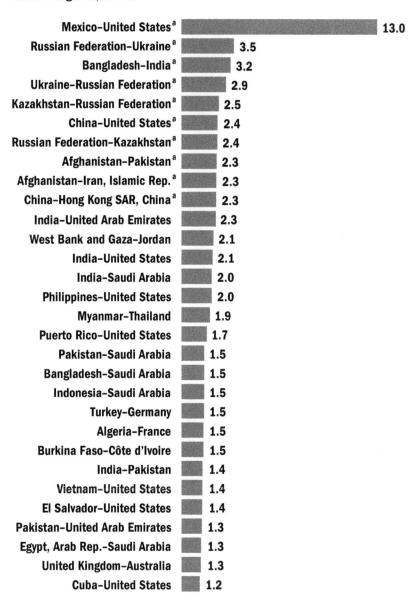

Corridor	Millions
Mexico–United States[a]	13.0
Russian Federation–Ukraine[a]	3.5
Bangladesh–India[a]	3.2
Ukraine–Russian Federation[a]	2.9
Kazakhstan–Russian Federation[a]	2.5
China–United States[a]	2.4
Russian Federation–Kazakhstan[a]	2.4
Afghanistan–Pakistan[a]	2.3
Afghanistan–Iran, Islamic Rep.[a]	2.3
China–Hong Kong SAR, China[a]	2.3
India–United Arab Emirates	2.3
West Bank and Gaza–Jordan	2.1
India–United States	2.1
India–Saudi Arabia	2.0
Philippines–United States	2.0
Myanmar–Thailand	1.9
Puerto Rico–United States	1.7
Pakistan–Saudi Arabia	1.5
Bangladesh–Saudi Arabia	1.5
Indonesia–Saudi Arabia	1.5
Turkey–Germany	1.5
Algeria–France	1.5
Burkina Faso–Côte d'Ivoire	1.5
India–Pakistan	1.4
Vietnam–United States	1.4
El Salvador–United States	1.4
Pakistan–United Arab Emirates	1.3
Egypt, Arab Rep.–Saudi Arabia	1.3
United Kingdom–Australia	1.3
Cuba–United States	1.2

Sources: Development Prospects Group, World Bank; UN Population Division 2013; national censuses.

a. Includes countries and territories (see Data Notes).

b. Top 10 country.

c. Puerto Rico is treated as a separate country and, therefore, Puerto Ricans residing in the United States are considered foreign born.

Top Source Countries for Refugees, 2014

Stock of migrants, millions

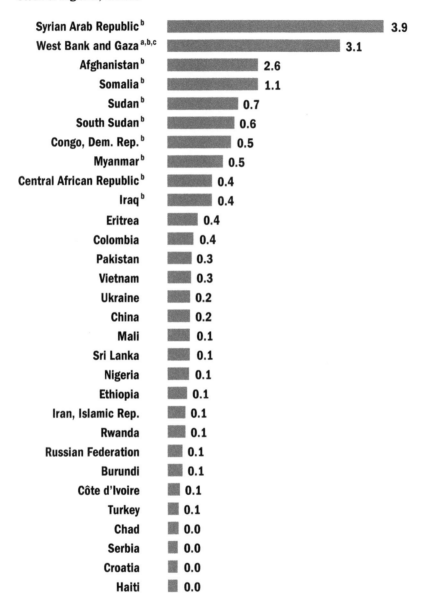

Syrian Arab Republic[b]	3.9
West Bank and Gaza[a,b,c]	3.1
Afghanistan[b]	2.6
Somalia[b]	1.1
Sudan[b]	0.7
South Sudan[b]	0.6
Congo, Dem. Rep.[b]	0.5
Myanmar[b]	0.5
Central African Republic[b]	0.4
Iraq[b]	0.4
Eritrea	0.4
Colombia	0.4
Pakistan	0.3
Vietnam	0.3
Ukraine	0.2
China	0.2
Mali	0.1
Sri Lanka	0.1
Nigeria	0.1
Ethiopia	0.1
Iran, Islamic Rep.	0.1
Rwanda	0.1
Russian Federation	0.1
Burundi	0.1
Côte d'Ivoire	0.1
Turkey	0.1
Chad	0.0
Serbia	0.0
Croatia	0.0
Haiti	0.0

Sources: UN Population Division, with data from UNHCR and UNRWA and some additional data from United Nations Department of Economic and Social Affairs (UNDESA).

a. Includes countries and territories (see Data Notes).

b. Top 10 country.

c. Refugees from West Bank and Gaza include those in Jordan, Lebanon, Syria, and West Bank and Gaza reported by UNRWA and those refugees in other countries reported by UNHCR.

Migration and Remittances Factbook 2016

Top Destination Countries for Refugees, 2014

Stock of migrants, millions

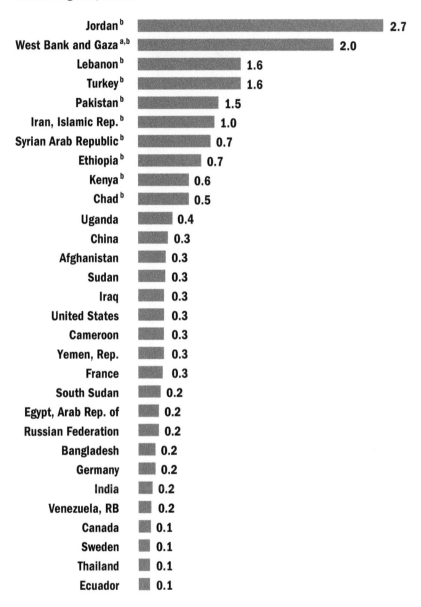

Jordan [b]	2.7
West Bank and Gaza [a,b]	2.0
Lebanon [b]	1.6
Turkey [b]	1.6
Pakistan [b]	1.5
Iran, Islamic Rep. [b]	1.0
Syrian Arab Republic [b]	0.7
Ethiopia [b]	0.7
Kenya [b]	0.6
Chad [b]	0.5
Uganda	0.4
China	0.3
Afghanistan	0.3
Sudan	0.3
Iraq	0.3
United States	0.3
Cameroon	0.3
Yemen, Rep.	0.3
France	0.3
South Sudan	0.2
Egypt, Arab Rep. of	0.2
Russian Federation	0.2
Bangladesh	0.2
Germany	0.2
India	0.2
Venezuela, RB	0.2
Canada	0.1
Sweden	0.1
Thailand	0.1
Ecuador	0.1

Sources: UN Population Division, with data from UNHCR and UNRWA and some additional data from UNDESA.

a. Includes countries and territories (see Data Notes).

b. Top 10 country.

Stock of Refugees, 1960 to mid-2015

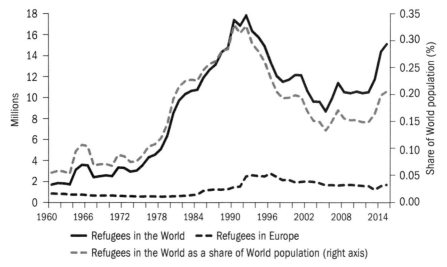

Refugees in the World   **Refugees in Europe**

Refugees in the World as a share of World population (right axis)

Source: UNHCR, excluding refugees listed by the UNRWA.

Stock of refugees and asylum seekers, 2010 to mid-2015

	2010	2011	2012	2013	2014	mid-2015
A. Stock of refugees (millions)						
World	10.5	10.4	10.5	11.7	14.4	15.1
Europe	1.6	1.5	1.5	1.2	1.5	1.6
B. Stock of asylum seekers (millions)						
World	0.8	0.9	0.9	1.2	1.8	2.3
Europe	0.3	0.3	0.3	0.4	0.6	0.7
C. Total stock of refugees and asylum seekers (millions)						
World	11.4	11.3	11.4	12.9	16.2	17.4
Europe	1.9	1.8	1.9	1.6	2.1	2.3
Refugees and asylum seekers as share of population						
World	0.16%	0.16%	0.16%	0.18%	0.22%	0.24%
Europe	0.26%	0.25%	0.25%	0.21%	0.28%	0.31%

Sources: UNHCR; and World Bank 2015b.

Migration and Remittances Factbook 2016

Top Emigration Countries of Tertiary Educated[a], 2010–11

Stock of migrants, thousands

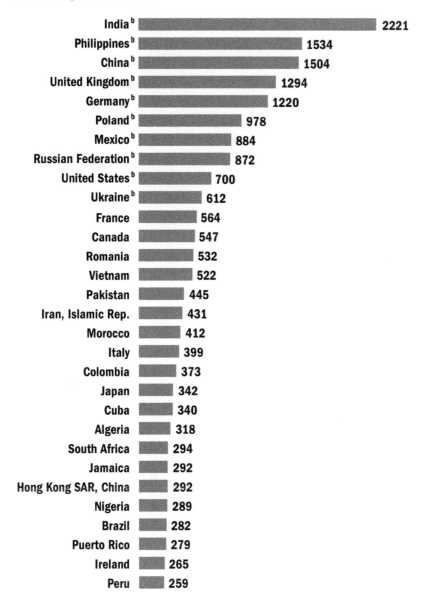

India[b]	2221
Philippines[b]	1534
China[b]	1504
United Kingdom[b]	1294
Germany[b]	1220
Poland[b]	978
Mexico[b]	884
Russian Federation[b]	872
United States[b]	700
Ukraine[b]	612
France	564
Canada	547
Romania	532
Vietnam	522
Pakistan	445
Iran, Islamic Rep.	431
Morocco	412
Italy	399
Colombia	373
Japan	342
Cuba	340
Algeria	318
South Africa	294
Jamaica	292
Hong Kong SAR, China	292
Nigeria	289
Brazil	282
Puerto Rico	279
Ireland	265
Peru	259

Source: OECD 2014.

a. Includes countries and territories (see Data Notes).

b. Top 10 country.

Top Emigration Countries of Tertiary Educated, 2010–11[a]

Emigration rate, percent of total

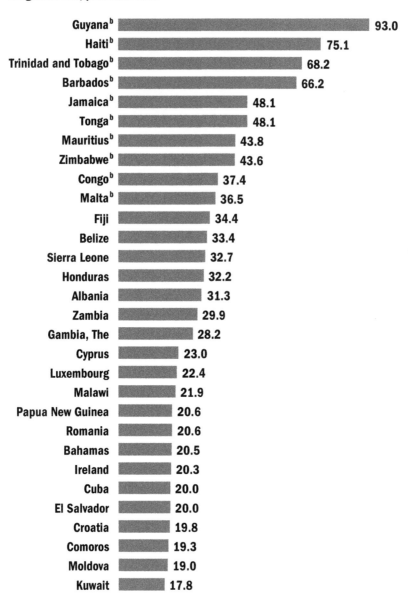

Guyana[b]	93.0
Haiti[b]	75.1
Trinidad and Tobago[b]	68.2
Barbados[b]	66.2
Jamaica[b]	48.1
Tonga[b]	48.1
Mauritius[b]	43.8
Zimbabwe[b]	43.6
Congo[b]	37.4
Malta[b]	36.5
Fiji	34.4
Belize	33.4
Sierra Leone	32.7
Honduras	32.2
Albania	31.3
Zambia	29.9
Gambia, The	28.2
Cyprus	23.0
Luxembourg	22.4
Malawi	21.9
Papua New Guinea	20.6
Romania	20.6
Bahamas	20.5
Ireland	20.3
Cuba	20.0
El Salvador	20.0
Croatia	19.8
Comoros	19.3
Moldova	19.0
Kuwait	17.8

Sources: Arslan et al. 2014; OECD 2014.

a. Includes countries and territories (see Data Notes).

b. Top 10 country.

South–South Migration versus South–North Migration

South–South migration (migration between developing countries) is larger than migration from the South to high-income countries.

Global Migrant Stock Estimates, 2013

	Migrants living in			
Migrants from	South (millions)	North (millions)	South (% of total migrants)	North (% of total migrants)
South	93.1	84.3	38%	34%
North	14.2	55.7	6%	23%
Total	107.3	140.0	43%	57%
	Remittances to			
Remittances from	South ($ billions)	North ($ billions)	South (% of total remittances)	North (% of total remittances)
South	206.7	27.9	34%	5%
North	223.8	143.0	37%	24%
Total	430.5	170.8	72%	28%

South–South migration Is Larger Than South–North Migration

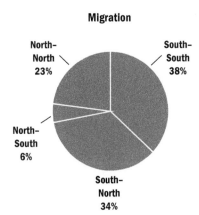

Migration

North–North 23%
South–South 38%
North–South 6%
South–North 34%

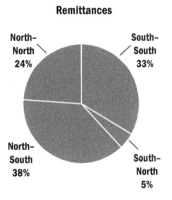

Remittances

North–North 24%
South–South 33%
North–South 38%
South–North 5%

Sources: World Bank staff calculations; UN Population Division 2013; and national censuses.

Note: Definition of the "North" and the "South" in this chart follows UN classification. The data on migration are for 2013, the latest year for which data are available. The data on remittances are forecasts for 2015. According to the UN, the term "North" refers to countries or regions traditionally classified for statistical purposes as "developed," while the term "South" refers to those classified as "developing." The developed regions include Europe and North America plus Australia, New Zealand, and Japan. Using World Bank classification of Developing Countries as "South" and High-Income Countries as "North" implies that South-South and South-North migrants constitute 56.4 million (23 percent) and 128.6 million (52 percent) of total international migrants, respectively.

Top Remittance-Receiving Countries[a], 2014

US$ billions

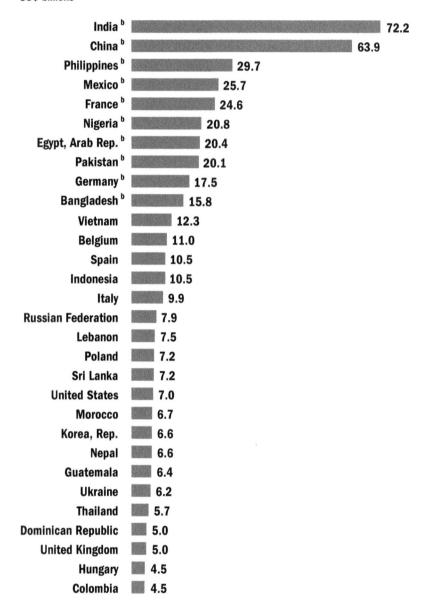

Country	US$ billions
India [b]	72.2
China [b]	63.9
Philippines [b]	29.7
Mexico [b]	25.7
France [b]	24.6
Nigeria [b]	20.8
Egypt, Arab Rep. [b]	20.4
Pakistan [b]	20.1
Germany [b]	17.5
Bangladesh [b]	15.8
Vietnam	12.3
Belgium	11.0
Spain	10.5
Indonesia	10.5
Italy	9.9
Russian Federation	7.9
Lebanon	7.5
Poland	7.2
Sri Lanka	7.2
United States	7.0
Morocco	6.7
Korea, Rep.	6.6
Nepal	6.6
Guatemala	6.4
Ukraine	6.2
Thailand	5.7
Dominican Republic	5.0
United Kingdom	5.0
Hungary	4.5
Colombia	4.5

Source: Migration and Remittances Unit, DECMR, of the World Bank.

a. Includes countries and territories (see Data Notes).

b. Top 10 country.

Top Remittance-Receiving Countries[a], 2014

Percentage of GDP

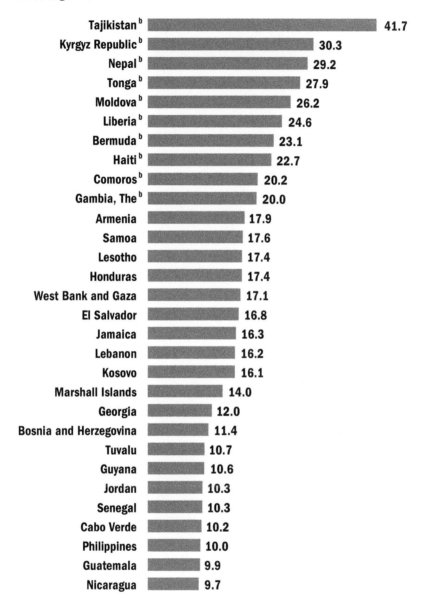

Tajikistan[b]	41.7
Kyrgyz Republic[b]	30.3
Nepal[b]	29.2
Tonga[b]	27.9
Moldova[b]	26.2
Liberia[b]	24.6
Bermuda[b]	23.1
Haiti[b]	22.7
Comoros[b]	20.2
Gambia, The[b]	20.0
Armenia	17.9
Samoa	17.6
Lesotho	17.4
Honduras	17.4
West Bank and Gaza	17.1
El Salvador	16.8
Jamaica	16.3
Lebanon	16.2
Kosovo	16.1
Marshall Islands	14.0
Georgia	12.0
Bosnia and Herzegovina	11.4
Tuvalu	10.7
Guyana	10.6
Jordan	10.3
Senegal	10.3
Cabo Verde	10.2
Philippines	10.0
Guatemala	9.9
Nicaragua	9.7

Source: Migration and Remittances Unit, DECMR, of the World Bank.

a. Includes countries and territories (see Data Notes).

b. Top 10 country.

Top Remittance-Sending Countries[a], 2014[b]

US$ billions

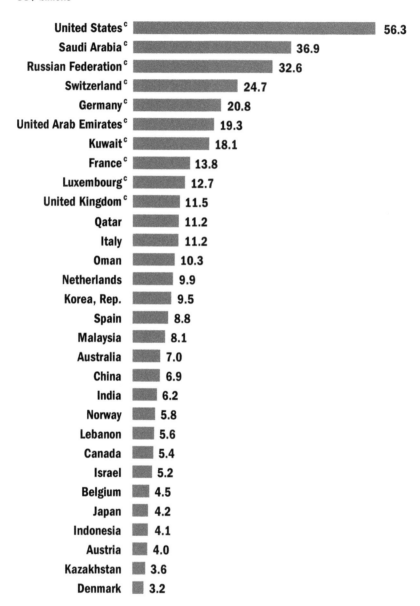

United States[c]	56.3
Saudi Arabia[c]	36.9
Russian Federation[c]	32.6
Switzerland[c]	24.7
Germany[c]	20.8
United Arab Emirates[c]	19.3
Kuwait[c]	18.1
France[c]	13.8
Luxembourg[c]	12.7
United Kingdom[c]	11.5
Qatar	11.2
Italy	11.2
Oman	10.3
Netherlands	9.9
Korea, Rep.	9.5
Spain	8.8
Malaysia	8.1
Australia	7.0
China	6.9
India	6.2
Norway	5.8
Lebanon	5.6
Canada	5.4
Israel	5.2
Belgium	4.5
Japan	4.2
Indonesia	4.1
Austria	4.0
Kazakhstan	3.6
Denmark	3.2

Source: Migration and Remittances Unit, DECMR, of the World Bank.
a. Includes countries and territories (see Data Notes).
b. Estimated outflows based on remittance inflows and the bilateral remittance matrix.
c. Top 10 country.

Migration and Remittances Factbook 2016

Top Remittance-Sending Countries[a], 2014

Percentage of GDP

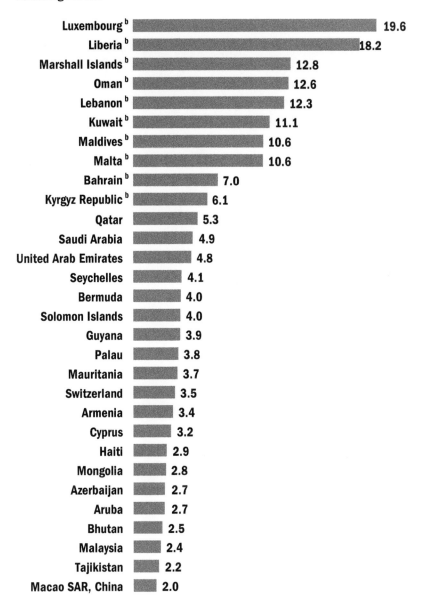

Luxembourg[b]	19.6
Liberia[b]	18.2
Marshall Islands[b]	12.8
Oman[b]	12.6
Lebanon[b]	12.3
Kuwait[b]	11.1
Maldives[b]	10.6
Malta[b]	10.6
Bahrain[b]	7.0
Kyrgyz Republic[b]	6.1
Qatar	5.3
Saudi Arabia	4.9
United Arab Emirates	4.8
Seychelles	4.1
Bermuda	4.0
Solomon Islands	4.0
Guyana	3.9
Palau	3.8
Mauritania	3.7
Switzerland	3.5
Armenia	3.4
Cyprus	3.2
Haiti	2.9
Mongolia	2.8
Azerbaijan	2.7
Aruba	2.7
Bhutan	2.5
Malaysia	2.4
Tajikistan	2.2
Macao SAR, China	2.0

Source: Migration and Remittances Unit, DECMR, of the World Bank.

a. Includes countries and territories (see Data Notes).

b. Top 10 country.

Top Remittance Corridors[a], 2015[b]

US$ billions

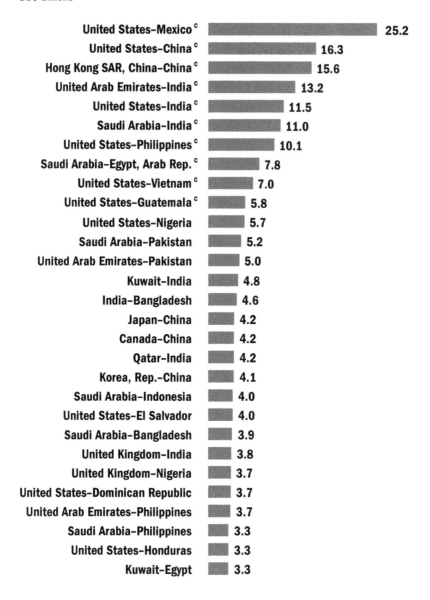

Corridor	US$ billions
United States–Mexico[c]	25.2
United States–China[c]	16.3
Hong Kong SAR, China–China[c]	15.6
United Arab Emirates–India[c]	13.2
United States–India[c]	11.5
Saudi Arabia–India[c]	11.0
United States–Philippines[c]	10.1
Saudi Arabia–Egypt, Arab Rep.[c]	7.8
United States–Vietnam[c]	7.0
United States–Guatemala[c]	5.8
United States–Nigeria	5.7
Saudi Arabia–Pakistan	5.2
United Arab Emirates–Pakistan	5.0
Kuwait–India	4.8
India–Bangladesh	4.6
Japan–China	4.2
Canada–China	4.2
Qatar–India	4.2
Korea, Rep.–China	4.1
Saudi Arabia–Indonesia	4.0
United States–El Salvador	4.0
Saudi Arabia–Bangladesh	3.9
United Kingdom–India	3.8
United Kingdom–Nigeria	3.7
United States–Dominican Republic	3.7
United Arab Emirates–Philippines	3.7
Saudi Arabia–Philippines	3.3
United States–Honduras	3.3
Kuwait–Egypt	3.3

Source: Migration and Remittances Unit, DECMR, of the World Bank.

a. Includes countries and territories (see Data Notes).

b. These data are not official—they are estimated using logical assumptions as explained in Ratha and Shaw (2007).

c. Top 10 country.

Migration and Remittances Factbook 2016

Remittances Compared with Other Resource Flows

Remittances to Developing Countries Are Large and More Stable Than Other External Financing

US$ billions

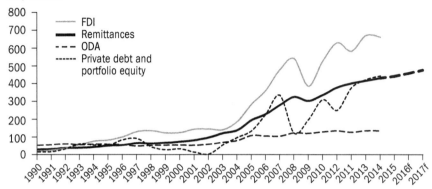

Resource Flows to Developing Countries

US$ billions

	1990	2000	2005	2006	2007	2008	2009	2010	2011	2012	2013	2014	2015e
Remittances	29	73	194	229	280	325	303	336	378	401	416	431	441
FDI	19	125	284	361	480	541	385	529	630	583	671	662	–
ODA[a]	53	54	108	105	105	123	121	129	135	127	135	135	–
Private debt and portfolio equity	16	32	134	228	334	122	197	309	250	376	422	443[b]	–

Sources: World Bank 2015; and World Bank Development Prospects Group (DECPG).

Note: Remittances are based on IMF BPM6. Private debt includes only medium- and long-term debt. FDI = foreign direct investment; ODA = official development assistance; and − = data not available.

a. OECD Development Assistance Committee (DAC) online database (http://www.oecd.org/dac).

b. Estimated flows.

1. Remittances resulting from migration constitute reliable sources of foreign exchange earnings, and cushion households' income during bad times. Remittance inflows to developing countries are more than three times official development aid (ODA); and even bigger than foreign direct investment inflows once China is excluded. Remittances have been growing steadily, showing their resilience to global headwinds, while other types of capital flows to the developing economies sharply respond to fluctuations of interest rates in advanced economies or growth prospects in developing countries.

2. Remittances are less volatile and more stable than all other external flows. Therefore, remittances help counter-balance fluctuations caused by weakening of capital flows to developing countries.

3. Small developing economies tend to show remittance dependency and need to upgrade their human capital to insulate themselves from external turbulence. For instance, remittances in 2014 accounted for 42 percent of GDP in Tajikistan, 30 percent in Kyrgyz Republic, and 29 percent in Nepal.

Lowest Cost Corridors of Sending Remittances for $200, Q3 of 2015

Percent

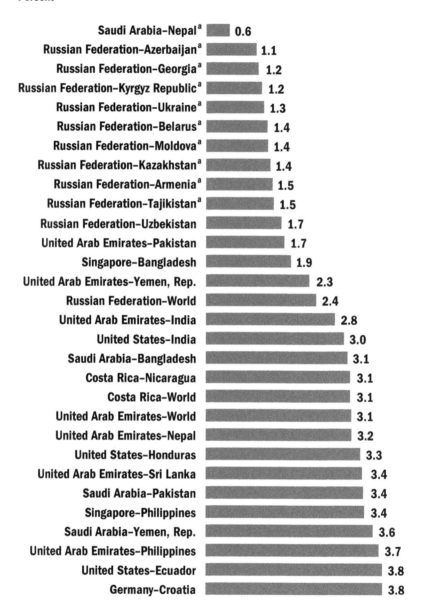

Corridor	Percent
Saudi Arabia–Nepal[a]	0.6
Russian Federation–Azerbaijan[a]	1.1
Russian Federation–Georgia[a]	1.2
Russian Federation–Kyrgyz Republic[a]	1.2
Russian Federation–Ukraine[a]	1.3
Russian Federation–Belarus[a]	1.4
Russian Federation–Moldova[a]	1.4
Russian Federation–Kazakhstan[a]	1.4
Russian Federation–Armenia[a]	1.5
Russian Federation–Tajikistan[a]	1.5
Russian Federation–Uzbekistan	1.7
United Arab Emirates–Pakistan	1.7
Singapore–Bangladesh	1.9
United Arab Emirates–Yemen, Rep.	2.3
Russian Federation–World	2.4
United Arab Emirates–India	2.8
United States–India	3.0
Saudi Arabia–Bangladesh	3.1
Costa Rica–Nicaragua	3.1
Costa Rica–World	3.1
United Arab Emirates–World	3.1
United Arab Emirates–Nepal	3.2
United States–Honduras	3.3
United Arab Emirates–Sri Lanka	3.4
Saudi Arabia–Pakistan	3.4
Singapore–Philippines	3.4
Saudi Arabia–Yemen, Rep.	3.6
United Arab Emirates–Philippines	3.7
United States–Ecuador	3.8
Germany–Croatia	3.8

Source: World Bank Remittance Prices Worldwide database, https://remittanceprices.worldbank.org/en.
a. Includes countries and territories (see Data Notes).

Migration and Remittances Factbook 2016

Highest Cost Corridors of Sending Remittances for $200, Q3 of 2015

Percent

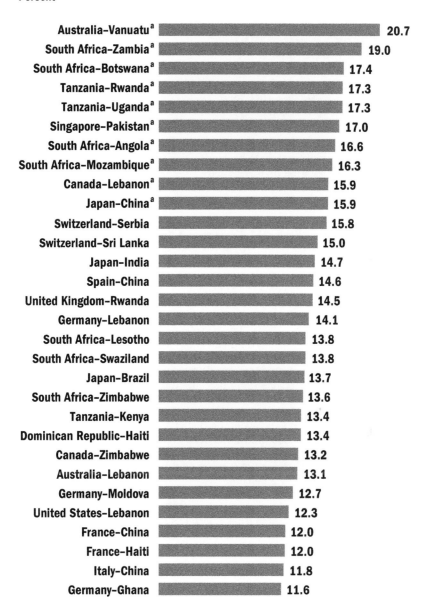

Corridor	Percent
Australia–Vanuatu[a]	20.7
South Africa–Zambia[a]	19.0
South Africa–Botswana[a]	17.4
Tanzania–Rwanda[a]	17.3
Tanzania–Uganda[a]	17.3
Singapore–Pakistan[a]	17.0
South Africa–Angola[a]	16.6
South Africa–Mozambique[a]	16.3
Canada–Lebanon[a]	15.9
Japan–China[a]	15.9
Switzerland–Serbia	15.8
Switzerland–Sri Lanka	15.0
Japan–India	14.7
Spain–China	14.6
United Kingdom–Rwanda	14.5
Germany–Lebanon	14.1
South Africa–Lesotho	13.8
South Africa–Swaziland	13.8
Japan–Brazil	13.7
South Africa–Zimbabwe	13.6
Tanzania–Kenya	13.4
Dominican Republic–Haiti	13.4
Canada–Zimbabwe	13.2
Australia–Lebanon	13.1
Germany–Moldova	12.7
United States–Lebanon	12.3
France–China	12.0
France–Haiti	12.0
Italy–China	11.8
Germany–Ghana	11.6

Source: World Bank Remittance Prices Worldwide database, https://remittanceprices.worldbank.org/en.
a. Includes countries and territories (see Data Notes).

World

Population (millions, 2014)	7,260.7
Population growth (avg. annual %, 2005–14)	1.2
Population density (people per sq km, 2014)	56.0
Labor force (millions, 2014)	3,384.1
Unemployment rate (% of labor force, 2014)	5.9
Urban population (% of pop., 2014)	53.4
Surface area (thousands of sq km, 2014)	134,325.2
GNI, Atlas method (current US$ billions, 2014)	78,323.8
GNI per capita, Atlas method (current US$, 2014)	10,787.4
GDP growth (avg. annual %, 2011–14)	2.5
Poverty headcount ratio at national poverty line (% of pop.)	—
Age dependency ratio (% of working-age pop., 2014)	53.9
Account at a formal financial institution (% age 15+)	60.7
Mobile cellular subscriptions (per 100 people, 2014)	96.3
Internet users (per 100 people, 2014)	40.7

Migration

- Stock of migrants, 2013: **247.2 million** or **3.4 percent** of population
- Top 10 emigration countries, 2013: India, Mexico, the Russian Federation, China, Bangladesh, Pakistan, the Philippines, Afghanistan, Ukraine, the United Kingdom
- Sources, 2013: high-income OECD countries (16.1 percent); high-income non-OECD countries (8.0 percent); developing countries (72.8 percent); unidentified (3.1 percent)
- As a percentage of population, top 10 source countries, 2013: Monaco (141.2 percent); Dominica (106.6 percent); the West Bank and Gaza (96.4 percent); Antigua and Barbuda (63.2 percent); Guyana (60.8 percent); Samoa (60.2 percent); Sint Maarten (Dutch part) (59.6 percent); St. Vincent and the Grenadines (55.4 percent); Grenada (54.7 percent); Tonga (53.6 percent)
- Top 10 immigration countries, 2013: the United States, Saudi Arabia, Germany, the Russian Federation, the United Arab Emirates, the United Kingdom, France, Canada, Spain, Australia
- Destinations, 2013: high-income OECD countries (49.4 percent); high-income non-OECD countries (21.0 percent); developing countries (29.3 percent); unidentified (0.2 percent)
- As a percentage of population, top 10 destination countries, 2013: Qatar (90.8 percent); the United Arab Emirates (88.5 percent); American Samoa (75.7 percent); Sint Maarten (Dutch part) (73.8 percent); Kuwait (72.1 percent); Monaco (64.7 percent); the Virgin Islands (U.S.) (60.4 percent); Andorra (59.4 percent); Macao SAR, China (58.7 percent); the Cayman Islands (57.7 percent)
- Top 10 migration corridors, 2013: Mexico–the United States; the Russian Federation–Ukraine; Bangladesh–India; Ukraine–the Russian Federation; Kazakhstan–the Russian Federation; China–the United States; the Russian Federation–Kazakhstan; Afghanistan–Pakistan; Afghanistan–the Islamic Republic of Iran; China–Hong Kong SAR, China

- Top 10 migration corridors excluding the former Soviet Union, 2013: Mexico–the United States; Bangladesh–India; China–the United States; Afghanistan–Pakistan; Afghanistan–the Islamic Republic of Iran; China–Hong Kong SAR, China; India–the United Arab Emirates; the West Bank and Gaza–Jordan; India–the United States; India–Saudi Arabia
- Tertiary-educated as a percentage of total migrants in OECD countries, 2011: **27.6 percent**
- Tertiary-educated women as a percentage of total women migrants in OECD countries, 2011: **28.0 percent**
- Number of refugees, 2014: **19.5 million**
- Women as percentage of migrants, 2013: **47.2 percent**
- Second generation diaspora in Australia, Europe, and the United States, 2012: **45.3 million**

Remittances

US$ billions	2006	2007	2008	2009	2010	2011	2012	2013	2014	2015e
Inward remittance flows^a	**330.3**	**398.6**	**460.2**	**429.4**	**463.7**	**525.9**	**547.0**	**572.3**	**592.9**	**601.3**
All developing countries	*228.6*	*279.5*	*324.8*	*302.9*	*335.7*	*377.9*	*400.7*	*416.2*	*431.1*	*440.5*
Outward remittance flows^a	**240.7**	**294.4**	**345.9**	**330.6**	**334.1**	**367.1**	**383.1**	**422.0**	**427.8**	—
All developing countries	*28.7*	*33.3*	*40.9*	*42.2*	*42.1*	*45.0*	*52.2*	*59.2*	*58.8*	—

Note: This table reports officially recorded remittances. The true size of remittances, including unrecorded flows through formal and informal channels, is believed to be larger.

a. For comparison: net FDI inflows US$1,951.9 billion, net ODA received US$150.09 billion in 2013. Inward remittance flows were 0.8 percent of GNI in 2013, outward remittance flows were 0.6 percent of GNI in 2013.

REMITTANCES

- Top 10 remittance recipients in 2015 ($US billions): India ($72.2bn), China ($63.9bn), the Philippines ($29.7bn), Mexico ($25.7bn), France ($24.6bn), Nigeria ($20.8bn), the Arab Republic of Egypt ($20.4bn), Pakistan ($20.1bn), Germany ($17.5bn), Bangladesh ($15.8bn)
- Top 10 remittance recipients in 2014 (percentage of GDP): Tajikistan (41.7 percent), the Kyrgyz Republic (30.3 percent), Nepal (29.2 percent), Tonga (27.9 percent), Moldova (26.2 percent), Liberia (24.6 percent), Bermuda (23.1 percent), Haiti (22.7 percent), Comoros (20.2 percent), The Gambia (20.0 percent)
- Top 10 remittance senders in 2014 ($US billions): the United States ($56.3bn), Saudi Arabia ($36.9bn), the Russian Federation ($32.6bn), Switzerland ($24.7bn), Germany ($20.8bn), the United Arab Emirates ($19.3bn), Kuwait ($18.1bn), France ($13.8bn), Luxembourg ($12.7bn), the United Kingdom ($11.5bn)
- Top 10 remittance senders in 2014 (percentage of GDP): Luxembourg (19.6 percent), Liberia (18.2 percent), the Marshall Islands (12.8 percent), Oman (12.6 percent), Lebanon (12.3 percent), Kuwait (11.1 percent), Maldives (10.6 percent), Malta (10.6 percent), Bahrain (7.0 percent), the Kyrgyz Republic (6.1 percent)

Developing Countries

Population (millions, 2014)	5,861.9
Population growth (avg. annual %, 2005–14)	1.4
Population density (people per sq km, 2014)	78.5
Labor force (millions, 2014)	2,694.5
Unemployment rate (% of labor force, 2014)	5.6
Urban population (% of pop., 2014)	47.0
Surface area (thousands of sq km, 2014)	76,600.0
GNI, Atlas method (current US$ billions, 2014)	24,844.8
GNI per capita, Atlas method (current US$, 2014)	4,238.3
GDP growth (avg. annual %, 2011–14)	5.3
Poverty headcount ratio at national poverty line (% of pop.)	—
Age dependency ratio (% of working-age pop., 2014)	54.6
Account at a formal financial institution (% age 15+, 2014)	53.1
Mobile cellular subscriptions (per 100 people, 2014)	89.8
Internet users (per 100 people, 2014)	31.1

Migration

EMIGRATION

- Stock of emigrants, 2013: **180.1 million** or **3.1 percent** of population
- Top 10 emigration countries, 2013: India, Mexico, China, Bangladesh, Pakistan, the Philippines, Afghanistan, Ukraine, Indonesia, the West Bank and Gaza
- Destinations, 2013: high-income OECD countries (44.0 percent); high-income non-OECD countries (26.3 percent); other developing countries (29.6 percent); unidentified (0.1 percent)
- Top 10 migration corridors, 2013: Mexico–the United States; Bangladesh–India; Ukraine–the Russian Federation; Kazakhstan–the Russian Federation; China–the United States; Afghanistan–Pakistan; Afghanistan–the Islamic Republic of Iran; China–Hong Kong SAR, China; India–the United Arab Emirates; the West Bank and Gaza–Jordan
- Top 10 migration corridors excluding the former Soviet Union, 2013: Mexico–the United States; Bangladesh–India; China–the United States; Afghanistan–Pakistan; Afghanistan–the Islamic Republic of Iran; China–Hong Kong SAR, China; India–the United Arab Emirates; the West Bank and Gaza–Jordan; India–the United States; India–Saudi Arabia
- Tertiary-educated as a percentage of total emigrants in OECD countries, 2011: **25.4 percent**
- Tertiary-educated women as a percentage of total women emigrants in OECD countries, 2011: **25.8 percent**
- Number of refugees, 2014: **19.1 million**
- Second generation diaspora in Australia, Europe, and the United States, 2012: **24.5 million**

IMMIGRATION

- Stock of immigrants, 2013: **72.4 million** or **1.2 percent** of population (compared to 247.2 million or 3.4 percent for the world)
- Top 10 immigration countries, 2013: Ukraine, India, Thailand, Pakistan, Jordan, Kazakhstan, South Africa, the Islamic Republic of Iran, Turkey, Côte d'Ivoire

Migration and Remittances Factbook 2016

- Sources, 2013: high-income OECD countries (7.4 percent); high-income non-OECD countries (13.3 percent); other developing countries (73.5 percent); unidentified (5.9 percent)
- Women as percentage of immigrants, 2013: **46.5 percent** (compared to 47.2 percent for the world)
- Number of refugees, 2014: **17.4 million**

Remittances

US$ billions	2006	2007	2008	2009	2010	2011	2012	2013	2014	2015e
Inward										
remittance flows[a]	**228.6**	**279.5**	**324.8**	**302.9**	**335.7**	**377.9**	**400.7**	**416.2**	**431.1**	**440.5**
World	330.3	398.6	460.2	429.4	463.7	525.9	547.0	572.3	592.9	601.3
Outward										
remittance flows[a]	**28.7**	**33.3**	**40.9**	**42.2**	**42.1**	**45.0**	**52.2**	**59.2**	**58.8**	–
World	240.7	294.4	345.9	330.6	334.1	367.1	383.1	422.0	427.8	–
Memorandum Items										
Developing countries										
FDI	361.3	480.2	540.9	385.2	528.8	630.5	582.7	671.3	661.8	–
ODA[b]	105.4	104.9	122.8	120.6	129.1	134.7	126.9	135.1	135.2	–
Private debt and portfolio equity	227.9	333.8	121.7	196.8	309.4	249.8	375.9	421.7	442.6[b]	–

Note: This table reports officially recorded remittances. The true size of remittances, including unrecorded flows through formal and informal channels, is believed to be larger. FDI = foreign direct investment; ODA = official development assistance; _ = data not available.

a. For comparison: net FDI inflows US$671.35 billion, net ODA received US$149.93 billion in 2013. Inward remittance flows were 2.0 percent of GNI in 2013, outward remittance flows were 0.3 percent of GNI in 2013.

b. OECD Development Assistance Committee (DAC) online database (http://www.oecd.org/dac).

REMITTANCES

- Top 10 remittance recipients in 2015 ($US billions): India ($72.2bn), China ($63.9bn), the Philippines ($29.7bn), Mexico ($25.7bn), Nigeria ($20.8bn), the Arab Republic of Egypt ($20.4bn), Pakistan ($20.1bn), Bangladesh ($15.8bn), Vietnam ($12.3bn), Indonesia ($10.5bn)
- Top 10 remittance recipients in 2014 (percentage of GDP): Tajikistan (41.7 percent), the Kyrgyz Republic (30.3 percent), Nepal (29.2 percent), Tonga (27.9 percent), Moldova (26.2 percent), Liberia (24.6 percent), Haiti (22.7 percent), Comoros (20.2 percent), The Gambia (20.0 percent), Armenia (17.9 percent)
- Top 10 remittance senders in 2014 ($US billions): Malaysia ($8.1bn), China ($6.9bn), India ($6.2bn), Lebanon ($5.6bn), Indonesia ($4.1bn), Kazakhstan ($3.6bn), Thailand ($3.1bn), Azerbaijan ($2.0bn), Ukraine ($1.7bn), Brazil ($1.5bn)
- Top 10 remittance senders in 2014 (percentage of GDP): Liberia (18.2 percent), the Marshall Islands (12.8 percent), Lebanon (12.3 percent), Maldives (10.6 percent), the Kyrgyz Republic (6.1 percent), Solomon Islands (4.0 percent), Guyana (3.9 percent), Palau (3.8 percent), Mauritania (3.7 percent), Armenia (3.4 percent)

Regional Tables

The country composition is based on the World Bank's analytical regions and may differ from the common geographic usage.

East Asia and Pacific (developing only: 24)

American Samoa, Cambodia, China, Fiji, Indonesia, Kiribati, Democratic Republic of Korea, Lao People's Democratic Republic, Malaysia, Marshall Islands, Federated States of Micronesia, Mongolia, Myanmar, Palau, Papua New Guinea, The Philippines, Samoa, Solomon Islands, Thailand, Timor-Leste, Tonga, Tuvalu, Vanuatu, Vietnam

Europe and Central Asia (developing only: 20)

Albania, Armenia, Azerbaijan, Belarus, Bosnia and Herzegovina, Bulgaria, Georgia, Kazakhstan, Kosovo, the Kyrgyz Republic, Former Yugoslav Republic of Macedonia, Moldova, Montenegro, Romania, Serbia, Tajikistan, Turkey, Turkmenistan, Ukraine, Uzbekistan

Latin America and the Caribbean (developing only: 24)

Belize, Plurinational State of Bolivia, Brazil, Colombia, Costa Rica, Cuba, Dominica, Dominican Republic, Ecuador, El Salvador, Grenada, Guatemala, Guyana, Haiti, Honduras, Jamaica, Mexico, Nicaragua, Panama, Paraguay, Peru, St. Lucia, St. Vincent and the Grenadines, Suriname

Middle East and North Africa (developing only: 13)

Algeria, Djibouti, Arab Republic of Egypt, Islamic Republic of Iran, Iraq, Jordan, Lebanon, Libya, Morocco, Syrian Arab Republic, Tunisia, West Bank and Gaza, Republic of Yemen

South Asia (8)

Afghanistan, Bangladesh, Nepal, Bhutan, India, Maldives, Pakistan, Sri Lanka

Sub-Saharan Africa (developing only: 46)

Angola, Benin, Botswana, Burkina Faso, Burundi, Cabo Verde, Cameroon, Central African Republic, Chad, Comoros, Democratic Republic of Congo, Republic of Congo, Côte d'Ivoire, Eritrea, Ethiopia, The Gambia, Gabon, Ghana, Guinea, Guinea-Bissau, Kenya, Lesotho, Liberia, Madagascar, Malawi, Mali, Mauritania, Mauritius, Mozambique, Namibia, Niger, Nigeria, Rwanda, São Tomé and Príncipe, Senegal, Sierra Leone, Somalia, South Africa, South Sudan, Sudan, Swaziland, Tanzania, Togo, Uganda, Zambia, Zimbabwe

East Asia and Pacific

Population (millions, 2014)	2,020.7
Population growth (avg. annual %, 2005–14)	0.7
Population density (people per sq km, 2014)	127.0
Labor force (millions, 2014)	1,145.2
Unemployment rate (% of labor force, 2014)	4.6
Urban population (% of pop., 2014)	51.9
Surface area (thousands of sq km, 2014)	16,270.9
GNI, Atlas method (current US$ billions, 2014)	12,439.2
GNI per capita, Atlas method (current US$, 2014)	6,156.0
GDP growth (avg. annual %, 2011–14)	7.5
Poverty headcount ratio at national poverty line (% of pop.)	–
Age dependency ratio (% of working-age pop., 2014)	40.1
Account at a formal financial institution (% age 15+, 2014)	68.8
Mobile cellular subscriptions (per 100 people, 2014)	100.5
Internet users (per 100 people, 2014)	42.1

Migration

EMIGRATION

- Stock of emigrants, 2013: **31.4 million** or **1.6 percent** of population
- Top 10 emigration countries, 2013: China, the Philippines, Indonesia, Myanmar, Vietnam, Malaysia, the Lao People's Democratic Republic, Cambodia, Thailand, the Democratic Republic of Korea
- Destinations, 2013: high-income OECD countries (45.9 percent); high-income non-OECD countries (29.2 percent); intra-regional (20.0 percent); other developing countries (5.0 percent); unidentified (0.0 percent)
- Top 10 migration corridors, 2013: China–the United States; China–Hong Kong SAR, China; the Philippines–the United States; Myanmar–Thailand; Indonesia–Saudi Arabia; Vietnam–the United States; Indonesia–Malaysia; Malaysia–Singapore; the Lao People's Democratic Republic–Thailand; Cambodia–Thailand
- Tertiary-educated as a percentage of total emigrants in OECD countries, 2011: **38.1 percent**
- Tertiary-educated women as a percentage of total women emigrants in OECD countries, 2011: **38.2 percent**
- Number of refugees, 2014: **1,044.0 thousands**
- Second generation diaspora in Australia, Europe, and the United States, 2012: **3.1 million**

IMMIGRATION

- Stock of immigrants, 2013: **9.0 million** or **0.4 percent** of population (compared to 247.2 million or 3.4 percent for the world)
- Top 10 immigration countries, 2013: Thailand, Malaysia, China, Indonesia, the Philippines, Myanmar, Cambodia, Vietnam, the Democratic Republic of Korea, American Samoa
- Sources, 2013: high-income OECD countries (12.0 percent); high-income non-OECD countries (1.7 percent); intra-regional (69.5 percent); other developing countries (8.3 percent); unidentified (8.5 percent)
- Women as percentage of immigrants, 2013: **44.4 percent** (compared to 47.2 percent for the world)
- Number of refugees, 2014: **544.6 thousands**

Remittances

US$ billions	2006	2007	2008	2009	2010	2011	2012	2013	2014	2015e
Inward										
remittance flows[a]	**56.2**	**71.3**	**84.3**	**79.3**	**95.1**	**107.3**	**107.4**	**114.7**	**122.9**	**129.0**
All developing										
countries	228.6	279.5	324.8	302.9	335.7	377.9	400.7	416.2	431.1	440.5
World	330.3	398.6	460.2	429.4	463.7	525.9	547.0	572.3	592.9	601.3
Outward										
remittance flows[a]	**10.5**	**13.0**	**16.0**	**17.1**	**14.8**	**17.8**	**19.5**	**21.1**	**23.8**	—
All developing										
countries	28.7	33.3	40.9	42.2	42.1	45.0	52.2	59.2	58.8	—
World	240.7	294.4	345.9	330.6	334.1	367.1	383.1	422.0	427.8	—

Note: This table reports officially recorded remittances. The true size of remittances, including unrecorded flows through formal and informal channels, is believed to be larger.

a. For comparison: net FDI inflows US$360.8 billion, net ODA received US$11.88 billion in 2013. Inward remittance flows were 1.2 percent of GNI in 2013, outward remittance flows were 0.2 percent of GNI in 2013.

REMITTANCES

- Top 10 remittance recipients in 2015 ($US billions): China ($63.9bn), the Philippines ($29.7bn), Vietnam ($12.3bn), Indonesia ($10.5bn), Thailand ($5.7bn), Myanmar ($3.5bn), Malaysia ($1.7bn), Cambodia ($0.9bn), Mongolia ($0.2bn), Fiji ($0.2bn)
- Top 10 remittance recipients in 2014 (percentage of GDP): Tonga (27.9 percent), Samoa (17.6 percent), the Marshall Islands (14.0 percent), Tuvalu (10.7 percent), the Philippines (10.0 percent), Kiribati (9.6 percent), the Federated States of Micronesia (6.9 percent), Vietnam (6.4 percent), Myanmar (4.8 percent), Fiji (4.5 percent)
- Top 10 remittance senders in 2014 ($US billions): Malaysia ($8.1bn), China ($6.9bn), Indonesia ($4.1bn), Thailand ($3.1bn), Myanmar ($0.8bn), Mongolia ($0.3bn), Cambodia ($0.2bn), the Philippines ($0.2bn), Solomon Islands ($0.0bn), Timor-Leste ($0.0bn)
- Top 10 remittance senders in 2014 (percentage of GDP): the Marshall Islands (12.8 percent), Solomon Islands (4.0 percent), Palau (3.8 percent), Mongolia (2.8 percent), Malaysia (2.4 percent), Timor-Leste (1.9 percent), Samoa (1.6 percent), Cambodia (1.3 percent), Myanmar (1.2 percent), Thailand (0.8 percent)

Europe and Central Asia

Population (millions, 2014)	264.4
Population growth (avg. annual %, 2005–14)	0.6
Population density (people per sq km, 2014)	42.3
Labor force (millions, 2014)	117.2
Unemployment rate (% of labor force, 2014)	9.3
Urban population (% of pop., 2014)	59.9
Surface area (thousands of sq km, 2014)	6,385.6
GNI, Atlas method (current US$ billions, 2014)	1,821.9
GNI per capita, Atlas method (current US$, 2014)	6,891.9
GDP growth (avg. annual %, 2011–14)	3.7
Poverty headcount ratio at national poverty line (% of pop.)	–
Age dependency ratio (% of working-age pop., 2014)	47.5
Account at a formal financial institution (% age 15+, 2014)	51.4
Mobile cellular subscriptions (per 100 people, 2014)	112.7
Internet users (per 100 people, 2014)	48.2

Migration

EMIGRATION

- Stock of emigrants, 2013: **31.9 million** or **12.2 percent** of population
- Top 10 emigration countries, 2013: Ukraine, Kazakhstan, Romania, Turkey, Uzbekistan, Bosnia and Herzegovina, Belarus, Bulgaria, Serbia, Azerbaijan
- Destinations, 2013: high-income OECD countries (46.0 percent); high-income non-OECD countries (36.4 percent); intra-regional (17.3 percent); other developing countries (0.4 percent); unidentified (0.0 percent)
- Top 10 migration corridors, 2013: Ukraine–the Russian Federation; Kazakhstan–the Russian Federation; Turkey–Germany; Uzbekistan–the Russian Federation; Romania–Italy; Romania–Spain; Azerbaijan–the Russian Federation; Belarus–the Russian Federation; Kazakhstan–Germany; Bulgaria–Turkey
- Tertiary-educated as a percentage of total emigrants in OECD countries, 2011: **19.6 percent**
- Tertiary-educated women as a percentage of total women emigrants in OECD countries, 2011: **21.0 percent**
- Number of refugees, 2014: **431.6 thousands**
- Second generation diaspora in Australia, Europe, and the United States, 2012: **2.5 million**

IMMIGRATION

- Stock of immigrants, 2013: **17.2 million** or **6.5 percent** of population (compared to 247.2 million or 3.4 percent for the world)
- Top 10 immigration countries, 2013: Ukraine, Kazakhstan, Turkey, Uzbekistan, Belarus, Serbia, Moldova, Armenia, Azerbaijan, Tajikistan
- Sources, 2013: high-income OECD countries (8.3 percent); high-income non-OECD countries (50.2 percent); intra-regional (32.1 percent); other developing countries (5.6 percent); unidentified (3.8 percent)
- Women as percentage of immigrants, 2013: **51.8 percent** (compared to 47.2 percent for the world)
- Number of refugees, 2014: **1,686.0 thousands**

Remittances

US$ billions	2006	2007	2008	2009	2010	2011	2012	2013	2014	2015e
Inward										
remittance flows[a]	**23.7**	**35.9**	**43.1**	**34.0**	**34.6**	**40.3**	**43.2**	**47.7**	**43.7**	**36.1**
All developing										
countries	228.6	279.5	324.8	302.9	335.7	377.9	400.7	416.2	431.1	440.5
World	330.3	398.6	460.2	429.4	463.7	525.9	547.0	572.3	592.9	601.3
Outward										
remittance flows[a]	**4.7**	**6.6**	**6.9**	**5.8**	**6.5**	**7.6**	**9.2**	**10.3**	**11.0**	–
All developing										
countries	28.7	33.3	40.9	42.2	42.1	45.0	52.2	59.2	58.8	–
World	240.7	294.4	345.9	330.6	334.1	367.1	383.1	422.0	427.8	–

Note: This table reports officially recorded remittances. The true size of remittances, including unrecorded flows through formal and informal channels, is believed to be larger.

a. For comparison: net FDI inflows US$48.31 billion, net ODA received US$9.03 billion in 2013. Inward remittance flows were 2.6 percent of GNI in 2013, outward remittance flows were 0.7 percent of GNI in 2013.

REMITTANCES

- Top 10 remittance recipients in 2015 ($US billions): Ukraine ($6.2bn), Serbia ($3.6bn), Romania ($3.2bn), Tajikistan ($3.0bn), Uzbekistan ($2.3bn), Bosnia and Herzegovina ($2.0bn), Moldova ($1.8bn), Bulgaria ($1.8bn), the Kyrgyz Republic ($1.7bn), Armenia ($1.7bn)
- Top 10 remittance recipients in 2014 (percentage of GDP): Tajikistan (41.7 percent), the Kyrgyz Republic (30.3 percent), Moldova (26.2 percent), Armenia (17.9 percent), Kosovo (16.1 percent), Georgia (12.0 percent), Bosnia and Herzegovina (11.4 percent), Montenegro (9.4 percent), Uzbekistan (9.0 percent), Albania (8.6 percent)
- Top 10 remittance senders in 2014 ($US billions): Kazakhstan ($3.6bn), Azerbaijan ($2.0bn), Ukraine ($1.7bn), Turkey ($0.9bn), Romania ($0.6bn), the Kyrgyz Republic ($0.5bn), Armenia ($0.4bn), Serbia ($0.3bn), Tajikistan ($0.2bn), Belarus ($0.2bn)
- Top 10 remittance senders in 2014 (percentage of GDP): the Kyrgyz Republic (6.1 percent), Armenia (3.4 percent), Azerbaijan (2.7 percent), Tajikistan (2.2 percent), Moldova (1.8 percent), Kazakhstan (1.6 percent), Montenegro (1.6 percent), Albania (1.4 percent), Kosovo (1.4 percent), Ukraine (1.3 percent)

Latin America and the Caribbean

Population (millions, 2014)	525.2
Population growth (avg. annual %, 2005–14)	1.2
Population density (people per sq km, 2014)	33.9
Labor force (millions, 2014)	259.3
Unemployment rate (% of labor force, 2014)	6.3
Urban population (% of pop., 2014)	77.8
Surface area (thousands of sq km, 2014)	15,769.3
GNI, Atlas method (current US$ billions, 2014)	4,721.1
GNI per capita, Atlas method (current US$, 2014)	8,989.5
GDP growth (avg. annual %, 2011–14)	3.0
Poverty headcount ratio at national poverty line (% of pop.)	–
Age dependency ratio (% of working-age pop., 2014)	50.3
Account at a formal financial institution (% age 15+, 2014)	51.1
Mobile cellular subscriptions (per 100 people, 2014)	111.3
Internet users (per 100 people, 2014)	47.5

Migration

EMIGRATION

- Stock of emigrants, 2013: **32.5 million** or **6.3 percent** of population
- Top 10 emigration countries, 2013: Mexico, Colombia, Brazil, El Salvador, Cuba, Peru, Haiti, the Dominican Republic, Ecuador, Jamaica
- Destinations, 2013: high-income OECD countries (84.5 percent); high-income non-OECD countries (8.9 percent); intra-regional (5.6 percent); other developing countries (0.6 percent); unidentified (0.4 percent)
- Top 10 migration corridors, 2013: Mexico–the United States; El Salvador–the United States; Cuba–the United States; the Dominican Republic–the United States; Guatemala–the United States; Colombia–República Bolivariana de Venezuela; Paraguay–Argentina; Jamaica–the United States; Colombia–the United States; Haiti–the United States
- Tertiary-educated as a percentage of total emigrants in OECD countries, 2011: **14.6 percent**
- Tertiary-educated women as a percentage of total women emigrants in OECD countries, 2011: **16.3 percent**
- Number of refugees, 2014: **452.7 thousands**
- Second generation diaspora in Australia, Europe, and the United States, 2012: **12.7 million**

IMMIGRATION

- Stock of immigrants, 2013: **4.2 million** or **0.8 percent** of population (compared to 247.2 million or 3.4 percent for the world)
- Top 10 immigration countries, 2013: Mexico, the Dominican Republic, Brazil, Costa Rica, Ecuador, Paraguay, Panama, Colombia, the Plurinational State of Bolivia, Peru
- Sources, 2013: high-income OECD countries (42.0 percent); high-income non-OECD countries (9.7 percent); intra-regional (43.6 percent); other developing countries (4.0 percent); unidentified (0.8 percent)
- Women as percentage of immigrants, 2013: **47.1 percent** (compared to 47.2 percent for the world)
- Number of refugees, 2014: **172.9 thousands**

Remittances

US$ billions	2006	2007	2008	2009	2010	2011	2012	2013	2014	2015e
Inward										
remittance flows[a]	**56.8**	**60.8**	**61.8**	**54.3**	**55.4**	**58.7**	**59.5**	**61.0**	**63.6**	**67.2**
All developing										
countries	*228.6*	*279.5*	*324.8*	*302.9*	*335.7*	*377.9*	*400.7*	*416.2*	*431.1*	*440.5*
World	330.3	398.6	460.2	429.4	463.7	525.9	547.0	572.3	592.9	601.3
Outward										
remittance flows[a]	**1.7**	**1.9**	**2.3**	**2.3**	**3.2**	**3.4**	**3.7**	**4.8**	**5.8**	–
All developing										
countries	*28.7*	*33.3*	*40.9*	*42.2*	*42.1*	*45.0*	*52.2*	*59.2*	*58.8*	–
World	240.7	294.4	345.9	330.6	334.1	367.1	383.1	422.0	427.8	–

Note: This table reports officially recorded remittances. The true size of remittances, including unrecorded flows through formal and informal channels, is believed to be larger.

a. For comparison: net FDI inflows US$168.7 billion, net ODA received US$10.2 billion in 2013. Inward remittance flows were 1.4 percent of GNI in 2013, outward remittance flows were 0.1 percent of GNI in 2013.

REMITTANCES

- Top 10 remittance recipients in 2015 ($US billions): Mexico ($25.7bn), Guatemala ($6.4bn), the Dominican Republic ($5.0bn), Colombia ($4.5bn), El Salvador ($4.4bn), Honduras ($3.8bn), Brazil ($2.8bn), Peru ($2.7bn), Ecuador ($2.4bn), Jamaica ($2.3bn)
- Top 10 remittance recipients in 2014 (percentage of GDP): Haiti (22.7 percent), Honduras (17.4 percent), El Salvador (16.8 percent), Jamaica (16.3 percent), Guyana (10.6 percent), Guatemala (9.9 percent), Nicaragua (9.7 percent), the Dominican Republic (7.5 percent), Belize (4.7 percent), Dominica (4.5 percent)
- Top 10 remittance senders in 2014 ($US billions): Brazil ($1.5bn), Mexico ($1.0bn), Panama ($0.8bn), the Dominican Republic ($0.6bn), Costa Rica ($0.4bn), Jamaica ($0.3bn), Haiti ($0.2bn), Colombia ($0.2bn), Ecuador ($0.2bn), the Plurinational State of Bolivia ($0.2bn)
- Top 10 remittance senders in 2014 (percentage of GDP): Guyana (3.9 percent), Haiti (2.9 percent), Belize (2.0 percent), Jamaica (2.0 percent), Panama (1.8 percent), the Dominican Republic (0.9 percent), Costa Rica (0.8 percent), the Plurinational State of Bolivia (0.6 percent), Suriname (0.4 percent), Honduras (0.2 percent)

Middle East and North Africa

Population (millions, 2014)	357.3
Population growth (avg. annual %, 2005–14)	1.8
Population density (people per sq km, 2014)	41.4
Labor force (millions, 2014)	115.1
Unemployment rate (% of labor force, 2014)	12.9
Urban population (% of pop., 2014)	60.0
Surface area (thousands of sq km, 2014)	8,775.4
GNI, Atlas method (current US$ billions, 2014)	1,655.9
GNI per capita, Atlas method (current US$, 2014)	4,722.4
GDP growth (avg. annual %, 2011–14)	1.0
Poverty headcount ratio at national poverty line (% of pop.)	—
Age dependency ratio (% of working-age pop., 2014)	57.3
Account at a formal financial institution (% age 15+)	14.0[a]
Mobile cellular subscriptions (per 100 people, 2014)	100.7
Internet users (per 100 people, 2014)	32.7

a. includes only Middle East

Migration

EMIGRATION

- Stock of emigrants, 2013: **23.9 million** or **6.8 percent** of population
- Top 10 emigration countries, 2013: the West Bank and Gaza, the Syrian Arab Republic, the Arab Republic of Egypt, Morocco, Iraq, Algeria, the Islamic Republic of Iran, the Republic of Yemen, Lebanon, Jordan
- Destinations, 2013: high-income OECD countries (37.7 percent); high-income non-OECD countries (27.7 percent); intra-regional (30.9 percent); other developing countries (3.7 percent); unidentified (0.0 percent)
- Top 10 migration corridors, 2013: the West Bank and Gaza–Jordan; Algeria–France; the Arab Republic of Egypt–Saudi Arabia; the Syrian Arab Republic–Saudi Arabia; Morocco–France; the Republic of Yemen–Saudi Arabia; Morocco–Spain; Iraq–the Syrian Arab Republic; the Syrian Arab Republic–Lebanon; the Syrian Arab Republic–Jordan
- Tertiary-educated as a percentage of total emigrants in OECD countries, 2011: **25.9 percent**
- Tertiary-educated women as a percentage of total women emigrants in OECD countries, 2011: **23.8 percent**
- Number of refugees, 2014: **9,618.2 thousands**
- Second generation diaspora in Australia, Europe, and the United States, 2012: **3.4 million**

IMMIGRATION

- Stock of immigrants, 2013: **11.7 million** or **3.3 percent** of population (compared to 247.2 million or 3.4 percent for the world)
- Top 10 immigration countries, 2013: Jordan, the Islamic Republic of Iran, Lebanon, the Syrian Arab Republic, Libya, the Arab Republic of Egypt, the Republic of Yemen, Algeria, the West Bank and Gaza, Iraq
- Sources, 2013: high-income OECD countries (1.5 percent); high-income non-OECD countries (1.6 percent); intra-regional (63.2 percent); other developing countries (26.7 percent); unidentified (7.0 percent)

- Women as percentage of immigrants, 2013: **44.2 percent** (compared to 47.2 percent for the world)
- Number of refugees, 2014: **8,998.5 thousands**

Remittances

US$ billions	2006	2007	2008	2009	2010	2011	2012	2013	2014	2015e
Inward remittance flows[a]	**25.9**	**31.4**	**35.2**	**33.0**	**38.9**	**41.6**	**48.5**	**48.8**	**50.9**	**51.7**
All developing countries	*228.6*	*279.5*	*324.8*	*302.9*	*335.7*	*377.9*	*400.7*	*416.2*	*431.1*	*440.5*
World	330.3	398.6	460.2	429.4	463.7	525.9	547.0	572.3	592.9	601.3
Outward remittance flows[a]	**6.2**	**5.1**	**6.7**	**8.6**	**7.8**	**6.2**	**8.5**	**9.9**	**6.4**	—
All developing countries	*28.7*	*33.3*	*40.9*	*42.2*	*42.1*	*45.0*	*52.2*	*59.2*	*58.8*	—
World	240.7	294.4	345.9	330.6	334.1	367.1	383.1	422.0	427.8	—

Note: This table reports officially recorded remittances. The true size of remittances, including unrecorded flows through formal and informal channels, is believed to be larger.

a. For comparison: net FDI inflows US$24.16 billion, net ODA received US$25.68 billion in 2013. Inward remittance flows were 3.3 percent of GNI in 2013, outward remittance flows were 0.4 percent of GNI in 2013.

REMITTANCES

- Top 10 remittance recipients in 2015 ($US billions): the Arab Republic of Egypt ($20.4bn), Lebanon ($7.5bn), Morocco ($6.7bn), Jordan ($3.8bn), the Republic of Yemen ($3.4bn), Tunisia ($2.3bn), the West Bank and Gaza ($2.3bn), Algeria ($2.0bn), the Syrian Arab Republic ($1.6bn), the Islamic Republic of Iran ($1.3bn)
- Top 10 remittance recipients in 2014 (percentage of GDP): the West Bank and Gaza (17.1 percent), Lebanon (16.2 percent), Jordan (10.3 percent), the Republic of Yemen (9.3 percent), the Arab Republic of Egypt (6.8 percent), Morocco (6.4 percent), Tunisia (4.8 percent), Djibouti (2.2 percent), Algeria (0.9 percent), the Islamic Republic of Iran (0.3 percent)
- Top 5 remittance senders in 2014 ($US billions): Lebanon ($5.6bn), the Arab Republic of Egypt ($0.4bn), the Republic of Yemen ($0.3bn), Algeria ($0.1bn), the West Bank and Gaza ($0.0bn)
- Top 5 remittance senders in 2014 (percentage of GDP): Lebanon (12.3 percent), the Republic of Yemen (0.9 percent), the West Bank and Gaza (0.3 percent), the Arab Republic of Egypt (0.1 percent), Tunisia (0.1 percent)

South Asia

Population (millions, 2014)	1,721.0
Population growth (avg. annual %, 2005–14)	1.5
Population density (people per sq km, 2014)	360.7
Labor force (millions, 2014)	674.3
Unemployment rate (% of labor force, 2014)	3.9
Urban population (% of pop., 2014)	32.6
Surface area (thousands of sq km, 2014)	5,136.2
GNI, Atlas method (current US$ billions, 2014)	2,575.3
GNI per capita, Atlas method (current US$, 2014)	1,496.4
GDP growth (avg. annual %, 2011–14)	6.2
Poverty headcount ratio at national poverty line (% of pop.)	–
Age dependency ratio (% of working-age pop., 2014)	55.4
Account at a formal financial institution (% age 15+, 2014)	45.5
Mobile cellular subscriptions (per 100 people, 2014)	75.0
Internet users (per 100 people, 2014)	16.6

Migration

EMIGRATION

- Stock of emigrants, 2013: **37.1 million** or **2.2 percent** of population
- Top 5 emigration countries, 2013: India, Bangladesh, Pakistan, Afghanistan, Nepal
- Destinations, 2013: high-income OECD countries (20.6 percent); high-income non-OECD countries (42.8 percent); intra-regional (28.2 percent); other developing countries (8.4 percent); unidentified (0.0 percent)
- Top 10 migration corridors, 2013: Bangladesh–India; Afghanistan–Pakistan; Afghanistan–the Islamic Republic of Iran; India–the United Arab Emirates; India–the United States; India–Saudi Arabia; Bangladesh–Saudi Arabia; Pakistan–Saudi Arabia; India–Pakistan; Pakistan–the United Arab Emirates
- Tertiary-educated as a percentage of total emigrants in OECD countries, 2011: **48.2 percent**
- Tertiary-educated women as a percentage of total women emigrants in OECD countries, 2011: **45.8 percent**
- Number of refugees, 2014: **3,104.6 thousands**
- Second generation diaspora in Australia, Europe, and the United States, 2012: **1.7 million**

IMMIGRATION

- Stock of immigrants, 2013: **12.4 million** or **0.7 percent** of population (compared to 247.2 million or 3.4 percent for the world)
- Top 5 immigration countries, 2013: India, Pakistan, Bangladesh, Nepal, Sri Lanka
- Sources, 2013: high-income OECD countries (1.0 percent); high-income non-OECD countries (0.9 percent); intra-regional (84.6 percent); other developing countries (9.3 percent); unidentified (4.2 percent)
- Women as percentage of immigrants, 2013: **44.3 percent** (compared to 47.2 percent for the world)
- Number of refugees, 2014: **2,277.3 thousands**

Remittances

US$ billions	2006	2007	2008	2009	2010	2011	2012	2013	2014	2015e
Inward remittance flows[a]	**42.5**	**54.0**	**71.7**	**74.9**	**82.0**	**96.4**	**108.0**	**110.8**	**115.5**	–
All developing countries	*228.6*	*279.5*	*324.8*	*302.9*	*335.7*	*377.9*	*400.7*	*416.2*	*431.1*	*440.5*
World	330.3	398.6	460.2	429.4	463.7	525.9	547.0	572.3	592.9	601.3
Outward remittance flows[a]	**4.2**	**5.2**	**9.3**	**7.8**	**10.0**	**10.7**	**12.5**	**15.9**	**15.6**	–
All developing countries	*28.7*	*33.3*	*40.9*	*42.2*	*42.1*	*45.0*	*52.2*	*59.2*	*58.8*	–
World	240.7	294.4	345.9	330.6	334.1	367.1	383.1	422.0	427.8	–

Note: This table reports officially recorded remittances. The true size of remittances, including unrecorded flows through formal and informal channels, is believed to be larger.

a. For comparison: net FDI inflows US$32.85 billion, net ODA received US$14.06 billion in 2013. Inward remittance flows were 4.9 percent of GNI in 2013, outward remittance flows were 0.7 percent of GNI in 2013.

REMITTANCES

- Top 5 remittance recipients in 2015 ($US billions): India ($72.2bn), Pakistan ($20.1bn), Bangladesh ($15.8bn), Sri Lanka ($7.2bn), Nepal ($6.6bn)
- Top 5 remittance recipients in 2014 (percentage of GDP): Nepal (29.2 percent), Sri Lanka (8.9 percent), Bangladesh (8.7 percent), Pakistan (7.0 percent), India (3.4 percent)
- Top 5 remittance senders in 2014 ($US billions): India ($6.2bn), Sri Lanka ($0.9bn), Maldives ($0.3bn), Afghanistan ($0.2bn), Bhutan ($0.0bn)
- Top 5 remittance senders in 2014 (percentage of GDP): Maldives (10.6 percent), Bhutan (2.5 percent), Afghanistan (1.2 percent), Sri Lanka (1.1 percent), India (0.3 percent)

Sub-Saharan Africa

Population (millions, 2014)	973.4
Population growth (avg. annual %, 2005–14)	2.8
Population density (people per sq km, 2014)	41.3
Labor force (millions, 2014)	383.3
Unemployment rate (% of labor force, 2014)	8.0
Urban population (% of pop., 2014)	37.2
Surface area (thousands of sq km, 2014)	24,262.6
GNI, Atlas method (current US$ billions, 2014)	1,594.6
GNI per capita, Atlas method (current US$, 2014)	1,638.2
GDP growth (avg. annual %, 2011–14)	4.3
Poverty headcount ratio at national poverty line (% of pop.)	—
Age dependency ratio (% of working-age pop., 2014)	86.8
Account at a formal financial institution (% age 15+, 2014)	28.9
Mobile cellular subscriptions (per 100 people, 2014)	71.1
Internet users (per 100 people, 2014)	19.2

Migration

EMIGRATION

- Stock of emigrants, 2013: **23.2 million** or **2.5 percent** of population
- Top 10 emigration countries, 2013: Somalia, Burkina Faso, Sudan, the Democratic Republic of Congo, Nigeria, Côte d'Ivoire, Zimbabwe, Mali, South Africa, South Sudan
- Destinations, 2013: high-income OECD countries (26.1 percent); high-income non-OECD countries (5.0 percent); intra-regional (65.6 percent); other developing countries (2.9 percent); unidentified (0.4 percent)
- Top 10 migration corridors, 2013: Burkina Faso–Côte d'Ivoire; Zimbabwe–South Africa; Côte d'Ivoire–Burkina Faso; Sudan–Saudi Arabia; Somalia–Kenya; Somalia–Ethiopia; Sudan–South Sudan; Mali–Côte d'Ivoire; Mozambique–South Africa; Lesotho–South Africa
- Tertiary-educated as a percentage of total emigrants in OECD countries, 2011: **33.4 percent**
- Tertiary-educated women as a percentage of total women emigrants in OECD countries, 2011: **31.4 percent**
- Number of refugees, 2014: **4,477.5 thousands**
- Second generation diaspora in Australia, Europe, and the United States, 2012: **1.1 million**

IMMIGRATION

- Stock of immigrants, 2013: **18.0 million** or **1.9 percent** of population (compared to 247.2 million or 3.4 percent for the world)
- Top 10 immigration countries, 2013: South Africa, Côte d'Ivoire, Nigeria, Kenya, Ethiopia, Burkina Faso, Tanzania, South Sudan, Cameroon, Uganda
- Sources, 2013: high-income OECD countries (4.2 percent); high-income non-OECD countries (0.7 percent); intra-regional (84.6 percent); other developing countries (2.2 percent); unidentified (8.2 percent)
- Women as percentage of immigrants, 2013: **45.3 percent** (compared to 47.2 percent for the world)
- Number of refugees, 2014: **3,745.4 thousands**

Remittances

US$ billions	2006	2007	2008	2009	2010	2011	2012	2013	2014	2015e
Inward										
remittance flows[a]	**23.5**	**26.1**	**28.7**	**27.4**	**29.7**	**33.6**	**34.1**	**33.2**	**34.5**	**34.8**
All developing										
countries	*228.6*	*279.5*	*324.8*	*302.9*	*335.7*	*377.9*	*400.7*	*416.2*	*431.1*	*440.5*
World	330.3	398.6	460.2	429.4	463.7	525.9	547.0	572.3	592.9	601.3
Outward										
remittance flows[a]	**3.5**	**4.0**	**4.2**	**4.5**	**4.7**	**4.7**	**5.1**	**5.2**	**4.1**	–
All developing										
countries	*28.7*	*33.3*	*40.9*	*42.2*	*42.1*	*45.0*	*52.2*	*59.2*	*58.8*	–
World	240.7	294.4	345.9	330.6	334.1	367.1	383.1	422.0	427.8	–

Note: This table reports officially recorded remittances. The true size of remittances, including unrecorded flows through formal and informal channels, is believed to be larger.

a. For comparison: net FDI inflows US$36.54 billion, net ODA received US$46.77 billion in 2013. Inward remittance flows were 2.4 percent of GNI in 2013, outward remittance flows were 0.3 percent of GNI in 2013.

REMITTANCES

- Top 10 remittance recipients in 2015 ($US billions): Nigeria ($20.8bn), Ghana ($2.0bn), Senegal ($1.6bn), Kenya ($1.6bn), South Africa ($1.0bn), Uganda ($0.9bn), Mali ($0.9bn), Ethiopia ($0.6bn), Liberia ($0.5bn), Sudan ($0.5bn)

- Top 10 remittance recipients in 2014 (percentage of GDP): Liberia (24.6 percent), Comoros (20.2 percent), The Gambia (20.0 percent), Lesotho (17.4 percent), Senegal (10.3 percent), Cabo Verde (10.2 percent), Togo (8.8 percent), São Tomé and Príncipe (8.0 percent), Mali (7.4 percent), Guinea-Bissau (6.2 percent)

- Top 10 remittance senders in 2014 ($US billions): Angola ($1.3bn), South Africa ($1.1bn), Liberia ($0.4bn), Uganda ($0.3bn), Mozambique ($0.2bn), Mauritania ($0.2bn), Kenya ($0.2bn), Rwanda ($0.1bn), Tanzania ($0.1bn), Zambia ($0.1bn)

- Top 10 remittance senders in 2014 (percentage of GDP): Liberia (18.2 percent), Mauritania (3.7 percent), Rwanda (1.6 percent), Mozambique (1.2 percent), Uganda (1.1 percent), Angola (0.9 percent), Cabo Verde (0.5 percent), São Tomé and Príncipe (0.4 percent), South Africa (0.3 percent), Zambia (0.3 percent)

Income-Group Tables

Low-Income Countries (31)

Afghanistan, Benin, Burkina Faso, Burundi, Cambodia, Central African Republic, Chad, Comoros, Democratic Republic of Congo, Eritrea, Ethiopia, The Gambia, Guinea, Guinea-Bissau, Haiti, Democratic Republic of Korea, Liberia, Madagascar, Malawi, Mali, Mozambique, Nepal, Niger, Rwanda, Sierra Leone, Somalia, South Sudan, Tanzania, Togo, Uganda, Zimbabwe

Middle-Income Countries (104)

Albania, Algeria, American Samoa, Angola, Armenia, Azerbaijan, Bangladesh, Belarus, Belize, Bhutan, Plurinational State of Bolivia, Bosnia and Herzegovina, Botswana, Brazil, Bulgaria, Cabo Verde, Cameroon, China, Colombia, Republic of Congo, Costa Rica, Côte d'Ivoire, Cuba, Djibouti, Dominica, Dominican Republic, Ecuador, Arab Republic of Egypt, El Salvador, Fiji, Gabon, Georgia, Ghana, Grenada, Guatemala, Guyana, Honduras, India, Indonesia, Islamic Republic of Iran, Iraq, Jamaica, Jordan, Kazakhstan, Kenya, Kiribati, Kosovo, Kyrgyz Republic, Lao People's Democratic Republic, Lebanon, Lesotho, Libya, Former Yugoslav Republic of Macedonia, Malaysia, Maldives, Marshall Islands, Mauritania, Mauritius, Mexico, Federated States of Micronesia, Moldova, Mongolia, Montenegro, Morocco, Myanmar, Namibia, Nicaragua, Nigeria, Pakistan, Palau, Panama, Papua New Guinea, Paraguay, Peru, The Philippines, Romania, Samoa, São Tomé and Príncipe, Senegal, Serbia, Solomon Islands, South Africa, Sri Lanka, St. Lucia, St. Vincent and the Grenadines, Sudan, Suriname, Swaziland, Syrian Arab Republic, Tajikistan, Thailand, Timor-Leste, Tonga, Tunisia, Turkey, Turkmenistan, Tuvalu, Ukraine, Uzbekistan, Vanuatu, Vietnam, West Bank and Gaza, Republic of Yemen, Zambia

High-Income OECD Countries (32)

Australia, Austria, Belgium, Canada, Chile, Czech Republic, Denmark, Estonia, Finland, France, Germany, Greece, Hungary, Iceland, Ireland, Israel, Italy, Japan, Republic of Korea, Luxembourg, The Netherlands, New Zealand, Norway, Poland, Portugal, Slovak Republic, Slovenia, Spain, Sweden, Switzerland, United Kingdom, United States

High-Income Non-OECD Countries (47)

Andorra, Argentina, Antigua and Barbuda, Aruba, The Bahamas, Bahrain, Barbados, Bermuda, Brunei Darussalam, Cayman Islands, Channel Islands, Croatia, Curaçao, Cyprus, Equatorial Guinea, Faeroe Islands, French Polynesia, Greenland, Guam, Hong Kong SAR China, Isle of Man, Kuwait, Latvia, Liechtenstein, Lithuania, Macao SAR China, Malta, Monaco, New Caledonia, Northern Mariana Islands, Oman, Puerto Rico, Qatar, Russian Federation, San Marino, Saudi Arabia, Seychelles, Singapore, Sint Maarten (Dutch part), St. Kitts and Nevis, St. Martin (French part), Trinidad and Tobago, Turks and Caicos Islands, United Arab Emirates, Uruguay, República Bolivariana de Venezuela, Virgin Islands (U.S.)

Low-Income Countries

Population (millions, 2014)	622.0
Population growth (avg. annual %, 2005–14)	2.7
Population density (people per sq km, 2014)	46.5
Labor force (millions, 2014)	271.0
Unemployment rate (% of labor force, 2014)	5.7
Urban population (% of pop., 2014)	29.8
Surface area (thousands of sq km, 2014)	14,455.8
GNI, Atlas method (current US$ billions, 2014)	391.0
GNI per capita, Atlas method (current US$, 2014)	628.6
GDP growth (avg. annual %, 2011–14)	6.3
Poverty headcount ratio at national poverty line (% of pop.)	—
Age dependency ratio (% of working-age pop., 2014)	87.0
Account at a formal financial institution (% age 15+, 2014)	22.3
Mobile cellular subscriptions (per 100 people, 2014)	57.2
Internet users (per 100 people, 2014)	6.3

Migration

EMIGRATION

- Stock of emigrants, 2013: **24.9 million** or **4.1 percent** of population
- Top 10 emigration countries, 2013: Afghanistan, Nepal, Somalia, Burkina Faso, Haiti, the Democratic Republic of Congo, Cambodia, Zimbabwe, Mali, South Sudan
- Destinations, 2013: high-income OECD countries (17.4 percent); high-income non-OECD countries (8.3 percent); developing countries (73.8 percent); unidentified (0.5 percent)
- Top 10 migration corridors, 2013: Afghanistan–Pakistan; Afghanistan–the Islamic Republic of Iran; Burkina Faso–Côte d'Ivoire; Cambodia–Thailand; Zimbabwe–South Africa; Haiti–the United States; Nepal–India; Nepal–Saudi Arabia; Afghanistan–Saudi Arabia; Somalia–Kenya
- Tertiary-educated as a percentage of total emigrants in OECD countries, 2011: **26.1 percent**
- Tertiary-educated women as a percentage of total women emigrants in OECD countries, 2011: **23.9 percent**
- Number of refugees, 2014: **6,177.1 thousands**
- Second generation diaspora in Australia, Europe, and the United States, 2012: **0.9 million**

IMMIGRATION

- Stock of immigrants, 2013: **8.9 million** or **1.4 percent** of population (compared to 247.2 million or 3.4 percent for the world)
- Top 10 immigration countries, 2013: Nepal, Ethiopia, Burkina Faso, Tanzania, South Sudan, Uganda, the Democratic Republic of Congo, Chad, Rwanda, Guinea
- Sources, 2013: high-income OECD countries (1.6 percent); high-income non-OECD countries (0.1 percent); developing countries (89.7 percent); unidentified (8.6 percent)
- Women as percentage of immigrants, 2013: **49.9 percent** (compared to 47.2 percent for the world)
- Number of refugees, 2014: **2,665.8 thousands**

Remittances

US$ billions	2006	2007	2008	2009	2010	2011	2012	2013	2014	2015e
Inward										
remittance flows[a]	**4.7**	**5.9**	**7.7**	**7.8**	**9.3**	**11.0**	**12.2**	**13.3**	**13.9**	**15.3**
All developing										
countries	228.6	279.5	324.8	302.9	335.7	377.9	400.7	416.2	431.1	440.5
World	330.3	398.6	460.2	429.4	463.7	525.9	547.0	572.3	592.9	601.3
Outward										
remittance flows[a]	**1.0**	**1.1**	**1.6**	**1.9**	**2.1**	**2.0**	**2.5**	**2.6**	**1.8**	—
All developing										
countries	28.7	33.3	40.9	42.2	42.1	45.0	52.2	59.2	58.8	—
World	240.7	294.4	345.9	330.6	334.1	367.1	383.1	422.0	427.8	—

Note: This table reports officially recorded remittances. The true size of remittances, including unrecorded flows through formal and informal channels, is believed to be larger.

a. For comparison: net FDI inflows US$17.98 billion, net ODA received US$43.86 billion in 2013. Inward remittance flows were 4.2 percent of GNI in 2013, outward remittance flows were 0.5 percent of GNI in 2013.

REMITTANCES

- Top 10 remittance recipients in 2015 ($US billions): Nepal ($6.6bn), Haiti ($2.0bn), Cambodia ($0.9bn), Uganda ($0.9bn), Mali ($0.9bn), Ethiopia ($0.6bn), Liberia ($0.5bn), Madagascar ($0.4bn), Tanzania ($0.4bn), Togo ($0.4bn)
- Top 10 remittance recipients in 2014 (percentage of GDP): Nepal (29.2 percent), Liberia (24.6 percent), Haiti (22.7 percent), Comoros (20.2 percent), The Gambia (20.0 percent), Togo (8.8 percent), Mali (7.4 percent), Guinea-Bissau (6.2 percent), Madagascar (4.0 percent), Uganda (3.3 percent)
- Top 10 remittance senders in 2014 ($US billions): Liberia ($0.4bn), Uganda ($0.3bn), Haiti ($0.2bn), Afghanistan ($0.2bn), Cambodia ($0.2bn), Mozambique ($0.2bn), Rwanda ($0.1bn), Tanzania ($0.1bn), the Democratic Republic of Congo ($0.0bn), Nepal ($0.0bn)
- Top 10 remittance senders in 2014 (percentage of GDP): Liberia (18.2 percent), Haiti (2.9 percent), Rwanda (1.6 percent), Cambodia (1.3 percent), Mozambique (1.2 percent), Afghanistan (1.2 percent), Uganda (1.1 percent), Tanzania (0.2 percent), the Democratic Republic of Congo (0.0 percent), Nepal (0.0 percent)

Middle-Income Countries

Population (millions, 2014)	5,239.9
Population growth (avg. annual %, 2005–14)	1.2
Population density (people per sq km, 2014)	85.5
Labor force (millions, 2014)	2,423.5
Unemployment rate (% of labor force, 2014)	5.6
Urban population (% of pop., 2014)	49.0
Surface area (thousands of sq km, 2014)	62,144.2
GNI, Atlas method (current US$ billions, 2014)	24,450.9
GNI per capita, Atlas method (current US$, 2014)	4,666.3
GDP growth (avg. annual %, 2011–14)	5.3
Poverty headcount ratio at national poverty line (% of pop.)	—
Age dependency ratio (% of working-age pop., 2014)	50.8
Account at a formal financial institution (% age 15+, 2014)	57.1
Mobile cellular subscriptions (per 100 people, 2014)	93.6
Internet users (per 100 people, 2014)	34.1

Migration

EMIGRATION

- Stock of emigrants, 2013: **155.2 million** or **3.0 percent** of population
- Top 10 emigration countries, 2013: India, Mexico, China, Bangladesh, Pakistan, the Philippines, Ukraine, Indonesia, the West Bank and Gaza, the Syrian Arab Republic
- Destinations, 2013: high-income OECD countries (48.3 percent); high-income non-OECD countries (29.2 percent); developing countries (22.5 percent); unidentified (0.1 percent)
- Top 10 migration corridors, 2013: Mexico–the United States; Bangladesh–India; Ukraine–the Russian Federation; Kazakhstan–the Russian Federation; China–the United States; China–Hong Kong SAR, China; India–the United Arab Emirates; the West Bank and Gaza–Jordan; India–the United States; India–Saudi Arabia
- Tertiary-educated as a percentage of total emigrants in OECD countries, 2011: **25.4 percent**
- Tertiary-educated women as a percentage of total women emigrants in OECD countries, 2011: **25.9 percent**
- Number of refugees, 2014: **12,951.4 thousands**
- Second generation diaspora in Australia, Europe, and the United States, 2012: **23.6 million**

IMMIGRATION

- Stock of immigrants, 2013: **63.6 million** or **1.2 percent** of population (compared to 247.2 million or 3.4 percent for the world)
- Top 10 immigration countries, 2013: Ukraine, India, Thailand, Pakistan, Jordan, Kazakhstan, South Africa, the Islamic Republic of Iran, Turkey, Côte d'Ivoire
- Sources, 2013: high-income OECD countries (8.2 percent); high-income non-OECD countries (15.1 percent); developing countries (71.2 percent); unidentified (5.5 percent)
- Women as percentage of immigrants, 2013: **46.0 percent** (compared to 47.2 percent for the world)
- Number of refugees, 2014: **14,758.9 thousands**

Remittances

US$ billions	2006	2007	2008	2009	2010	2011	2012	2013	2014	2015e
Inward										
remittance flows[a]	**223.9**	**273.7**	**317.2**	**295.1**	**326.3**	**366.9**	**388.5**	**402.8**	**417.2**	**425.2**
All developing										
countries	*228.6*	*279.5*	*324.8*	*302.9*	*335.7*	*377.9*	*400.7*	*416.2*	*431.1*	*440.5*
World	330.3	398.6	460.2	429.4	463.7	525.9	547.0	572.3	592.9	601.3
Outward										
remittance flows[a]	**27.7**	**32.2**	**39.3**	**40.3**	**40.0**	**43.0**	**49.7**	**56.6**	**57.0**	—
All developing										
countries	*28.7*	*33.3*	*40.9*	*42.2*	*42.1*	*45.0*	*52.2*	*59.2*	*58.8*	—
World	240.7	294.4	345.9	330.6	334.1	367.1	383.1	422.0	427.8	—

Note: This table reports officially recorded remittances. The true size of remittances, including unrecorded flows through formal and informal channels, is believed to be larger.

a. For comparison: net FDI inflows US$653.37 billion, net ODA received US$61.29 billion in 2013. Inward remittance flows were 2.0 percent of GNI in 2013, outward remittance flows were 0.3 percent of GNI in 2013.

REMITTANCES

- Top 10 remittance recipients in 2015 ($US billions): India ($72.2bn), China ($63.9bn), the Philippines ($29.7bn), Mexico ($25.7bn), Nigeria ($20.8bn), the Arab Republic of Egypt ($20.4bn), Pakistan ($20.1bn), Bangladesh ($15.8bn), Vietnam ($12.3bn), Indonesia ($10.5bn)
- Top 10 remittance recipients in 2014 (percentage of GDP): Tajikistan (41.7 percent), the Kyrgyz Republic (30.3 percent), Tonga (27.9 percent), Moldova (26.2 percent), Armenia (17.9 percent), Samoa (17.6 percent), Lesotho (17.4 percent), Honduras (17.4 percent), the West Bank and Gaza (17.1 percent), El Salvador (16.8 percent)
- Top 10 remittance senders in 2014 ($US billions): Malaysia ($8.1bn), China ($6.9bn), India ($6.2bn), Lebanon ($5.6bn), Indonesia ($4.1bn), Kazakhstan ($3.6bn), Thailand ($3.1bn), Azerbaijan ($2.0bn), Ukraine ($1.7bn), Brazil ($1.5bn)
- Top 10 remittance senders in 2014 (percentage of GDP): the Marshall Islands (12.8 percent), Lebanon (12.3 percent), Maldives (10.6 percent), the Kyrgyz Republic (6.1 percent), Solomon Islands (4.0 percent), Guyana (3.9 percent), Palau (3.8 percent), Mauritania (3.7 percent), Armenia (3.4 percent), Mongolia (2.8 percent)

High-Income OECD Countries

Population (millions, 2014)	1,070.0
Population growth (avg. annual %, 2005–14)	0.5
Population density (people per sq km, 2014)	33.8
Labor force (millions, 2014)	536.4
Unemployment rate (% of labor force, 2014)	7.5
Urban population (% of pop., 2014)	80.7
Surface area (thousands of sq km, 2014)	33,449.1
GNI, Atlas method (current US$ billions, 2014)	47,372.5
GNI per capita, Atlas method (current US$, 2014)	44,272.3
GDP growth (avg. annual %, 2011–14)	1.5
Poverty headcount ratio at national poverty line (% of pop.)	—
Age dependency ratio (% of working-age pop., 2014)	52.1
Account at a formal financial institution (% age 15+, 2014)	94.0
Mobile cellular subscriptions (per 100 people, 2014)	114.7
Internet users (per 100 people, 2014)	83.8

Migration

EMIGRATION

- Stock of emigrants, 2013: **39.7 million** or **3.7 percent** of population
- Top 10 emigration countries, 2013: the United Kingdom, Germany, Poland, the United States, Italy, the Republic of Korea, France, Portugal, Canada, Spain
- Destinations, 2013: high-income OECD countries (80.2 percent); high-income non-OECD countries (5.7 percent); developing countries (13.5 percent); unidentified (0.7 percent)
- Top 10 migration corridors, 2013: the United Kingdom–Australia; Poland–Germany; the Republic of Korea–the United States; Canada–the United States; the United States–Mexico; the United Kingdom–the United States; the Republic of Korea–Japan; Germany–the United States; the United Kingdom–Canada; Poland–the United Kingdom
- Tertiary-educated as a percentage of total emigrants in OECD countries, 2011: **31.5 percent**
- Tertiary-educated women as a percentage of total women emigrants in OECD countries, 2011: **31.3 percent**
- Number of refugees, 2014: **12.7 thousands**
- Second generation diaspora in Australia, Europe, and the United States, 2012: **18.8 million**

IMMIGRATION

- Stock of immigrants, 2013: **122.2 million** or **11.4 percent** of population (compared to 247.2 million or 3.4 percent for the world)
- Top 10 immigration countries, 2013: the United States, Germany, the United Kingdom, France, Canada, Spain, Australia, Italy, Switzerland, Japan
- Sources, 2013: high-income OECD countries (26.0 percent); high-income non-OECD countries (7.4 percent); developing countries (64.9 percent); unidentified (1.7 percent)
- Women as percentage of immigrants, 2013: **51.2 percent** (compared to 47.2 percent for the world)
- Number of refugees, 2014: **1,672.5 thousands**

Remittances

US$ billions	2006	2007	2008	2009	2010	2011	2012	2013	2014	2015e
Inward										
remittance flows[a]	**89.5**	**104.7**	**118.8**	**111.7**	**113.2**	**130.6**	**129.8**	**137.8**	**142.3**	**141.3**
All developing countries	*228.6*	*279.5*	*324.8*	*302.9*	*335.7*	*377.9*	*400.7*	*416.2*	*431.1*	*440.5*
World	330.3	398.6	460.2	429.4	463.7	525.9	547.0	572.3	592.9	601.3
Outward										
remittance flows[a]	**162.5**	**191.0**	**213.5**	**198.4**	**198.8**	**216.2**	**211.6**	**224.2**	**231.2**	—
All developing countries	*28.7*	*33.3*	*40.9*	*42.2*	*42.1*	*45.0*	*52.2*	*59.2*	*58.8*	—
World	240.7	294.4	345.9	330.6	334.1	367.1	383.1	422.0	427.8	—

Note: This table reports officially recorded remittances. The true size of remittances, including unrecorded flows through formal and informal channels, is believed to be larger.

a. For comparison: net FDI inflows US$997.05 billion, net ODA received US$.08 billion in 2013. Inward remittance flows were 0.3 percent of GNI in 2013, outward remittance flows were 0.5 percent of GNI in 2013.

REMITTANCES

- Top 10 remittance recipients in 2015 ($US billions): France ($24.6bn), Germany ($17.5bn), Belgium ($11.0bn), Spain ($10.5bn), Italy ($9.9bn), Poland ($7.2bn), the United States ($7.0bn), the Republic of Korea ($6.6bn), the United Kingdom ($5.0bn), Hungary ($4.5bn)
- Top 10 remittance recipients in 2014 (percentage of GDP): Hungary (3.4 percent), Luxembourg (2.7 percent), the Slovak Republic (2.4 percent), Belgium (2.2 percent), Estonia (2.1 percent), Portugal (1.9 percent), Slovenia (1.5 percent), Poland (1.4 percent), Iceland (1.2 percent), the Czech Republic (0.9 percent)
- Top 10 remittance senders in 2014 ($US billions): the United States ($56.3bn), Switzerland ($24.7bn), Germany ($20.8bn), France ($13.8bn), Luxembourg ($12.7bn), the United Kingdom ($11.5bn), Italy ($11.2bn), the Netherlands ($9.9bn), the Republic of Korea ($9.5bn), Spain ($8.8bn)
- Top 10 remittance senders in 2014 (percentage of GDP): Luxembourg (19.6 percent), Switzerland (3.5 percent), Israel (1.7 percent), Norway (1.2 percent), the Netherlands (1.1 percent), Austria (0.9 percent), Denmark (0.9 percent), Belgium (0.8 percent), Ireland (0.8 percent), Hungary (0.8 percent)

High-Income Non-OECD Countries

Population (millions, 2014)	328.8
Population growth (avg. annual %, 2005–14)	0.9
Population density (people per sq km, 2014)	14.0
Labor force (millions, 2014)	153.2
Unemployment rate (% of labor force, 2014)	6.1
Urban population (% of pop., 2014)	80.6
Surface area (thousands of sq km, 2014)	24,276.2
GNI, Atlas method (current US$ billions, 2014)	6,226.4
GNI per capita, Atlas method (current US$, 2014)	18,938.7
GDP growth (avg. annual %, 2011–14)	3.3
Poverty headcount ratio at national poverty line (% of pop.)	—
Age dependency ratio (% of working-age pop., 2014)	44.7
Account at a formal financial institution (% age 15+, 2014)	72.8
Mobile cellular subscriptions (per 100 people, 2014)	151.8
Internet users (per 100 people, 2014)	69.9

Migration

EMIGRATION

- Stock of emigrants, 2013: **19.8 million** or **6.1 percent** of population
- Top 10 emigration countries, 2013: the Russian Federation, Puerto Rico, Argentina, Croatia, Hong Kong SAR, China, República Bolivariana de Venezuela, Lithuania, Trinidad and Tobago, Latvia, Uruguay
- Destinations, 2013: high-income OECD countries (45.4 percent); high-income non-OECD countries (6.1 percent); developing countries (48.4 percent); unidentified (0.1 percent)
- Top 10 migration corridors, 2013: the Russian Federation–Ukraine; the Russian Federation–Kazakhstan; Puerto Rico–the United States; the Russian Federation–Germany; the Russian Federation–Belarus; the Russian Federation–Uzbekistan; the Russian Federation–the United States; Argentina–Spain; Croatia–Serbia; Hong Kong SAR, China–Canada
- Tertiary-educated as a percentage of total emigrants in OECD countries, 2011: **32.5 percent**
- Tertiary-educated women as a percentage of total women emigrants in OECD countries, 2011: **34.4 percent**
- Number of refugees, 2014: **124.7 thousands**
- Second generation diaspora in Australia, Europe, and the United States, 2012: **2.1 million**

IMMIGRATION

- Stock of immigrants, 2013: **52.0 million** or **15.8 percent** of population (compared to 247.2 million or 3.4 percent for the world)
- Top 10 immigration countries, 2013: Saudi Arabia, the Russian Federation, the United Arab Emirates, Hong Kong SAR, China, Kuwait, Argentina, Singapore, Qatar, República Bolivariana de Venezuela, Oman
- Sources, 2013: high-income OECD countries (4.4 percent); high-income non-OECD countries (2.3 percent); developing countries (91.0 percent); unidentified (2.3 percent)
- Women as percentage of immigrants, 2013: **38.7 percent** (compared to 47.2 percent for the world)
- Number of refugees, 2014: **428.4 thousands**

Remittances

US$ billions	2006	2007	2008	2009	2010	2011	2012	2013	2014	2015e
Inward										
remittance flows[a]	**12.2**	**14.4**	**16.5**	**14.7**	**14.9**	**17.5**	**16.6**	**18.3**	**19.5**	**19.4**
All developing										
countries	228.6	279.5	324.8	302.9	335.7	377.9	400.7	416.2	431.1	440.5
World	330.3	398.6	460.2	429.4	463.7	525.9	547.0	572.3	592.9	601.3
Outward										
remittance flows[a]	**49.5**	**70.1**	**91.6**	**90.0**	**93.2**	**105.9**	**119.3**	**138.5**	**137.8**	—
All developing										
countries	28.7	33.3	40.9	42.2	42.1	45.0	52.2	59.2	58.8	—
World	240.7	294.4	345.9	330.6	334.1	367.1	383.1	422.0	427.8	—

Note: This table reports officially recorded remittances. The true size of remittances, including unrecorded flows through formal and informal channels, is believed to be larger.

a. For comparison: net FDI inflows US$283.51 billion, net ODA received US$.07 billion in 2013. Inward remittance flows were 0.3 percent of GNI in 2013, outward remittance flows were 2.4 percent of GNI in 2013.

REMITTANCES

- Top 5 remittance recipients in 2015 ($US billions): the Russian Federation ($7.9bn), Croatia ($2.1bn), Lithuania ($2.0bn), Latvia ($1.7bn), Bermuda ($1.3bn)
- Top 5 remittance recipients in 2014 (percentage of GDP): Bermuda (23.1 percent), the Faeroe Islands (6.1 percent), St. Kitts and Nevis (6.1 percent), Latvia (5.7 percent), Lithuania (4.4 percent)
- Top 5 remittance senders in 2014 ($US billions): Saudi Arabia ($36.9bn), the Russian Federation ($32.6bn), the United Arab Emirates ($19.3bn), Kuwait ($18.1bn), Qatar ($11.2bn)
- Top 5 remittance senders in 2014 (percentage of GDP): Oman (12.6 percent), Kuwait (11.1 percent), Malta (10.6 percent), Bahrain (7.0 percent), Qatar (5.3 percent)

Other Country Group Tables

Least Developed Countries, United Nations Classification (48)

Afghanistan, Angola, Bangladesh, Benin, Bhutan, Burkina Faso, Burundi, Central African Republic, Cambodia, Chad, Comoros, Democratic Republic of Congo, Djibouti, Equatorial Guinea, Eritrea, The Gambia, Ethiopia, Guinea, Guinea-Bissau, Haiti, Kiribati, Lao People's Democratic Republic, Lesotho, Liberia, Madagascar, Malawi, Mali, Mauritania, Mozambique, Myanmar, Nepal, Niger, Republic of Yemen, Rwanda, São Tomé and Príncipe, Senegal, Sierra Leone, Solomon Islands, Somalia, South Sudan, Sudan, Tanzania, Timor-Leste, Togo, Tuvalu, Uganda, Vanuatu, Zambia

Fragile States (35)

Afghanistan, Bosnia and Herzegovina, Burundi, Central African Republic, Chad, Comoros, Côte d'Ivoire, Democratic Republic of Congo, Eritrea, Federated States of Micronesia, The Gambia, Guinea-Bissau, Haiti, Iraq, Kiribati, Kosovo, Lebanon, Liberia, Libya, Madagascar, Mali, Marshall Islands, Myanmar, Republic of Yemen, Sierra Leone, Solomon Islands, Somalia, South Sudan, Sudan, Syrian Arab Republic, Timor-Leste, Togo, Tuvalu, West Bank and Gaza, Zimbabwe

Small States[a] (developing only: 39)

Antigua and Barbuda, Barbados, Belize, Bhutan, Botswana, Cabo Verde, Comoros, Djibouti, Dominica, Equatorial Guinea, Fiji, Gabon, The Gambia, Grenada, Guinea-Bissau, Guyana, Jamaica, Kiribati, Lesotho, Maldives, Marshall Islands, Mauritius, Federated States of Micronesia, Montenegro, Namibia, Palau, Samoa, São Tomé and Príncipe, Solomon Islands, St. Kitts and Nevis, St. Lucia, St. Vincent and the Grenadines, Suriname, Swaziland, Timor-Leste, Tonga, Trinidad and Tobago, Tuvalu, Vanuatu

---

a. Countries with a population below 1.5 million are considered as small states according to the World Bank classification.

Least Developed Countries[a]

Population (millions, 2014)	932.0
Population growth (avg. annual %, 2005–14)	2.4
Population density (people per sq km, 2014)	46.2
Labor force (millions, 2014)	406.5
Unemployment rate (% of labor force, 2014)	6.1
Urban population (% of pop., 2014)	31.0
Surface area (thousands of sq km, 2014)	20,818.2
GNI, Atlas method (current US$ billions, 2014)	786.6
GNI per capita, Atlas method (current US$, 2014)	844.0
GDP growth (avg. annual %, 2011–14)	5.1
Poverty headcount ratio at national poverty line (% of pop.)	–
Age dependency ratio (% of working-age pop., 2014)	80.0
Account at a formal financial institution (% age 15+)	–
Mobile cellular subscriptions (per 100 people, 2014)	63.1
Internet users (per 100 people, 2014)	8.6

Migration

EMIGRATION

- Stock of emigrants, 2013: **40.6 million** or **4.5 percent** of population
- Top 10 emigration countries, 2013: Bangladesh, Afghanistan, Myanmar, Nepal, Somalia, Burkina Faso, Sudan, Haiti, the Democratic Republic of Congo, the Lao People's Democratic Republic
- Destinations, 2013: high-income OECD countries (15.1 percent); high-income non-OECD countries (19.2 percent); developing countries (65.4 percent); unidentified (0.3 percent)
- Top 10 migration corridors, 2013: Bangladesh–India; Afghanistan–Pakistan; Afghanistan–the Islamic Republic of Iran; Myanmar–Thailand; Bangladesh–Saudi Arabia; Burkina Faso–Côte d'Ivoire; Bangladesh–the United Arab Emirates; the Lao People's Democratic Republic–Thailand; the Republic of Yemen–Saudi Arabia; Cambodia–Thailand
- Tertiary-educated as a percentage of total emigrants in OECD countries, 2011: **25.8 percent**
- Tertiary-educated women as a percentage of total women emigrants in OECD countries, 2011: **23.5 percent**
- Number of refugees, 2014: **7,410.9 thousands**
- Second generation diaspora in Australia, Europe, and the United States, 2012: **1.3 million**

IMMIGRATION

- Stock of immigrants, 2013: **11.5 million** or **1.2 percent** of population (compared to 247.2 million or 3.4 percent for the world)
- Top 10 immigration countries, 2013: Bangladesh, Nepal, Ethiopia, Burkina Faso, Tanzania, South Sudan, Uganda, the Democratic Republic of Congo, Chad, Rwanda
- Sources, 2013: high-income OECD countries (2.3 percent); high-income non-OECD countries (0.7 percent); developing countries (87.2 percent); unidentified (9.8 percent)

---

a. According to the United Nations classification.

- Women as percentage of immigrants, 2013: **45.0 percent** (compared to 47.2 percent for the world)
- Number of refugees, 2014: **3,579.1 thousand**

Remittances

US$ billions	2006	2007	2008	2009	2010	2011	2012	2013	2014	2015e
Inward										
remittance flows[a]	**14.0**	**16.8**	**22.0**	**23.1**	**25.3**	**27.7**	**32.9**	**35.0**	**38.2**	**40.8**
All developing										
countries	*228.6*	*279.5*	*324.8*	*302.9*	*335.7*	*377.9*	*400.7*	*416.2*	*431.1*	*440.5*
World	330.3	398.6	460.2	429.4	463.7	525.9	547.0	572.3	592.9	601.3
Outward										
remittance flows[a]	**1.9**	**2.4**	**3.0**	**3.4**	**3.7**	**3.6**	**4.1**	**4.7**	**4.7**	—
All developing										
countries	*28.7*	*33.3*	*40.9*	*42.2*	*42.1*	*45.0*	*52.2*	*59.2*	*58.8*	—
World	240.7	294.4	345.9	330.6	334.1	367.1	383.1	422.0	427.8	—

Note: This table reports officially recorded remittances. The true size of remittances, including unrecorded flows through formal and informal channels, is believed to be larger.

a. For comparison: net FDI inflows US$22.39 billion, net ODA received US$47.45 billion in 2013. Inward remittance flows were 5.6 percent of GNI in 2013, outward remittance flows were 0.7 percent of GNI in 2013.

Remittances

- Top 10 remittance recipients in 2015 ($US billions): Bangladesh ($15.8bn), Nepal ($6.6bn), Myanmar ($3.5bn), the Republic of Yemen ($3.4bn), Haiti ($2.0bn), Senegal ($1.6bn), Cambodia ($0.9bn), Uganda ($0.9bn), Mali ($0.9bn), Ethiopia ($0.6bn)
- Top 10 remittance recipients in 2014 (percentage of GDP): Nepal (29.2 percent), Liberia (24.6 percent), Haiti (22.7 percent), Comoros (20.2 percent), The Gambia (20.0 percent), Lesotho (17.4 percent), Tuvalu (10.7 percent), Senegal (10.3 percent), Kiribati (9.6 percent), the Republic of Yemen (9.3 percent)
- Top 10 remittance senders in 2014 ($US billions): Angola ($1.3bn), Myanmar ($0.8bn), Liberia ($0.4bn), the Republic of Yemen ($0.3bn), Uganda ($0.3bn), Haiti ($0.2bn), Afghanistan ($0.2bn), Cambodia ($0.2bn), Mozambique ($0.2bn), Mauritania ($0.2bn)
- Top 10 remittance senders in 2014 (percentage of GDP): Liberia (18.2 percent), Solomon Islands (4.0 percent), Mauritania (3.7 percent), Haiti (2.9 percent), Bhutan (2.5 percent), Timor-Leste (1.9 percent), Rwanda (1.6 percent), Cambodia (1.3 percent), Mozambique (1.2 percent), Afghanistan (1.2 percent)

Fragile States

Population (millions, 2014)	473.0
Population growth (avg. annual %, 2005–14)	2.5
Population density (people per sq km, 2014)	32.8
Labor force (millions, 2014)	175.4
Unemployment rate (% of labor force, 2014)	8.2
Urban population (% of pop., 2014)	40.7
Surface area (thousands of sq km, 2014)	14,778.3
GNI, Atlas method (current US$ billions, 2014)	734.2
GNI per capita, Atlas method (current US$, 2014)	1,552.3
GDP growth (avg. annual %, 2011–14)	1.4
Poverty headcount ratio at national poverty line (% of pop.)	–
Age dependency ratio (% of working-age pop., 2014)	80.2
Account at a formal financial institution (% age 15+)	–
Mobile cellular subscriptions (per 100 people, 2014)	67.6
Internet users (per 100 people, 2014)	11.5

Migration

EMIGRATION

- Stock of emigrants, 2013: **36.6 million** or **7.9 percent** of population
- Top 10 emigration countries, 2013: Afghanistan, the West Bank and Gaza, the Syrian Arab Republic, Myanmar, Iraq, Somalia, Bosnia and Herzegovina, Sudan, Haiti, the Democratic Republic of Congo
- Destinations, 2013: high-income OECD countries (18.2 percent); high-income non-OECD countries (15.9 percent); developing countries (65.6 percent); unidentified (0.3 percent)
- Top 10 migration corridors, 2013: Afghanistan–Pakistan; Afghanistan–the Islamic Republic of Iran; the West Bank and Gaza–Jordan; Myanmar–Thailand; the Syrian Arab Republic–Saudi Arabia; the Republic of Yemen–Saudi Arabia; Iraq–the Syrian Arab Republic; the Syrian Arab Republic–Lebanon; the Syrian Arab Republic–Jordan; Zimbabwe–South Africa
- Tertiary-educated as a percentage of total emigrants in OECD countries, 2011: **23.8 percent**
- Tertiary-educated women as a percentage of total women emigrants in OECD countries, 2011: **22.0 percent**
- Number of refugees, 2014: **16,711.8 thousands**
- Second generation diaspora in Australia, Europe, and the United States, 2012: **1.0 million**

IMMIGRATION

- Stock of immigrants, 2013: **11.1 million** or **2.3 percent** of population (compared to 247.2 million or 3.4 percent for the world)
- Top 10 immigration countries, 2013: Côte d'Ivoire, Lebanon, the Syrian Arab Republic, Libya, South Sudan, the Democratic Republic of Congo, Chad, Sudan, Zimbabwe, the Republic of Yemen
- Sources, 2013: high-income OECD countries (1.8 percent); high-income non-OECD countries (1.4 percent); developing countries (88.0 percent); unidentified (8.8 percent)
- Women as percentage of immigrants, 2013: **44.8 percent** (compared to 47.2 percent for the world)
- Number of refugees, 2014: **6,469.5 thousands**

Remittances

US$ billions	2006	2007	2008	2009	2010	2011	2012	2013	2014	2015e
Inward										
remittance flows[a]	**14.1**	**16.1**	**19.3**	**19.1**	**19.3**	**19.6**	**22.2**	**25.2**	**27.2**	**27.9**
All developing										
countries	*228.6*	*279.5*	*324.8*	*302.9*	*335.7*	*377.9*	*400.7*	*416.2*	*431.1*	*440.5*
World	330.3	398.6	460.2	429.4	463.7	525.9	547.0	572.3	592.9	601.3
Outward										
remittance flows[a]	**6.6**	**5.5**	**7.4**	**9.6**	**8.9**	**7.4**	**10.0**	**11.9**	**7.9**	—
All developing										
countries	*28.7*	*33.3*	*40.9*	*42.2*	*42.1*	*45.0*	*52.2*	*59.2*	*58.8*	—
World	240.7	294.4	345.9	330.6	334.1	367.1	383.1	422.0	427.8	—

Note: This table reports officially recorded remittances. The true size of remittances, including unrecorded flows through formal and informal channels, is believed to be larger.

a. For comparison: net FDI inflows US$16.98 billion, net ODA received US$33.98 billion in 2013. Inward remittance flows were 4.0 percent of GNI in 2013, outward remittance flows were 1.2 percent of GNI in 2013.

REMITTANCES

- Top 10 remittance recipients in 2015 ($US billions): Lebanon ($7.5bn), Myanmar ($3.5bn), the Republic of Yemen ($3.4bn), the West Bank and Gaza ($2.3bn), Bosnia and Herzegovina ($2.0bn), Haiti ($2.0bn), the Syrian Arab Republic ($1.6bn), Kosovo ($1.2bn), Mali ($0.9bn), Liberia ($0.5bn)
- Top 10 remittance recipients in 2014 (percentage of GDP): Liberia (24.6 percent), Haiti (22.7 percent), Comoros (20.2 percent), The Gambia (20.0 percent), the West Bank and Gaza (17.1 percent), Lebanon (16.2 percent), Kosovo (16.1 percent), the Marshall Islands (14.0 percent), Bosnia and Herzegovina (11.4 percent), Tuvalu (10.7 percent)
- Top 10 remittance senders in 2014 ($US billions): Lebanon ($5.6bn), Myanmar ($0.8bn), Liberia ($0.4bn), the Republic of Yemen ($0.3bn), Haiti ($0.2bn), Afghanistan ($0.2bn), Kosovo ($0.1bn), Bosnia and Herzegovina ($0.1bn), Solomon Islands ($0.0bn), the West Bank and Gaza ($0.0bn)
- Top 10 remittance senders in 2014 (percentage of GDP): Liberia (18.2 percent), the Marshall Islands (12.8 percent), Lebanon (12.3 percent), Solomon Islands (4.0 percent), Haiti (2.9 percent), Timor-Leste (1.9 percent), Kosovo (1.4 percent), Afghanistan (1.2 percent), Myanmar (1.2 percent), the Republic of Yemen (0.9 percent)

Small States

Population (millions, 2014)	30.3
Population growth (avg. annual %, 2005–14)	1.5
Population density (people per sq km, 2014)	13.0
Labor force (millions, 2014)	12.7
Unemployment rate (% of labor force, 2014)	12.7
Urban population (% of pop., 2014)	46.2
Surface area (thousands of sq km, 2014)	2,396.9
GNI, Atlas method (current US$ billions, 2014)	171.2
GNI per capita, Atlas method (current US$, 2014)	5,656.7
GDP growth (avg. annual %, 2011–14)	2.9
Poverty headcount ratio at national poverty line (% of pop.)	–
Age dependency ratio (% of working-age pop., 2014)	63.6
Account at a formal financial institution (% age 15+)	–
Mobile cellular subscriptions (per 100 people, 2014)	108.4
Internet users (per 100 people, 2014)	26.4

Migration

EMIGRATION

- Stock of emigrants, 2013: **5.1 million or 17.0 percent** of population
- Top 10 emigration countries, 2013: Jamaica, Guyana, Trinidad and Tobago, Lesotho, Montenegro, Suriname, Fiji, Cabo Verde, Mauritius, Namibia
- Destinations, 2013: high-income OECD countries (69.1 percent); high-income non-OECD countries (3.9 percent); developing countries (24.5 percent); unidentified (2.4 percent)
- Top 10 migration corridors, 2013: Jamaica–the United States; Lesotho–South Africa; Guyana–the United States; Trinidad and Tobago–the United States; Suriname–the Netherlands; Jamaica–the United Kingdom; Jamaica–Canada; Namibia–South Africa; Guyana–Canada; Swaziland–South Africa
- Tertiary-educated as a percentage of total emigrants in OECD countries, 2011: **27.0 percent**
- Tertiary-educated women as a percentage of total women emigrants in OECD countries, 2011: **29.0 percent**
- Number of refugees, 2014: **41.3 thousands**
- Second generation diaspora in Australia, Europe, and the United States, 2012: **0.8 million**

IMMIGRATION

- Stock of immigrants, 2013: **1.6 million** or **5.4 percent** of population (compared to 247.2 million or 3.4 percent for the world)
- Top 10 immigration countries, 2013: Gabon, The Gambia, Botswana, Djibouti, Maldives, Namibia, The Bahamas, Bhutan, Belize, Montenegro
- Sources, 2013: high-income OECD countries (8.7 percent); high-income non-OECD countries (7.4 percent); developing countries (74.3 percent); unidentified (9.7 percent)
- Women as percentage of immigrants, 2013: **45.6 percent** (compared to 47.2 percent for the world)
- Number of refugees, 2014: **53.3 thousands**

Remittances

US$ billions	2006	2007	2008	2009	2010	2011	2012	2013	2014	2015e
Inward										
remittance flows[a]	**4.4**	**5.0**	**5.0**	**4.8**	**5.1**	**5.5**	**5.6**	**5.5**	**5.5**	**5.7**
All developing										
countries	228.6	279.5	324.8	302.9	335.7	377.9	400.7	416.2	431.1	440.5
World	330.3	398.6	460.2	429.4	463.7	525.9	547.0	572.3	592.9	601.3
Outward										
remittance flows[a]	**1.0**	**1.2**	**1.2**	**1.2**	**1.4**	**1.6**	**1.7**	**1.4**	**1.3**	—
All developing										
countries	28.7	33.3	40.9	42.2	42.1	45.0	52.2	59.2	58.8	—
World	240.7	294.4	345.9	330.6	334.1	367.1	383.1	422.0	427.8	—

Note: This table reports officially recorded remittances. The true size of remittances, including unrecorded flows through formal and informal channels, is believed to be larger.

a. For comparison: net FDI inflows US$8.57 billion, net ODA received US$3.74 billion in 2013. Inward remittance flows were 3.5 percent of GNI in 2013, outward remittance flows were 0.8 percent of GNI in 2013.

REMITTANCES

- Top 10 remittance recipients in 2015 ($US billions): Jamaica ($2.3bn), Montenegro ($0.4bn), Lesotho ($0.4bn), Guyana ($0.3bn), Mauritius ($0.2bn), Fiji ($0.2bn), Cabo Verde ($0.2bn), The Gambia ($0.2bn), Samoa ($0.2bn), Comoros ($0.1bn)
- Top 10 remittance recipients in 2014 (percentage of GDP): Tonga (27.9 percent), Comoros (20.2 percent), The Gambia (20.0 percent), Samoa (17.6 percent), Lesotho (17.4 percent), Jamaica (16.3 percent), the Marshall Islands (14.0 percent), Tuvalu (10.7 percent), Guyana (10.6 percent), Cabo Verde (10.2 percent)
- Top 10 remittance senders in 2014 ($US billions): Maldives ($0.3bn), Jamaica ($0.3bn), The Bahamas ($0.2bn), Guyana ($0.1bn), Montenegro ($0.1bn), Seychelles ($0.1bn), Bhutan ($0.0bn), Solomon Islands ($0.0bn), Belize ($0.0bn), Timor-Leste ($0.0bn)
- Top 10 remittance senders in 2014 (percentage of GDP): the Marshall Islands (12.8 percent), Maldives (10.6 percent), Seychelles (4.1 percent), Solomon Islands (4.0 percent), Guyana (3.9 percent), Palau (3.8 percent), Bhutan (2.5 percent), Belize (2.0 percent), Jamaica (2.0 percent), Timor-Leste (1.9 percent)

References

OECD (Organisation for Economic Co-operation and Development). 2014. Database on Immigrants in OECD and non-OECD Countries: DIOC 2010/11. Paris: OECD. http://www.oecd.org/els/mig/dioc.htm

Ratha, Dilip, and William Shaw. 2007. "South–South Migration and Remittances." Working Paper 102, World Bank, Washington, DC.

UNHCR (United Nations High Commissioner for Refugees). 2015. Global Trends: Forced Displacement in 2014. http://unhcr.org/556725e69 .html

UN Population Division. 2013. Trends in international migrant stock: The 2013 Revision. New York: UN Department of Economic and Social Affairs. http://www.un.org/en/development/desa/population/migration /data/index.shtml

World Bank. 2015. *World Development Indicators.* Washington, DC: World Bank. http://data.worldbank.org/products/wdi

Country Tables

Afghanistan

Population (millions, 2014)	31.6
Population growth (avg. annual %, 2005–14)	3.0
Population density (people per sq km, 2014)	48.4
Labor force (millions, 2014)	8.3
Unemployment rate (% of labor force, 2014)	9.1
Urban population (% of pop., 2014)	26.3
Surface area (thousands of sq km, 2014)	652.9
GNI, Atlas method (current US$ billions, 2014)	21.4
GNI per capita, Atlas method (current US$, 2014)	680.0
GDP growth (avg. annual %, 2011–14)	6.0
Poverty headcount ratio at national poverty line (% of pop., 2011)	35.8
Age dependency ratio (% of working-age pop., 2014)	89.8
Account at a formal financial institution (% age 15+, 2014)	10.0
Mobile cellular subscriptions (per 100 people, 2014)	74.9
Internet users (per 100 people, 2014)	6.4

Migration

EMIGRATION

- Stock of emigrants, 2013: **5,632.2 thousands**
- Stock of emigrants as percentage of population, 2013: **18.4 percent**
- Top destination countries, 2013: Pakistan, the Islamic Republic of Iran, Saudi Arabia, Germany, the United States, the United Kingdom, Canada, the Netherlands, Australia, Sweden
- Tertiary-educated as a percentage of total emigrants in OECD countries, 2011: **21.6 percent**
- Tertiary-educated women as a percentage of total women emigrants in OECD countries, 2011: **20.7 percent**
- Number of refugees, 2014: **2,593,332**
- Second generation diaspora in Australia, Europe, and the United States, 2012: **68.0 thousands**

IMMIGRATION

- Stock of immigrants, 2013: **105.1 thousands**
- Stock of immigrants as percentage of population, 2013: **0.3 percent**
- Top source countries, 2013: Pakistan, Tajikistan, Uzbekistan
- Women as percentage of immigrants, 2013: **43.5 percent**
- Number of refugees, 2014: **300,421**

Remittances

US$ millions	2006	2007	2008	2009	2010	2011	2012	2013	2014	2015e
Inward remittance flows[a]	—	—	**106**	**152**	**342**	**185**	**252**	**314**	**268**	**272**
of which										
Compensation of employees	—	—	72	75	151	107	121	169	181	—
Personal transfers	—	—	34	77	191	79	130	145	87	—
Outward remittance flows	—	—	**189**	**324**	**328**	**258**	**193**	**282**	**244**	—
of which										
Compensation of employees	—	—	128	135	131	166	109	131	170	—
Personal transfers	—	—	61	189	197	91	84	151	74	—

a. Net FDI inflows US$0.04 billion, net ODA received US$5.27 billion in 2013.

Albania

Population (millions, 2014)	2.9
Population growth (avg. annual %, 2005–14)	-0.4
Population density (people per sq km, 2014)	105.6
Labor force (millions, 2014)	1.3
Unemployment rate (% of labor force, 2014)	16.1
Urban population (% of pop., 2014)	56.4
Surface area (thousands of sq km, 2014)	28.8
GNI, Atlas method (current US$ billions, 2014)	12.9
GNI per capita, Atlas method (current US$, 2014)	4,450.0
GDP growth (avg. annual %, 2011–14)	1.8
Poverty headcount ratio at national poverty line (% of pop., 2012)	14.3
Age dependency ratio (% of working-age pop., 2014)	44.9
Account at a formal financial institution (% age 15+, 2014)	38.0
Mobile cellular subscriptions (per 100 people, 2014)	105.5
Internet users (per 100 people, 2014)	60.1

Migration

EMIGRATION

- Stock of emigrants, 2013: **1,264.2 thousands**
- Stock of emigrants as percentage of population, 2013: **43.6 percent**
- Top destination countries, 2013: Greece, Italy, the United States, Germany, the Former Yugoslav Republic of Macedonia, Montenegro, the United Kingdom, Canada, France, Belgium
- Tertiary-educated as a percentage of total emigrants in OECD countries, 2011: **9.9 percent**
- Tertiary-educated women as a percentage of total women emigrants in OECD countries, 2011: **11.2 percent**
- Number of refugees, 2014: **10,123**
- Second generation diaspora in Australia, Europe, and the United States, 2012: **42.6 thousands**

IMMIGRATION

- Stock of immigrants, 2013: **180.7 thousands**
- Stock of immigrants as percentage of population, 2013: **6.2 percent**
- Top source countries, 2013: Greece, Serbia, Bosnia and Herzegovina, Croatia, Montenegro, the Former Yugoslav Republic of Macedonia, Turkey, the United States, Italy, Slovenia
- Women as percentage of immigrants, 2013: **51.5 percent**
- Number of refugees, 2014: **76**

Remittances

US$ millions	2006	2007	2008	2009	2010	2011	2012	2013	2014	2015e
Inward remittance flows[a]	**1,359**	**1,468**	**1,495**	**1,318**	**1,156**	**1,126**	**1,027**	**1,094**	**1,142**	**1,102**
of which										
Compensation of employees	184	163	269	227	232	193	152	64	52	—
Personal transfers	1,176	1,305	1,226	1,091	924	932	875	1,030	1,090	—
Outward remittance flows	**27**	**10**	**16**	**10**	**24**	**21**	**44**	**191**	**179**	**—**
of which										
Compensation of employees	27	10	16	9	15	14	37	47	41	—
Personal transfers	0	0	—	1	9	7	6	144	138	—

a. Net FDI inflows US$1.25 billion, net ODA received US$0.30 billion in 2013.

Algeria

Population (millions, 2014)	38.9
Population growth (avg. annual %, 2005–14)	1.7
Population density (people per sq km, 2014)	16.3
Labor force (millions, 2014)	12.4
Unemployment rate (% of labor force, 2014)	9.5
Urban population (% of pop., 2014)	70.1
Surface area (thousands of sq km, 2014)	2,381.7
GNI, Atlas method (current US$ billions, 2014)	213.8
GNI per capita, Atlas method (current US$, 2014)	5,490.0
GDP growth (avg. annual %, 2011–14)	3.2
Poverty headcount ratio at national poverty line (% of pop.)	–
Age dependency ratio (% of working-age pop., 2014)	51.5
Account at a formal financial institution (% age 15+, 2014)	50.5
Mobile cellular subscriptions (per 100 people, 2014)	93.3
Internet users (per 100 people, 2014)	18.1

Migration

EMIGRATION

- Stock of emigrants, 2013: **1,784.5 thousands**
- Stock of emigrants as percentage of population, 2013: **4.7 percent**
- Top destination countries, 2013: France, Spain, Israel, Canada, Belgium, Italy, the United Kingdom, the United States, Germany, Morocco
- Tertiary-educated as a percentage of total emigrants in OECD countries, 2011: **20.3 percent**
- Tertiary-educated women as a percentage of total women emigrants in OECD countries, 2011: **19.1 percent**
- Number of refugees, 2014: **3,478**
- Second generation diaspora in Australia, Europe, and the United States, 2012: **1,423.5 thousands**

IMMIGRATION

- Stock of immigrants, 2013: **270.4 thousands**
- Stock of immigrants as percentage of population, 2013: **0.7 percent**
- Top source countries, 2013: the West Bank and Gaza, Somalia, Iraq, Saudi Arabia, the Syrian Arab Republic, the Republic of Yemen, Libya, Jordan, Sudan, Indonesia
- Women as percentage of immigrants, 2013: **45.0 percent**
- Number of refugees, 2014: **94,104**

Remittances

US$ millions	2006	2007	2008	2009	2010	2011	2012	2013	2014	2015e
Inward remittance flows[a]	1,610	2,120	2,202	2,059	2,044	1,942	1,942	2,000	2,000	2,000
of which										
Compensation of employees	–	62	59	77	130	151	164	175	207	–
Personal transfers	189	37	44	73	66	52	51	35	98	–
Outward remittance flows	35	49	27	46	28	31	44	39	53	–
of which										
Compensation of employees	–	–	–	–	–	–	–	–	–	–
Personal transfers	35	49	27	46	28	31	44	39	53	–

a. Net FDI inflows US$1.69 billion, net ODA received US$0.21 billion in 2013.

American Samoa

	MIDDLE INCOME
Population (thousands, 2013)	55.4
Population growth (avg. annual %, 2005–14)	-0.7
Population density (people per sq km, 2014)	277.2
Labor force, total	–
Unemployment rate (% of labor force)	–
Urban population (% of pop., 2014)	87.3
Surface area (thousands of sq km, 2014)	0.2
GNI, Atlas method (current US$ billions)	–
GNI per capita, Atlas method (current US$)	–
GDP growth (avg. annual %)	–
Poverty headcount ratio at national poverty line (% of pop.)	–
Age dependency ratio (% of working-age pop.)	–
Account at a formal financial institution (% age 15+)	–
Mobile cellular subscriptions (per 100 people, 2004)	3.8
Internet users (per 100 people)	–

Migration

EMIGRATION

- Stock of emigrants, 2013: **3.3 thousands**
- Stock of emigrants as percentage of population, 2013: **6.0 percent**
- Top destination countries, 2013: Samoa, France, Australia, Canada, the Russian Federation, Mexico, Greece, Seychelles, Cuba, Bermuda
- Tertiary-educated as a percentage of total emigrants in OECD countries, 2011: **15.9 percent**
- Tertiary-educated women as a percentage of total women emigrants in OECD countries, 2011: **14.6 percent**
- Number of refugees, 2014: Not available
- Second generation diaspora in Australia, Europe, and the United States, 2012: Not available

IMMIGRATION

- Stock of immigrants, 2013: **41.8 thousands**
- Stock of immigrants as percentage of population, 2013: **75.7 percent**
- Top source countries, 2013: Samoa, the United States, Tonga, the Philippines, New Zealand, China, Fiji, the Republic of Korea, Vietnam
- Women as percentage of immigrants, 2013: **49.0 percent**
- Number of refugees, 2014: Not available

Remittances

US$ millions	2006	2007	2008	2009	2010	2011	2012	2013	2014	2015e
Inward remittance flows	–	–	–	–	–	–	–	–	–	–
of which										
Compensation of employees	–	–	–	–	–	–	–	–	–	–
Personal transfers	–	–	–	–	–	–	–	–	–	–
Outward remittance flows	–	–	–	–	–	–	–	–	–	–
of which										
Compensation of employees	–	–	–	–	–	–	–	–	–	–
Personal transfers	–	–	–	–	–	–	–	–	–	–

Andorra

Population (thousands, 2013)	72.8
Population growth (avg. annual %, 2005–14)	-0.7
Population density (people per sq km, 2014)	154.9
Labor force, total	—
Unemployment rate (% of labor force)	—
Urban population (% of pop., 2014)	85.6
Surface area (thousands of sq km, 2014)	0.5
GNI, Atlas method (current US$ billions, 2014)	3.3
GNI per capita, Atlas method (current US$, 2014)	43,270.0
GDP growth (avg. annual %, 2011–14)	-1.7
Poverty headcount ratio at national poverty line (% of pop.)	—
Age dependency ratio (% of working-age pop.)	—
Account at a formal financial institution (% age 15+)	—
Mobile cellular subscriptions (per 100 people, 2014)	82.6
Internet users (per 100 people, 2014)	95.9

Migration

EMIGRATION

- Stock of emigrants, 2013: **7.4 thousands**
- Stock of emigrants as percentage of population, 2013: **9.7 percent**
- Top destination countries, 2013: Spain, France, Portugal, the United States, Malaysia, Italy, Switzerland, Argentina, Colombia, Canada
- Tertiary-educated as a percentage of total emigrants in OECD countries, 2011: **25.0 percent**
- Tertiary-educated women as a percentage of total women emigrants in OECD countries, 2011: **24.4 percent**
- Number of refugees, 2014: Not available
- Second generation diaspora in Australia, Europe, and the United States, 2012: Not available

IMMIGRATION

- Stock of immigrants, 2013: **45.1 thousands**
- Stock of immigrants as percentage of population, 2013: **59.4 percent**
- Top source countries, 2013: Spain, Portugal, France, the United Kingdom, Argentina, Morocco, Italy, the Philippines, Germany, the Netherlands
- Women as percentage of immigrants, 2013: **47.3 percent**
- Number of refugees, 2014: Not available

Remittances

US$ millions	2006	2007	2008	2009	2010	2011	2012	2013	2014	2015e
Inward **remittance flows**	—	—	—	—	—	—	—	—	—	—
of which										
Compensation of employees	—	—	—	—	—	—	—	—	—	—
Personal transfers	—	—	—	—	—	—	—	—	—	—
Outward **remittance flows**	—	—	—	—	—	—	—	—	—	—
of which										
Compensation of employees	—	—	—	—	—	—	—	—	—	—
Personal transfers	—	—	—	—	—	—	—	—	—	—

Angola

Population (millions, 2014)	24.2
Population growth (avg. annual %, 2005–14)	3.4
Population density (people per sq km, 2014)	19.4
Labor force (millions, 2014)	8.8
Unemployment rate (% of labor force, 2014)	6.8
Urban population (% of pop., 2014)	43.3
Surface area (thousands of sq km, 2014)	1,246.7
GNI, Atlas method (current US$ billions, 2002)	10.3
GNI per capita, Atlas method (current US$, 2002)	640.0
GDP growth (avg. annual %)	1,382.2
Poverty headcount ratio at national poverty line (% of pop., 2008)	36.6
Age dependency ratio (% of working-age pop., 2014)	100.6
Account at a formal financial institution (% age 15+, 2014)	29.3
Mobile cellular subscriptions (per 100 people, 2014)	63.5
Internet users (per 100 people, 2014)	21.3

Migration

EMIGRATION

- Stock of emigrants, 2013: **518.7 thousands**
- Stock of emigrants as percentage of population, 2013: **2.2 percent**
- Top destination countries, 2013: Portugal, the Democratic Republic of Congo, Zambia, South Africa, the Republic of Congo, France, Namibia, the United Kingdom, Switzerland, Brazil
- Tertiary-educated as a percentage of total emigrants in OECD countries, 2011: **22.8 percent**
- Tertiary-educated women as a percentage of total women emigrants in OECD countries, 2011: **24.3 percent**
- Number of refugees, 2014: **9,476**
- Second generation diaspora in Australia, Europe, and the United States, 2012: Not available

IMMIGRATION

- Stock of immigrants, 2013: **87.4 thousands**
- Stock of immigrants as percentage of population, 2013: **0.4 percent**
- Top source countries, 2013: the Democratic Republic of Congo, Portugal, Cabo Verde, São Tomé and Príncipe, South Africa, Rwanda, the Republic of Congo, Namibia, Guinea, Zambia
- Women as percentage of immigrants, 2013: **51.8 percent**
- Number of refugees, 2014: **15,458**

Remittances

US$ millions	2006	2007	2008	2009	2010	2011	2012	2013	2014	2015e
Inward remittance flows[a]	–	–	82	11	29	11	11	11	11	11
of which Compensation of employees	–	–	11	11	11	11	11	–	–	–
Personal transfers	–	–	71	0	18	0	0	–	–	–
Outward remittance flows	413	603	669	716	714	564	523	670	1,299	–
of which Compensation of employees	241	374	447	321	304	334	297	298	579	–
Personal transfers	172	228	222	395	411	231	226	372	719	–

a. Net FDI inflows US$-7.12 billion, net ODA received US$0.29 billion in 2013.

Antigua and Barbuda

Population (thousands, 2013)	90.9
Population growth (avg. annual %, 2005–14)	1.1
Population density (people per sq km, 2014)	206.6
Labor force, total	–
Unemployment rate (% of labor force)	–
Urban population (% of pop., 2014)	24.2
Surface area (thousands of sq km, 2014)	0.4
GNI, Atlas method (current US$ billions, 2014)	1.2
GNI per capita, Atlas method (current US$, 2014)	13,300.0
GDP growth (avg. annual %, 2011–14)	1.7
Poverty headcount ratio at national poverty line (% of pop.)	–
Age dependency ratio (% of working-age pop., 2014)	46.3
Account at a formal financial institution (% age 15+)	–
Mobile cellular subscriptions (per 100 people, 2014)	120.0
Internet users (per 100 people, 2014)	64.0

Migration

EMIGRATION

- Stock of emigrants, 2013: **56.8 thousands**
- Stock of emigrants as percentage of population, 2013: **63.2 percent**
- Top destination countries, 2013: the United States, Bangladesh, the Virgin Islands (U.S.), Canada, Vietnam, Sint Maarten (Dutch part), Dominica, the Dominican Republic, Barbados, Jamaica
- Tertiary-educated as a percentage of total emigrants in OECD countries, 2011: **31.6 percent**
- Tertiary-educated women as a percentage of total women emigrants in OECD countries, 2011: **35.2 percent**
- Number of refugees, 2014: **48**
- Second generation diaspora in Australia, Europe, and the United States, 2012: Not available

IMMIGRATION

- Stock of immigrants, 2013: **28.7 thousands**
- Stock of immigrants as percentage of population, 2013: **31.9 percent**
- Top source countries, 2013: Guyana, Dominica, Jamaica, the United States, the Dominican Republic, Ethiopia, the United Kingdom, St. Vincent and the Grenadines, the Virgin Islands (U.S.), Trinidad and Tobago
- Women as percentage of immigrants, 2013: **52.0 percent**
- Number of refugees, 2014: Not available

Remittances

US$ millions	2006	2007	2008	2009	2010	2011	2012	2013	2014	2015e
Inward remittance flows[a]	19	21	22	21	20	20	21	21	21	22
of which										
Compensation of employees	7	8	9	9	8	8	8	8	–	–
Personal transfers	12	12	13	12	13	13	13	13	–	–
Outward remittance flows	2	2	2	2	2	2	2	2	–	–
of which										
Compensation of employees	–	–	–	–	–	–	–	–	–	–
Personal transfers	2	2	2	2	2	2	2	2	–	–

a. Net FDI inflows US$0.13 billion, net ODA received US$0.00 billion in 2013.

Argentina

Population (millions, 2014)	43.0
Population growth (avg. annual %, 2005–14)	1.0
Population density (people per sq km, 2014)	15.7
Labor force (millions, 2014)	19.5
Unemployment rate (% of labor force, 2014)	8.2
Urban population (% of pop., 2014)	91.6
Surface area (thousands of sq km, 2014)	2,780.4
GNI, Atlas method (current US$ billions, 2014)	579.2
GNI per capita, Atlas method (current US$, 2014)	13,480.0
GDP growth (avg. annual %, 2011–14)	3.1
Poverty headcount ratio at national poverty line (% of pop.)	–
Age dependency ratio (% of working-age pop., 2014)	56.6
Account at a formal financial institution (% age 15+, 2014)	50.2
Mobile cellular subscriptions (per 100 people, 2014)	158.7
Internet users (per 100 people, 2014)	64.7

Migration

EMIGRATION

- Stock of emigrants, 2013: **986.8 thousands**
- Stock of emigrants as percentage of population, 2013: **2.3 percent**
- Top destination countries, 2013: Spain, the United States, Italy, Paraguay, Chile, Israel, the Plurinational State of Bolivia, Brazil, Uruguay, Canada
- Tertiary-educated as a percentage of total emigrants in OECD countries, 2011: **35.9 percent**
- Tertiary-educated women as a percentage of total women emigrants in OECD countries, 2011: **37.5 percent**
- Number of refugees, 2014: **301**
- Second generation diaspora in Australia, Europe, and the United States, 2012: **169.4 thousands**

IMMIGRATION

- Stock of immigrants, 2013: **2,396.4 thousands**
- Stock of immigrants as percentage of population, **2013: 5.6 percent**
- Top source countries, 2013: Paraguay, the Plurinational State of Bolivia, Peru, Chile, Italy, Uruguay, Spain, Brazil, Colombia, the United States
- Women as percentage of immigrants, 2013: **53.8 percent**
- Number of refugees, 2014: **3,433**

Remittances

US$ millions	2006	2007	2008	2009	2010	2011	2012	2013	2014	2015e
Inward remittance flows[a]	**541**	**606**	**698**	**621**	**639**	**698**	**576**	**535**	**502**	**502**
of which										
Compensation of employees	56	65	92	91	104	143	154	178	168	–
Personal transfers	486	541	606	529	535	555	422	357	334	–
Outward remittance flows	**356**	**463**	**630**	**767**	**1,040**	**1,146**	**979**	**889**	**771**	**–**
of which										
Compensation of employees	115	137	150	159	166	197	219	245	244	–
Personal transfers	240	325	481	608	874	949	761	644	527	–

a. Net FDI inflows US$8.92 billion, net ODA received US$0.03 billion in 2013.

Armenia

Population (millions, 2014)	3.0
Population growth (avg. annual %, 2005–14)	-0.1
Population density (people per sq km, 2014)	105.6
Labor force (millions, 2014)	1.6
Unemployment rate (% of labor force, 2014)	17.1
Urban population (% of pop., 2014)	62.8
Surface area (thousands of sq km, 2014)	29.7
GNI, Atlas method (current US$ billions, 2014)	12.1
GNI per capita, Atlas method (current US$, 2014)	4,020.0
GDP growth (avg. annual %, 2011–14)	4.7
Poverty headcount ratio at national poverty line (% of pop., 2013)	32.0
Age dependency ratio (% of working-age pop., 2014)	41.3
Account at a formal financial institution (% age 15+, 2014)	17.2
Mobile cellular subscriptions (per 100 people, 2014)	115.9
Internet users (per 100 people, 2014)	46.3

Migration

EMIGRATION

- Stock of emigrants, 2013: **785.7 thousands**
- Stock of emigrants as percentage of population, 2013: **26.3 percent**
- Top destination countries, 2013: the Russian Federation, the United States, Ukraine, France, Uzbekistan, Germany, Spain, Kazakhstan, Greece, Belgium
- Tertiary-educated as a percentage of total emigrants in OECD countries, 2011: **38.3 percent**
- Tertiary-educated women as a percentage of total women emigrants in OECD countries, 2011: **42.8 percent**
- Number of refugees, 2014: **11,811**
- Second generation diaspora in Australia, Europe, and the United States, 2012: **75.8 thousands**

IMMIGRATION

- Stock of immigrants, 2013: **328.0 thousands**
- Stock of immigrants as percentage of population, 2013: **11.0 percent**
- Top source countries, 2013: Azerbaijan, Georgia, the Democratic Republic of Korea, the Russian Federation, the Syrian Arab Republic, the Islamic Republic of Iran, Ukraine, Turkey, Greece, Uzbekistan
- Women as percentage of immigrants, 2013: **54.1 percent**
- Number of refugees, 2014: **17,635**

Remittances

US$ millions	2006	2007	2008	2009	2010	2011	2012	2013	2014	2015e
Inward remittance flows[a]	1,169	1,644	1,904	1,440	1,669	1,799	1,915	2,192	2,079	1,675
of which										
Compensation of employees	608	889	1,067	838	1,008	1,009	1,071	1,228	1,169	–
Personal transfers	561	756	837	602	661	790	844	964	910	–
Outward remittance flows	182	239	224	180	227	300	315	355	391	–
of which										
Compensation of employees	75	100	94	77	99	153	156	177	194	–
Personal transfers	107	139	130	103	128	148	159	178	197	–

a. Net FDI inflows US$0.38 billion, net ODA received US$0.29 billion in 2013.

Aruba

	HIGH INCOME NON-OECD
Population (thousands, 2013)	103.4
Population growth (avg. annual %, 2005–14)	0.5
Population density (people per sq km, 2014)	574.7
Labor force, total	–
Unemployment rate (% of labor force)	–
Urban population (% of pop., 2014)	41.8
Surface area (thousands of sq km, 2014)	0.2
GNI, Atlas method (current US$ billions)	–
GNI per capita, Atlas method (current US$)	–
GDP growth (avg. annual %, 2005–08)	-3.5
Poverty headcount ratio at national poverty line (% of pop.)	–
Age dependency ratio (% of working-age pop., 2014)	44.1
Account at a formal financial institution (% age 15+)	–
Mobile cellular subscriptions (per 100 people, 2014)	135.1
Internet users (per 100 people, 2014)	83.8

Migration

EMIGRATION

- Stock of emigrants, 2013: **17.1 thousands**
- Stock of emigrants as percentage of population, 2013: **16.6 percent**
- Top destination countries, 2013: the United States, the Netherlands, Curaçao, Sint Maarten (Dutch part), Canada, the Virgin Islands (U.S.), the Dominican Republic, República Bolivariana de Venezuela, Colombia, Greece
- Tertiary-educated as a percentage of total emigrants in OECD countries, 2011: **46.3 percent**
- Tertiary-educated women as a percentage of total women emigrants in OECD countries, 2011: **49.2 percent**
- Number of refugees, 2014: Not available
- Second generation diaspora in Australia, Europe, and the United States, 2012: Not available

IMMIGRATION

- Stock of immigrants, 2013: **34.5 thousands**
- Stock of immigrants as percentage of population, 2013: **33.5 percent**
- Top source countries, 2013: Colombia, the Netherlands, the Dominican Republic, República Bolivariana de Venezuela, Haiti, Suriname, Peru, China, the Philippines, Jamaica
- Women as percentage of immigrants, 2013: **48.1 percent**
- Number of refugees, 2014: Not available

Remittances

US$ millions	2006	2007	2008	2009	2010	2011	2012	2013	2014	2015e
Inward remittance flows[a]	1	5	7	9	5	5	5	6	7	10
of which										
Compensation of employees	1	5	5	5	1	1	2	3	3	–
Personal transfers	0	0	2	4	4	5	3	3	4	–
Outward remittance flows	72	73	76	73	65	64	68	67	70	–
of which										
Compensation of employees	9	10	5	2	2	2	3	3	5	–
Personal transfers	63	63	70	71	63	62	65	64	65	–

a. Net FDI inflows US$0.23 billion in 2013.

Australia

	HIGH INCOME OECD
Population (millions, 2014)	23.5
Population growth (avg. annual %, 2005–14)	1.5
Population density (people per sq km, 2014)	3.1
Labor force (millions, 2014)	12.4
Unemployment rate (% of labor force, 2014)	6.0
Urban population (% of pop., 2014)	89.3
Surface area (thousands of sq km, 2014)	7,741.2
GNI, Atlas method (current US$ billions, 2014)	1,516.2
GNI per capita, Atlas method (current US$, 2014)	64,540.0
GDP growth (avg. annual %, 2011–14)	2.7
Poverty headcount ratio at national poverty line (% of pop.)	–
Age dependency ratio (% of working-age pop., 2014)	50.2
Account at a formal financial institution (% age 15+, 2014)	98.9
Mobile cellular subscriptions (per 100 people, 2014)	131.2
Internet users (per 100 people, 2014)	84.6

Migration

EMIGRATION

- Stock of emigrants, 2013: **487.3 thousands**
- Stock of emigrants as percentage of population, 2013: **2.1 percent**
- Top destination countries, 2013: the United Kingdom, the United States, New Zealand, Canada, Italy, Japan, China, Germany, Thailand, the Netherlands
- Tertiary-educated as a percentage of total emigrants in OECD countries, 2011: **44.7 percent**
- Tertiary-educated women as a percentage of total women emigrants in OECD countries, 2011: **45.2 percent**
- Number of refugees, 2014: **17**
- Second generation diaspora in Australia, Europe, and the United States, 2012: **95.8 thousands**

IMMIGRATION

- Stock of immigrants, 2013: **6,468.6 thousands**
- Stock of immigrants as percentage of population, 2013: **28.0 percent**
- Top source countries, 2013: the United Kingdom, New Zealand, China, India, Italy, Vietnam, the Philippines, South Africa, Malaysia, Germany
- Women as percentage of immigrants, 2013: **50.3 percent**
- Number of refugees, 2014: **35,490**

Remittances

US$ millions	2006	2007	2008	2009	2010	2011	2012	2013	2014	2015e
Inward remittance flows[a]	1,015	1,342	1,526	1,335	1,864	2,449	2,441	2,460	2,332	2,331
of which										
Compensation of employees	1,015	1,342	1,526	1,335	1,864	2,449	2,441	2,460	2,332	–
Personal transfers	–	–	–	–	–	–	–	–	–	–
Outward remittance flows	2,051	2,981	3,366	3,224	4,655	6,598	7,288	7,353	7,000	–
of which										
Compensation of employees	1,555	2,370	2,695	2,575	3,833	5,578	6,195	6,234	5,899	–
Personal transfers	496	611	672	649	822	1,020	1,093	1,119	1,101	–

a. Net FDI inflows US$54.55 billion in 2013.

Austria

	HIGH INCOME OECD
Population (millions, 2014)	8.5
Population growth (avg. annual %, 2005–14)	0.4
Population density (people per sq km, 2014)	103.4
Labor force (millions, 2014)	4.5
Unemployment rate (% of labor force, 2014)	5.0
Urban population (% of pop., 2014)	65.9
Surface area (thousands of sq km, 2014)	83.9
GNI, Atlas method (current US$ billions, 2014)	423.9
GNI per capita, Atlas method (current US$, 2014)	49,670.0
GDP growth (avg. annual %, 2011–14)	1.1
Poverty headcount ratio at national poverty line (% of pop.)	—
Age dependency ratio (% of working-age pop., 2014)	49.0
Account at a formal financial institution (% age 15+, 2014)	96.7
Mobile cellular subscriptions (per 100 people, 2014)	151.9
Internet users (per 100 people, 2014)	81.0

Migration

EMIGRATION

- Stock of emigrants, 2013: **529.6 thousands**
- Stock of emigrants as percentage of population, 2013: **6.2 percent**
- Top destination countries, 2013: Germany, Switzerland, the United States, Canada, Australia, Turkey, the United Kingdom, France, Italy, Spain
- Tertiary-educated as a percentage of total emigrants in OECD countries, 2011: **32.3 percent**
- Tertiary-educated women as a percentage of total women emigrants in OECD countries, 2011: **24.7 percent**
- Number of refugees, 2014: **5**
- Second generation diaspora in Australia, Europe, and the United States, 2012: **491.6 thousands**

IMMIGRATION

- Stock of immigrants, 2013: **1,397.8 thousands**
- Stock of immigrants as percentage of population, 2013: **16.5 percent**
- Top source countries, 2013: Germany, Turkey, Bosnia and Herzegovina, Serbia, Romania, Poland, Hungary, the Czech Republic, Croatia, Kosovo
- Women as percentage of immigrants, 2013: **51.1 percent**
- Number of refugees, 2014: **55,560**

Remittances

US$ millions	2006	2007	2008	2009	2010	2011	2012	2013	2014	2015e
Inward remittance flows[a]	**2,099**	**2,449**	**2,671**	**2,591**	**2,526**	**2,815**	**2,656**	**3,262**	**3,315**	**3,251**
of which Compensation of employees	2,099	2,449	2,671	2,591	2,526	2,815	2,656	2,879	2,944	–
Personal transfers	–	–	–	–	–	–	–	383	371	–
Outward remittance flows	**1,406**	**1,594**	**1,913**	**1,881**	**2,017**	**2,613**	**2,520**	**3,896**	**4,037**	**–**
of which Compensation of employees	1,406	1,594	1,913	1,881	2,017	2,613	2,520	2,910	3,017	–
Personal transfers	–	–	–	–	–	–	–	986	1,020	–

a. Net FDI inflows US$0.45 billion in 2013.

Azerbaijan

Population (millions, 2014)	9.5
Population growth (avg. annual %, 2005–14)	1.4
Population density (people per sq km, 2014)	115.4
Labor force (millions, 2014)	5.0
Unemployment rate (% of labor force, 2014)	5.2
Urban population (% of pop., 2014)	54.4
Surface area (thousands of sq km, 2014)	86.6
GNI, Atlas method (current US$ billions, 2014)	72.4
GNI per capita, Atlas method (current US$, 2014)	7,590.0
GDP growth (avg. annual %, 2011–14)	2.5
Poverty headcount ratio at national poverty line (% of pop., 2013)	5.3
Age dependency ratio (% of working-age pop., 2014)	38.1
Account at a formal financial institution (% age 15+, 2014)	29.2
Mobile cellular subscriptions (per 100 people, 2014)	110.9
Internet users (per 100 people, 2014)	61.0

Migration

EMIGRATION

- Stock of emigrants, 2013: **1,287.4 thousands**
- Stock of emigrants as percentage of population, 2013: **13.7 percent**
- Top destination countries, 2013: the Russian Federation, Armenia, Ukraine, Kazakhstan, Uzbekistan, Turkey, the United States, Germany, Israel, Belarus
- Tertiary-educated as a percentage of total emigrants in OECD countries, 2011: **42.9 percent**
- Tertiary-educated women as a percentage of total women emigrants in OECD countries, 2011: **43.0 percent**
- Number of refugees, 2014: **10,509**
- Second generation diaspora in Australia, Europe, and the United States, 2012: Not available

IMMIGRATION

- Stock of immigrants, 2013: **323.8 thousands**
- Stock of immigrants as percentage of population, 2013: **3.4 percent**
- Top source countries, 2013: the Russian Federation, Ukraine, Kazakhstan, Belarus, Uzbekistan, Georgia, Poland, Moldova, Lithuania, Armenia
- Women as percentage of immigrants, 2013: **52.5 percent**
- Number of refugees, 2014: **1,298**

Remittances

US$ millions	2006	2007	2008	2009	2010	2011	2012	2013	2014	2015e
Inward remittance flows[a]	790	1,268	1,518	1,255	1,410	1,893	1,990	1,733	1,846	1,538
of which										
Compensation of employees	128	76	102	73	72	121	138	120	138	–
Personal transfers	662	1,192	1,416	1,182	1,338	1,772	1,852	1,613	1,709	–
Outward remittance flows	274	405	567	638	954	1,280	2,073	1,903	2,031	–
of which										
Compensation of employees	125	131	168	116	114	141	180	223	287	–
Personal transfers	149	273	399	522	840	1,138	1,892	1,680	1,745	–

a. Net FDI inflows US$2.62 billion, net ODA received US$-0.06 billion in 2013.

Bahamas, The

	HIGH INCOME NON-OECD
Population (thousands, 2013)	383.1
Population growth (avg. annual %, 2005–14)	1.7
Population density (people per sq km, 2014)	38.3
Labor force (thousands, 2013)	224.0
Unemployment rate (% of labor force, 2014)	15.4
Urban population (% of pop., 2014)	82.8
Surface area (thousands of sq km, 2014)	13.9
GNI, Atlas method (current US$ billions, 2014)	8.0
GNI per capita, Atlas method (current US$, 2014)	20,980.0
GDP growth (avg. annual %, 2011–14)	1.0
Poverty headcount ratio at national poverty line (% of pop.)	—
Age dependency ratio (% of working-age pop., 2014)	41.0
Account at a formal financial institution (% age 15+)	—
Mobile cellular subscriptions (per 100 people, 2014)	71.4
Internet users (per 100 people, 2014)	76.9

Migration

EMIGRATION

- Stock of emigrants, 2013: **46.0 thousands**
- Stock of emigrants as percentage of population, 2013: **12.2 percent**
- Top destination countries, 2013: the United States, the United Kingdom, Canada, Jamaica, Australia, the Cayman Islands, Switzerland, the Dominican Republic, Italy, Nicaragua
- Tertiary-educated as a percentage of total emigrants in OECD countries, 2011: **35.5 percent**
- Tertiary-educated women as a percentage of total women emigrants in OECD countries, 2011: **36.4 percent**
- Number of refugees, 2014: **211**
- Second generation diaspora in Australia, Europe, and the United States, 2012: Not available

IMMIGRATION

- Stock of immigrants, 2013: **61.3 thousands**
- Stock of immigrants as percentage of population, 2013: **16.2 percent**
- Top source countries, 2013: Haiti, Jamaica, the United States, the United Kingdom, Canada, Guyana, the Philippines, India, the Turks and Caicos Islands, Cuba
- Women as percentage of immigrants, 2013: **49.1 percent**
- Number of refugees, 2014: **12**

Remittances

US$ millions	2006	2007	2008	2009	2010	2011	2012	2013	2014	2015e
Inward remittance flows[a]	—	—	—	—	—	—	—	—	—	—
of which										
Compensation of employees	—	—	—	—	—	—	—	—	—	—
Personal transfers	—	—	—	—	—	—	—	—	—	—
Outward remittance flows	100	95	66	63	88	120	140	139	164	—
of which										
Compensation of employees	93	85	27	12	27	48	45	36	63	—
Personal transfers	7	10	39	52	61	72	95	103	101	—

a. Net FDI inflows US$0.38 billion in 2013.

Bahrain

Population (millions, 2014)	1.4
Population growth (avg. annual %, 2005–14)	5.2
Population density (people per sq km, 2014)	1,768.7
Labor force (thousands, 2013)	750.1
Unemployment rate (% of labor force, 2014)	3.9
Urban population (% of pop., 2014)	88.7
Surface area (thousands of sq km, 2014)	0.8
GNI, Atlas method (current US$ billions, 2014)	28.4
GNI per capita, Atlas method (current US$, 2014)	21,060.0
GDP growth (avg. annual %, 2011–14)	3.9
Poverty headcount ratio at national poverty line (% of pop.)	—
Age dependency ratio (% of working-age pop., 2014)	30.9
Account at a formal financial institution (% age 15+, 2014)	81.9
Mobile cellular subscriptions (per 100 people, 2014)	173.3
Internet users (per 100 people, 2014)	91.0

Migration

EMIGRATION

- Stock of emigrants, 2013: **61.6 thousands**
- Stock of emigrants as percentage of population, 2013: **4.6 percent**
- Top destination countries, 2013: Bangladesh, the West Bank and Gaza, the United Kingdom, the United Arab Emirates, the United States, Canada, Vietnam, Australia, Libya, Kuwait
- Tertiary-educated as a percentage of total emigrants in OECD countries, 2011: **48.0 percent**
- Tertiary-educated women as a percentage of total women emigrants in OECD countries, 2011: **49.4 percent**
- Number of refugees, 2014: **334**
- Second generation diaspora in Australia, Europe, and the United States, 2012: **1.5 thousands**

IMMIGRATION

- Stock of immigrants, 2013: **729.4 thousands**
- Stock of immigrants as percentage of population, 2013: **54.0 percent**
- Top source countries, 2013: India, Bangladesh, Pakistan, the Arab Republic of Egypt, the Philippines, Indonesia, the Republic of Yemen, Sudan, Jordan, Sri Lanka
- Women as percentage of immigrants, 2013: **27.8 percent**
- Number of refugees, 2014: **310**

Remittances

US$ millions	2006	2007	2008	2009	2010	2011	2012	2013	2014	2015e
Inward remittance flows[a]	–	–	–	–	–	–	–	–	–	–
of which										
Compensation of employees	–	–	–	–	–	–	–	–	–	–
Personal transfers	–	–	–	–	–	–	–	–	–	–
Outward remittance flows	1,531	1,483	1,774	1,391	1,642	2,050	2,074	2,166	2,364	–
of which										
Compensation of employees	–	–	–	–	–	–	–	–	–	–
Personal transfers	1,531	1,483	1,774	1,391	1,642	2,050	2,074	2,166	2,364	–

a. Net FDI inflows US$0.99 billion in 2013.

Bangladesh

	MIDDLE INCOME
Population (millions, 2014)	159.1
Population growth (avg. annual %, 2005–14)	1.2
Population density (people per sq km, 2014)	1,222.1
Labor force (millions, 2014)	79.0
Unemployment rate (% of labor force, 2014)	4.3
Urban population (% of pop., 2014)	33.5
Surface area (thousands of sq km, 2014)	148.5
GNI, Atlas method (current US$ billions, 2014)	171.3
GNI per capita, Atlas method (current US$, 2014)	1,080.0
GDP growth (avg. annual %, 2011–14)	6.3
Poverty headcount ratio at national poverty line (% of pop., 2010)	31.5
Age dependency ratio (% of working-age pop., 2014)	53.7
Account at a formal financial institution (% age 15+, 2014)	29.1
Mobile cellular subscriptions (per 100 people, 2014)	75.9
Internet users (per 100 people, 2014)	9.6

Migration

EMIGRATION

- Stock of emigrants, 2013: **7,572.1 thousands**
- Stock of emigrants as percentage of population, 2013: **4.8 percent**
- Top destination countries, 2013: India, Saudi Arabia, the United Arab Emirates, Kuwait, the United Kingdom, the United States, Pakistan, Oman, Qatar, Malaysia
- Tertiary-educated as a percentage of total emigrants in OECD countries, 2011: **35.1 percent**
- Tertiary-educated women as a percentage of total women emigrants in OECD countries, 2011: **30.7 percent**
- Number of refugees, 2014: **10,834**
- Second generation diaspora in Australia, Europe, and the United States, 2012: **117.0 thousands**

IMMIGRATION

- Stock of immigrants, 2013: **1,396.5 thousands**
- Stock of immigrants as percentage of population, 2013: **0.9 percent**
- Top source countries, 2013: Malaysia, Myanmar, China, Indonesia, the Lao People's Democratic Republic, the United States, Nepal, India, the United Kingdom, Bahrain
- Women as percentage of immigrants, 2013: **12.8 percent**
- Number of refugees, 2014: **232,468**

Remittances

US$ millions	2006	2007	2008	2009	2010	2011	2012	2013	2014	2015e
Inward remittance flows[a]	**5,428**	**6,562**	**8,941**	**10,521**	**10,850**	**12,071**	**14,120**	**13,867**	**14,983**	**15,771**
of which										
Compensation of employees	10	9	15	13	14	17	18	21	21	–
Personal transfers	5,418	6,553	8,925	10,508	10,836	12,054	14,102	13,846	14,962	–
Outward remittance flows	**3**	**3**	**14**	**8**	**9**	**12**	**12**	**20**	**33**	**–**
of which										
Compensation of employees	1	1	9	2	2	2	2	2	2	–
Personal transfers	2	2	6	6	7	9	9	17	30	–

a. Net FDI inflows US$1.91 billion, net ODA received US$2.67 billion in 2013.

Barbados

Population (thousands, 2013)	283.4
Population growth (avg. annual %, 2005–14)	0.4
Population density (people per sq km, 2014)	659.0
Labor force (thousands, 2013)	162.3
Unemployment rate (% of labor force, 2014)	12.0
Urban population (% of pop., 2014)	31.6
Surface area (thousands of sq km, 2014)	0.4
GNI, Atlas method (current US$ billions, 2012)	4.3
GNI per capita, Atlas method (current US$, 2012)	15,310.0
GDP growth (avg. annual %, 2011–14)	0.3
Poverty headcount ratio at national poverty line (% of pop.)	–
Age dependency ratio (% of working-age pop., 2014)	49.7
Account at a formal financial institution (% age 15+)	–
Mobile cellular subscriptions (per 100 people, 2014)	106.8
Internet users (per 100 people, 2014)	76.7

Migration

EMIGRATION

- Stock of emigrants, 2013: **100.5 thousands**
- Stock of emigrants as percentage of population, 2013: **35.6 percent**
- Top destination countries, 2013: the United States, the United Kingdom, Canada, Trinidad and Tobago, Jamaica, St. Lucia, St. Vincent and the Grenadines, Australia, the Virgin Islands (U.S.), Bermuda
- Tertiary-educated as a percentage of total emigrants in OECD countries, 2011: **34.8 percent**
- Tertiary-educated women as a percentage of total women emigrants in OECD countries, 2011: **38.1 percent**
- Number of refugees, 2014: **82**
- Second generation diaspora in Australia, Europe, and the United States, 2012: **91.3 thousands**

IMMIGRATION

- Stock of immigrants, 2013: **32.3 thousands**
- Stock of immigrants as percentage of population, 2013: **11.4 percent**
- Top source countries, 2013: St. Vincent and the Grenadines, St. Lucia, the United Kingdom, Guyana, Trinidad and Tobago, the United States, Canada, Jamaica, Grenada, Dominica
- Women as percentage of immigrants, 2013: **59.6 percent**
- Number of refugees, 2014: Not available

Remittances

US$ millions	2006	2007	2008	2009	2010	2011	2012	2013	2014	2015e
Inward remittance flows[a]	87	139	101	114	82	147	121	108	108	110
of which										
Compensation of employees	32	49	46	62	31	74	69	60	–	–
Personal transfers	55	90	55	53	51	73	52	48	–	–
Outward remittance flows	36	55	39	37	35	57	36	46	–	–
of which										
Compensation of employees	5	9	10	10	7	10	9	13	–	–
Personal transfers	31	46	29	27	28	46	28	33	–	–

a. Net FDI inflows US$-0.01 billion in 2013.

Belarus

Population (millions, 2014)	9.5
Population growth (avg. annual %, 2005–14)	-0.3
Population density (people per sq km, 2014)	46.7
Labor force (millions, 2014)	4.5
Unemployment rate (% of labor force, 2014)	5.9
Urban population (% of pop., 2014)	76.3
Surface area (thousands of sq km, 2014)	207.6
GNI, Atlas method (current US$ billions, 2014)	69.5
GNI per capita, Atlas method (current US$, 2014)	7,340.0
GDP growth (avg. annual %, 2011–14)	2.5
Poverty headcount ratio at national poverty line (% of pop., 2013)	5.5
Age dependency ratio (% of working-age pop., 2014)	42.3
Account at a formal financial institution (% age 15+, 2014)	72.0
Mobile cellular subscriptions (per 100 people, 2014)	122.5
Internet users (per 100 people, 2014)	59.0

Migration

EMIGRATION

- Stock of emigrants, 2013: **1,620.2 thousands**
- Stock of emigrants as percentage of population, 2013: **17.1 percent**
- Top destination countries, 2013: the Russian Federation, Ukraine, Poland, Uzbekistan, the United States, Lithuania, Latvia, Kazakhstan, Germany, Moldova
- Tertiary-educated as a percentage of total emigrants in OECD countries, 2011: **43.8 percent**
- Tertiary-educated women as a percentage of total women emigrants in OECD countries, 2011: **43.4 percent**
- Number of refugees, 2014: **4,273**
- Second generation diaspora in Australia, Europe, and the United States, 2012: Not available

IMMIGRATION

- Stock of immigrants, 2013: **1,085.4 thousands**
- Stock of immigrants as percentage of population, 2013: **11.5 percent**
- Top source countries, 2013: the Russian Federation, Ukraine, Kazakhstan, Lithuania, Uzbekistan, Azerbaijan, Latvia, Georgia, Moldova, Armenia
- Women as percentage of immigrants, 2013: **54.2 percent**
- Number of refugees, 2014: **919**

Remittances

US$ millions	2006	2007	2008	2009	2010	2011	2012	2013	2014	2015e
Inward remittance flows[a]	**268**	**288**	**583**	**504**	**575**	**891**	**1,053**	**1,214**	**1,231**	**1,061**
of which										
Compensation of employees	175	157	414	334	328	495	595	621	709	–
Personal transfers	93	132	170	170	248	396	459	593	522	–
Outward remittance flows	**70**	**103**	**171**	**133**	**116**	**134**	**142**	**151**	**181**	**–**
of which										
Compensation of employees	3	5	11	10	12	12	16	26	51	–
Personal transfers	68	98	160	123	104	121	126	125	130	–

a. Net FDI inflows US$2.25 billion, net ODA received US$0.10 billion in 2013.

Belgium

Population (millions, 2014)	11.2
Population growth (avg. annual %, 2005–14)	0.7
Population density (people per sq km, 2014)	370.7
Labor force (millions, 2014)	5.0
Unemployment rate (% of labor force, 2014)	8.5
Urban population (% of pop., 2014)	97.8
Surface area (thousands of sq km, 2014)	30.5
GNI, Atlas method (current US$ billions, 2014)	530.6
GNI per capita, Atlas method (current US$, 2014)	47,260.0
GDP growth (avg. annual %, 2011–14)	0.8
Poverty headcount ratio at national poverty line (% of pop.)	–
Age dependency ratio (% of working-age pop., 2014)	53.6
Account at a formal financial institution (% age 15+, 2014)	98.1
Mobile cellular subscriptions (per 100 people, 2014)	114.3
Internet users (per 100 people, 2014)	85.0

Migration

EMIGRATION

- Stock of emigrants, 2013: **530.4 thousands**
- Stock of emigrants as percentage of population, 2013: **4.7 percent**
- Top destination countries, 2013: France, the Netherlands, Italy, Spain, the United Kingdom, Germany, the United States, Canada, Luxembourg, Switzerland
- Tertiary-educated as a percentage of total emigrants in OECD countries, 2011: **35.9 percent**
- Tertiary-educated women as a percentage of total women emigrants in OECD countries, 2011: **33.9 percent**
- Number of refugees, 2014: **71**
- Second generation diaspora in Australia, Europe, and the United States, 2012: **541.4 thousands**

IMMIGRATION

- Stock of immigrants, 2013: **1,702.5 thousands**
- Stock of immigrants as percentage of population, 2013: **15.2 percent**
- Top source countries, 2013: Morocco, France, the Netherlands, Italy, Turkey, Germany, the Democratic Republic of Congo, Poland, Romania, the United Kingdom
- Women as percentage of immigrants, 2013: **49.7 percent**
- Number of refugees, 2014: **29,115**

Remittances

US$ millions	2006	2007	2008	2009	2010	2011	2012	2013	2014	2015e
Inward remittance flows[a]	7,266	8,993	10,480	10,638	10,351	11,066	10,626	11,234	11,453	11,020
of which										
Compensation of employees	7,239	8,879	10,341	10,501	10,227	10,896	10,495	11,097	11,341	–
Personal transfers	27	114	139	137	123	169	131	137	111	–
Outward remittance flows	2,564	3,202	4,124	4,479	4,185	4,556	4,239	4,482	4,505	–
of which										
Compensation of employees	2,135	2,727	3,539	3,865	3,591	3,847	3,607	3,770	3,773	–
Personal transfers	429	476	585	614	594	710	632	712	732	–

a. Net FDI inflows US$-35.82 billion in 2013.

Belize

	MIDDLE INCOME
Population (thousands, 2013)	351.7
Population growth (avg. annual %, 2005–14)	2.4
Population density (people per sq km, 2014)	15.4
Labor force (thousands, 2013)	154.6
Unemployment rate (% of labor force, 2014)	11.5
Urban population (% of pop., 2014)	44.1
Surface area (thousands of sq km, 2014)	23.0
GNI, Atlas method (current US$ billions, 2014)	1.5
GNI per capita, Atlas method (current US$, 2014)	4,350.0
GDP growth (avg. annual %, 2011–14)	2.8
Poverty headcount ratio at national poverty line (% of pop.)	–
Age dependency ratio (% of working-age pop., 2014)	58.3
Account at a formal financial institution (% age 15+, 2014)	48.2
Mobile cellular subscriptions (per 100 people, 2014)	50.7
Internet users (per 100 people, 2014)	38.7

Migration

EMIGRATION

- Stock of emigrants, 2013: **61.8 thousands**
- Stock of emigrants as percentage of population, 2013: **18.0 percent**
- Top destination countries, 2013: the United States, Mexico, Canada, Guatemala, the Plurinational State of Bolivia, the Cayman Islands, El Salvador, Honduras, Costa Rica, the Dominican Republic
- Tertiary-educated as a percentage of total emigrants in OECD countries, 2011: **25.8 percent**
- Tertiary-educated women as a percentage of total women emigrants in OECD countries, 2011: **26.7 percent**
- Number of refugees, 2014: **42**
- Second generation diaspora in Australia, Europe, and the United States, 2012: **20.3 thousands**

IMMIGRATION

- Stock of immigrants, 2013: **50.9 thousands**
- Stock of immigrants as percentage of population, 2013: **14.8 percent**
- Top source countries, 2013: Guatemala, El Salvador, Mexico, Honduras, the United States, China, Canada, Jamaica, the United Kingdom, India
- Women as percentage of immigrants, 2013: **49.5 percent**
- Number of refugees, 2014: **10**

Remittances

US$ millions	2006	2007	2008	2009	2010	2011	2012	2013	2014	2015e
Inward remittance flows[a]	**64**	**73**	**76**	**79**	**78**	**75**	**76**	**74**	**80**	**83**
of which										
Compensation of employees	6	2	2	2	2	2	2	2	2	–
Personal transfers	58	71	74	76	76	73	74	72	78	–
Outward remittance flows	**21**	**21**	**28**	**23**	**22**	**24**	**26**	**32**	**33**	**–**
of which										
Compensation of employees	6	5	6	6	6	5	5	6	7	–
Personal transfers	15	16	22	17	16	18	21	25	27	–

a. Net FDI inflows US$0.09 billion, net ODA received US$0.05 billion in 2013.

Benin

Population (millions, 2014)	10.6
Population growth (avg. annual %, 2005–14)	2.9
Population density (people per sq km, 2014)	94.0
Labor force (millions, 2014)	4.4
Unemployment rate (% of labor force, 2014)	1.0
Urban population (% of pop., 2014)	43.5
Surface area (thousands of sq km, 2014)	114.8
GNI, Atlas method (current US$ billions, 2014)	9.5
GNI per capita, Atlas method (current US$, 2014)	890.0
GDP growth (avg. annual %, 2011–14)	5.3
Poverty headcount ratio at national poverty line (% of pop., 2011)	36.2
Age dependency ratio (% of working-age pop., 2014)	83.0
Account at a formal financial institution (% age 15+, 2014)	16.0
Mobile cellular subscriptions (per 100 people, 2014)	101.7
Internet users (per 100 people, 2014)	5.3

Migration

EMIGRATION

- Stock of emigrants, 2013: **486.8 thousands**
- Stock of emigrants as percentage of population, 2013: **4.7 percent**
- Top destination countries, 2013: Nigeria, Côte d'Ivoire, Togo, Gabon, France, Ghana, Niger, the Republic of Congo, Burkina Faso, Cameroon
- Tertiary-educated as a percentage of total emigrants in OECD countries, 2011: **43.2 percent**
- Tertiary-educated women as a percentage of total women emigrants in OECD countries, 2011: **35.5 percent**
- Number of refugees, 2014: **330**
- Second generation diaspora in Australia, Europe, and the United States, 2012: **7.9 thousands**

IMMIGRATION

- Stock of immigrants, 2013: **234.2 thousands**
- Stock of immigrants as percentage of population, 2013: **2.3 percent**
- Top source countries, 2013: Niger, Togo, Nigeria, Côte d'Ivoire, Ghana, Burkina Faso, the Republic of Congo, France, Mali, Chad
- Women as percentage of immigrants, 2013: **44.1 percent**
- Number of refugees, 2014: **404**

Remittances

US$ millions	2006	2007	2008	2009	2010	2011	2012	2013	2014	2015e
Inward remittance flows[a]	195	240	207	126	139	172	208	249	249	249
of which										
Compensation of employees	9	6	7	3	12	19	19	19	–	–
Personal transfers	186	234	200	123	127	153	189	229	–	–
Outward remittance flows	61	108	74	70	63	62	88	101	–	–
of which										
Compensation of employees	9	5	6	3	2	12	14	13	–	–
Personal transfers	52	102	68	67	62	50	74	88	–	–

a. Net FDI inflows US$0.36 billion, net ODA received US$0.65 billion in 2013.

Bermuda

Population (thousands, 2013)	65.2
Population growth (avg. annual %, 2005–14)	0.2
Population density (people per sq km, 2014)	1,303.6
Labor force, total	–
Unemployment rate (% of labor force)	–
Urban population (% of pop., 2014)	100.0
Surface area (thousands of sq km, 2014)	0.1
GNI, Atlas method (current US$ billions, 2014)	6.9
GNI per capita, Atlas method (current US$, 2014)	106,140.0
GDP growth (avg. annual %, 2011–14)	-3.3
Poverty headcount ratio at national poverty line (% of pop.)	–
Age dependency ratio (% of working-age pop.)	–
Account at a formal financial institution (% age 15+)	–
Mobile cellular subscriptions (per 100 people, 2014)	90.9
Internet users (per 100 people, 2014)	96.8

Migration

EMIGRATION

- Stock of emigrants, 2013: **12.5 thousands**
- Stock of emigrants as percentage of population, 2013: **19.2** percent
- Top destination countries, 2013: the United States, Canada, Australia, Ireland, France, South Africa, the Cayman Islands, the Netherlands, The Bahamas, Austria
- Tertiary-educated as a percentage of total emigrants in OECD countries, 2011: **39.6 percent**
- Tertiary-educated women as a percentage of total women emigrants in OECD countries, 2011: **39.9 percent**
- Number of refugees, 2014: Not available
- Second generation diaspora in Australia, Europe, and the United States, 2012: Not available

IMMIGRATION

- Stock of immigrants, 2013: **20.2 thousands**
- Stock of immigrants as percentage of population, 2013: **31.0 percent**
- Top source countries, 2013: the United Kingdom, the United States, Canada, Haiti, Portugal, Jamaica, the Philippines, India, Barbados, Ireland
- Women as percentage of immigrants, 2013: **45.3 percent**
- Number of refugees, 2014: Not available

Remittances

US$ millions	2006	2007	2008	2009	2010	2011	2012	2013	2014	2015e
Inward remittance flows[a]	**1,182**	**1,450**	**1,391**	**1,346**	**1,261**	**1,175**	**1,191**	**1,225**	**1,290**	**1,325**
of which										
Compensation of employees	1,182	1,450	1,391	1,345	1,260	1,174	1,189	1,223	1,289	–
Personal transfers	–	–	0	1	1	2	1	2	2	–
Outward remittance flows	**172**	**178**	**191**	**213**	**239**	**215**	**217**	**219**	**223**	–
of which										
Compensation of employees	67	69	68	71	86	64	67	64	66	–
Personal transfers	105	109	123	142	153	151	150	154	157	–

a. Net FDI inflows US$0.05 billion in 2013.

Bhutan

Population (thousands, 2013)	765.0
Population growth (avg. annual %, 2005–14)	1.9
Population density (people per sq km, 2014)	20.1
Labor force (thousands, 2013)	404.1
Unemployment rate (% of labor force, 2014)	2.8
Urban population (% of pop., 2014)	37.9
Surface area (thousands of sq km, 2014)	38.4
GNI, Atlas method (current US$ billions, 2014)	1.8
GNI per capita, Atlas method (current US$, 2014)	2,370.0
GDP growth (avg. annual %, 2011–14)	5.1
Poverty headcount ratio at national poverty line (% of pop., 2012)	12.0
Age dependency ratio (% of working-age pop., 2014)	47.9
Account at a formal financial institution (% age 15+, 2014)	33.7
Mobile cellular subscriptions (per 100 people, 2014)	82.1
Internet users (per 100 people, 2014)	34.4

Migration

EMIGRATION

- Stock of emigrants, 2013: **90.8 thousands**
- Stock of emigrants as percentage of population, 2013: **12.0 percent**
- Top destination countries, 2013: Nepal, India, Australia, Denmark, China, Norway, the Netherlands, Canada, the United States, France
- Tertiary-educated as a percentage of total emigrants in OECD countries, 2011: **16.3 percent**
- Tertiary-educated women as a percentage of total women emigrants in OECD countries, 2011: **12.9 percent**
- Number of refugees, 2014: **23,618**
- Second generation diaspora in Australia, Europe, and the United States, 2012: Not available

IMMIGRATION

- Stock of immigrants, 2013: **50.9 thousands**
- Stock of immigrants as percentage of population, 2013: **6.7 percent**
- Top source countries, 2013: India, China, Nepal, the United States, Japan, Thailand, Bangladesh, Denmark, Canada, the United Kingdom
- Women as percentage of immigrants, 2013: **18.9 percent**
- Number of refugees, 2014: Not available

Remittances

US$ millions	2006	2007	2008	2009	2010	2011	2012	2013	2014	2015e
Inward remittance flows[a]	**2**	**3**	**4**	**5**	**8**	**10**	**18**	**12**	**14**	**15**
of which										
Compensation of employees	1	1	2	2	2	1	1	2	1	—
Personal transfers	1	2	2	3	7	9	17	10	12	—
Outward remittance flows	**75**	**61**	**61**	**48**	**71**	**92**	**74**	**58**	**49**	**—**
of which										
Compensation of employees	16	11	13	14	27	47	38	40	35	—
Personal transfers	59	50	48	33	43	46	36	18	14	—

a. Net FDI inflows US$0.05 billion, net ODA received US$0.13 billion in 2013.

Bolivia, Plurinational State of

Population (millions, 2014)	10.6
Population growth (avg. annual %, 2005-14)	1.6
Population density (people per sq km, 2014)	9.7
Labor force (millions, 2014)	5.1
Unemployment rate (% of labor force, 2014)	2.7
Urban population (% of pop., 2014)	68.1
Surface area (thousands of sq km, 2014)	1,098.6
GNI, Atlas method (current US$ billions, 2014)	30.3
GNI per capita, Atlas method (current US$, 2014)	2,870.0
GDP growth (avg. annual %, 2011-14)	5.6
Poverty headcount ratio at national poverty line (% of pop., 2011)	45.0
Age dependency ratio (% of working-age pop., 2014)	64.6
Account at a formal financial institution (% age 15+, 2014)	40.7
Mobile cellular subscriptions (per 100 people, 2014)	96.3
Internet users (per 100 people, 2014)	39.0

Migration

EMIGRATION

- Stock of emigrants, 2013: **879.0 thousands**
- Stock of emigrants as percentage of population, 2013: **8.5 percent**
- Top destination countries, 2013: Argentina, Spain, the United States, Brazil, Chile, Italy, Peru, Canada, Sweden, Switzerland
- Tertiary-educated as a percentage of total emigrants in OECD countries, 2011: **19.4 percent**
- Tertiary-educated women as a percentage of total women emigrants in OECD countries, 2011: **18.6 percent**
- Number of refugees, 2014: **583**
- Second generation diaspora in Australia, Europe, and the United States, 2012: **42.4 thousands**

IMMIGRATION

- Stock of immigrants, 2013: **119.0 thousands**
- Stock of immigrants as percentage of population, 2013: **1.1 percent**
- Top source countries, 2013: Argentina, Brazil, Spain, Peru, Mexico, the United States, Chile, Paraguay, Colombia, Germany
- Women as percentage of immigrants, 2013: **47.8 percent**
- Number of refugees, 2014: **741**

Remittances

US$ millions	2006	2007	2008	2009	2010	2011	2012	2013	2014	2015e
Inward remittance flows[a]	603	1,055	1,135	1,058	960	1,043	1,111	1,201	1,184	1,200
of which										
Compensation of employees	33	35	37	35	21	31	16	20	20	–
Personal transfers	569	1,020	1,097	1,023	939	1,012	1,094	1,182	1,164	–
Outward remittance flows	73	79	106	103	102	117	147	172	189	–
of which										
Compensation of employees	7	7	7	7	2	3	4	9	11	–
Personal transfers	66	72	98	96	100	114	144	164	178	–

a. Net FDI inflows US$1.75 billion, net ODA received US$0.70 billion in 2013.

Bosnia and Herzegovina

Population (millions, 2014)	3.8
Population growth (avg. annual %, 2005–14)	0.0
Population density (people per sq km, 2014)	74.6
Labor force (millions, 2014)	1.5
Unemployment rate (% of labor force, 2014)	27.9
Urban population (% of pop., 2014)	39.6
Surface area (thousands of sq km, 2014)	51.2
GNI, Atlas method (current US$ billions, 2014)	18.2
GNI per capita, Atlas method (current US$, 2014)	4,760.0
GDP growth (avg. annual %, 2011–14)	0.8
Poverty headcount ratio at national poverty line (% of pop., 2011)	17.9
Age dependency ratio (% of working-age pop., 2014)	40.1
Account at a formal financial institution (% age 15+, 2014)	52.7
Mobile cellular subscriptions (per 100 people, 2014)	91.3
Internet users (per 100 people, 2014)	60.8

Migration

EMIGRATION

- Stock of emigrants, 2013: **1,699.9 thousands**
- Stock of emigrants as percentage of population, 2013: **44.5 percent**
- Top destination countries, 2013: Croatia, Serbia, Germany, Austria, the United States, Slovenia, Sweden, Switzerland, Australia, Canada
- Tertiary-educated as a percentage of total emigrants in OECD countries, 2011: **14.0 percent**
- Tertiary-educated women as a percentage of total women emigrants in OECD countries, 2011: **14.8 percent**
- Number of refugees, 2014: **21,877**
- Second generation diaspora in Australia, Europe, and the United States, 2012: Not available

IMMIGRATION

- Stock of immigrants, 2013: **23.2 thousands**
- Stock of immigrants as percentage of population, 2013: **0.6 percent**
- Top source countries, 2013: Croatia, Serbia, Montenegro, the Slovak Republic, the Former Yugoslav Republic of Macedonia, Slovenia, Germany, Romania, Austria, the Russian Federation
- Women as percentage of immigrants, 2013: **50.1 percent**
- Number of refugees, 2014: **6,873**

Remittances

US$ millions	2006	2007	2008	2009	2010	2011	2012	2013	2014	2015e
Inward remittance flows[a]	**2,149**	**2,686**	**2,718**	**2,127**	**1,822**	**1,958**	**1,846**	**1,947**	**2,086**	**2,017**
of which										
Compensation of employees	560	739	818	695	479	530	472	471	519	–
Personal transfers	1,589	1,947	1,899	1,432	1,343	1,429	1,374	1,475	1,567	–
Outward remittance flows	**55**	**65**	**55**	**55**	**46**	**52**	**47**	**48**	**51**	–
of which										
Compensation of employees	14	15	17	15	13	13	11	11	9	–
Personal transfers	41	50	38	40	34	39	36	38	42	–

a. Net FDI inflows US$0.34 billion, net ODA received US$0.55 billion in 2013.

Botswana

Population (millions, 2014)	2.2
Population growth (avg. annual %, 2005–14)	1.9
Population density (people per sq km, 2014)	3.9
Labor force (millions, 2014)	1.2
Unemployment rate (% of labor force, 2014)	18.2
Urban population (% of pop., 2014)	57.2
Surface area (thousands of sq km, 2014)	581.7
GNI, Atlas method (current US$ billions, 2014)	16.1
GNI per capita, Atlas method (current US$, 2014)	7,240.0
GDP growth (avg. annual %, 2011–14)	6.2
Poverty headcount ratio at national poverty line (% of pop., 2009)	19.3
Age dependency ratio (% of working-age pop., 2014)	55.6
Account at a formal financial institution (% age 15+, 2014)	49.2
Mobile cellular subscriptions (per 100 people, 2014)	167.3
Internet users (per 100 people, 2014)	18.5

Migration

EMIGRATION

- Stock of emigrants, 2013: **57.5 thousands**
- Stock of emigrants as percentage of population, 2013: **2.6 percent**
- Top destination countries, 2013: South Africa, Zimbabwe, Australia, Kenya, the United States, Canada, Tanzania, Namibia, Ireland, the Netherlands
- Tertiary-educated as a percentage of total emigrants in OECD countries, 2011: **36.3 percent**
- Tertiary-educated women as a percentage of total women emigrants in OECD countries, 2011: **38.8 percent**
- Number of refugees, 2014: **234**
- Second generation diaspora in Australia, Europe, and the United States, 2012: Not available

IMMIGRATION

- Stock of immigrants, 2013: **146.5 thousands**
- Stock of immigrants as percentage of population, 2013: **6.7 percent**
- Top source countries, 2013: South Africa, Zimbabwe, Zambia, India, the United Kingdom, Malawi, China, Angola, the Democratic Republic of Congo, Lesotho
- Women as percentage of immigrants, 2013: **45.3 percent**
- Number of refugees, 2014: **2,637**

Remittances

US$ millions	2006	2007	2008	2009	2010	2011	2012	2013	2014	2015e
Inward remittance flows[a]	104	92	47	15	22	20	18	36	42	43
of which										
Compensation of employees	25	12	20	12	19	17	16	31	–	–
Personal transfers	79	80	27	3	3	3	2	5	–	–
Outward remittance flows	97	99	56	60	85	107	108	81	–	–
of which										
Compensation of employees	87	89	17	26	36	37	29	24	–	–
Personal transfers	10	10	39	34	49	70	78	57	–	–

a. Net FDI inflows US$0.19 billion, net ODA received US$0.11 billion in 2013.

Brazil

Population (millions, 2014)	206.1
Population growth (avg. annual %, 2005–14)	1.0
Population density (people per sq km, 2014)	24.7
Labor force (millions, 2014)	109.8
Unemployment rate (% of labor force, 2014)	6.8
Urban population (% of pop., 2014)	85.4
Surface area (thousands of sq km, 2014)	8,515.8
GNI, Atlas method (current US$ billions, 2014)	2,375.3
GNI per capita, Atlas method (current US$, 2014)	11,530.0
GDP growth (avg. annual %, 2011–14)	2.1
Poverty headcount ratio at national poverty line (% of pop., 2013)	8.9
Age dependency ratio (% of working-age pop., 2014)	45.1
Account at a formal financial institution (% age 15+, 2014)	68.1
Mobile cellular subscriptions (per 100 people, 2014)	139.0
Internet users (per 100 people, 2014)	57.6

Migration

EMIGRATION

- Stock of emigrants, 2013: **1,804.3 thousands**
- Stock of emigrants as percentage of population, 2013: **0.9 percent**
- Top destination countries, 2013: the United States, Japan, Portugal, Spain, China, Italy, Paraguay, Germany, France, the United Kingdom
- Tertiary-educated as a percentage of total emigrants in OECD countries, 2011: **26.0 percent**
- Tertiary-educated women as a percentage of total women emigrants in OECD countries, 2011: **27.9 percent**
- Number of refugees, 2014: **957**
- Second generation diaspora in Australia, Europe, and the United States, 2012: **187.4 thousands**

IMMIGRATION

- Stock of immigrants, 2013: **599.7 thousands**
- Stock of immigrants as percentage of population, 2013: **0.3 percent**
- Top source countries, 2013: Portugal, Japan, Paraguay, the Plurinational State of Bolivia, Italy, Spain, Argentina, Uruguay, the United States, China
- Women as percentage of immigrants, 2013: **46.0 percent**
- Number of refugees, 2014: **7,423**

Remittances

US$ millions	2006	2007	2008	2009	2010	2011	2012	2013	2014	2015e
Inward remittance flows[a]	**3,287**	**3,306**	**3,643**	**2,889**	**2,754**	**2,798**	**2,583**	**2,537**	**2,645**	**2,809**
of which										
Compensation of employees	397	497	730	665	565	665	593	593	520	–
Personal transfers	2,890	2,809	2,913	2,224	2,189	2,134	1,990	1,944	2,125	–
Outward remittance flows	**529**	**563**	**813**	**731**	**922**	**910**	**897**	**1,019**	**1,535**	**–**
of which										
Compensation of employees	220	49	185	62	66	98	82	82	163	–
Personal transfers	309	514	628	669	855	811	815	937	1,372	–

a. Net FDI inflows US$80.84 billion, net ODA received US$1.15 billion in 2013.

Brunei Darussalam

Population (thousands, 2013)	417.4
Population growth (avg. annual %, 2005–14)	1.6
Population density (people per sq km, 2014)	79.2
Labor force (thousands, 2013)	203.3
Unemployment rate (% of labor force, 2014)	3.8
Urban population (% of pop., 2014)	76.9
Surface area (thousands of sq km, 2014)	5.8
GNI, Atlas method (current US$ billions, 2012)	15.1
GNI per capita, Atlas method (current US$, 2012)	37,320.0
GDP growth (avg. annual %, 2011–14)	0.1
Poverty headcount ratio at national poverty line (% of pop.)	—
Age dependency ratio (% of working-age pop., 2014)	38.3
Account at a formal financial institution (% age 15+)	—
Mobile cellular subscriptions (per 100 people, 2014)	110.1
Internet users (per 100 people, 2014)	68.8

Migration

EMIGRATION

- Stock of emigrants, 2013: **43.1 thousands**
- Stock of emigrants as percentage of population, 2013: **10.5 percent**
- Top destination countries, 2013: India, the United Kingdom, Canada, Australia, the United States, Malaysia, the Netherlands, Brazil, Vietnam, the Philippines
- Tertiary-educated as a percentage of total emigrants in OECD countries, 2011: **47.5 percent**
- Tertiary-educated women as a percentage of total women emigrants in OECD countries, 2011: **47.6 percent**
- Number of refugees, 2014: Not available
- Second generation diaspora in Australia, Europe, and the United States, 2012: Not available

IMMIGRATION

- Stock of immigrants, 2013: **206.2 thousands**
- Stock of immigrants as percentage of population, 2013: **50.1 percent**
- Top source countries, 2013: Japan, Thailand, New Zealand, India, the Republic of Korea, Hong Kong SAR, China, the United Kingdom, Sri Lanka, the Philippines, Singapore
- Women as percentage of immigrants, 2013: **43.5 percent**
- Number of refugees, 2014: Not available

Remittances

US$ millions	2006	2007	2008	2009	2010	2011	2012	2013	2014	2015e
Inward remittance flows[a]	–	–	–	–	–	–	–	–	–	–
of which										
Compensation of employees	–	–	–	–	–	–	–	–	–	–
Personal transfers	–	–	–	–	–	–	–	–	–	–
Outward remittance flows	405	430	420	445	–	–	–	–	–	–
of which										
Compensation of employees	–	–	–	–	–	–	–	–	–	–
Personal transfers	405	430	420	445	–	–	–	–	–	–

a. Net FDI inflows US$0.78 billion in 2013.

Bulgaria

Population (millions, 2014)	7.2
Population growth (avg. annual %, 2005–14)	–0.6
Population density (people per sq km, 2014)	66.6
Labor force (millions, 2014)	3.3
Unemployment rate (% of labor force, 2014)	11.6
Urban population (% of pop., 2014)	73.6
Surface area (thousands of sq km, 2014)	111.0
GNI, Atlas method (current US$ billions, 2014)	55.0
GNI per capita, Atlas method (current US$, 2014)	7,620.0
GDP growth (avg. annual %, 2011–14)	1.2
Poverty headcount ratio at national poverty line (% of pop., 2013)	21.0
Age dependency ratio (% of working-age pop., 2014)	50.8
Account at a formal financial institution (% age 15+, 2014)	63.0
Mobile cellular subscriptions (per 100 people, 2014)	137.7
Internet users (per 100 people, 2014)	55.5

Migration

EMIGRATION

- Stock of emigrants, 2013: **1,416.6 thousands**
- Stock of emigrants as percentage of population, 2013: **19.5 percent**
- Top destination countries, 2013: Turkey, Spain, Germany, the United States, the United Kingdom, Italy, Greece, Belgium, Canada, Romania
- Tertiary-educated as a percentage of total emigrants in OECD countries, 2011: **24.0 percent**
- Tertiary-educated women as a percentage of total women emigrants in OECD countries, 2011: **26.6 percent**
- Number of refugees, 2014: **1,639**
- Second generation diaspora in Australia, Europe, and the United States, 2012: **49.3 thousands**

IMMIGRATION

- Stock of immigrants, 2013: **84.1 thousands**
- Stock of immigrants as percentage of population, 2013: **1.2 percent**
- Top source countries, 2013: the Russian Federation, Romania, Ukraine, Greece, Turkey, the United Kingdom, the Former Yugoslav Republic of Macedonia, Serbia, Azerbaijan, Germany
- Women as percentage of immigrants, 2013: **55.5 percent**
- Number of refugees, 2014: **11,006**

Remittances

US$ millions	2006	2007	2008	2009	2010	2011	2012	2013	2014	2015e
Inward remittance flows[a]	**1,716**	**1,694**	**1,919**	**1,592**	**1,448**	**1,483**	**1,449**	**1,667**	**1,684**	**1,752**
of which										
Compensation of employees	1,297	788	894	593	403	409	420	539	586	–
Personal transfers	420	905	1,025	999	1,045	1,074	1,029	1,128	1,099	–
Outward remittance flows	**50**	**103**	**162**	**101**	**20**	**24**	**28**	**21**	**22**	**–**
of which										
Compensation of employees	29	69	128	88	14	14	21	13	17	–
Personal transfers	21	33	33	14	7	9	7	8	6	–

a. Net FDI inflows US$1.99 billion in 2013.

Burkina Faso

Population (millions, 2014)	17.6
Population growth (avg. annual %, 2005–14)	3.0
Population density (people per sq km, 2014)	64.3
Labor force (millions, 2014)	7.9
Unemployment rate (% of labor force, 2014)	3.1
Urban population (% of pop., 2014)	29.0
Surface area (thousands of sq km, 2014)	274.2
GNI, Atlas method (current US$ billions, 2014)	12.3
GNI per capita, Atlas method (current US$, 2014)	700.0
GDP growth (avg. annual %, 2011–14)	5.2
Poverty headcount ratio at national poverty line (% of pop., 2009)	46.7
Age dependency ratio (% of working-age pop., 2014)	93.1
Account at a formal financial institution (% age 15+, 2014)	13.4
Mobile cellular subscriptions (per 100 people, 2014)	71.7
Internet users (per 100 people, 2014)	9.4

Migration

EMIGRATION

- Stock of emigrants, 2013: **1,642.6 thousands**
- Stock of emigrants as percentage of population, 2013: **9.6 percent**
- Top destination countries, 2013: Côte d'Ivoire, Ghana, Mali, Niger, Italy, Benin, France, Nigeria, Gabon, Germany
- Tertiary-educated as a percentage of total emigrants in OECD countries, 2011: **21.5 percent**
- Tertiary-educated women as a percentage of total women emigrants in OECD countries, 2011: **22.7 percent**
- Number of refugees, 2014: **1,823**
- Second generation diaspora in Australia, Europe, and the United States, 2012: **6.5 thousands**

IMMIGRATION

- Stock of immigrants, 2013: **697.0 thousands**
- Stock of immigrants as percentage of population, 2013: **4.1 percent**
- Top source countries, 2013: Côte d'Ivoire, Mali, Ghana, Togo, Niger, Benin, Nigeria, Senegal
- Women as percentage of immigrants, 2013: **52.4 percent**
- Number of refugees, 2014: **31,889**

Remittances

US$ millions	2006	2007	2008	2009	2010	2011	2012	2013	2014	2015e
Inward remittance flows[a]	68	84	99	96	120	120	120	120	120	120
of which										
Compensation of employees	7	8	14	12	15	–	–	–	–	–
Personal transfers	61	76	85	84	106	–	–	–	–	–
Outward remittance flows	86	93	100	99	112	–	–	–	–	–
of which										
Compensation of employees	15	16	16	17	17	–	–	–	–	–
Personal transfers	71	77	84	83	94	–	–	–	–	–

a. Net FDI inflows US$0.49 billion, net ODA received US$1.04 billion in 2013.

Burundi

LOW INCOME

Population (millions, 2014)	10.8
Population growth (avg. annual %, 2005–14)	3.4
Population density (people per sq km, 2014)	421.2
Labor force (millions, 2014)	5.0
Unemployment rate (% of labor force, 2014)	6.9
Urban population (% of pop., 2014)	11.8
Surface area (thousands of sq km, 2014)	27.8
GNI, Atlas method (current US$ billions, 2014)	2.9
GNI per capita, Atlas method (current US$, 2014)	270.0
GDP growth (avg. annual %, 2011–14)	4.4
Poverty headcount ratio at national poverty line (% of pop., 2006)	66.9
Age dependency ratio (% of working-age pop., 2014)	89.1
Account at a formal financial institution (% age 15+, 2014)	6.9
Mobile cellular subscriptions (per 100 people, 2014)	30.5
Internet users (per 100 people, 2014)	1.4

Migration

EMIGRATION

- Stock of emigrants, 2013: **378.8 thousands**
- Stock of emigrants as percentage of population, 2013: **3.6 percent**
- Top destination countries, 2013: Tanzania, Rwanda, the Democratic Republic of Congo, Uganda, Canada, Malawi, South Africa, Sweden, Belgium, the Netherlands
- Tertiary-educated as a percentage of total emigrants in OECD countries, 2011: **33.9 percent**
- Tertiary-educated women as a percentage of total women emigrants in OECD countries, 2011: **31.9 percent**
- Number of refugees, 2014: **72,463**
- Second generation diaspora in Australia, Europe, and the United States, 2012: **2.6 thousands**

IMMIGRATION

- Stock of immigrants, 2013: **254.5 thousands**
- Stock of immigrants as percentage of population, 2013: **2.4 percent**
- Top source countries, 2013: the Democratic Republic of Congo, Rwanda, Tanzania, Kenya, Uganda, Belgium, France
- Women as percentage of immigrants, 2013: **50.8 percent**
- Number of refugees, 2014: **52,931**

Remittances

US$ millions	2006	2007	2008	2009	2010	2011	2012	2013	2014	2015e
Inward remittance flows[a]	0	0	4	28	34	45	46	49	49	50
of which										
Compensation of employees	–	–	–	–	–	6	10	13	–	–
Personal transfers	0	0	4	28	34	39	36	36	–	–
Outward remittance flows	0	0	0	1	5	6	5	7	–	–
of which										
Compensation of employees	–	–	–	–	–	3	3	3	–	–
Personal transfers	0	0	0	1	5	4	3	4	–	–

a. Net FDI inflows US$0.01 billion, net ODA received US$0.55 billion in 2013.

Cabo Verde

Population (thousands, 2013)	513.9
Population growth (avg. annual %, 2005–14)	0.9
Population density (people per sq km, 2014)	127.5
Labor force (thousands, 2013)	244.0
Unemployment rate (% of labor force, 2014)	9.2
Urban population (% of pop., 2014)	64.8
Surface area (thousands of sq km, 2014)	4.0
GNI, Atlas method (current US$ billions, 2014)	1.8
GNI per capita, Atlas method (current US$, 2014)	3,450.0
GDP growth (avg. annual %, 2011–14)	2.2
Poverty headcount ratio at national poverty line (% of pop., 2007)	26.6
Age dependency ratio (% of working-age pop., 2014)	53.1
Account at a formal financial institution (% age 15+)	–
Mobile cellular subscriptions (per 100 people, 2014)	121.8
Internet users (per 100 people, 2014)	40.3

Migration

EMIGRATION

- Stock of emigrants, 2013: **173.0 thousands**
- Stock of emigrants as percentage of population, 2013: **34.1 percent**
- Top destination countries, 2013: Portugal, the United States, France, the Netherlands, Angola, Mozambique, Italy, Spain, Nigeria, Switzerland
- Tertiary-educated as a percentage of total emigrants in OECD countries, 2011: **7.5 percent**
- Tertiary-educated women as a percentage of total women emigrants in OECD countries, 2011: **8.0 percent**
- Number of refugees, 2014: **17**
- Second generation diaspora in Australia, Europe, and the United States, 2012: Not available

IMMIGRATION

- Stock of immigrants, 2013: **14.9 thousands**
- Stock of immigrants as percentage of population, 2013: **2.9 percent**
- Top source countries, 2013: Guinea-Bissau, São Tomé and Príncipe, Senegal, Portugal, the Russian Federation, Nigeria, Guinea, Italy, Angola, the United States
- Women as percentage of immigrants, 2013: **49.4 percent**
- Number of refugees, 2014: Not available

Remittances

US$ millions	2006	2007	2008	2009	2010	2011	2012	2013	2014	2015e
Inward remittance flows[a]	137	139	155	137	131	177	178	176	191	195
of which Compensation of employees	1	0	1	0	1	1	2	2	2	–
Personal transfers	136	138	154	136	130	176	175	174	189	–
Outward remittance flows	6	6	10	12	8	9	10	10	9	–
of which Compensation of employees	1	1	2	5	2	2	2	2	3	–
Personal transfers	5	5	8	7	6	7	8	8	6	–

a. Net FDI inflows US$0.09 billion, net ODA received US$0.24 billion in 2013.

Cambodia

LOW INCOME

Population (millions, 2014)	15.3
Population growth (avg. annual %, 2005–14)	1.6
Population density (people per sq km, 2014)	86.8
Labor force (millions, 2014)	8.6
Unemployment rate (% of labor force, 2014)	0.4
Urban population (% of pop., 2014)	20.5
Surface area (thousands of sq km, 2014)	181.0
GNI, Atlas method (current US$ billions, 2014)	15.6
GNI per capita, Atlas method (current US$, 2014)	1,020.0
GDP growth (avg. annual %, 2011–14)	7.2
Poverty headcount ratio at national poverty line (% of pop., 2012)	17.7
Age dependency ratio (% of working-age pop., 2014)	55.8
Account at a formal financial institution (% age 15+, 2014)	12.6
Mobile cellular subscriptions (per 100 people, 2014)	155.1
Internet users (per 100 people, 2014)	9.0

Migration

EMIGRATION

- Stock of emigrants, 2013: **1,118.9 thousands**
- Stock of emigrants as percentage of population, 2013: **7.4 percent**
- Top destination countries, 2013: Thailand, the United States, France, Australia, Canada, Bangladesh, Malaysia, the Republic of Korea, New Zealand, Japan
- Tertiary-educated as a percentage of total emigrants in OECD countries, 2011: **18.3 percent**
- Tertiary-educated women as a percentage of total women emigrants in OECD countries, 2011: **15.6 percent**
- Number of refugees, 2014: **13,056**
- Second generation diaspora in Australia, Europe, and the United States, 2012: **120.4 thousands**

IMMIGRATION

- Stock of immigrants, 2013: **75.6 thousands**
- Stock of immigrants as percentage of population, 2013: **0.5 percent**
- Top source countries, 2013: Vietnam, Thailand, China, France, the Lao People's Democratic Republic, the United States, Malaysia, the Philippines, Japan, Singapore
- Women as percentage of immigrants, 2013: **46.3 percent**
- Number of refugees, 2014: **59**

Remittances

US$ millions	2006	2007	2008	2009	2010	2011	2012	2013	2014	2015e
Inward remittance flows[a]	**184**	**186**	**188**	**142**	**153**	**160**	**172**	**176**	**377**	**731**
of which										
Compensation of employees	4	4	4	5	5	5	5	7	11	–
Personal transfers	180	182	184	138	148	155	167	169	366	–
Outward remittance flows	**120**	**118**	**171**	**159**	**171**	**150**	**134**	**181**	**219**	–
of which										
Compensation of employees	100	94	147	140	151	129	54	66	82	–
Personal transfers	20	24	24	19	20	21	80	114	137	–

a. Net FDI inflows US$1.35 billion, net ODA received US$0.80 billion in 2013.

Cameroon

	MIDDLE INCOME
Population (millions, 2014)	22.8
Population growth (avg. annual %, 2005–14)	2.5
Population density (people per sq km, 2014)	48.2
Labor force (millions, 2014)	9.2
Unemployment rate (% of labor force, 2014)	4.3
Urban population (% of pop., 2014)	53.8
Surface area (thousands of sq km, 2014)	475.4
GNI, Atlas method (current US$ billions, 2014)	30.8
GNI per capita, Atlas method (current US$, 2014)	1,350.0
GDP growth (avg. annual %, 2011–14)	5.1
Poverty headcount ratio at national poverty line (% of pop., 2007)	39.9
Age dependency ratio (% of working-age pop., 2014)	85.1
Account at a formal financial institution (% age 15+, 2014)	11.4
Mobile cellular subscriptions (per 100 people, 2014)	75.7
Internet users (per 100 people, 2014)	11.0

Migration

EMIGRATION

- Stock of emigrants, 2013: **360.6 thousands**
- Stock of emigrants as percentage of population, 2013: **1.6 percent**
- Top destination countries, 2013: France, the United States, Gabon, Nigeria, Chad, Belgium, Germany, the United Kingdom, Central African Republic, Italy
- Tertiary-educated as a percentage of total emigrants in OECD countries, 2011: **37.4 percent**
- Tertiary-educated women as a percentage of total women emigrants in OECD countries, 2011: **32.1 percent**
- Number of refugees, 2014: **10,724**
- Second generation diaspora in Australia, Europe, and the United States, 2012: **35.7 thousands**

IMMIGRATION

- Stock of immigrants, 2013: **596.9 thousands**
- Stock of immigrants as percentage of population, 2013: **2.7 percent**
- Top source countries, 2013: Nigeria, Chad, Central African Republic, Niger, Gabon, France, Mali, Senegal, the Republic of Congo, the Democratic Republic of Congo
- Women as percentage of immigrants, 2013: **28.0 percent**
- Number of refugees, 2014: **264,102**

Remittances

US$ millions	2006	2007	2008	2009	2010	2011	2012	2013	2014	2015e
Inward remittance flows[a]	130	167	162	184	115	219	210	244	244	244
of which										
Compensation of employees	12	15	25	36	21	61	77	90	–	–
Personal transfers	118	152	137	149	94	158	134	154	–	–
Outward remittance flows	92	90	56	130	54	81	73	65	–	–
of which										
Compensation of employees	44	48	36	71	26	37	30	36	–	–
Personal transfers	48	42	20	59	28	43	43	29	–	–

a. Net FDI inflows US$0.55 billion, net ODA received US$0.74 billion in 2013.

Canada

	HIGH INCOME OECD
Population (millions, 2014)	35.5
Population growth (avg. annual %, 2005-14)	1.1
Population density (people per sq km, 2014)	3.9
Labor force (millions, 2014)	19.7
Unemployment rate (% of labor force, 2014)	6.9
Urban population (% of pop., 2014)	81.7
Surface area (thousands of sq km, 2014)	9,984.7
GNI, Atlas method (current US$ billions, 2014)	1,835.1
GNI per capita, Atlas method (current US$, 2014)	51,630.0
GDP growth (avg. annual %, 2011-14)	2.3
Poverty headcount ratio at national poverty line (% of pop.)	
Age dependency ratio (% of working-age pop., 2014)	46.5
Account at a formal financial institution (% age 15+, 2014)	99.1
Mobile cellular subscriptions (per 100 people, 2014)	83.0
Internet users (per 100 people, 2014)	87.1

Migration

EMIGRATION

- Stock of emigrants, 2013: **1,335.2 thousands**
- Stock of emigrants as percentage of population, 2013: **3.8 percent**
- Top destination countries, 2013: the United States, the United Kingdom, Australia, Italy, France, Germany, China, the Republic of Korea, Hong Kong SAR, China, Japan
- Tertiary-educated as a percentage of total emigrants in OECD countries, 2011: **45.2 percent**
- Tertiary-educated women as a percentage of total women emigrants in OECD countries, 2011: **43.7 percent**
- Number of refugees, 2014: **89**
- Second generation diaspora in Australia, Europe, and the United States, 2012: **1,072.3 thousands**

IMMIGRATION

- Stock of immigrants, 2013: **7,404.2 thousands**
- Stock of immigrants as percentage of population, 2013: **21.1 percent**
- Top source countries, 2013: the United Kingdom, China, India, the Philippines, Italy, the United States, Hong Kong SAR, China, Germany, Poland, Vietnam
- Women as percentage of immigrants, 2013: **52.2 percent**
- Number of refugees, 2014: **149,134**

Remittances

US$ millions	2006	2007	2008	2009	2010	2011	2012	2013	2014	2015e
Inward										
remittance flows[a]	1,049	1,152	1,195	1,160	1,222	1,167	1,206	1,199	1,184	1,206
of which										
Compensation of employees	1,049	1,152	1,195	1,160	1,222	1,167	1,206	1,199	1,184	–
Personal transfers	–	–	–	–	–	–	–	–	–	–
Outward										
remittance flows	3,353	4,644	4,944	4,657	5,290	5,556	5,630	5,612	5,393	–
of which										
Compensation of employees	1,880	2,458	2,828	2,530	2,891	3,150	3,180	3,185	3,062	–
Personal transfers	1,472	2,186	2,116	2,127	2,400	2,406	2,451	2,427	2,331	–

a. Net FDI inflows US$70.75 billion in 2013.

Cayman Islands

HIGH INCOME NON-OECD

Population (thousands, 2013)	59.2
Population growth (avg. annual %, 2005–14)	2.2
Population density (people per sq km, 2014)	246.6
Labor force, total	—
Unemployment rate (% of labor force)	—
Urban population (% of pop., 2014)	100.0
Surface area (thousands of sq km, 2014)	0.3
GNI, Atlas method (current US$ billions)	—
GNI per capita, Atlas method (current US$)	—
GDP growth (avg. annual %)	—
Poverty headcount ratio at national poverty line (% of pop.)	—
Age dependency ratio (% of working-age pop.)	—
Account at a formal financial institution (% age 15+)	—
Mobile cellular subscriptions (per 100 people, 2014)	153.7
Internet users (per 100 people, 2014)	74.1

Migration

EMIGRATION

- Stock of emigrants, 2013: **4.4 thousands**
- Stock of emigrants as percentage of population, 2013: **7.5 percent**
- Top destination countries, 2013: the United States, Canada, Ireland, Honduras, Greece, Australia, the Dominican Republic, Colombia, The Bahamas, Cuba
- Tertiary-educated as a percentage of total emigrants in OECD countries, 2011: **18.0 percent**
- Tertiary-educated women as a percentage of total women emigrants in OECD countries, 2011: **17.6 percent**
- Number of refugees, 2014: **6**
- Second generation diaspora in Australia, Europe, and the United States, 2012: Not available

IMMIGRATION

- Stock of immigrants, 2013: **33.7 thousands**
- Stock of immigrants as percentage of population, 2013: **57.7 percent**
- Top source countries, 2013: Jamaica, the United States, the United Kingdom, the Philippines, Honduras, Canada, Cuba, India, Colombia, Nicaragua
- Women as percentage of immigrants, 2013: **50.4 percent**
- Number of refugees, 2014: Not available

Remittances

US$ millions	2006	2007	2008	2009	2010	2011	2012	2013	2014	2015e
Inward remittance flows[a]	—	—	—	—	—	—	—	—	—	—
of which										
Compensation of employees	—	—	—	—	—	—	—	—	—	—
Personal transfers	—	—	—	—	—	—	—	—	—	—
Outward remittance flows	—	—	—	—	—	—	—	—	—	—
of which										
Compensation of employees	—	—	—	—	—	—	—	—	—	—
Personal transfers	—	—	—	—	—	—	—	—	—	—

a. Net FDI inflows US$12.64 billion in 2013.

Central African Republic

LOW INCOME

Population (millions, 2014)	4.8
Population growth (avg. annual %, 2005–14)	1.9
Population density (people per sq km, 2014)	7.7
Labor force (millions, 2014)	2.3
Unemployment rate (% of labor force, 2014)	7.4
Urban population (% of pop., 2014)	39.8
Surface area (thousands of sq km, 2014)	623.0
GNI, Atlas method (current US$ billions, 2014)	1.6
GNI per capita, Atlas method (current US$, 2014)	320.0
GDP growth (avg. annual %, 2011–14)	-6.9
Poverty headcount ratio at national poverty line (% of pop., 2008)	62.0
Age dependency ratio (% of working-age pop., 2014)	76.2
Account at a formal financial institution (% age 15+)	–
Mobile cellular subscriptions (per 100 people, 2014)	31.4
Internet users (per 100 people, 2014)	4.0

Migration

EMIGRATION

- Stock of emigrants, 2013: **342.0 thousands**
- Stock of emigrants as percentage of population, 2013: **7.3 percent**
- Top destination countries, 2013: Cameroon, Chad, the Democratic Republic of Congo, the Republic of Congo, France, Sudan, South Sudan, Kenya, the United States, Mali
- Tertiary-educated as a percentage of total emigrants in OECD countries, 2011: **31.9 percent**
- Tertiary-educated women as a percentage of total women emigrants in OECD countries, 2011: **26.3 percent**
- Number of refugees, 2014: **412,018**
- Second generation diaspora in Australia, Europe, and the United States, 2012: Not available

IMMIGRATION

- Stock of immigrants, 2013: **134.2 thousands**
- Stock of immigrants as percentage of population, 2013: **2.8 percent**
- Top source countries, 2013: Chad, the Democratic Republic of Congo, Cameroon, France, Senegal, Nigeria, the Republic of Congo, South Sudan, Mali, Niger
- Women as percentage of immigrants, 2013: **44.9 percent**
- Number of refugees, 2014: **7,687**

Remittances

US$ millions	2006	2007	2008	2009	2010	2011	2012	2013	2014	2015e
Inward remittance flows[a]	–	–	–	–	–	–	–	–	–	–
of which										
Compensation of employees	–	–	–	–	–	–	–	–	–	–
Personal transfers	–	–	–	–	–	–	–	–	–	–
Outward remittance flows	–	–	–	–	–	–	–	–	–	–
of which										
Compensation of employees	–	–	–	–	–	–	–	–	–	–
Personal transfers	–	–	–	–	–	–	–	–	–	–

a. Net FDI inflows US$0.00 billion, net ODA received US$0.19 billion in 2013.

Chad

	LOW INCOME
Population (millions, 2014)	13.6
Population growth (avg. annual %, 2005–14)	3.4
Population density (people per sq km, 2014)	10.8
Labor force (millions, 2014)	5.1
Unemployment rate (% of labor force, 2014)	7.0
Urban population (% of pop., 2014)	22.3
Surface area (thousands of sq km, 2014)	1,284.0
GNI, Atlas method (current US$ billions, 2014)	13.3
GNI per capita, Atlas method (current US$, 2014)	980.0
GDP growth (avg. annual %, 2011–14)	5.5
Poverty headcount ratio at national poverty line (% of pop., 2011)	46.7
Age dependency ratio (% of working-age pop., 2014)	101.8
Account at a formal financial institution (% age 15+, 2014)	7.7
Mobile cellular subscriptions (per 100 people, 2014)	39.8
Internet users (per 100 people, 2014)	2.5

Migration

EMIGRATION

- Stock of emigrants, 2013: **403.9 thousands**
- Stock of emigrants as percentage of population, 2013: **3.1 percent**
- Top destination countries, 2013: Cameroon, Sudan, Central African Republic, Nigeria, Saudi Arabia, the Republic of Congo, France, the United Arab Emirates, South Sudan, Gabon
- Tertiary-educated as a percentage of total emigrants in OECD countries, 2011: **37.9 percent**
- Tertiary-educated women as a percentage of total women emigrants in OECD countries, 2011: **33.1 percent**
- Number of refugees, 2014: **48,211**
- Second generation diaspora in Australia, Europe, and the United States, 2012: Not available

IMMIGRATION

- Stock of immigrants, 2013: **490.6 thousands**
- Stock of immigrants as percentage of population, 2013: **3.7 percent**
- Top source countries, 2013: South Sudan, Sudan, Central African Republic, Cameroon, Nigeria, Niger, Libya, France, the Republic of Congo, the Democratic Republic of Congo
- Women as percentage of immigrants, 2013: **48.0 percent**
- Number of refugees, 2014: **452,877**

Remittances

US$ millions	2006	2007	2008	2009	2010	2011	2012	2013	2014	2015e
Inward remittance flows[a]	–	–	–	–	–	–	–	–	–	–
of which										
Compensation of employees	–	–	–	–	–	–	–	–	–	–
Personal transfers	–	–	–	–	–	–	–	–	–	–
Outward remittance flows	–	–	–	–	–	–	–	–	–	–
of which										
Compensation of employees	–	–	–	–	–	–	–	–	–	–
Personal transfers	–	–	–	–	–	–	–	–	–	–

a. Net FDI inflows US$0.54 billion, net ODA received US$0.40 billion in 2013.

Channel Islands

Population (thousands, 2013)	162.9
Population growth (avg. annual %, 2005–14)	0.6
Population density (people per sq km, 2014)	857.5
Labor force (thousands, 2013)	81.6
Unemployment rate (% of labor force)	–
Urban population (% of pop., 2014)	31.4
Surface area (thousands of sq km, 2014)	0.2
GNI, Atlas method (current US$ billions, 2007)	10.2
GNI per capita, Atlas method (current US$, 2007)	65,430.0
GDP growth (avg. annual %, 2003–06)	3.1
Poverty headcount ratio at national poverty line (% of pop.)	–
Age dependency ratio (% of working-age pop., 2014)	46.5
Account at a formal financial institution (% age 15+)	–
Mobile cellular subscriptions (per 100 people)	–
Internet users (per 100 people)	–

Migration

EMIGRATION

- Stock of emigrants, 2013: **26.5 thousands**
- Stock of emigrants as percentage of population, 2013: **16.3 percent**
- Top destination countries, 2013: the United Kingdom, Australia, the Isle of Man, the Cayman Islands, the Russian Federation, Greece, Turkey, Panama, Uruguay
- Tertiary-educated as a percentage of total emigrants in OECD countries, 2011: Not available
- Tertiary-educated women as a percentage of total women emigrants in OECD countries, 2011: Not available
- Number of refugees, 2014: Not available
- Second generation diaspora in Australia, Europe, and the United States, 2012: **4.6 thousands**

IMMIGRATION

- Stock of immigrants, 2013: **82.6 thousands**
- Stock of immigrants as percentage of population, 2013: **50.9 percent**
- Top source countries, 2013: the United Kingdom, Portugal, Ireland, France
- Women as percentage of immigrants, 2013: **52.2 percent**
- Number of refugees, 2014: Not available

Remittances

US$ millions	2006	2007	2008	2009	2010	2011	2012	2013	2014	2015e
Inward **remittance flows**	–	–	–	–	–	–	–	–	–	–
of which										
Compensation of employees	–	–	–	–	–	–	–	–	–	–
Personal transfers	–	–	–	–	–	–	–	–	–	–
Outward **remittance flows**	–	–	–	–	–	–	–	–	–	–
of which										
Compensation of employees	–	–	–	–	–	–	–	–	–	–
Personal transfers	–	–	–	–	–	–	–	–	–	–

Chile

	HIGH INCOME OECD
Population (millions, 2014)	17.8
Population growth (avg. annual %, 2005-14)	1.1
Population density (people per sq km, 2014)	23.9
Labor force (millions, 2014)	8.7
Unemployment rate (% of labor force, 2014)	6.4
Urban population (% of pop., 2014)	89.4
Surface area (thousands of sq km, 2014)	756.1
GNI, Atlas method (current US$ billions, 2014)	264.8
GNI per capita, Atlas method (current US$, 2014)	14,910.0
GDP growth (avg. annual %, 2011-14)	4.4
Poverty headcount ratio at national poverty line (% of pop., 2013)	14.4
Age dependency ratio (% of working-age pop., 2014)	45.3
Account at a formal financial institution (% age 15+, 2014)	63.2
Mobile cellular subscriptions (per 100 people, 2014)	133.3
Internet users (per 100 people, 2014)	72.3

Migration

EMIGRATION

- Stock of emigrants, 2013: **610.2 thousands**
- Stock of emigrants as percentage of population, 2013: **3.5 percent**
- Top destination countries, 2013: Argentina, the United States, Spain, Canada, Australia, Sweden, Ecuador, Brazil, France, Italy
- Tertiary-educated as a percentage of total emigrants in OECD countries, 2011: **34.6 percent**
- Tertiary-educated women as a percentage of total women emigrants in OECD countries, 2011: **34.6 percent**
- Number of refugees, 2014: **571**
- Second generation diaspora in Australia, Europe, and the United States, 2012: **69.8 thousands**

IMMIGRATION

- Stock of immigrants, 2013: **415.5 thousands**
- Stock of immigrants as percentage of population, 2013: **2.4 percent**
- Top source countries, 2013: Peru, Argentina, the Plurinational State of Bolivia, Ecuador, Colombia, South Africa, Spain, Brazil, the United States, the United Kingdom
- Women as percentage of immigrants, 2013: **53.0 percent**
- Number of refugees, 2014: **1,749**

Remittances

US$ millions	2006	2007	2008	2009	2010	2011	2012	2013	2014	2015e
Inward remittance flows[a]	3	3	3	4	–	–	170	137	136	141
of which										
Compensation of employees	3	3	3	4	–	–	170	137	136	–
Personal transfers	–	–	–	–	–	–	–	–	–	–
Outward remittance flows	6	6	6	6	2	0	225	308	280	–
of which										
Compensation of employees	6	6	6	6	2	0	225	308	280	–
Personal transfers	–	–	–	–	–	–	–	–	–	–

a. Net FDI inflows US$19.26 billion, net ODA received US$0.08 billion in 2013.

China

	MIDDLE INCOME
Population (millions, 2014)	1,364.3
Population growth (avg. annual %, 2005–14)	0.5
Population density (people per sq km, 2014)	145.3
Labor force (millions, 2014)	806.5
Unemployment rate (% of labor force, 2014)	4.7
Urban population (% of pop., 2014)	54.4
Surface area (thousands of sq km, 2014)	9,562.9
GNI, Atlas method (current US$ billions, 2014)	10,097.0
GNI per capita, Atlas method (current US$, 2014)	7,400.0
GDP growth (avg. annual %, 2011–14)	8.0
Poverty headcount ratio at national poverty line (% of pop.)	–
Age dependency ratio (% of working-age pop., 2014)	35.8
Account at a formal financial institution (% age 15+, 2014)	78.9
Mobile cellular subscriptions (per 100 people, 2014)	92.3
Internet users (per 100 people, 2014)	49.3

Migration

EMIGRATION

- Stock of emigrants, 2013: **9,651.2 thousands**
- Stock of emigrants as percentage of population, 2013: **0.7 percent**
- Top destination countries, 2013: the United States, Hong Kong SAR, China, the Republic of Korea, Japan, Canada, Australia, Singapore, Macao SAR, China, Italy, Bangladesh
- Tertiary-educated as a percentage of total emigrants in OECD countries, 2011: **39.1 percent**
- Tertiary-educated women as a percentage of total women emigrants in OECD countries, 2011: **37.7 percent**
- Number of refugees, 2014: **210,701**
- Second generation diaspora in Australia, Europe, and the United States, 2012: **662.0 thousands**

IMMIGRATION

- Stock of immigrants, 2013: **1,133.3 thousands**
- Stock of immigrants as percentage of population, **2013: 0.1 percent**
- Top source countries, 2013: the Republic of Korea, the Philippines, Brazil, the United States, Japan, Indonesia, Myanmar, Vietnam, Macao SAR, China, Thailand
- Women as percentage of immigrants, 2013: **40.0 percent**
- Number of refugees, 2014: **301,047**

Remittances

US$ millions	2006	2007	2008	2009	2010	2011	2012	2013	2014	2015e
Inward										
remittance flows[a]	**27,565**	**38,395**	**47,743**	**41,600**	**52,460**	**61,576**	**57,987**	**59,491**	**62,332**	**63,899**
of which										
Compensation of employees	4,319	6,833	9,137	9,209	13,636	16,568	17,066	17,790	–	–
Personal transfers†	23,246	31,562	38,606	32,391	38,824	45,008	40,921	41,701	–	–
Outward										
remittance flows	**3,025**	**4,372**	**6,349**	**4,444**	**1,754**	**3,566**	**4,274**	**4,443**	**6,884**	**–**
of which										
Compensation of employees	2,330	2,493	2,736	2,052	1,455	1,618	1,788	1,714	4,155	–
Personal transfers	695	1,879	3,612	2,393	299	1,948	2,486	2,729	2,729	–

a. Net FDI inflows US$290.93 billion, net ODA received US$-0.65 billion in 2013.
†Includes "personal transfers" and two-thirds of "other current transfers."

Colombia

	MIDDLE INCOME
Population (millions, 2014)	47.8
Population growth (avg. annual %, 2005–14)	1.1
Population density (people per sq km, 2014)	43.1
Labor force (millions, 2014)	24.3
Unemployment rate (% of labor force, 2014)	10.1
Urban population (% of pop., 2014)	76.2
Surface area (thousands of sq km, 2014)	1,141.7
GNI, Atlas method (current US$ billions, 2014)	381.0
GNI per capita, Atlas method (current US$, 2014)	7,970.0
GDP growth (avg. annual %, 2011–14)	5.0
Poverty headcount ratio at national poverty line (% of pop., 2013)	30.6
Age dependency ratio (% of working-age pop., 2014)	45.9
Account at a formal financial institution (% age 15+, 2014)	38.4
Mobile cellular subscriptions (per 100 people, 2014)	113.1
Internet users (per 100 people, 2014)	52.6

Migration

EMIGRATION

- Stock of emigrants, 2013: **2,530.5 thousands**
- Stock of emigrants as percentage of population, 2013: **5.3 percent**
- Top destination countries, 2013: República Bolivariana de Venezuela, the United States, Spain, Ecuador, Argentina, Canada, Panama, Italy, the United Kingdom, France
- Tertiary-educated as a percentage of total emigrants in OECD countries, 2011: **29.2 percent**
- Tertiary-educated women as a percentage of total women emigrants in OECD countries, 2011: **30.3 percent**
- Number of refugees, 2014: **360,281**
- Second generation diaspora in Australia, Europe, and the United States, 2012: **324.9 thousands**

IMMIGRATION

- Stock of immigrants, 2013: **129.6 thousands**
- Stock of immigrants as percentage of population, 2013: **0.3 percent**
- Top source countries, 2013: República Bolivariana de Venezuela, the United States, Ecuador, Spain, Peru, Argentina, Mexico, Italy, Germany, Brazil
- Women as percentage of immigrants, 2013: **46.8 percent**
- Number of refugees, 2014: **173**

Remittances

US$ millions	2006	2007	2008	2009	2010	2011	2012	2013	2014	2015e
Inward remittance flows[a]	**3,899**	**4,460**	**4,827**	**4,125**	**4,031**	**4,101**	**4,019**	**4,450**	**4,166**	**4,514**
of which										
Compensation of employees	38	30	42	35	34	37	49	49	73	–
Personal transfers	3,861	4,430	4,785	4,090	3,996	4,064	3,970	4,401	4,093	–
Outward remittance flows	66	95	88	92	112	117	128	147	204	–
of which										
Compensation of employees	19	29	29	33	40	39	48	69	144	–
Personal transfers	47	66	59	60	72	78	79	78	60	–

a. Net FDI inflows US$16.21 billion, net ODA received US$0.85 billion in 2013.

Comoros

Population (thousands, 2013)	770.0
Population growth (avg. annual %, 2005–14)	2.4
Population density (people per sq km, 2014)	413.8
Labor force (thousands, 2013)	264.0
Unemployment rate (% of labor force, 2014)	6.5
Urban population (% of pop., 2014)	28.2
Surface area (thousands of sq km, 2014)	1.9
GNI, Atlas method (current US$ billions, 2014)	0.6
GNI per capita, Atlas method (current US$, 2014)	790.0
GDP growth (avg. annual %, 2011–14)	2.8
Poverty headcount ratio at national poverty line (% of pop., 2004)	44.8
Age dependency ratio (% of working-age pop., 2014)	76.3
Account at a formal financial institution (% age 15+)	–
Mobile cellular subscriptions (per 100 people, 2014)	50.9
Internet users (per 100 people, 2014)	7.0

Migration

EMIGRATION

- Stock of emigrants, 2013: **111.2 thousands**
- Stock of emigrants as percentage of population, 2013: **14.8 percent**
- Top destination countries, 2013: France, Madagascar, Libya, Kenya, the Arab Republic of Egypt, Algeria, Tanzania, Eritrea, South Africa, the Russian Federation
- Tertiary-educated as a percentage of total emigrants in OECD countries, 2011: **13.4 percent**
- Tertiary-educated women as a percentage of total women emigrants in OECD countries, 2011: **12.3 percent**
- Number of refugees, 2014: **565**
- Second generation diaspora in Australia, Europe, and the United States, 2012: Not available

IMMIGRATION

- Stock of immigrants, 2013: **12.5 thousands**
- Stock of immigrants as percentage of population, 2013: **1.7 percent**
- Top source countries, 2013: Madagascar, France, Tanzania, Kenya
- Women as percentage of immigrants, 2013: **51.7 percent**
- Number of refugees, 2014: Not available

Remittances

US$ millions	2006	2007	2008	2009	2010	2011	2012	2013	2014	2015e
Inward remittance flows[a]	63	74	101	100	87	108	110	116	126	134
of which										
Compensation of employees	–	–	–	–	–	–	–	–	–	–
Personal transfers	63	74	101	100	87	108	110	–	–	–
Outward remittance flows	0	0	1	1	1	1	1	–	–	–
of which										
Compensation of employees	–	–	–	–	–	–	–	–	–	–
Personal transfers	0	0	1	1	1	1	1	–	–	–

a. Net FDI inflows US$0.01 billion, net ODA received US$0.08 billion in 2013.

Congo, Democratic Republic of

Population (millions, 2014)	74.9
Population growth (avg. annual %, 2005–14)	3.2
Population density (people per sq km, 2014)	33.0
Labor force (millions, 2014)	29.0
Unemployment rate (% of labor force, 2014)	8.0
Urban population (% of pop., 2014)	42.0
Surface area (thousands of sq km, 2014)	2,344.9
GNI, Atlas method (current US$ billions, 2014)	28.7
GNI per capita, Atlas method (current US$, 2014)	380.0
GDP growth (avg. annual %, 2011–14)	7.9
Poverty headcount ratio at national poverty line (% of pop., 2012)	63.6
Age dependency ratio (% of working-age pop., 2014)	96.6
Account at a formal financial institution (% age 15+, 2014)	10.9
Mobile cellular subscriptions (per 100 people, 2014)	53.5
Internet users (per 100 people, 2014)	3.0

Migration

EMIGRATION

- Stock of emigrants, 2013: **1,306.0 thousands**
- Stock of emigrants as percentage of population, 2013: **1.8 percent**
- Top destination countries, 2013: the Republic of Congo, Rwanda, Uganda, Burundi, Tanzania, Belgium, South Sudan, France, Angola, Central African Republic
- Tertiary-educated as a percentage of total emigrants in OECD countries, 2011: **30.6 percent**
- Tertiary-educated women as a percentage of total women emigrants in OECD countries, 2011: **26.3 percent**
- Number of refugees, 2014: **516,734**
- Second generation diaspora in Australia, Europe, and the United States, 2012: **29.6 thousands**

IMMIGRATION

- Stock of immigrants, 2013: **503.0 thousands**
- Stock of immigrants as percentage of population, 2013: **0.7 percent**
- Top source countries, 2013: Angola, Rwanda, Central African Republic, Burundi, South Sudan, Uganda, the Republic of Congo, Sudan
- Women as percentage of immigrants, 2013: **46.1 percent**
- Number of refugees, 2014: **119,747**

Remittances

US$ millions	2006	2007	2008	2009	2010	2011	2012	2013	2014	2015e
Inward remittance flows[a]	13	9	15	20	16	115	12	33	22	23
of which										
Compensation of employees	13	9	15	20	16	115	12	33	22	–
Personal transfers	–	–	–	–	–	–	–	–	–	–
Outward remittance flows	32	26	37	31	57	40	55	136	16	–
of which										
Compensation of employees	32	26	37	31	57	40	55	136	16	–
Personal transfers	–	–	–	–	–	–	–	–	–	–

a. Net FDI inflows US$-0.40 billion, net ODA received US$2.57 billion in 2013.

Congo, Republic of

MIDDLE INCOME

Population (millions, 2014)	4.5
Population growth (avg. annual %, 2005–14)	2.8
Population density (people per sq km, 2014)	13.2
Labor force (millions, 2014)	1.8
Unemployment rate (% of labor force, 2014)	6.5
Urban population (% of pop., 2014)	65.0
Surface area (thousands of sq km, 2014)	342.0
GNI, Atlas method (current US$ billions, 2014)	12.3
GNI per capita, Atlas method (current US$, 2014)	2,720.0
GDP growth (avg. annual %, 2011–14)	4.4
Poverty headcount ratio at national poverty line (% of pop., 2011)	46.5
Age dependency ratio (% of working-age pop., 2014)	86.1
Account at a formal financial institution (% age 15+, 2014)	16.7
Mobile cellular subscriptions (per 100 people, 2014)	108.1
Internet users (per 100 people, 2014)	7.1

Migration

EMIGRATION

- Stock of emigrants, 2013: **177.3 thousands**
- Stock of emigrants as percentage of population, 2013: **4.0 percent**
- Top destination countries, 2013: France, South Africa, Germany, Gabon, the United Kingdom, Cameroon, Mali, Kenya, Italy, Central African Republic
- Tertiary-educated as a percentage of total emigrants in OECD countries, 2011: **35.0 percent**
- Tertiary-educated women as a percentage of total women emigrants in OECD countries, 2011: **30.7 percent**
- Number of refugees, 2014: **14,435**
- Second generation diaspora in Australia, Europe, and the United States, 2012: **38.8 thousands**

IMMIGRATION

- Stock of immigrants, 2013: **431.5 thousands**
- Stock of immigrants as percentage of population, 2013: **9.8 percent**
- Top source countries, 2013: the Democratic Republic of Congo, Angola, Mali, Central African Republic, Rwanda, Benin, Senegal, Cameroon, Chad, France
- Women as percentage of immigrants, 2013: **46.8 percent**
- Number of refugees, 2014: **54,827**

Remittances

US$ millions	2006	2007	2008	2009	2010	2011	2012	2013	2014	2015e
Inward **remittance flows**[a]	13	15	–	–	–	–	–	–	–	–
of which Compensation of employees	13	15	–	–	–	–	–	–	–	–
Personal transfers	–	–	–	–	–	–	–	–	–	–
Outward **remittance flows**	81	102	–	–	–	–	–	–	–	–
of which Compensation of employees	73	93	–	–	–	–	–	–	–	–
Personal transfers	8	9	–	–	–	–	–	–	–	–

a. Net FDI inflows US$2.91 billion, net ODA received US$0.15 billion in 2013.

Costa Rica

Population (millions, 2014)	4.8
Population growth (avg. annual %, 2005–14)	1.3
Population density (people per sq km, 2014)	93.2
Labor force (millions, 2014)	2.3
Unemployment rate (% of labor force, 2014)	8.3
Urban population (% of pop., 2014)	75.9
Surface area (thousands of sq km, 2014)	51.1
GNI, Atlas method (current US$ billions, 2014)	48.1
GNI per capita, Atlas method (current US$, 2014)	10,120.0
GDP growth (avg. annual %, 2011–14)	4.2
Poverty headcount ratio at national poverty line (% of pop., 2014)	22.4
Age dependency ratio (% of working-age pop., 2014)	45.6
Account at a formal financial institution (% age 15+, 2014)	64.6
Mobile cellular subscriptions (per 100 people, 2014)	143.8
Internet users (per 100 people, 2014)	49.4

Migration

EMIGRATION

- Stock of emigrants, 2013: **131.2 thousands**
- Stock of emigrants as percentage of population, 2013: **2.8 percent**
- Top destination countries, 2013: the United States, Nicaragua, Panama, Canada, Spain, Mexico, the Dominican Republic, Italy, Ecuador, Guatemala
- Tertiary-educated as a percentage of total emigrants in OECD countries, 2011: **28.4 percent**
- Tertiary-educated women as a percentage of total women emigrants in OECD countries, 2011: **30.5 percent**
- Number of refugees, 2014: **409**
- Second generation diaspora in Australia, Europe, and the United States, 2012: **47.1 thousands**

IMMIGRATION

- Stock of immigrants, 2013: **413.7 thousands**
- Stock of immigrants as percentage of population, 2013: **8.8 percent**
- Top source countries, 2013: Nicaragua, Colombia, the United States, El Salvador, China, Cuba, Panama, República Bolivariana de Venezuela, Peru, Mexico
- Women as percentage of immigrants, 2013: **51.4 percent**
- Number of refugees, 2014: **20,701**

Remittances

US$ millions	2006	2007	2008	2009	2010	2011	2012	2013	2014	2015e
Inward remittance flows[a]	**513**	**618**	**605**	**513**	**531**	**520**	**562**	**596**	**594**	**608**
of which										
Compensation of employees	23	22	21	25	25	33	36	35	35	—
Personal transfers	490	596	584	489	505	487	527	561	559	—
Outward remittance flows	**246**	**271**	**269**	**239**	**259**	**291**	**346**	**403**	**419**	—
of which										
Compensation of employees	13	14	14	15	32	33	65	70	91	—
Personal transfers	233	258	254	224	227	258	281	333	328	—

a. Net FDI inflows US$3.29 billion, net ODA received US$0.04 billion in 2013.

Migration and Remittances Factbook 2016

Côte d'Ivoire

Population (millions, 2014)	22.2
Population growth (avg. annual %, 2005–14)	2.2
Population density (people per sq km, 2014)	69.7
Labor force (millions, 2014)	8.5
Unemployment rate (% of labor force, 2014)	4.0
Urban population (% of pop., 2014)	53.5
Surface area (thousands of sq km, 2014)	322.5
GNI, Atlas method (current US$ billions, 2014)	32.2
GNI per capita, Atlas method (current US$, 2014)	1,450.0
GDP growth (avg. annual %, 2011–14)	6.0
Poverty headcount ratio at national poverty line (% of pop., 2008)	42.7
Age dependency ratio (% of working-age pop., 2014)	84.4
Account at a formal financial institution (% age 15+, 2014)	15.1
Mobile cellular subscriptions (per 100 people, 2014)	106.2
Internet users (per 100 people, 2014)	14.6

Migration

EMIGRATION

- Stock of emigrants, 2013: **1,020.4 thousands**
- Stock of emigrants as percentage of population, 2013: **4.7 percent**
- Top destination countries, 2013: Burkina Faso, Liberia, France, Mali, Ghana, Italy, Benin, the United States, Guinea, Togo
- Tertiary-educated as a percentage of total emigrants in OECD countries, 2011: **27.3 percent**
- Tertiary-educated women as a percentage of total women emigrants in OECD countries, 2011: **23.8 percent**
- Number of refugees, 2014: **71,894**
- Second generation diaspora in Australia, Europe, and the United States, 2012: **35.3 thousands**

IMMIGRATION

- Stock of immigrants, 2013: **2,446.2 thousands**
- Stock of immigrants as percentage of population, 2013: **11.3 percent**
- Top source countries, 2013: Burkina Faso, Mali, Guinea, Liberia, Benin, Togo, Niger, Ghana, Nigeria, Senegal
- Women as percentage of immigrants, 2013: **43.7 percent**
- Number of refugees, 2014: **1,898**

Remittances

US$ millions	2006	2007	2008	2009	2010	2011	2012	2013	2014	2015e
Inward remittance flows[a]	**167**	**185**	**199**	**315**	**373**	**397**	**367**	**385**	**385**	**385**
of which										
Compensation of employees	165	182	196	187	182	192	180	189	–	–
Personal transfers	2	2	3	128	192	204	187	196	–	–
Outward remittance flows	**660**	**698**	**756**	**743**	**726**	**728**	**694**	**736**	–	–
of which										
Compensation of employees	17	19	21	20	20	21	20	21	–	–
Personal transfers	643	679	735	723	706	706	675	715	–	–

a. Net FDI inflows US$0.41 billion, net ODA received US$1.26 billion in 2013.

Croatia

Population (millions, 2014)	4.2
Population growth (avg. annual %, 2005–14)	-0.2
Population density (people per sq km, 2014)	75.7
Labor force (millions, 2014)	1.8
Unemployment rate (% of labor force, 2014)	16.7
Urban population (% of pop., 2014)	58.7
Surface area (thousands of sq km, 2014)	56.6
GNI, Atlas method (current US$ billions, 2014)	55.0
GNI per capita, Atlas method (current US$, 2014)	12,990.0
GDP growth (avg. annual %, 2011–14)	-1.0
Poverty headcount ratio at national poverty line (% of pop., 2012)	19.5
Age dependency ratio (% of working-age pop., 2014)	50.5
Account at a formal financial institution (% age 15+, 2014)	86.0
Mobile cellular subscriptions (per 100 people, 2014)	104.4
Internet users (per 100 people, 2014)	68.6

Migration

EMIGRATION

- Stock of emigrants, 2013: **888.2 thousands**
- Stock of emigrants as percentage of population, 2013: **20.9 percent**
- Top destination countries, 2013: Serbia, Germany, Australia, Slovenia, Canada, the United States, Austria, Italy, Switzerland, Albania
- Tertiary-educated as a percentage of total emigrants in OECD countries, 2011: **13.7 percent**
- Tertiary-educated women as a percentage of total women emigrants in OECD countries, 2011: **13.5 percent**
- Number of refugees, 2014: **40,115**
- Second generation diaspora in Australia, Europe, and the United States, 2012: **293.3 thousands**

IMMIGRATION

- Stock of immigrants, 2013: **757.0 thousands**
- Stock of immigrants as percentage of population, 2013: **17.8 percent**
- Top source countries, 2013: Bosnia and Herzegovina, Serbia, Slovenia, Montenegro, the Former Yugoslav Republic of Macedonia, Germany, Italy, Hungary, Austria, the United States
- Women as percentage of immigrants, 2013: **53.0 percent**
- Number of refugees, 2014: **689**

Remittances

US$ millions	2006	2007	2008	2009	2010	2011	2012	2013	2014	2015e
Inward remittance flows[a]	**1,611**	**1,854**	**2,065**	**1,890**	**1,900**	**2,092**	**2,085**	**2,174**	**2,149**	**2,149**
of which										
Compensation of employees	510	724	878	869	871	938	963	1,007	994	–
Personal transfers	1,102	1,130	1,187	1,021	1,029	1,154	1,122	1,168	1,155	–
Outward remittance flows	**183**	**237**	**267**	**235**	**236**	**249**	**247**	**267**	**297**	–
of which										
Compensation of employees	39	46	52	52	48	54	49	60	44	–
Personal transfers	144	191	215	183	188	195	198	207	253	–

a. Net FDI inflows US$0.93 billion in 2013.

Cuba

Population (millions, 2014)	11.4
Population growth (avg. annual %, 2005–14)	0.1
Population density (people per sq km, 2014)	106.9
Labor force (millions, 2014)	5.4
Unemployment rate (% of labor force, 2014)	3.3
Urban population (% of pop., 2014)	77.0
Surface area (thousands of sq km, 2014)	109.9
GNI, Atlas method (current US$ billions, 2011)	66.6
GNI per capita, Atlas method (current US$, 2011)	5,880.0
GDP growth (avg. annual %, 2011–14)	2.8
Poverty headcount ratio at national poverty line (% of pop.)	—
Age dependency ratio (% of working-age pop., 2014)	43.2
Account at a formal financial institution (% age 15+)	-
Mobile cellular subscriptions (per 100 people, 2014)	22.5
Internet users (per 100 people, 2014)	30.0

Migration

EMIGRATION

- Stock of emigrants, 2013: **1,485.1 thousands**
- Stock of emigrants as percentage of population, 2013: **13.1 percent**
- Top destination countries, 2013: the United States, Spain, Italy, Puerto Rico, Mexico, Germany, Canada, the Dominican Republic, República Bolivariana de Venezuela, Costa Rica
- Tertiary-educated as a percentage of total emigrants in OECD countries, 2011: **27.3 percent**
- Tertiary-educated women as a percentage of total women emigrants in OECD countries, 2011: **27.3 percent**
- Number of refugees, 2014: **7,467**
- Second generation diaspora in Australia, Europe, and the United States, 2012: **453.9 thousands**

IMMIGRATION

- Stock of immigrants, 2013: **16.2 thousands**
- Stock of immigrants as percentage of population, 2013: **0.1 percent**
- Top source countries, 2013: Spain, the Russian Federation, Haiti, Ukraine, the United States, Mexico, Germany, China, Jamaica, Nicaragua
- Women as percentage of immigrants, 2013: **55.1 percent**
- Number of refugees, 2014: **271**

Remittances

US$ millions	2006	2007	2008	2009	2010	2011	2012	2013	2014	2015e
Inward remittance flows[a]	–	–	–	–	–	–	–	–	–	–
of which										
Compensation of employees	–	–	–	–	–	–	–	–	–	–
Personal transfers	–	–	–	–	–	–	–	–	–	–
Outward remittance flows	–	–	–	–	–	–	–	–	–	–
of which										
Compensation of employees	–	–	–	–	–	–	–	–	–	–
Personal transfers	–	–	–	–	–	–	–	–	–	–

a. Net ODA received US$0.10 billion in 2013.

Curaçao

	HIGH INCOME NON-OECD
Population (thousands, 2013)	155.9
Population growth (avg. annual %, 2005–14)	1.5
Population density (people per sq km, 2014)	351.1
Labor force, total	–
Unemployment rate (% of labor force)	–
Urban population (% of pop., 2014)	89.4
Surface area (thousands of sq km, 2014)	0.4
GNI, Atlas method (current US$ billions)	–
GNI per capita, Atlas method (current US$)	–
GDP growth (avg. annual %)	–
Poverty headcount ratio at national poverty line (% of pop.)	–
Age dependency ratio (% of working-age pop., 2014)	50.4
Account at a formal financial institution (% age 15+)	–
Mobile cellular subscriptions (per 100 people, 2014)	121.6
Internet users (per 100 people)	–

Migration

EMIGRATION

- Stock of emigrants, 2013: **80.1 thousands**
- Stock of emigrants as percentage of population, 2013: **52.1 percent**
- Top destination countries, 2013: the Netherlands, South Africa, the United States, Sint Maarten (Dutch part), República Bolivariana de Venezuela, Canada, the Virgin Islands (U.S.), Australia, Colombia, Portugal
- Tertiary-educated as a percentage of total emigrants in OECD countries, 2011: Not available
- Tertiary-educated women as a percentage of total women emigrants in OECD countries, 2011: Not available
- Number of refugees, 2014: **35**
- Second generation diaspora in Australia, Europe, and the United States, 2012: Not available

IMMIGRATION

- Stock of immigrants, 2013: **36.9 thousands**
- Stock of immigrants as percentage of population, 2013: **24.0 percent**
- Top source countries, 2013: the Netherlands, the Dominican Republic, Colombia, Haiti, Suriname, República Bolivariana de Venezuela, Aruba, Jamaica, Portugal, India
- Women as percentage of immigrants, 2013: **55.2 percent**
- Number of refugees, 2014: **34**

Remittances

US$ millions	2006	2007	2008	2009	2010	2011	2012	2013	2014	2015e
Inward remittance flows[a]	–	–	–	–	–	150	136	133	143	143
of which										
Compensation of employees	–	–	–	–	–	34	30	33	44	–
Personal transfers	–	–	–	–	–	116	106	100	99	–
Outward remittance flows	–	–	–	–	–	133	135	117	121	–
of which										
Compensation of employees	–	–	–	–	–	6	7	6	10	–
Personal transfers	–	–	–	–	–	127	128	111	111	–

a. Net FDI inflows US$0.02 billion in 2013.

Cyprus

Population (millions, 2014)	1.2
Population growth (avg. annual %, 2005–14)	1.3
Population density (people per sq km, 2014)	124.9
Labor force (thousands, 2013)	613.7
Unemployment rate (% of labor force, 2014)	15.6
Urban population (% of pop., 2014)	67.0
Surface area (thousands of sq km, 2014)	9.3
GNI, Atlas method (current US$ billions, 2014)	22.5
GNI per capita, Atlas method (current US$, 2014)	26,370.0
GDP growth (avg. annual %, 2011–14)	-2.4
Poverty headcount ratio at national poverty line (% of pop.)	—
Age dependency ratio (% of working-age pop., 2014)	41.5
Account at a formal financial institution (% age 15+, 2014)	90.2
Mobile cellular subscriptions (per 100 people, 2014)	96.3
Internet users (per 100 people, 2014)	69.3

Migration

EMIGRATION

- Stock of emigrants, 2013: **148.8 thousands**
- Stock of emigrants as percentage of population, 2013: **13.0 percent**
- Top destination countries, 2013: the United Kingdom, Australia, the United States, Turkey, Greece, Canada, South Africa, Germany, France, Italy
- Tertiary-educated as a percentage of total emigrants in OECD countries, 2011: **31.2 percent**
- Tertiary-educated women as a percentage of total women emigrants in OECD countries, 2011: **29.0 percent**
- Number of refugees, 2014: Not available
- Second generation diaspora in Australia, Europe, and the United States, 2012: Not available

IMMIGRATION

- Stock of immigrants, 2013: **207.3 thousands**
- Stock of immigrants as percentage of population, 2013: **18.2 percent**
- Top source countries, 2013: the United Kingdom, Greece, Georgia, the Russian Federation, Sri Lanka, the Philippines, Bulgaria, Romania, the Arab Republic of Egypt, South Africa
- Women as percentage of immigrants, 2013: **56.4 percent**
- Number of refugees, 2014: **5,075**

Remittances

US$ millions	2006	2007	2008	2009	2010	2011	2012	2013	2014	2015e
Inward remittance flows[a]	**104**	**142**	**234**	**127**	**135**	**127**	**117**	**274**	**260**	**261**
of which										
Compensation of employees	35	44	87	39	40	42	40	72	67	—
Personal transfers	70	99	147	88	95	84	76	201	193	—
Outward remittance flows	**240**	**305**	**501**	**345**	**363**	**460**	**468**	**720**	**743**	—
of which										
Compensation of employees	184	223	386	226	210	314	331	73	88	—
Personal transfers	55	81	115	119	154	146	137	647	655	—

a. Net FDI inflows US$3.77 billion in 2013.

Czech Republic

	HIGH INCOME OECD
Population (millions, 2014)	10.5
Population growth (avg. annual %, 2005–14)	0.3
Population density (people per sq km, 2014)	136.1
Labor force (millions, 2014)	5.3
Unemployment rate (% of labor force, 2014)	6.2
Urban population (% of pop., 2014)	73.0
Surface area (thousands of sq km, 2014)	78.9
GNI, Atlas method (current US$ billions, 2014)	193.1
GNI per capita, Atlas method (current US$, 2014)	18,370.0
GDP growth (avg. annual %, 2011–14)	0.6
Poverty headcount ratio at national poverty line (% of pop., 2012)	8.6
Age dependency ratio (% of working-age pop., 2014)	47.9
Account at a formal financial institution (% age 15+, 2014)	82.2
Mobile cellular subscriptions (per 100 people, 2014)	130.0
Internet users (per 100 people, 2014)	79.7

Migration

EMIGRATION

- Stock of emigrants, 2013: **524.4 thousands**
- Stock of emigrants as percentage of population, 2013: **5.0 percent**
- Top destination countries, 2013: Germany, the Slovak Republic, the United States, Austria, the United Kingdom, Canada, Australia, Switzerland, the Russian Federation, France
- Tertiary-educated as a percentage of total emigrants in OECD countries, 2011: **28.3 percent**
- Tertiary-educated women as a percentage of total women emigrants in OECD countries, 2011: **26.9 percent**
- Number of refugees, 2014: **1,321**
- Second generation diaspora in Australia, Europe, and the United States, 2012: **262.5 thousands**

IMMIGRATION

- Stock of immigrants, 2013: **745.2 thousands**
- Stock of immigrants as percentage of population, 2013: **7.1 percent**
- Top source countries, 2013: the Slovak Republic, Ukraine, Vietnam, the Russian Federation, Poland, Germany, Romania, Belarus, Moldova, Bulgaria
- Women as percentage of immigrants, 2013: **42.7 percent**
- Number of refugees, 2014: **3,079**

Remittances

US$ millions	2006	2007	2008	2009	2010	2011	2012	2013	2014	2015e
Inward										
remittance flows[a]	**1,688**	**1,897**	**1,134**	**1,196**	**1,229**	**1,394**	**1,409**	**1,738**	**1,893**	**2,191**
of which										
Compensation of employees	1,109	1,226	1,134	1,196	1,229	1,394	1,409	1,738	1,893	–
Personal transfers	579	671	–	–	–	–	–	–	–	–
Outward										
remittance flows	**1,460**	**2,075**	**2,586**	**2,045**	**1,497**	**1,522**	**1,335**	**1,079**	**822**	**–**
of which										
Compensation of employees	966	1,416	2,586	2,045	1,497	1,522	1,335	1,079	822	–
Personal transfers	495	659	–	–	–	–	–	–	–	–

a. Net FDI inflows US$7.36 billion in 2013.

Denmark

Population (millions, 2014)	5.6
Population growth (avg. annual %, 2005–14)	0.4
Population density (people per sq km, 2014)	132.9
Labor force (millions, 2014)	2.9
Unemployment rate (% of labor force, 2014)	6.6
Urban population (% of pop., 2014)	87.5
Surface area (thousands of sq km, 2014)	43.1
GNI, Atlas method (current US$ billions, 2014)	345.8
GNI per capita, Atlas method (current US$, 2014)	61,310.0
GDP growth (avg. annual %, 2011–14)	0.3
Poverty headcount ratio at national poverty line (% of pop.)	—
Age dependency ratio (% of working-age pop., 2014)	55.2
Account at a formal financial institution (% age 15+, 2014)	100.0
Mobile cellular subscriptions (per 100 people, 2014)	126.0
Internet users (per 100 people, 2014)	96.0

Migration

EMIGRATION

- Stock of emigrants, 2013: **265.5 thousands**
- Stock of emigrants as percentage of population, 2013: **4.7 percent**
- Top destination countries, 2013: Sweden, the United States, Germany, Norway, the United Kingdom, Canada, Spain, Australia, France, Belgium
- Tertiary-educated as a percentage of total emigrants in OECD countries, 2011: **37.6 percent**
- Tertiary-educated women as a percentage of total women emigrants in OECD countries, 2011: **38.1 percent**
- Number of refugees, 2014: **6**
- Second generation diaspora in Australia, Europe, and the United States, 2012: **126.2 thousands**

IMMIGRATION

- Stock of immigrants, 2013: **556.8 thousands**
- Stock of immigrants as percentage of population, 2013: **9.9 percent**
- Top source countries, 2013: Germany, Turkey, Poland, Sweden, Iraq, Norway, Bosnia and Herzegovina, the United Kingdom, Greenland, the Islamic Republic of Iran
- Women as percentage of immigrants, 2013: **51.6 percent**
- Number of refugees, 2014: **17,737**

Remittances

US$ millions	2006	2007	2008	2009	2010	2011	2012	2013	2014	2015e
Inward remittance flows[a]	982	823	1,295	1,219	1,078	1,357	1,274	1,217	1,377	1,378
of which										
Compensation of employees	982	823	1,295	1,219	1,078	1,357	1,274	1,217	1,377	—
Personal transfers	—	—	—	—	—	—	—	—	—	—
Outward remittance flows	1,766	3,020	3,977	3,425	2,826	3,134	2,949	3,060	3,152	—
of which										
Compensation of employees	1,766	3,020	3,977	3,425	2,826	3,134	2,949	3,060	3,152	—
Personal transfers	—	—	—	—	—	—	—	—	—	—

a. Net FDI inflows US$-0.86 billion in 2013.

Djibouti

Population (thousands, 2013)	876.2
Population growth (avg. annual %, 2005–14)	1.3
Population density (people per sq km, 2014)	37.8
Labor force (thousands, 2013)	307.0
Unemployment rate (% of labor force)	–
Urban population (% of pop., 2014)	77.3
Surface area (thousands of sq km, 2014)	23.2
GNI, Atlas method (current US$ billions, 2005)	0.8
GNI per capita, Atlas method (current US$, 2005)	1,030.0
GDP growth (avg. annual %, 2011–14)	5.1
Poverty headcount ratio at national poverty line (% of pop.)	–
Age dependency ratio (% of working-age pop., 2014)	59.0
Account at a formal financial institution (% age 15+)	–
Mobile cellular subscriptions (per 100 people, 2014)	32.4
Internet users (per 100 people, 2014)	10.7

Migration

EMIGRATION

- Stock of emigrants, 2013: **14.9 thousands**
- Stock of emigrants as percentage of population, 2013: **1.7 percent**
- Top destination countries, 2013: France, Ethiopia, Libya, Kenya, Canada, the Arab Republic of Egypt, Algeria, Sweden, Australia, Italy
- Tertiary-educated as a percentage of total emigrants in OECD countries, 2011: **31.1 percent**
- Tertiary-educated women as a percentage of total women emigrants in OECD countries, 2011: **27.2 percent**
- Number of refugees, 2014: **860**
- Second generation diaspora in Australia, Europe, and the United States, 2012: Not available

IMMIGRATION

- Stock of immigrants, 2013: **123.5 thousands**
- Stock of immigrants as percentage of population, 2013: **14.3 percent**
- Top source countries, 2013: Somalia, Ethiopia, the Republic of Yemen
- Women as percentage of immigrants, 2013: **44.5 percent**
- Number of refugees, 2014: **20,520**

Remittances

US$ millions	2006	2007	2008	2009	2010	2011	2012	2013	2014	2015e
Inward remittance flows[a]	**28**	**29**	**30**	**32**	**33**	**32**	**33**	**36**	**36**	**36**
of which										
Compensation of employees	25	25	26	27	26	26	27	28	–	–
Personal transfers	4	4	4	6	7	6	7	8	–	–
Outward remittance flows	**5**	**5**	**5**	**6**	**12**	**13**	**12**	**13**	–	–
of which										
Compensation of employees	–	–	–	–	–	–	–	–	–	–
Personal transfers	5	5	5	6	12	13	12	13	–	–

a. Net FDI inflows US$0.29 billion, net ODA received US$0.15 billion in 2013.

Dominica

Population (thousands, 2013)	72.3
Population growth (avg. annual %, 2005–14)	0.3
Population density (people per sq km, 2014)	96.5
Labor force, total	–
Unemployment rate (% of labor force)	–
Urban population (% of pop., 2014)	69.3
Surface area (thousands of sq km, 2014)	0.8
GNI, Atlas method (current US$ billions, 2014)	0.5
GNI per capita, Atlas method (current US$, 2014)	6,930.0
GDP growth (avg. annual %, 2011–14)	0.8
Poverty headcount ratio at national poverty line (% of pop.)	–
Age dependency ratio (% of working-age pop.)	–
Account at a formal financial institution (% age 15+)	–
Mobile cellular subscriptions (per 100 people, 2014)	127.5
Internet users (per 100 people, 2014)	62.9

Migration

EMIGRATION

- Stock of emigrants, 2013: **76.8 thousands**
- Stock of emigrants as percentage of population, 2013: **106.6 percent**
- Top destination countries, 2013: the United States, France, the Virgin Islands (U.S.), the United Kingdom, Antigua and Barbuda, Canada, Puerto Rico, Sint Maarten (Dutch part), Spain, Barbados
- Tertiary-educated as a percentage of total emigrants in OECD countries, 2011: **22.8 percent**
- Tertiary-educated women as a percentage of total women emigrants in OECD countries, 2011: **25.5 percent**
- Number of refugees, 2014: **35**
- Second generation diaspora in Australia, Europe, and the United States, 2012: Not available

IMMIGRATION

- Stock of immigrants, 2013: **6.4 thousands**
- Stock of immigrants as percentage of population, 2013: **8.9 percent**
- Top source countries, 2013: the United Kingdom, the United States, Antigua and Barbuda, Trinidad and Tobago, St. Lucia, Guyana, Canada, Barbados, Jamaica, St. Vincent and the Grenadines
- Women as percentage of immigrants, 2013: **43.9 percent**
- Number of refugees, 2014: Not available

Remittances

US$ millions	2006	2007	2008	2009	2010	2011	2012	2013	2014	2015e
Inward remittance flows[a]	**22**	**22**	**23**	**22**	**23**	**23**	**23**	**24**	**24**	**24**
of which										
Compensation of employees	1	1	1	1	1	1	1	1	–	–
Personal transfers	21	22	22	21	22	22	22	23	–	–
Outward remittance flows	**0**	**0**	**0**	**0**	**0**	**0**	**2**	**2**	–	–
of which										
Compensation of employees	–	–	–	–	–	–	–	–	–	–
Personal transfers	0	0	0	0	0	0	2	2	–	–

a. Net FDI inflows US$0.02 billion, net ODA received US$0.02 billion in 2013.

Dominican Republic

Population (millions, 2014)	10.4
Population growth (avg. annual %, 2005–14)	1.3
Population density (people per sq km, 2014)	215.4
Labor force (millions, 2014)	4.7
Unemployment rate (% of labor force, 2014)	15.0
Urban population (% of pop., 2014)	78.1
Surface area (thousands of sq km, 2014)	48.7
GNI, Atlas method (current US$ billions, 2014)	62.9
GNI per capita, Atlas method (current US$, 2014)	6,040.0
GDP growth (avg. annual %, 2011–14)	4.4
Poverty headcount ratio at national poverty line (% of pop., 2013)	41.1
Age dependency ratio (% of working-age pop., 2014)	58.1
Account at a formal financial institution (% age 15+, 2014)	54.0
Mobile cellular subscriptions (per 100 people, 2014)	78.9
Internet users (per 100 people, 2014)	49.6

Migration

EMIGRATION

- Stock of emigrants, 2013: **1,375.5 thousands**
- Stock of emigrants as percentage of population, 2013: **13.4 percent**
- Top destination countries, 2013: the United States, Spain, Puerto Rico, Italy, República Bolivariana de Venezuela, Switzerland, Argentina, Germany, the Netherlands, Canada
- Tertiary-educated as a percentage of total emigrants in OECD countries, 2011: **16.0 percent**
- Tertiary-educated women as a percentage of total women emigrants in OECD countries, 2011: **17.0 percent**
- Number of refugees, 2014: **328**
- Second generation diaspora in Australia, Europe, and the United States, 2012: **600.5 thousands**

IMMIGRATION

- Stock of immigrants, 2013: **607.3 thousands**
- Stock of immigrants as percentage of population, 2013: **5.9 percent**
- Top source countries, 2013: Haiti, República Bolivariana de Venezuela, the United States, Puerto Rico, Spain, Italy, Cuba, Germany, Colombia, China
- Women as percentage of immigrants, 2013: **38.3 percent**
- Number of refugees, 2014: **603**

Remittances

US$ millions	2006	2007	2008	2009	2010	2011	2012	2013	2014	2015e
Inward remittance flows[a]	3,054	3,397	3,606	3,415	3,887	4,241	4,262	4,486	4,810	4,985
of which										
Compensation of employees	316	351	384	373	204	232	217	223	239	–
Personal transfers	2,738	3,046	3,222	3,042	3,683	4,008	4,045	4,262	4,571	–
Outward remittance flows	27	28	35	27	519	566	565	559	591	–
of which										
Compensation of employees	27	28	35	27	148	159	167	167	173	–
Personal transfers	–	–	–	–	371	407	398	392	418	–

a. Net FDI inflows US$1.60 billion, net ODA received US$0.15 billion in 2013.

Ecuador

	MIDDLE INCOME
Population (millions, 2014)	15.9
Population growth (avg. annual %, 2005–14)	1.6
Population density (people per sq km, 2014)	64.0
Labor force (millions, 2014)	7.7
Unemployment rate (% of labor force, 2014)	4.6
Urban population (% of pop., 2014)	63.5
Surface area (thousands of sq km, 2014)	256.4
GNI, Atlas method (current US$ billions, 2014)	96.8
GNI per capita, Atlas method (current US$, 2014)	6,090.0
GDP growth (avg. annual %, 2011–14)	5.4
Poverty headcount ratio at national poverty line (% of pop., 2014)	22.5
Age dependency ratio (% of working-age pop., 2014)	55.9
Account at a formal financial institution (% age 15+, 2014)	46.2
Mobile cellular subscriptions (per 100 people, 2014)	103.9
Internet users (per 100 people, 2014)	43.0

Migration

EMIGRATION

- Stock of emigrants, 2013: **1,160.8 thousands**
- Stock of emigrants as percentage of population, 2013: **7.4 percent**
- Top destination countries, 2013: the United States, Spain, Italy, República Bolivariana de Venezuela, Chile, Canada, Colombia, Argentina, Germany, the United Kingdom
- Tertiary-educated as a percentage of total emigrants in OECD countries, 2011: **14.8 percent**
- Tertiary-educated women as a percentage of total women emigrants in OECD countries, 2011: **16.0 percent**
- Number of refugees, 2014: **778**
- Second generation diaspora in Australia, Europe, and the United States, 2012: **216.5 thousands**

IMMIGRATION

- Stock of immigrants, 2013: **359.3 thousands**
- Stock of immigrants as percentage of population, 2013: **2.3 percent**
- Top source countries, 2013: Colombia, the United States, Peru, Chile, República Bolivariana de Venezuela, Spain, Argentina, Germany, Italy, Cuba
- Women as percentage of immigrants, 2013: **48.4 percent**
- Number of refugees, 2014: **122,079**

Remittances

US$ millions	2006	2007	2008	2009	2010	2011	2012	2013	2014	2015e
Inward remittance flows[a]	**2,934**	**3,341**	**3,089**	**2,742**	**2,599**	**2,681**	**2,476**	**2,459**	**2,472**	**2,434**
of which										
Compensation of employees	6	6	6	7	8	8	9	9	11	–
Personal transfers	2,928	3,335	3,083	2,736	2,591	2,672	2,467	2,450	2,462	–
Outward remittance flows	**62**	**83**	**66**	**95**	**136**	**148**	**154**	**167**	**196**	**–**
of which										
Compensation of employees	5	5	6	6	7	8	8	10	11	–
Personal transfers	57	78	60	89	129	141	146	157	184	–

a. Net FDI inflows US$0.73 billion, net ODA received US$0.15 billion in 2013.

Egypt, Arab Republic of

Population (millions, 2014)	89.6
Population growth (avg. annual %, 2005–14)	2.0
Population density (people per sq km, 2014)	90.0
Labor force (millions, 2014)	29.6
Unemployment rate (% of labor force, 2014)	13.2
Urban population (% of pop., 2014)	43.1
Surface area (thousands of sq km, 2014)	1,001.5
GNI, Atlas method (current US$ billions, 2014)	273.1
GNI per capita, Atlas method (current US$, 2014)	3,050.0
GDP growth (avg. annual %, 2011–14)	2.1
Poverty headcount ratio at national poverty line (% of pop., 2010)	25.2
Age dependency ratio (% of working-age pop., 2014)	61.7
Account at a formal financial institution (% age 15+, 2014)	13.7
Mobile cellular subscriptions (per 100 people, 2014)	114.3
Internet users (per 100 people, 2014)	31.7

Migration

EMIGRATION

- Stock of emigrants, 2013: **3,386.1 thousands**
- Stock of emigrants as percentage of population, 2013: **3.9 percent**
- Top destination countries, 2013: Saudi Arabia, Kuwait, the United Arab Emirates, Jordan, the United States, Qatar, Italy, Lebanon, Bahrain, Canada
- Tertiary-educated as a percentage of total emigrants in OECD countries, 2011: **46.7 percent**
- Tertiary-educated women as a percentage of total women emigrants in OECD countries, 2011: **43.0 percent**
- Number of refugees, 2014: **15,824**
- Second generation diaspora in Australia, Europe, and the United States, 2012: **160.3 thousands**

IMMIGRATION

- Stock of immigrants, 2013: **416.3 thousands**
- Stock of immigrants as percentage of population, 2013: **0.5 percent**
- Top source countries, 2013: the Syrian Arab Republic, the West Bank and Gaza, Somalia, Iraq, Saudi Arabia, the Republic of Yemen, Libya, Jordan, Sudan, Indonesia
- Women as percentage of immigrants, 2013: **43.2 percent**
- Number of refugees, 2014: **236,050**

Remittances

US$ millions	2006	2007	2008	2009	2010	2011	2012	2013	2014	2015e
Inward remittance flows[a]	**5,330**	**7,656**	**8,694**	**7,150**	**12,453**	**14,324**	**19,236**	**17,833**	**19,570**	**20,391**
of which										
Compensation of employees	–	–	–	–	–	–	–	–	–	–
Personal transfers	5,330	7,656	8,694	7,150	12,453	14,324	19,236	17,833	19,570	–
Outward remittance flows	**135**	**180**	**241**	**255**	**305**	**293**	**293**	**355**	**351**	**–**
of which										
Compensation of employees	–	–	–	–	–	–	–	–	–	–
Personal transfers	135	180	241	255	305	293	293	355	351	–

a. Net FDI inflows US$4.19 billion, net ODA received US$5.51 billion in 2013.

El Salvador

Population (millions, 2014)	6.1
Population growth (avg. annual %, 2005–14)	0.3
Population density (people per sq km, 2014)	294.8
Labor force (millions, 2014)	2.7
Unemployment rate (% of labor force, 2014)	6.2
Urban population (% of pop., 2014)	66.3
Surface area (thousands of sq km, 2014)	21.0
GNI, Atlas method (current US$ billions, 2014)	23.9
GNI per capita, Atlas method (current US$, 2014)	3,920.0
GDP growth (avg. annual %, 2011–14)	2.0
Poverty headcount ratio at national poverty line (% of pop., 2013)	29.6
Age dependency ratio (% of working-age pop., 2014)	55.3
Account at a formal financial institution (% age 15+, 2014)	34.6
Mobile cellular subscriptions (per 100 people, 2014)	144.0
Internet users (per 100 people, 2014)	29.7

Migration

EMIGRATION

- Stock of emigrants, 2013: **1,525.4 thousands**
- Stock of emigrants as percentage of population, 2013: **25.0 percent**
- Top destination countries, 2013: the United States, Canada, Guatemala, Australia, Belize, Italy, Costa Rica, Mexico, Spain, Honduras
- Tertiary-educated as a percentage of total emigrants in OECD countries, 2011: **10.1 percent**
- Tertiary-educated women as a percentage of total women emigrants in OECD countries, 2011: **10.8 percent**
- Number of refugees, 2014: **10,943**
- Second generation diaspora in Australia, Europe, and the United States, 2012: **685.1 thousands**

IMMIGRATION

- Stock of immigrants, 2013: **41.6 thousands**
- Stock of immigrants as percentage of population, 2013: **0.7 percent**
- Top source countries, 2013: Honduras, Guatemala, Nicaragua, the United States, Mexico, Costa Rica, Colombia, Spain, Panama, Belize
- Women as percentage of immigrants, 2013: **52.5 percent**
- Number of refugees, 2014: **23**

Remittances

US$ millions	2006	2007	2008	2009	2010	2011	2012	2013	2014	2015e
Inward remittance flows[a]	**3,483**	**3,709**	**3,755**	**3,402**	**3,472**	**3,644**	**3,910**	**3,971**	**4,235**	**4,357**
of which										
Compensation of employees	12	14	13	15	17	16	16	18	18	–
Personal transfers	3,471	3,695	3,742	3,387	3,455	3,627	3,894	3,954	4,217	–
Outward remittance flows	**28**	**28**	**19**	**20**	**22**	**27**	**27**	**28**	**51**	**–**
of which										
Compensation of employees	28	28	19	20	22	27	27	28	28	–
Personal transfers	–	–	–	–	–	–	–	–	23	–

a. Net FDI inflows US$0.24 billion, net ODA received US$0.17 billion in 2013.

Equatorial Guinea

Population (thousands, 2013)	820.9
Population growth (avg. annual %, 2005–14)	3.0
Population density (people per sq km, 2014)	29.3
Labor force (thousands, 2013)	431.1
Unemployment rate (% of labor force, 2014)	7.9
Urban population (% of pop., 2014)	39.8
Surface area (thousands of sq km, 2014)	28.1
GNI, Atlas method (current US$ billions, 2014)	8.4
GNI per capita, Atlas method (current US$, 2014)	10,210.0
GDP growth (avg. annual %, 2011–14)	0.2
Poverty headcount ratio at national poverty line (% of pop., 2006)	76.8
Age dependency ratio (% of working-age pop., 2014)	73.3
Account at a formal financial institution (% age 15+)	–
Mobile cellular subscriptions (per 100 people, 2014)	66.4
Internet users (per 100 people, 2014)	18.9

Migration

EMIGRATION

- Stock of emigrants, 2013: **126.1 thousands**
- Stock of emigrants as percentage of population, 2013: **15.8 percent**
- Top destination countries, 2013: Gabon, Spain, Nigeria, Belgium, Cameroon, Kenya, the Republic of Congo, the United States, France, São Tomé and Príncipe
- Tertiary-educated as a percentage of total emigrants in OECD countries, 2011: **23.1 percent**
- Tertiary-educated women as a percentage of total women emigrants in OECD countries, 2011: **18.3 percent**
- Number of refugees, 2014: **163**
- Second generation diaspora in Australia, Europe, and the United States, 2012: Not available

IMMIGRATION

- Stock of immigrants, 2013: **10.1 thousands**
- Stock of immigrants as percentage of population, 2013: **1.3 percent**
- Top source countries, 2013: France, São Tomé and Príncipe, Spain, Cameroon, Nigeria, Gabon
- Women as percentage of immigrants, 2013: **44.9 percent**
- Number of refugees, 2014: Not available

Remittances

US$ millions	2006	2007	2008	2009	2010	2011	2012	2013	2014	2015e
Inward remittance flows[a]	–	–	–	–	–	–	–	–	–	–
of which										
Compensation of employees	–	–	–	–	–	–	–	–	–	–
Personal transfers	–	–	–	–	–	–	–	–	–	–
Outward remittance flows	–	–	–	–	–	–	–	–	–	–
of which										
Compensation of employees	–	–	–	–	–	–	–	–	–	–
Personal transfers	–	–	–	–	–	–	–	–	–	–

a. Net FDI inflows US$1.91 billion, net ODA received US$0.01 billion in 2013.

Eritrea

Population (millions, 2014)	5.1
Population growth (avg. annual %, 2005–14)	2.3
Population density (people per sq km, 2014)	50.6
Labor force (millions, 2014)	2.5
Unemployment rate (% of labor force, 2014)	7.2
Urban population (% of pop., 2014)	22.2
Surface area (thousands of sq km, 2014)	117.6
GNI, Atlas method (current US$ billions, 2014)	3.5
GNI per capita, Atlas method (current US$, 2014)	680.0
GDP growth (avg. annual %, 2011–14)	4.7
Poverty headcount ratio at national poverty line (% of pop.)	–
Age dependency ratio (% of working-age pop., 2014)	83.1
Account at a formal financial institution (% age 15+)	–
Mobile cellular subscriptions (per 100 people, 2014)	6.4
Internet users (per 100 people, 2014)	1.0

Migration

EMIGRATION

- Stock of emigrants, 2013: **387.4 thousands**
- Stock of emigrants as percentage of population, 2013: **7.8 percent**
- Top destination countries, 2013: Sudan, Saudi Arabia, the United States, Ethiopia, the United Kingdom, the United Arab Emirates, Sweden, Italy, Norway, Germany
- Tertiary-educated as a percentage of total emigrants in OECD countries, 2011: **21.3 percent**
- Tertiary-educated women as a percentage of total women emigrants in OECD countries, 2011: **17.5 percent**
- Number of refugees, 2014: **363,026**
- Second generation diaspora in Australia, Europe, and the United States, 2012: **12.5 thousands**

IMMIGRATION

- Stock of immigrants, 2013: **15.8 thousands**
- Stock of immigrants as percentage of population, 2013: **0.3 percent**
- Top source countries, 2013: Somalia, the Democratic Republic of Congo, Uganda, South Sudan, Mozambique, Burundi, Malawi, Tanzania, Rwanda, France
- Women as percentage of immigrants, 2013: **44.7 percent**
- Number of refugees, 2014: **2,898**

Remittances

US$ millions	2006	2007	2008	2009	2010	2011	2012	2013	2014	2015e
Inward remittance flows[a]	–	–	–	–	–	–	–	–	–	–
of which										
Compensation of employees	–	–	–	–	–	–	–	–	–	–
Personal transfers	–	–	–	–	–	–	–	–	–	–
Outward remittance flows	–	–	–	–	–	–	–	–	–	–
of which										
Compensation of employees	–	–	–	–	–	–	–	–	–	–
Personal transfers	–	–	–	–	–	–	–	–	–	–

a. Net FDI inflows US$0.04 billion, net ODA received US$0.08 billion in 2013.

Estonia

Population (millions, 2014)	1.3
Population growth (avg. annual %, 2005–14)	-0.4
Population density (people per sq km, 2014)	31.0
Labor force (thousands, 2013)	686.7
Unemployment rate (% of labor force, 2014)	7.7
Urban population (% of pop., 2014)	67.6
Surface area (thousands of sq km, 2014)	45.2
GNI, Atlas method (current US$ billions, 2014)	25.0
GNI per capita, Atlas method (current US$, 2014)	19,030.0
GDP growth (avg. annual %, 2011–14)	4.3
Poverty headcount ratio at national poverty line (% of pop., 2012)	18.6
Age dependency ratio (% of working-age pop., 2014)	52.3
Account at a formal financial institution (% age 15+, 2014)	97.7
Mobile cellular subscriptions (per 100 people, 2014)	160.7
Internet users (per 100 people, 2014)	84.2

Migration

EMIGRATION

- Stock of emigrants, 2013: **191.2 thousands**
- Stock of emigrants as percentage of population, 2013: **14.5 percent**
- Top destination countries, 2013: the Russian Federation, Finland, Germany, the United States, Ukraine, Sweden, the United Kingdom, Canada, Norway, Uzbekistan
- Tertiary-educated as a percentage of total emigrants in OECD countries, 2011: **29.6 percent**
- Tertiary-educated women as a percentage of total women emigrants in OECD countries, 2011: **34.3 percent**
- Number of refugees, 2014: **330**
- Second generation diaspora in Australia, Europe, and the United States, 2012: **28.5 thousands**

IMMIGRATION

- Stock of immigrants, 2013: **197.6 thousands**
- Stock of immigrants as percentage of population, 2013: **15.0 percent**
- Top source countries, 2013: the Russian Federation, Ukraine, Belarus, Latvia, Kazakhstan, Finland, Lithuania, Azerbaijan, Georgia, Germany
- Women as percentage of immigrants, 2013: **58.6 percent**
- Number of refugees, **2014: 57**

Remittances

US$ millions	2006	2007	2008	2009	2010	2011	2012	2013	2014	2015e
Inward remittance flows[a]	**402**	**411**	**362**	**340**	**357**	**438**	**461**	**568**	**544**	**481**
of which										
Compensation of employees	392	381	302	249	265	345	351	419	415	–
Personal transfers	10	30	60	91	92	93	110	149	129	–
Outward remittance flows	**75**	**93**	**98**	**92**	**123**	**113**	**113**	**100**	**114**	–
of which										
Compensation of employees	74	91	96	76	91	81	82	67	73	–
Personal transfers	2	2	2	17	33	32	31	33	40	–

a. Net FDI inflows US$0.87 billion in 2013.

Ethiopia

Population (millions, 2014)	97.0
Population growth (avg. annual %, 2005–14)	2.6
Population density (people per sq km, 2014)	97.0
Labor force (millions, 2014)	47.0
Unemployment rate (% of labor force, 2014)	5.2
Urban population (% of pop., 2014)	19.0
Surface area (thousands of sq km, 2014)	1,104.3
GNI, Atlas method (current US$ billions, 2014)	53.6
GNI per capita, Atlas method (current US$, 2014)	550.0
GDP growth (avg. annual %, 2011–14)	10.2
Poverty headcount ratio at national poverty line (% of pop., 2010)	29.6
Age dependency ratio (% of working-age pop., 2014)	83.6
Account at a formal financial institution (% age 15+, 2014)	21.8
Mobile cellular subscriptions (per 100 people, 2014)	31.6
Internet users (per 100 people, 2014)	2.9

Migration

EMIGRATION

- Stock of emigrants, 2013: **749.1 thousands**
- Stock of emigrants as percentage of population, 2013: **0.8 percent**
- Top destination countries, 2013: the United States, Saudi Arabia, Israel, Sudan, Italy, South Africa, Canada, Kenya, the United Kingdom, Sweden
- Tertiary-educated as a percentage of total emigrants in OECD countries, 2011: **23.7 percent**
- Tertiary-educated women as a percentage of total women emigrants in OECD countries, 2011: **19.7 percent**
- Number of refugees, 2014: **86,773**
- Second generation diaspora in Australia, Europe, and the United States, 2012: **52.7 thousands**

IMMIGRATION

- Stock of immigrants, 2013: **774.8 thousands**
- Stock of immigrants as percentage of population, 2013: **0.8 percent**
- Top source countries, 2013: Somalia, South Sudan, Eritrea, Sudan, Djibouti, Uganda, Rwanda, the Republic of Yemen, the Democratic Republic of Congo, Burundi
- Women as percentage of immigrants, 2013: **46.2 percent**
- Number of refugees, 2014: **659,510**

Remittances

US$ millions	2006	2007	2008	2009	2010	2011	2012	2013	2014	2015e
Inward remittance flows[a]	**172**	**358**	**387**	**262**	**345**	**513**	**624**	**624**	**624**	**635**
of which										
Compensation of employees	3	2	0	0	0	0	0	–	–	–
Personal transfers	169	356	387	262	345	513	624	–	–	–
Outward remittance flows	**14**	**15**	**21**	**27**	**66**	**21**	**22**	**–**	**–**	**–**
of which										
Compensation of employees	–	–	0	0	2	2	2	–	–	–
Personal transfers	14	15	21	27	64	19	20	–	–	–

a. Net FDI inflows US$0.95 billion, net ODA received US$3.83 billion in 2013.

Faeroe Islands

Population (thousands, 2013)	48.2
Population growth (avg. annual %, 2005–14)	0.0
Population density (people per sq km, 2014)	34.5
Labor force, total	—
Unemployment rate (% of labor force)	—
Urban population (% of pop., 2014)	41.7
Surface area (thousands of sq km, 2014)	1.4
GNI, Atlas method (current US$ billions)	—
GNI per capita, Atlas method (current US$)	—
GDP growth (avg. annual %)	—
Poverty headcount ratio at national poverty line (% of pop.)	—
Age dependency ratio (% of working-age pop.)	—
Account at a formal financial institution (% age 15+)	—
Mobile cellular subscriptions (per 100 people, 2014)	124.1
Internet users (per 100 people, 2014)	94.7

Migration

EMIGRATION

- Stock of emigrants, 2013: **13.4 thousands**
- Stock of emigrants as percentage of population, 2013: **27.7 percent**
- Top destination countries, 2013: Denmark, Norway, Iceland, the United States, Australia, Ecuador, Ireland, the Netherlands, Chile, France
- Tertiary-educated as a percentage of total emigrants in OECD countries, 2011: Not available
- Tertiary-educated women as a percentage of total women emigrants in OECD countries, 2011: Not available
- Number of refugees, 2014: Not available
- Second generation diaspora in Australia, Europe, and the United States, 2012: Not available

IMMIGRATION

- Stock of immigrants, 2013: **3.6 thousands**
- Stock of immigrants as percentage of population, 2013: **7.5 percent**
- Top source countries, 2013: Iceland, Norway, Poland, the United Kingdom, Thailand, Romania, the Philippines, Serbia, Sweden, the Russian Federation
- Women as percentage of immigrants, 2013: **43.1 percent**
- Number of refugees, 2014: Not available

Remittances

US$ millions	2006	2007	2008	2009	2010	2011	2012	2013	2014	2015e
Inward remittance flows	89	109	137	139	146	158	158	158	158	162
of which										
Compensation of employees	89	109	137	139	146	158	—	—	—	—
Personal transfers	—	—	—	—	—	—	—	—	—	—
Outward remittance flows	23	33	41	31	31	34	—	—	—	—
of which										
Compensation of employees	23	33	41	31	31	34	—	—	—	—
Personal transfers	—	—	—	—	—	—	—	—	—	—

Fiji

	MIDDLE INCOME
Population (thousands, 2013)	886.5
Population growth (avg. annual %, 2005–14)	0.8
Population density (people per sq km, 2014)	48.5
Labor force (thousands, 2013)	347.2
Unemployment rate (% of labor force, 2014)	7.9
Urban population (% of pop., 2014)	53.4
Surface area (thousands of sq km, 2014)	18.3
GNI, Atlas method (current US$ billions, 2014)	4.3
GNI per capita, Atlas method (current US$, 2014)	4,870.0
GDP growth (avg. annual %, 2011–14)	2.7
Poverty headcount ratio at national poverty line (% of pop., 2008)	35.2
Age dependency ratio (% of working-age pop., 2014)	52.5
Account at a formal financial institution (% age 15+)	–
Mobile cellular subscriptions (per 100 people, 2014)	98.8
Internet users (per 100 people, 2014)	41.8

Migration

EMIGRATION

- Stock of emigrants, 2013: **201.5 thousands**
- Stock of emigrants as percentage of population, 2013: **22.9 percent**
- Top destination countries, 2013: Australia, New Zealand, the United States, Canada, the United Kingdom, Tonga, Kiribati, American Samoa, Vanuatu, India
- Tertiary-educated as a percentage of total emigrants in OECD countries, 2011: **28.6 percent**
- Tertiary-educated women as a percentage of total women emigrants in OECD countries, 2011: **29.0 percent**
- Number of refugees, 2014: **917**
- Second generation diaspora in Australia, Europe, and the United States, 2012: **15.2 thousands**

IMMIGRATION

- Stock of immigrants, 2013: **22.8 thousands**
- Stock of immigrants as percentage of population, 2013: **2.6 percent**
- Top source countries, 2013: India, Bangladesh, Australia, Pakistan, New Zealand, the United Kingdom
- Women as percentage of immigrants, 2013: **46.2 percent**
- Number of refugees, 2014: **7**

Remittances

US$ millions	2006	2007	2008	2009	2010	2011	2012	2013	2014	2015e
Inward remittance flows[a]	**205**	**183**	**147**	**171**	**174**	**160**	**191**	**204**	**206**	**208**
of which										
Compensation of employees	39	45	50	48	62	60	51	42	–	–
Personal transfers	166	138	97	123	112	100	140	161	–	–
Outward remittance flows	**10**	**9**	**13**	**7**	**10**	**11**	**8**	**8**	**–**	**–**
of which										
Compensation of employees	5	5	8	4	5	6	5	4	–	–
Personal transfers	5	4	5	3	4	4	3	5	–	–

a. Net FDI inflows US$0.16 billion, net ODA received US$0.09 billion in 2013.

Finland

	HIGH INCOME OECD
Population (millions, 2014)	5.5
Population growth (avg. annual %, 2005–14)	0.4
Population density (people per sq km, 2014)	18.0
Labor force (millions, 2014)	2.7
Unemployment rate (% of labor force, 2014)	8.6
Urban population (% of pop., 2014)	84.1
Surface area (thousands of sq km, 2014)	338.4
GNI, Atlas method (current US$ billions, 2014)	264.6
GNI per capita, Atlas method (current US$, 2014)	48,420.0
GDP growth (avg. annual %, 2011–14)	-0.1
Poverty headcount ratio at national poverty line (% of pop.)	—
Age dependency ratio (% of working-age pop., 2014)	56.6
Account at a formal financial institution (% age 15+, 2014)	100.0
Mobile cellular subscriptions (per 100 people, 2014)	139.7
Internet users (per 100 people, 2014)	92.4

Migration

EMIGRATION

- Stock of emigrants, 2013: **314.1 thousands**
- Stock of emigrants as percentage of population, 2013: **5.8 percent**
- Top destination countries, 2013: Sweden, the United States, Germany, Canada, the United Kingdom, Spain, Australia, Norway, Belgium, Switzerland
- Tertiary-educated as a percentage of total emigrants in OECD countries, 2011: **28.0 percent**
- Tertiary-educated women as a percentage of total women emigrants in OECD countries, 2011: **31.7 percent**
- Number of refugees, 2014: **5**
- Second generation diaspora in Australia, Europe, and the United States, 2012: **293.5 thousands**

IMMIGRATION

- Stock of immigrants, 2013: **293.2 thousands**
- Stock of immigrants as percentage of population, 2013: **5.4 percent**
- Top source countries, 2013: the Russian Federation, Sweden, Estonia, Somalia, Iraq, China, Thailand, Germany, Turkey, the United Kingdom
- Women as percentage of immigrants, 2013: **49.2 percent**
- Number of refugees, 2014: **11,708**

Remittances

US$ millions	2006	2007	2008	2009	2010	2011	2012	2013	2014	2015e
Inward remittance flows[a]	691	766	908	875	848	751	866	973	974	977
of which										
Compensation of employees	691	766	908	875	848	751	866	973	974	—
Personal transfers	—	—	—	—	—	—	—	—	—	—
Outward remittance flows	331	391	457	454	517	467	821	862	862	—
of which										
Compensation of employees	309	367	428	429	493	442	795	835	835	—
Personal transfers	22	24	30	25	24	25	26	27	27	—

a. Net FDI inflows US$-4.98 billion in 2013.

France

Population (millions, 2014)	66.2
Population growth (avg. annual %, 2005–14)	0.5
Population density (people per sq km, 2014)	120.9
Labor force (millions, 2014)	30.1
Unemployment rate (% of labor force, 2014)	9.9
Urban population (% of pop., 2014)	79.3
Surface area (thousands of sq km, 2014)	549.1
GNI, Atlas method (current US$ billions, 2014)	2,844.3
GNI per capita, Atlas method (current US$, 2014)	42,960.0
GDP growth (avg. annual %, 2011–14)	0.8
Poverty headcount ratio at national poverty line (% of pop.)	–
Age dependency ratio (% of working-age pop., 2014)	59.2
Account at a formal financial institution (% age 15+, 2014)	96.6
Mobile cellular subscriptions (per 100 people, 2014)	100.4
Internet users (per 100 people, 2014)	83.8

Migration

EMIGRATION

- Stock of emigrants, 2013: **2,184.5 thousands**
- Stock of emigrants as percentage of population, 2013: **3.3 percent**
- Top destination countries, 2013: Spain, the United States, Belgium, Germany, Switzerland, Italy, the United Kingdom, Canada, Portugal, Israel
- Tertiary-educated as a percentage of total emigrants in OECD countries, 2011: **40.1 percent**
- Tertiary-educated women as a percentage of total women emigrants in OECD countries, 2011: **38.9 percent**
- Number of refugees, 2014: **79**
- Second generation diaspora in Australia, Europe, and the United States, 2012: **933.1 thousands**

IMMIGRATION

- Stock of immigrants, 2013: **7,456.1 thousands**
- Stock of immigrants as percentage of population, 2013: **11.3 percent**
- Top source countries, 2013: Algeria, Morocco, Portugal, Tunisia, Italy, Spain, Turkey, Germany, Belgium, Vietnam
- Women as percentage of immigrants, 2013: **51.3 percent**
- Number of refugees, 2014: **252,228**

Remittances

US$ millions	2006	2007	2008	2009	2010	2011	2012	2013	2014	2015e
Inward remittance flows[a]	**15,529**	**17,589**	**20,085**	**19,649**	**19,903**	**22,927**	**22,674**	**24,406**	**25,195**	**24,633**
of which										
Compensation of employees	14,412	16,380	18,915	18,579	18,881	21,962	21,996	23,689	24,568	–
Personal transfers	1,117	1,210	1,170	1,071	1,022	965	679	717	627	–
Outward remittance flows	**10,281**	**11,947**	**13,269**	**11,757**	**12,029**	**12,849**	**12,566**	**13,318**	**13,835**	**–**
of which										
Compensation of employees	1,297	1,432	1,437	1,414	1,457	1,307	1,297	1,397	1,372	–
Personal transfers	8,984	10,515	11,832	10,343	10,572	11,543	11,269	11,921	12,463	–

a. Net FDI inflows US$33.55 billion in 2013.

French Polynesia

	HIGH INCOME NON-OECD
Population (thousands, 2013)	279.8
Population growth (avg. annual %, 2005–14)	1.1
Population density (people per sq km, 2014)	76.4
Labor force (thousands, 2013)	121.0
Unemployment rate (% of labor force)	–
Urban population (% of pop., 2014)	56.0
Surface area (thousands of sq km, 2014)	4.0
GNI, Atlas method (current US$ billions, 2000)	3.8
GNI per capita, Atlas method (current US$, 2000)	15,990.0
GDP growth (avg. annual %)	–
Poverty headcount ratio at national poverty line (% of pop.)	–
Age dependency ratio (% of working-age pop., 2014)	42.5
Account at a formal financial institution (% age 15+)	–
Mobile cellular subscriptions (per 100 people, 2014)	85.7
Internet users (per 100 people, 2014)	60.7

Migration

EMIGRATION

- Stock of emigrants, 2013: **3.8 thousands**
- Stock of emigrants as percentage of population, 2013: **1.4 percent**
- Top destination countries, 2013: the United States, Australia, New Caledonia, Solomon Islands, Canada, Greece, Kenya, the Netherlands, Ukraine, Chile
- Tertiary-educated as a percentage of total emigrants in OECD countries, 2011: Not available
- Tertiary-educated women as a percentage of total women emigrants in OECD countries, 2011: Not available
- Number of refugees, 2014: Not available
- Second generation diaspora in Australia, Europe, and the United States, 2012: Not available

IMMIGRATION

- Stock of immigrants, 2013: **34.8 thousands**
- Stock of immigrants as percentage of population, 2013: **12.6 percent**
- Top source countries, 2013: France, New Caledonia, Algeria, China, the United States, Germany, Vanuatu, Italy, Canada, Switzerland
- Women as percentage of immigrants, 2013: **44.2 percent**
- Number of refugees, 2014: Not available

Remittances

US$ millions	2006	2007	2008	2009	2010	2011	2012	2013	2014	2015e
Inward remittance flows[a]	**622**	**689**	**763**	**728**	**694**	**756**	**669**	**689**	**689**	**706**
of which										
Compensation of employees	607	675	752	712	681	745	659	676	–	–
Personal transfers	14	14	11	16	13	11	10	13	–	–
Outward remittance flows	51	56	69	64	71	56	58	65	–	–
of which										
Compensation of employees	15	16	28	30	24	21	17	17	–	–
Personal transfers	36	40	42	34	47	35	41	48	–	–

a. Net FDI inflows US$0.10 billion in 2013.

Gabon

MIDDLE INCOME

Population (millions, 2014)	1.7
Population growth (avg. annual %, 2005–14)	2.3
Population density (people per sq km, 2014)	6.5
Labor force (thousands, 2013)	645.6
Unemployment rate (% of labor force, 2014)	19.7
Urban population (% of pop., 2014)	86.9
Surface area (thousands of sq km, 2014)	267.7
GNI, Atlas method (current US$ billions, 2014)	16.4
GNI per capita, Atlas method (current US$, 2014)	9,720.0
GDP growth (avg. annual %, 2011–14)	5.6
Poverty headcount ratio at national poverty line (% of pop., 2005)	32.7
Age dependency ratio (% of working-age pop., 2014)	73.8
Account at a formal financial institution (% age 15+, 2014)	30.2
Mobile cellular subscriptions (per 100 people, 2014)	210.4
Internet users (per 100 people, 2014)	9.8

Migration

EMIGRATION

- Stock of emigrants, 2013: **48.9 thousands**
- Stock of emigrants as percentage of population, 2013: **3.0 percent**
- Top destination countries, 2013: France, Cameroon, Mali, the Republic of Congo, Kenya, Canada, Portugal, Germany, the United States, Italy
- Tertiary-educated as a percentage of total emigrants in OECD countries, 2011: **40.3 percent**
- Tertiary-educated women as a percentage of total women emigrants in OECD countries, 2011: **37.4 percent**
- Number of refugees, 2014: **154**
- Second generation diaspora in Australia, Europe, and the United States, 2012: **0.9 thousands**

IMMIGRATION

- Stock of immigrants, 2013: **395.0 thousands**
- Stock of immigrants as percentage of population, 2013: **23.9 percent**
- Top source countries, 2013: Equatorial Guinea, Mali, Benin, Cameroon, Senegal, Nigeria, Togo, the Republic of Congo, France, the Democratic Republic of Congo
- Women as percentage of immigrants, 2013: **40.9 percent**
- Number of refugees, 2014: **992**

Remittances

US$ millions	2006	2007	2008	2009	2010	2011	2012	2013	2014	2015e
Inward remittance flows[a]	–	–	–	–	–	–	–	–	–	–
of which										
Compensation of employees	–	–	–	–	–	–	–	–	–	6.5
Personal transfers	–	–	–	–	–	–	–	–	–	–
Outward remittance flows	–	–	–	–	–	–	–	–	–	–
of which										
Compensation of employees	–	–	–	–	–	–	–	–	–	–
Personal transfers	–	–	–	–	–	–	–	–	–	–

a. Net FDI inflows US$0.97 billion, net ODA received US$0.09 billion in 2013.

Gambia, The

Population (millions, 2014)	1.9
Population growth (avg. annual %, 2005–14)	3.2
Population density (people per sq km, 2014)	190.5
Labor force (thousands, 2013)	801.2
Unemployment rate (% of labor force, 2014)	7.0
Urban population (% of pop., 2014)	59.0
Surface area (thousands of sq km, 2014)	11.3
GNI, Atlas method (current US$ billions, 2014)	0.9
GNI per capita, Atlas method (current US$, 2014)	500.0
GDP growth (avg. annual %, 2011–14)	2.8
Poverty headcount ratio at national poverty line (% of pop., 2010)	48.4
Age dependency ratio (% of working-age pop., 2014)	94.8
Account at a formal financial institution (% age 15+)	–
Mobile cellular subscriptions (per 100 people, 2014)	119.6
Internet users (per 100 people, 2014)	15.6

Migration

EMIGRATION

- Stock of emigrants, 2013: **71.0 thousands**
- Stock of emigrants as percentage of population, 2013: **3.8 percent**
- Top destination countries, 2013: Spain, the United Kingdom, the United States, Nigeria, Sweden, Senegal, Germany, Sierra Leone, France, Guinea-Bissau
- Tertiary-educated as a percentage of total emigrants in OECD countries, 2011: **19.2 percent**
- Tertiary-educated women as a percentage of total women emigrants in OECD countries, 2011: **18.9 percent**
- Number of refugees, 2014: **5,085**
- Second generation diaspora in Australia, Europe, and the United States, 2012: **0.8 thousands**

IMMIGRATION

- Stock of immigrants, 2013: **162.9 thousands**
- Stock of immigrants as percentage of population, 2013: **8.7 percent**
- Top source countries, 2013: Senegal, Guinea, Guinea-Bissau, Mali, Mauritania, Sierra Leone
- Women as percentage of immigrants, 2013: **51.0 percent**
- Number of refugees, 2014: **11,601**

Remittances

US$ millions	2006	2007	2008	2009	2010	2011	2012	2013	2014	2015e
Inward remittance flows[a]	**64**	**56**	**65**	**80**	**116**	**108**	**141**	**181**	**181**	**181**
of which										
Compensation of employees	1	2	9	8	8	8	9	–	–	–
Personal transfers	63	54	56	72	107	99	132	–	–	–
Outward remittance flows	**1**	**15**	**3**	**8**	**58**	**37**	**48**	**–**	**–**	**–**
of which										
Compensation of employees	1	1	1	2	4	10	12	–	–	–
Personal transfers	–	13	2	7	54	26	36	–	–	–

a. Net FDI inflows US$0.04 billion, net ODA received US$0.11 billion in 2013.

Georgia

Population (millions, 2014)	4.5
Population growth (avg. annual %, 2005–14)	0.4
Population density (people per sq km, 2014)	78.8
Labor force (millions, 2014)	2.4
Unemployment rate (% of labor force, 2014)	13.4
Urban population (% of pop., 2014)	53.5
Surface area (thousands of sq km, 2014)	69.7
GNI, Atlas method (current US$ billions, 2014)	16.7
GNI per capita, Atlas method (current US$, 2014)	3,720.0
GDP growth (avg. annual %, 2011–14)	5.4
Poverty headcount ratio at national poverty line (% of pop., 2012)	14.8
Age dependency ratio (% of working-age pop., 2014)	45.6
Account at a formal financial institution (% age 15+, 2014)	39.7
Mobile cellular subscriptions (per 100 people, 2014)	124.9
Internet users (per 100 people, 2014)	48.9

Migration

EMIGRATION

- Stock of emigrants, 2013: **746.0 thousands**
- Stock of emigrants as percentage of population, 2013: **16.6 percent**
- Top destination countries, 2013: the Russian Federation, Ukraine, Greece, Armenia, Uzbekistan, Cyprus, Germany, the United States, Spain, Turkey
- Tertiary-educated as a percentage of total emigrants in OECD countries, 2011: **31.9 percent**
- Tertiary-educated women as a percentage of total women emigrants in OECD countries, 2011: **34.8 percent**
- Number of refugees, 2014: **6,698**
- Second generation diaspora in Australia, Europe, and the United States, 2012: Not available

IMMIGRATION

- Stock of immigrants, 2013: **190.3 thousands**
- Stock of immigrants as percentage of population, 2013: **4.2 percent**
- Top source countries, 2013: the Russian Federation, Ukraine, Kazakhstan, Belarus, Uzbekistan, Azerbaijan, Poland, Moldova, Lithuania, Armenia
- Women as percentage of immigrants, 2013: **52.4 percent**
- Number of refugees, 2014: **843**

Remittances

US$ millions	2006	2007	2008	2009	2010	2011	2012	2013	2014	2015e
Inward remittance flows[a]	627	883	1,065	1,112	1,184	1,547	1,770	1,945	1,986	1,625
of which										
Compensation of employees	315	406	419	392	381	510	650	714	739	–
Personal transfers	312	477	646	720	803	1,037	1,120	1,231	1,248	–
Outward remittance flows	27	32	51	34	55	77	87	88	86	–
of which										
Compensation of employees	20	26	44	30	49	70	83	83	76	–
Personal transfers	7	5	7	4	6	7	4	4	10	–

a. Net FDI inflows US$0.71 billion, net ODA received US$0.65 billion in 2013.

Germany

	HIGH INCOME OECD
Population (millions, 2014)	80.9
Population growth (avg. annual %, 2005–14)	-0.2
Population density (people per sq km, 2014)	232.1
Labor force (millions, 2014)	42.2
Unemployment rate (% of labor force, 2014)	5.0
Urban population (% of pop., 2014)	75.1
Surface area (thousands of sq km, 2014)	357.2
GNI, Atlas method (current US$ billions, 2014)	3,853.6
GNI per capita, Atlas method (current US$, 2014)	47,640.0
GDP growth (avg. annual %, 2011–14)	1.5
Poverty headcount ratio at national poverty line (% of pop.)	–
Age dependency ratio (% of working-age pop., 2014)	51.6
Account at a formal financial institution (% age 15+, 2014)	98.8
Mobile cellular subscriptions (per 100 people, 2014)	120.4
Internet users (per 100 people, 2014)	86.2

Migration

EMIGRATION

- Stock of emigrants, 2013: **4,141.4 thousands**
- Stock of emigrants as percentage of population, 2013: **5.1 percent**
- Top destination countries, 2013: the United States, Turkey, Switzerland, the United Kingdom, France, Spain, Italy, Austria, Canada, Australia
- Tertiary-educated as a percentage of total emigrants in OECD countries, 2011: **33.6 percent**
- Tertiary-educated women as a percentage of total women emigrants in OECD countries, 2011: **32.1 percent**
- Number of refugees, 2014: **165**
- Second generation diaspora in Australia, Europe, and the United States, 2012: **2,393.2 thousands**

IMMIGRATION

- Stock of immigrants, 2013: **11,110.9 thousands**
- Stock of immigrants as percentage of population, 2013: **13.8 percent**
- Top source countries, 2013: Turkey, Poland, the Russian Federation, Kazakhstan, Romania, Italy, Greece, Croatia, Ukraine, Serbia
- Women as percentage of immigrants, 2013: **51.3 percent**
- Number of refugees, 2014: **216,921**

Remittances

US$ millions	2006	2007	2008	2009	2010	2011	2012	2013	2014	2015e
Inward remittance flows[a]	7,481	9,769	10,974	12,335	12,792	16,995	16,434	16,989	17,629	17,491
of which Compensation of employees	7,481	9,769	10,974	12,335	12,792	16,995	16,434	16,984	17,604	–
Personal transfers	–	–	–	–	–	–	–	5	26	–
Outward remittance flows	12,700	14,082	15,234	15,324	14,685	16,566	15,533	19,870	20,836	–
of which Compensation of employees	9,024	9,976	10,704	11,152	10,659	12,427	11,739	15,555	16,219	–
Personal transfers	3,676	4,106	4,530	4,172	4,026	4,140	3,794	4,315	4,617	–

a. Net FDI inflows US$59.01 billion in 2013.

Ghana

	MIDDLE INCOME
Population (millions, 2014)	26.8
Population growth (avg. annual %, 2005–14)	2.5
Population density (people per sq km, 2014)	117.7
Labor force (millions, 2014)	11.4
Unemployment rate (% of labor force, 2014)	2.4
Urban population (% of pop., 2014)	53.4
Surface area (thousands of sq km, 2014)	238.5
GNI, Atlas method (current US$ billions, 2014)	42.7
GNI per capita, Atlas method (current US$, 2014)	1,590.0
GDP growth (avg. annual %, 2011–14)	8.7
Poverty headcount ratio at national poverty line (% of pop., 2012)	24.2
Age dependency ratio (% of working-age pop., 2014)	73.4
Account at a formal financial institution (% age 15+, 2014)	34.6
Mobile cellular subscriptions (per 100 people, 2014)	114.8
Internet users (per 100 people, 2014)	18.9

Migration

EMIGRATION

- Stock of emigrants, 2013: **737.2 thousands**
- Stock of emigrants as percentage of population, 2013: **2.8 percent**
- Top destination countries, 2013: Nigeria, the United States, the United Kingdom, Côte d'Ivoire, Italy, Togo, Burkina Faso, Germany, Canada, Spain
- Tertiary-educated as a percentage of total emigrants in OECD countries, 2011: **35.2 percent**
- Tertiary-educated women as a percentage of total women emigrants in OECD countries, 2011: **31.7 percent**
- Number of refugees, 2014: **22,100**
- Second generation diaspora in Australia, Europe, and the United States, 2012: **61.5 thousands**

IMMIGRATION

- Stock of immigrants, 2013: **439.3 thousands**
- Stock of immigrants as percentage of population, 2013: **1.7 percent**
- Top source countries, 2013: Togo, Burkina Faso, Nigeria, Côte d'Ivoire, Liberia, Benin, Niger, Mali, the United Kingdom, Sierra Leone
- Women as percentage of immigrants, 2013: **45.3 percent**
- Number of refugees, 2014: **18,438**

Remittances

US$ millions	2006	2007	2008	2009	2010	2011	2012	2013	2014	2015e
Inward remittance flows[a]	105	117	126	114	136	2,135	2,155	–	2,008	2,008
of which										
Compensation of employees	–	–	–	–	–	–	–	–	–	–
Personal transfers	105	117	126	114	136	2,135	2,155	–	2,008	–
Outward remittance flows	–	–	–	–	–	–	8	5	9	–
of which										
Compensation of employees	–	–	–	–	–	–	–	–	–	–
Personal transfers	–	–	–	–	–	–	8	5	9	–

a. Net FDI inflows US$3.23 billion, net ODA received US$1.33 billion in 2013.

Greece

	HIGH INCOME OECD
Population (millions, 2014)	11.0
Population growth (avg. annual %, 2005-14)	-0.1
Population density (people per sq km, 2014)	85.0
Labor force (millions, 2014)	5.0
Unemployment rate (% of labor force, 2014)	26.3
Urban population (% of pop., 2014)	77.7
Surface area (thousands of sq km, 2014)	132.0
GNI, Atlas method (current US$ billions, 2014)	250.1
GNI per capita, Atlas method (current US$, 2014)	22,680.0
GDP growth (avg. annual %, 2011-14)	-4.7
Poverty headcount ratio at national poverty line (% of pop.)	–
Age dependency ratio (% of working-age pop., 2014)	55.1
Account at a formal financial institution (% age 15+, 2014)	87.5
Mobile cellular subscriptions (per 100 people, 2014)	115.0
Internet users (per 100 people, 2014)	63.2

Migration

EMIGRATION

Stock of emigrants, 2013: **1,000.1 thousands**
Stock of emigrants as percentage of population, 2013: **9.1 percent**
Top destination countries, 2013: Germany, the United States, Australia, Turkey, Canada, Albania, the United Kingdom, Belgium, Cyprus, Italy
Tertiary-educated as a percentage of total emigrants in OECD countries, 2011: **19.2 percent**
Tertiary-educated women as a percentage of total women emigrants in OECD countries, 2011: **17.6 percent**
Number of refugees, 2014: **108**
Second generation diaspora in Australia, Europe, and the United States, 2012: **477.8 thousands**

IMMIGRATION

Stock of immigrants, 2013: **988.2 thousands**
Stock of immigrants as percentage of population, 2013: **9.0 percent**
Top source countries, 2013: Albania, Bulgaria, Romania, Georgia, Pakistan, Monaco, Bangladesh, the Russian Federation, Ukraine, Poland
Women as percentage of immigrants, 2013: **46.1 percent**
Number of refugees, 2014: **10,262**

Remittances

US$ millions	2006	2007	2008	2009	2010	2011	2012	2013	2014	2015e
Inward remittance flows[a]	**1,543**	**2,484**	**2,687**	**2,020**	**1,499**	**1,186**	**681**	**805**	**735**	**736**
of which										
Compensation of employees	400	504	509	411	265	261	258	278	279	–
Personal transfers	1,143	1,980	2,178	1,609	1,234	925	423	527	456	–
Outward remittance flows	**982**	**1,460**	**1,912**	**1,843**	**1,932**	**1,941**	**1,438**	**1,291**	**1,424**	–
of which										
Compensation of employees	353	457	596	575	501	654	602	601	650	–
Personal transfers	629	1,003	1,316	1,268	1,431	1,287	836	690	774	–

a. Net FDI inflows US$2.95 billion in 2013.

Greenland

	HIGH INCOME NON-OECD
Population (thousands, 2013)	56.3
Population growth (avg. annual %, 2005–14)	-0.1
Population density (people per sq km, 2014)	0.1
Labor force, total	–
Unemployment rate (% of labor force)	–
Urban population (% of pop., 2014)	86.0
Surface area (thousands of sq km, 2014)	410.5
GNI, Atlas method (current US$ billions, 2009)	1.5
GNI per capita, Atlas method (current US$, 2009)	26,020.0
GDP growth (avg. annual %, 2005–08)	1.2
Poverty headcount ratio at national poverty line (% of pop.)	–
Age dependency ratio (% of working-age pop.)	–
Account at a formal financial institution (% age 15+)	–
Mobile cellular subscriptions (per 100 people, 2014)	106.4
Internet users (per 100 people, 2014)	66.7

Migration

EMIGRATION

- Stock of emigrants, 2013: **17.7 thousands**
- Stock of emigrants as percentage of population, 2013: **31.3 percent**
- Top destination countries, 2013: Denmark, the United States, Guatemala, Norway, Cuba, Iceland, Canada, Australia, Greece, France
- Tertiary-educated as a percentage of total emigrants in OECD countries, 2011: Not available
- Tertiary-educated women as a percentage of total women emigrants in OECD countries, 2011: Not available
- Number of refugees, 2014: Not available
- Second generation diaspora in Australia, Europe, and the United States, 2012: Not available

IMMIGRATION

- Stock of immigrants, 2013: **5.7 thousands**
- Stock of immigrants as percentage of population, 2013: **10.1 percent**
- Top source countries, 2013: Denmark, Iceland, Sweden, Norway, Canada, the United States, Finland
- Women as percentage of immigrants, 2013: **33.5 percent**
- Number of refugees, 2014: Not available

Remittances

US$ millions	2006	2007	2008	2009	2010	2011	2012	2013	2014	2015e
Inward remittance flows	–	–	–	–	–	–	–	–	–	–
of which										
Compensation of employees	–	–	–	–	–	–	–	–	–	–
Personal transfers	–	–	–	–	–	–	–	–	–	–
Outward remittance flows	–	–	–	–	–	–	–	–	–	–
of which										
Compensation of employees	–	–	–	–	–	–	–	–	–	–
Personal transfers	–	–	–	–	–	–	–	–	–	–

Grenada

	MIDDLE INCOME
Population (thousands, 2013)	106.3
Population growth (avg. annual %, 2005–14)	0.4
Population density (people per sq km, 2014)	312.8
Labor force, total	–
Unemployment rate (% of labor force)	–
Urban population (% of pop., 2014)	35.6
Surface area (thousands of sq km, 2014)	0.3
GNI, Atlas method (current US$ billions, 2014)	0.8
GNI per capita, Atlas method (current US$, 2014)	7,910.0
GDP growth (avg. annual %, 2011–14)	1.9
Poverty headcount ratio at national poverty line (% of pop.)	–
Age dependency ratio (% of working-age pop., 2014)	50.9
Account at a formal financial institution (% age 15+)	–
Mobile cellular subscriptions (per 100 people, 2014)	126.5
Internet users (per 100 people, 2014)	37.4

Migration

EMIGRATION

- Stock of emigrants, 2013: **57.9 thousands**
- Stock of emigrants as percentage of population, 2013: **54.7 percent**
- Top destination countries, 2013: the United States, Canada, the United Kingdom, Trinidad and Tobago, Barbados, the Virgin Islands (U.S.), Jamaica, Aruba, Guyana, Antigua and Barbuda
- Tertiary-educated as a percentage of total emigrants in OECD countries, 2011: **29.1 percent**
- Tertiary-educated women as a percentage of total women emigrants in OECD countries, 2011: **31.7 percent**
- Number of refugees, 2014: **324**
- Second generation diaspora in Australia, Europe, and the United States, 2012: Not available

IMMIGRATION

- Stock of immigrants, 2013: **11.4 thousands**
- Stock of immigrants as percentage of population, 2013: **10.7 percent**
- Top source countries, 2013: Trinidad and Tobago, the Virgin Islands (U.S.), St. Vincent and the Grenadines, Guyana, República Bolivariana de Venezuela, Canada, Barbados, St. Lucia, Jamaica, Dominica
- Women as percentage of immigrants, 2013: **49.6 percent**
- Number of refugees, 2014: Not available

Remittances

US$ millions	2006	2007	2008	2009	2010	2011	2012	2013	2014	2015e
Inward remittance flows[a]	28	29	29	28	28	29	29	30	30	30
of which										
Compensation of employees	1	0	0	0	0	0	0	0	–	–
Personal transfers	28	28	29	27	28	29	29	29	–	–
Outward remittance flows	1	2	2	1	2	2	2	2	–	–
of which										
Compensation of employees	–	–	–	–	–	–	–	–	–	–
Personal transfers	1	2	2	1	2	2	2	2	–	–

a. Net FDI inflows US$0.07 billion, net ODA received US$0.01 billion in 2013.

Guam

	HIGH INCOME NON-OECD
Population (thousands, 2013)	167.5
Population growth (avg. annual %, 2005–14)	0.6
Population density (people per sq km, 2014)	310.3
Labor force (thousands, 2013)	77.6
Unemployment rate (% of labor force)	–
Urban population (% of pop., 2014)	94.4
Surface area (thousands of sq km, 2014)	0.5
GNI, Atlas method (current US$ billions)	–
GNI per capita, Atlas method (current US$)	–
GDP growth (avg. annual %)	–
Poverty headcount ratio at national poverty line (% of pop.)	–
Age dependency ratio (% of working-age pop., 2014)	52.1
Account at a formal financial institution (% age 15+)	–
Mobile cellular subscriptions (per 100 people, 2004)	61.9
Internet users (per 100 people, 2014)	69.3

Migration

EMIGRATION

- Stock of emigrants, 2013: **2.8 thousands**
- Stock of emigrants as percentage of population, 2013: **1.7 percent**
- Top destination countries, 2013: the Philippines, the Northern Mariana Islands, the Federated States of Micronesia, Palau, Vietnam, Australia, Canada, Chile, Costa Rica, Greece
- Tertiary-educated as a percentage of total emigrants in OECD countries, 2011: **29.8 percent**
- Tertiary-educated women as a percentage of total women emigrants in OECD countries, 2011: **34.9 percent**
- Number of refugees, 2014: Not available
- Second generation diaspora in Australia, Europe, and the United States, 2012: Not available

IMMIGRATION

- Stock of immigrants, 2013: **80.8 thousands**
- Stock of immigrants as percentage of population, 2013: **48.9 percent**
- Top source countries, 2013: the Philippines, the United States, the Federated States of Micronesia, the Republic of Korea, China, Japan, the Northern Mariana Islands, Palau, Vietnam, the Marshall Islands
- Women as percentage of immigrants, 2013: **42.5 percent**
- Number of refugees, 2014: Not available

Remittances

US$ millions	2006	2007	2008	2009	2010	2011	2012	2013	2014	2015e
Inward remittance flows	–	–	–	–	–	–	–	–	–	–
of which										
Compensation of employees	–	–	–	–	–	–	–	–	–	–
Personal transfers	–	–	–	–	–	–	–	–	–	–
Outward remittance flows	–	–	–	–	–	–	–	–	–	–
of which										
Compensation of employees	–	–	–	–	–	–	–	–	–	–
Personal transfers	–	–	–	–	–	–	–	–	–	–

Guatemala

Population (millions, 2014)	16.0
Population growth (avg. annual %, 2005–14)	2.2
Population density (people per sq km, 2014)	149.5
Labor force (millions, 2014)	6.8
Unemployment rate (% of labor force, 2014)	2.9
Urban population (% of pop., 2014)	51.1
Surface area (thousands of sq km, 2014)	108.9
GNI, Atlas method (current US$ billions, 2014)	55.0
GNI per capita, Atlas method (current US$, 2014)	3,430.0
GDP growth (avg. annual %, 2011–14)	3.8
Poverty headcount ratio at national poverty line (% of pop., 2011)	53.7
Age dependency ratio (% of working-age pop., 2014)	72.1
Account at a formal financial institution (% age 15+, 2014)	40.8
Mobile cellular subscriptions (per 100 people, 2014)	106.6
Internet users (per 100 people, 2014)	23.4

Migration

EMIGRATION

- Stock of emigrants, 2013: **1,051.8 thousands**
- Stock of emigrants as percentage of population, 2013: **6.7 percent**
- Top destination countries, 2013: the United States, Mexico, Belize, Canada, El Salvador, Spain, Honduras, Costa Rica, France, Italy
- Tertiary-educated as a percentage of total emigrants in OECD countries, 2011: **9.1 percent**
- Tertiary-educated women as a percentage of total women emigrants in OECD countries, 2011: **10.5 percent**
- Number of refugees, 2014: **7,462**
- Second generation diaspora in Australia, Europe, and the United States, 2012: **429.6 thousands**

IMMIGRATION

- Stock of immigrants, 2013: **72.8 thousands**
- Stock of immigrants as percentage of population, 2013: **0.5 percent**
- Top source countries, 2013: El Salvador, Mexico, the United States, Nicaragua, Honduras, the Republic of Korea, Spain, Costa Rica, Colombia, Belize
- Women as percentage of immigrants, 2013: **52.9 percent**
- Number of refugees, 2014: **160**

Remittances

US$ millions	2006	2007	2008	2009	2010	2011	2012	2013	2014	2015e
Inward remittance flows[a]	**3,700**	**4,236**	**4,460**	**4,019**	**4,232**	**4,524**	**5,031**	**5,379**	**5,837**	**6,408**
of which										
Compensation of employees	20	29	40	53	69	112	97	115	118	-
Personal transfers	3,680	4,207	4,419	3,966	4,162	4,412	4,933	5,265	5,718	-
Outward remittance flows	**46**	**17**	**26**	**22**	**21**	**27**	**28**	**28**	**25**	-
of which										
Compensation of employees	11	10	10	7	5	10	10	9	6	-
Personal transfers	35	7	16	15	15	16	18	19	19	-

a. Net FDI inflows US$1.35 billion, net ODA received US$0.49 billion in 2013.

Guinea

Population (millions, 2014)	12.3
Population growth (avg. annual %, 2005–14)	2.6
Population density (people per sq km, 2014)	50.0
Labor force (millions, 2014)	5.1
Unemployment rate (% of labor force, 2014)	1.8
Urban population (% of pop., 2014)	36.7
Surface area (thousands of sq km, 2014)	245.9
GNI, Atlas method (current US$ billions, 2014)	5.8
GNI per capita, Atlas method (current US$, 2014)	470.0
GDP growth (avg. annual %, 2011–14)	2.6
Poverty headcount ratio at national poverty line (% of pop., 2012)	55.2
Age dependency ratio (% of working-age pop., 2014)	84.5
Account at a formal financial institution (% age 15+, 2014)	6.2
Mobile cellular subscriptions (per 100 people, 2014)	72.1
Internet users (per 100 people, 2014)	1.7

Migration

EMIGRATION

- Stock of emigrants, 2013: **398.5 thousands**
- Stock of emigrants as percentage of population, 2013: **3.3 percent**
- Top destination countries, 2013: Côte d'Ivoire, Sierra Leone, Senegal, Liberia, The Gambia, France, Mali, the United States, Spain, Mauritania
- Tertiary-educated as a percentage of total emigrants in OECD countries, 2011: **20.0 percent**
- Tertiary-educated women as a percentage of total women emigrants in OECD countries, 2011: **16.8 percent**
- Number of refugees, 2014: **15,213**
- Second generation diaspora in Australia, Europe, and the United States, 2012: **10.0 thousands**

IMMIGRATION

- Stock of immigrants, 2013: **378.5 thousands**
- Stock of immigrants as percentage of population, 2013: **3.2 percent**
- Top source countries, 2013: Sierra Leone, Liberia, Mali, Côte d'Ivoire, Senegal, Guinea-Bissau, Benin, France, Togo, Niger
- Women as percentage of immigrants, 2013: **51.7 percent**
- Number of refugees, 2014: **8,748**

Remittances

US$ millions	2006	2007	2008	2009	2010	2011	2012	2013	2014	2015e
Inward remittance flows[a]	**30**	**15**	**62**	**52**	**46**	**65**	**66**	**93**	**93**	**93**
of which										
Compensation of employees	–	–	2	1	1	1	4	1	–	–
Personal transfers	30	15	60	51	45	64	62	92	–	–
Outward remittance flows	**52**	**39**	**56**	**45**	**41**	**39**	**51**	**81**	**–**	**–**
of which										
Compensation of employees	3	5	20	14	9	7	6	12	–	–
Personal transfers	49	34	36	31	32	32	45	69	–	–

a. Net FDI inflows US$0.00 billion, net ODA received US$0.50 billion in 2013.

Guinea-Bissau

	LOW INCOME
Population (millions, 2014)	1.8
Population growth (avg. annual %, 2005–14)	2.3
Population density (people per sq km, 2014)	64.0
Labor force (thousands, 2013)	780.0
Unemployment rate (% of labor force, 2014)	6.9
Urban population (% of pop., 2014)	48.5
Surface area (thousands of sq km, 2014)	36.1
GNI, Atlas method (current US$ billions, 2014)	1.0
GNI per capita, Atlas method (current US$, 2014)	550.0
GDP growth (avg. annual %, 2011–14)	2.4
Poverty headcount ratio at national poverty line (% of pop., 2010)	69.3
Age dependency ratio (% of working-age pop., 2014)	79.0
Account at a formal financial institution (% age 15+)	–
Mobile cellular subscriptions (per 100 people, 2014)	63.5
Internet users (per 100 people, 2014)	3.3

Migration

EMIGRATION

- Stock of emigrants, 2013: **91.2 thousands**
- Stock of emigrants as percentage of population, 2013: **5.2 percent**
- Top destination countries, 2013: Portugal, Senegal, The Gambia, Spain, Cabo Verde, Nigeria, France, Mauritania, Guinea, Brazil
- Tertiary-educated as a percentage of total emigrants in OECD countries, 2011: **11.7 percent**
- Tertiary-educated women as a percentage of total women emigrants in OECD countries, 2011: **12.0 percent**
- Number of refugees, 2014: **1,286**
- Second generation diaspora in Australia, Europe, and the United States, 2012: Not available

IMMIGRATION

- Stock of immigrants, 2013: **18.0 thousands**
- Stock of immigrants as percentage of population, 2013: **1.0 percent**
- Top source countries, 2013: Senegal, Guinea, The Gambia, Liberia, Portugal, Sierra Leone, Mauritania, Cabo Verde, the United States, France
- Women as percentage of immigrants, 2013: **49.1 percent**
- Number of refugees, 2014: **8,680**

Remittances

US$ millions	2006	2007	2008	2009	2010	2011	2012	2013	2014	2015e
Inward remittance flows[a]	**26**	**43**	**49**	**49**	**46**	**52**	**46**	**64**	**64**	**64**
of which										
Compensation of employees	–	–	–	–	2	1	0	8	–	–
Personal transfers	26	43	49	49	44	51	45	56	–	–
Outward remittance flows	**4**	**4**	**17**	**20**	**20**	**30**	**25**	**35**	**–**	**–**
of which										
Compensation of employees	0	0	0	0	0	2	4	9	–	–
Personal transfers	4	4	16	20	19	28	21	26	–	–

a. Net FDI inflows US$0.02 billion, net ODA received US$0.10 billion in 2013.

Guyana

Population (thousands, 2013)	763.9
Population growth (avg. annual %, 2005–14)	0.3
Population density (people per sq km, 2014)	3.9
Labor force (thousands, 2013)	328.7
Unemployment rate (% of labor force, 2014)	11.1
Urban population (% of pop., 2014)	28.5
Surface area (thousands of sq km, 2014)	215.0
GNI, Atlas method (current US$ billions, 2014)	3.0
GNI per capita, Atlas method (current US$, 2014)	3,940.0
GDP growth (avg. annual %, 2011–14)	5.2
Poverty headcount ratio at national poverty line (% of pop.)	–
Age dependency ratio (% of working-age pop., 2014)	53.1
Account at a formal financial institution (% age 15+)	–
Mobile cellular subscriptions (per 100 people, 2014)	70.5
Internet users (per 100 people, 2014)	37.3

Migration

EMIGRATION

- Stock of emigrants, 2013: **462.6 thousands**
- Stock of emigrants as percentage of population, 2013: **60.8 percent**
- Top destination countries, 2013: the United States, Canada, the United Kingdom, Suriname, República Bolivariana de Venezuela, Antigua and Barbuda, Trinidad and Tobago, France, Barbados, the Netherlands
- Tertiary-educated as a percentage of total emigrants in OECD countries, 2011: **30.7 percent**
- Tertiary-educated women as a percentage of total women emigrants in OECD countries, 2011: **30.8 percent**
- Number of refugees, 2014: **700**
- Second generation diaspora in Australia, Europe, and the United States, 2012: Not available

IMMIGRATION

- Stock of immigrants, 2013: **14.8 thousands**
- Stock of immigrants as percentage of population, 2013: **1.9 percent**
- Top source countries, 2013: Suriname, Brazil, República Bolivariana de Venezuela, the United States, China, Trinidad and Tobago, the United Kingdom, Canada, St. Vincent and the Grenadines, Jamaica
- Women as percentage of immigrants, 2013: **45.6 percent**
- Number of refugees, 2014: **7**

Remittances

US$ millions	2006	2007	2008	2009	2010	2011	2012	2013	2014	2015e
Inward remittance flows[a]	**218**	**278**	**274**	**262**	**368**	**412**	**469**	**328**	**330**	**337**
of which										
Compensation of employees	–	–	–	–	–	–	–	–	–	–
Personal transfers	218	278	274	262	368	412	469	328	330	–
Outward remittance flows	**48**	**61**	**72**	**86**	**128**	**138**	**184**	**123**	**122**	–
of which										
Compensation of employees	6	7	4	3	3	3	3	5	6	–
Personal transfers	42	54	69	83	125	135	180	118	116	–

a. Net FDI inflows US$0.20 billion, net ODA received US$0.10 billion in 2013.

Haiti

Population (millions, 2014)	10.6
Population growth (avg. annual %, 2005–14)	1.5
Population density (people per sq km, 2014)	383.6
Labor force (millions, 2014)	4.6
Unemployment rate (% of labor force, 2014)	6.8
Urban population (% of pop., 2014)	57.4
Surface area (thousands of sq km, 2014)	27.8
GNI, Atlas method (current US$ billions, 2014)	8.7
GNI per capita, Atlas method (current US$, 2014)	820.0
GDP growth (avg. annual %, 2011–14)	3.9
Poverty headcount ratio at national poverty line (% of pop., 2012)	58.5
Age dependency ratio (% of working-age pop., 2014)	63.2
Account at a formal financial institution (% age 15+, 2014)	17.5
Mobile cellular subscriptions (per 100 people, 2014)	64.7
Internet users (per 100 people, 2014)	11.4

Migration

EMIGRATION

- Stock of emigrants, 2013: **1,377.7 thousands**
- Stock of emigrants as percentage of population, 2013: **13.2 percent**
- Top destination countries, 2013: the United States, the Dominican Republic, France, Canada, The Bahamas, the Turks and Caicos Islands, Sint Maarten (Dutch part), Curaçao, Switzerland, Bermuda
- Tertiary-educated as a percentage of total emigrants in OECD countries, 2011: **22.4 percent**
- Tertiary-educated women as a percentage of total women emigrants in OECD countries, 2011: **21.1 percent**
- Number of refugees, 2014: **37,142**
- Second generation diaspora in Australia, Europe, and the United States, 2012: **312.1 thousands**

IMMIGRATION

- Stock of immigrants, 2013: **38.1 thousands**
- Stock of immigrants as percentage of population, 2013: **0.4 percent**
- Top source countries, 2013: República Bolivariana de Venezuela, the Dominican Republic, the United States, Puerto Rico, Spain, Italy, Cuba, Germany, Colombia, Canada
- Women as percentage of immigrants, 2013: **42.4 percent**
- Number of refugees, 2014: Not available

Remittances

US$ millions	2006	2007	2008	2009	2010	2011	2012	2013	2014	2015e
Inward remittance flows[a]	1,063	1,222	1,370	1,376	1,474	1,551	1,612	1,781	1,977	2,020
of which										
Compensation of employees	–	–	–	–	–	–	–	–	–	–
Personal transfers	1,063	1,222	1,370	1,376	1,474	1,551	1,612	1,781	1,977	–
Outward remittance flows	76	96	117	135	167	240	232	248	249	–
of which										
Compensation of employees	–	–	–	–	–	–	–	–	–	–
Personal transfers	76	96	117	135	167	240	232	248	249	–

a. Net FDI inflows US$0.16 billion, net ODA received US$1.17 billion in 2013.

Honduras

Population (millions, 2014)	8.0
Population growth (avg. annual %, 2005–14)	1.6
Population density (people per sq km, 2014)	71.2
Labor force (millions, 2014)	3.4
Unemployment rate (% of labor force, 2014)	3.9
Urban population (% of pop., 2014)	54.1
Surface area (thousands of sq km, 2014)	112.5
GNI, Atlas method (current US$ billions, 2014)	18.1
GNI per capita, Atlas method (current US$, 2014)	2,270.0
GDP growth (avg. annual %, 2011–14)	3.5
Poverty headcount ratio at national poverty line (% of pop., 2013)	64.5
Age dependency ratio (% of working-age pop., 2014)	59.4
Account at a formal financial institution (% age 15+, 2014)	30.0
Mobile cellular subscriptions (per 100 people, 2014)	93.5
Internet users (per 100 people, 2014)	19.1

Migration

EMIGRATION

- Stock of emigrants, 2013: **658.8 thousands**
- Stock of emigrants as percentage of population, 2013: **8.4 percent**
- Top destination countries, 2013: the United States, Spain, Nicaragua, Mexico, El Salvador, Guatemala, Canada, Belize, Costa Rica, the Cayman Islands
- Tertiary-educated as a percentage of total emigrants in OECD countries, 2011: **10.9 percent**
- Tertiary-educated women as a percentage of total women emigrants in OECD countries, 2011: **13.3 percent**
- Number of refugees, 2014: **4,147**
- Second generation diaspora in Australia, Europe, and the United States, 2012: **235.7 thousands**

IMMIGRATION

- Stock of immigrants, 2013: **27.5 thousands**
- Stock of immigrants as percentage of population, 2013: **0.4 percent**
- Top source countries, 2013: El Salvador, Nicaragua, the United States, Guatemala, Mexico, Colombia, Costa Rica, Cuba, China, Spain
- Women as percentage of immigrants, 2013: **47.3 percent**
- Number of refugees, 2014: **13**

Remittances

US$ millions	2006	2007	2008	2009	2010	2011	2012	2013	2014	2015e
Inward remittance flows[a]	2,337	2,614	2,821	2,477	2,618	2,811	2,920	3,098	3,370	3,931
of which										
Compensation of employees	30	33	14	9	9	13	29	16	16	–
Personal transfers	2,307	2,581	2,807	2,468	2,609	2,798	2,892	3,083	3,353	–
Outward remittance flows	2	2	37	27	27	33	36	41	42	–
of which										
Compensation of employees	2	2	37	27	27	33	36	41	42	–
Personal transfers	–	–	–	–	–	–	–	–	–	–

a. Net FDI inflows US$1.07 billion, net ODA received US$0.63 billion in 2013.

Hong Kong SAR, China

	HIGH INCOME NON-OECD
Population (millions, 2014)	7.2
Population growth (avg. annual %, 2005–14)	0.7
Population density (people per sq km, 2014)	6,896.9
Labor force (millions, 2014)	3.7
Unemployment rate (% of labor force, 2014)	3.2
Urban population (% of pop., 2014)	100.0
Surface area (thousands of sq km, 2014)	1.1
GNI, Atlas method (current US$ billions, 2014)	292.0
GNI per capita, Atlas method (current US$, 2014)	40,320.0
GDP growth (avg. annual %, 2011–14)	3.0
Poverty headcount ratio at national poverty line (% of pop.)	–
Age dependency ratio (% of working-age pop., 2014)	35.9
Account at a formal financial institution (% age 15+, 2014)	96.1
Mobile cellular subscriptions (per 100 people, 2014)	239.3
Internet users (per 100 people, 2014)	74.6

Migration

EMIGRATION

- Stock of emigrants, 2013: **784.1 thousands**
- Stock of emigrants as percentage of population, 2013: **10.9 percent**
- Top destination countries, 2013: Canada, the United States, Australia, the United Kingdom, Singapore, Macao SAR, China, New Zealand, China, Brunei Darussalam, Thailand
- Tertiary-educated as a percentage of total emigrants in OECD countries, 2011: **55.5 percent**
- Tertiary-educated women as a percentage of total women emigrants in OECD countries, 2011: **53.5 percent**
- Number of refugees, 2014: **20**
- Second generation diaspora in Australia, Europe, and the United States, 2012: Not available

IMMIGRATION

- Stock of immigrants, 2013: **2,804.8 thousands**
- Stock of immigrants as percentage of population, 2013: **39.0 percent**
- Top source countries, 2013: China, Indonesia, the Philippines, Macao SAR, China, Thailand, India, the United Kingdom, Malaysia, Canada, Japan
- Women as percentage of immigrants, 2013: **59.2 percent**
- Number of refugees, 2014: **130**

Remittances

US$ millions	2006	2007	2008	2009	2010	2011	2012	2013	2014	2015e
Inward remittance flows[a]	294	317	355	348	340	352	367	360	372	380
of which Compensation of employees	294	317	355	348	340	352	367	360	372	–
Personal transfers	–	–	–	–	–	–	–	–	–	–
Outward remittance flows	377	388	393	413	483	554	607	656	712	–
of which Compensation of employees	377	388	393	413	483	554	607	656	712	–
Personal transfers	–	–	–	–	–	–	–	–	–	–

a. Net FDI inflows US$76.86 billion in 2013.

Hungary

Population (millions, 2014)	9.9
Population growth (avg. annual %, 2005–14)	-0.2
Population density (people per sq km, 2014)	108.9
Labor force (millions, 2014)	4.4
Unemployment rate (% of labor force, 2014)	7.8
Urban population (% of pop., 2014)	70.8
Surface area (thousands of sq km, 2014)	93.0
GNI, Atlas method (current US$ billions, 2014)	131.6
GNI per capita, Atlas method (current US$, 2014)	13,340.0
GDP growth (avg. annual %, 2011–14)	1.4
Poverty headcount ratio at national poverty line (% of pop., 2012)	14.3
Age dependency ratio (% of working-age pop., 2014)	47.2
Account at a formal financial institution (% age 15+, 2014)	72.3
Mobile cellular subscriptions (per 100 people, 2014)	118.1
Internet users (per 100 people, 2014)	76.1

Migration

EMIGRATION

- Stock of emigrants, 2013: **570.2 thousands**
- Stock of emigrants as percentage of population, 2013: **5.8 percent**
- Top destination countries, 2013: Germany, the United States, Canada, the United Kingdom, Austria, Australia, Switzerland, the Slovak Republic, the Russian Federation, Sweden
- Tertiary-educated as a percentage of total emigrants in OECD countries, 2011: **35.1 percent**
- Tertiary-educated women as a percentage of total women emigrants in OECD countries, 2011: **37.0 percent**
- Number of refugees, 2014: **1,254**
- Second generation diaspora in Australia, Europe, and the United States, 2012: **383.7 thousands**

IMMIGRATION

- Stock of immigrants, 2013: **472.8 thousands**
- Stock of immigrants as percentage of population, 2013: **4.8 percent**
- Top source countries, 2013: Romania, Germany, Ukraine, Serbia, the Slovak Republic, China, Austria, the United States, the United Kingdom, the Russian Federation
- Women as percentage of immigrants, 2013: **51.6 percent**
- Number of refugees, 2014: **2,819**

Remittances

US$ millions	2006	2007	2008	2009	2010	2011	2012	2013	2014	2015e
Inward remittance flows[a]	2,073	2,309	2,522	1,747	2,069	2,785	3,530	4,592	4,656	4,538
of which										
Compensation of employees	2,019	2,252	2,461	1,503	1,830	2,425	3,030	3,914	3,949	–
Personal transfers	54	57	61	244	239	360	500	678	707	–
Outward remittance flows	981	1,367	1,526	1,192	1,133	1,195	1,089	1,100	1,053	–
of which										
Compensation of employees	874	1,256	1,405	1,071	1,005	1,059	968	967	922	–
Personal transfers	107	111	122	121	128	136	121	133	131	–

a. Net FDI inflows US$-3.85 billion in 2013.

Iceland

HIGH INCOME OECD

Population (thousands, 2013)	327.6
Population growth (avg. annual %, 2005–14)	1.1
Population density (people per sq km, 2014)	3.3
Labor force (thousands, 2013)	192.7
Unemployment rate (% of labor force, 2014)	5.0
Urban population (% of pop., 2014)	94.0
Surface area (thousands of sq km, 2014)	103.0
GNI, Atlas method (current US$ billions, 2014)	15.0
GNI per capita, Atlas method (current US$, 2014)	46,350.0
GDP growth (avg. annual %, 2011–14)	2.2
Poverty headcount ratio at national poverty line (% of pop.)	–
Age dependency ratio (% of working-age pop., 2014)	50.9
Account at a formal financial institution (% age 15+)	–
Mobile cellular subscriptions (per 100 people, 2014)	111.1
Internet users (per 100 people, 2014)	98.2

Migration

EMIGRATION

- Stock of emigrants, 2013: **36.9 thousands**
- Stock of emigrants as percentage of population, 2013: **11.4 percent**
- Top destination countries, 2013: Denmark, Norway, Sweden, the United States, Germany, Spain, Canada, Malaysia, Australia, the Faeroe Islands
- Tertiary-educated as a percentage of total emigrants in OECD countries, 2011: **32.3 percent**
- Tertiary-educated women as a percentage of total women emigrants in OECD countries, 2011: **33.5 percent**
- Number of refugees, 2014: Not available
- Second generation diaspora in Australia, Europe, and the United States, 2012: **2.1 thousands**

IMMIGRATION

- Stock of immigrants, 2013: **35.4 thousands**
- Stock of immigrants as percentage of population, 2013: **10.9 percent**
- Top source countries, 2013: Poland, Denmark, the United States, Sweden, the Philippines, Germany, Lithuania, the United Kingdom, Thailand, Norway
- Women as percentage of immigrants, 2013: **51.5 percent**
- Number of refugees, 2014: **58**

Remittances

US$ millions	2006	2007	2008	2009	2010	2011	2012	2013	2014	2015e
Inward remittance flows[a]	80	110	120	94	135	151	157	189	206	208
of which										
Compensation of employees	73	94	100	90	128	145	152	182	196	–
Personal transfers	8	16	20	4	7	6	5	7	10	–
Outward remittance flows	82	115	101	68	67	73	68	74	102	–
of which										
Compensation of employees	68	94	55	37	37	41	36	37	61	–
Personal transfers	14	20	46	31	31	32	32	37	41	–

a. Net FDI inflows US$0.47 billion in 2013.

India

Population (millions, 2014)	1,295.3
Population growth (avg. annual %, 2005–14)	1.4
Population density (people per sq km, 2014)	435.7
Labor force (millions, 2014)	497.0
Unemployment rate (% of labor force, 2014)	3.6
Urban population (% of pop., 2014)	32.4
Surface area (thousands of sq km, 2014)	3,287.3
GNI, Atlas method (current US$ billions, 2014)	2,028.0
GNI per capita, Atlas method (current US$, 2014)	1,570.0
GDP growth (avg. annual %, 2011–14)	6.5
Poverty headcount ratio at national poverty line (% of pop., 2011)	21.9
Age dependency ratio (% of working-age pop., 2014)	53.1
Account at a formal financial institution (% age 15+, 2014)	52.8
Mobile cellular subscriptions (per 100 people, 2014)	74.5
Internet users (per 100 people, 2014)	18.0

Migration

EMIGRATION

- Stock of emigrants, 2013: **13,885.1 thousands**
- Stock of emigrants as percentage of population, 2013: **1.1 percent**
- Top destination countries, 2013: the United Arab Emirates, the United States, Saudi Arabia, Pakistan, Nepal, the United Kingdom, Kuwait, Oman, Canada, Qatar
- Tertiary-educated as a percentage of total emigrants in OECD countries, 2011: **58.7 percent**
- Tertiary-educated women as a percentage of total women emigrants in OECD countries, 2011: **55.9 percent**
- Number of refugees, 2014: **10,393**
- Second generation diaspora in Australia, Europe, and the United States, 2012: **1,023.6 thousands**

IMMIGRATION

- Stock of immigrants, 2013: **5,338.5 thousands**
- Stock of immigrants as percentage of population, 2013: **0.4 percent**
- Top source countries, 2013: Bangladesh, Pakistan, Nepal, Sri Lanka, Myanmar, Brunei Darussalam, Malaysia, the United Arab Emirates, Afghanistan, China
- Women as percentage of immigrants, 2013: **48.7 percent**
- Number of refugees, 2014: **199,916**

Remittances

US$ millions	2006	2007	2008	2009	2010	2011	2012	2013	2014	2015e
Inward										
remittance flows[a]	28,334	37,217	49,977	49,204	53,480	62,499	68,821	69,970	70,389	72,163
of which										
Compensation										
of employees	309	447	798	872	990	2,240	2,859	3,171	3,557	–
Personal transfers	28,025	36,770	49,180	48,332	52,490	60,259	65,962	66,799	66,832	–
Outward										
remittance flows	1,562	2,059	3,812	2,890	3,829	4,078	4,963	6,413	6,222	–
of which										
Compensation										
of employees	858	1,055	1,330	1,525	1,948	1,955	2,157	2,537	2,878	–
Personal transfers	704	1,004	2,482	1,365	1,881	2,123	2,806	3,876	3,344	–

a. Net FDI inflows US$28.15 billion, net ODA received US$2.44 billion in 2013.

Indonesia

MIDDLE INCOME

Population (millions, 2014)	254.5
Population growth (avg. annual %, 2005–14)	1.3
Population density (people per sq km, 2014)	140.5
Labor force (millions, 2014)	124.1
Unemployment rate (% of labor force, 2014)	6.2
Urban population (% of pop., 2014)	53.0
Surface area (thousands of sq km, 2014)	1,910.9
GNI, Atlas method (current US$ billions, 2014)	923.7
GNI per capita, Atlas method (current US$, 2014)	3,630.0
GDP growth (avg. annual %, 2011–14)	5.7
Poverty headcount ratio at national poverty line (% of pop., 2014)	11.3
Age dependency ratio (% of working-age pop., 2014)	49.5
Account at a formal financial institution (% age 15+, 2014)	35.9
Mobile cellular subscriptions (per 100 people, 2014)	126.2
Internet users (per 100 people, 2014)	17.1

Migration

EMIGRATION

- Stock of emigrants, 2013: **4,116.6 thousands**
- Stock of emigrants as percentage of population, 2013: **1.6 percent**
- Top destination countries, 2013: Saudi Arabia, Malaysia, the United Arab Emirates, Bangladesh, Singapore, the Netherlands, Hong Kong SAR, China, the United States, Kuwait, Australia
- Tertiary-educated as a percentage of total emigrants in OECD countries, 2011: **41.7 percent**
- Tertiary-educated women as a percentage of total women emigrants in OECD countries, 2011: **39.3 percent**
- Number of refugees, 2014: **14,393**
- Second generation diaspora in Australia, Europe, and the United States, 2012: **324.7 thousands**

IMMIGRATION

- Stock of immigrants, 2013: **295.4 thousands**
- Stock of immigrants as percentage of population, 2013: **0.1 percent**
- Top source countries, 2013: China, the Republic of Korea, the United Kingdom, Singapore, Timor-Leste, Thailand, Japan, the United States, Jordan, India
- Women as percentage of immigrants, 2013: **38.1 percent**
- Number of refugees, 2014: **4,262**

Remittances

US$ millions	2006	2007	2008	2009	2010	2011	2012	2013	2014	2015e
Inward remittance flows[a]	**5,722**	**6,174**	**6,794**	**6,793**	**6,916**	**6,924**	**7,212**	**7,614**	**8,551**	**10,487**
of which										
Compensation of employees	162	171	176	175	181	188	194	200	206	–
Personal transfers	5,560	6,004	6,618	6,618	6,735	6,736	7,018	7,415	8,345	–
Outward remittance flows	**1,359**	**1,654**	**1,971**	**2,702**	**2,840**	**3,164**	**3,634**	**3,951**	**4,119**	–
of which										
Compensation of employees	299	483	560	953	962	1,073	1,231	1,338	1,406	–
Personal transfers	1,060	1,171	1,412	1,748	1,877	2,091	2,402	2,613	2,713	–

a. Net FDI inflows US$23.28 billion, net ODA received US$0.05 billion in 2013.

Migration and Remittances Factbook 2016

Iran, Islamic Republic of

Population (millions, 2014)	78.1
Population growth (avg. annual %, 2005–14)	1.2
Population density (people per sq km, 2014)	48.0
Labor force (millions, 2014)	27.1
Unemployment rate (% of labor force, 2014)	12.8
Urban population (% of pop., 2014)	72.9
Surface area (thousands of sq km, 2014)	1,745.2
GNI, Atlas method (current US$ billions, 2014)	549.0
GNI per capita, Atlas method (current US$, 2014)	7,120.0
GDP growth (avg. annual %, 2011–14)	-0.1
Poverty headcount ratio at national poverty line (% of pop.)	—
Age dependency ratio (% of working-age pop., 2014)	39.8
Account at a formal financial institution (% age 15+, 2014)	92.2
Mobile cellular subscriptions (per 100 people, 2014)	87.8
Internet users (per 100 people, 2014)	39.3

Migration

EMIGRATION

- Stock of emigrants, 2013: **1,604.8 thousands**
- Stock of emigrants as percentage of population, 2013: **2.1 percent**
- Top destination countries, 2013: the United Arab Emirates, the United States, Germany, Canada, the United Kingdom, Sweden, Israel, Kuwait, Australia, Qatar
- Tertiary-educated as a percentage of total emigrants in OECD countries, 2011: **50.9 percent**
- Tertiary-educated women as a percentage of total women emigrants in OECD countries, 2011: **48.4 percent**
- Number of refugees, 2014: **82,111**
- Second generation diaspora in Australia, Europe, and the United States, 2012: **161.4 thousands**

IMMIGRATION

- Stock of immigrants, 2013: **2,649.5 thousands**
- Stock of immigrants as percentage of population, 2013: **3.4 percent**
- Top source countries, 2013: Afghanistan, Iraq, Pakistan, Azerbaijan, Turkmenistan, Armenia, Turkey
- Women as percentage of immigrants, 2013: **39.2 percent**
- Number of refugees, 2014: **982,025**

Remittances

US$ millions	2006	2007	2008	2009	2010	2011	2012	2013	2014	2015e
Inward remittance flows[a]	1,032	1,115	1,115	1,072	1,181	1,330	1,330	1,330	1,330	1,342
of which										
Compensation of employees	–	–	–	–	–	–	–	–	–	–
Personal transfers	–	–	–	–	–	–	–	–	–	–
Outward remittance flows	–	–	–	–	–	–	–	–	–	–
of which										
Compensation of employees	–	–	–	–	–	–	–	–	–	–
Personal transfers	–	–	–	–	–	–	–	–	–	–

a. Net FDI inflows US$3.05 billion, net ODA received US$0.13 billion in 2013.

Iraq

Population (millions, 2014)	34.8
Population growth (avg. annual %, 2005–14)	2.8
Population density (people per sq km, 2014)	80.2
Labor force (millions, 2014)	8.7
Unemployment rate (% of labor force, 2014)	16.4
Urban population (% of pop., 2014)	69.4
Surface area (thousands of sq km, 2014)	435.2
GNI, Atlas method (current US$ billions, 2014)	226.3
GNI per capita, Atlas method (current US$, 2014)	6,500.0
GDP growth (avg. annual %, 2011–14)	6.5
Poverty headcount ratio at national poverty line (% of pop., 2012)	18.9
Age dependency ratio (% of working-age pop., 2014)	79.2
Account at a formal financial institution (% age 15+, 2014)	11.0
Mobile cellular subscriptions (per 100 people, 2014)	94.9
Internet users (per 100 people, 2014)	11.3

Migration

EMIGRATION

- Stock of emigrants, 2013: **2,370.2 thousands**
- Stock of emigrants as percentage of population, 2013: **7.0 percent**
- Top destination countries, 2013: the Syrian Arab Republic, Jordan, the United States, Lebanon, Sweden, Germany, the Islamic Republic of Iran, the United Kingdom, Israel, Libya
- Tertiary-educated as a percentage of total emigrants in OECD countries, 2011: **26.4 percent**
- Tertiary-educated women as a percentage of total women emigrants in OECD countries, 2011: **24.4 percent**
- Number of refugees, 2014: **369,850**
- Second generation diaspora in Australia, Europe, and the United States, 2012: **48.7 thousands**

IMMIGRATION

- Stock of immigrants, 2013: **245.0 thousands**
- Stock of immigrants as percentage of population, 2013: **0.7 percent**
- Top source countries, 2013: the Syrian Arab Republic, the Islamic Republic of Iran, the West Bank and Gaza, the Arab Republic of Egypt, Turkey, Jordan, Sudan, the Republic of Yemen, Lebanon, Pakistan
- Women as percentage of immigrants, 2013: **32.4 percent**
- Number of refugees, 2014: **271,137**

Remittances

US$ millions	2006	2007	2008	2009	2010	2011	2012	2013	2014	2015e
Inward remittance flows[a]	389	3	71	152	177	223	271	271	271	277
of which										
Compensation of employees	128	1	7	15	18	22	32	–	–	–
Personal transfers	261	3	64	137	159	201	239	–	–	–
Outward remittance flows	781	17	31	27	48	78	548	–	–	–
of which										
Compensation of employees	153	2	2	1	2	4	8	–	–	–
Personal transfers	629	16	30	25	46	74	540	–	–	–

a. Net FDI inflows US$5.13 billion, net ODA received US$1.54 billion in 2013.

Ireland

Population (millions, 2014)	4.6
Population growth (avg. annual %, 2005–14)	1.3
Population density (people per sq km, 2014)	67.0
Labor force (millions, 2014)	2.2
Unemployment rate (% of labor force, 2014)	11.6
Urban population (% of pop., 2014)	63.0
Surface area (thousands of sq km, 2014)	70.3
GNI, Atlas method (current US$ billions, 2014)	214.7
GNI per capita, Atlas method (current US$, 2014)	46,550.0
GDP growth (avg. annual %, 2011–14)	2.3
Poverty headcount ratio at national poverty line (% of pop.)	—
Age dependency ratio (% of working-age pop., 2014)	52.3
Account at a formal financial institution (% age 15+, 2014)	94.7
Mobile cellular subscriptions (per 100 people, 2014)	104.3
Internet users (per 100 people, 2014)	79.7

Migration

EMIGRATION

- Stock of emigrants, 2013: **782.8 thousands**
- Stock of emigrants as percentage of population, 2013: **17.0 percent**
- Top destination countries, 2013: the United Kingdom, the United States, Australia, Canada, Spain, Germany, South Africa, France, New Zealand, Poland
- Tertiary-educated as a percentage of total emigrants in OECD countries, 2011: **34.6 percent**
- Tertiary-educated women as a percentage of total women emigrants in OECD countries, 2011: **35.7 percent**
- Number of refugees, 2014: **7**
- Second generation diaspora in Australia, Europe, and the United States, 2012: **1,375.1 thousands**

IMMIGRATION

- Stock of immigrants, 2013: **752.5 thousands**
- Stock of immigrants as percentage of population, 2013: **16.4 percent**
- Top source countries, 2013: the United Kingdom, Poland, Lithuania, the United States, Latvia, Nigeria, Romania, India, the Philippines, Germany
- Women as percentage of immigrants, 2013: **51.7 percent**
- Number of refugees, 2014: **5,797**

Remittances

US$ millions	2006	2007	2008	2009	2010	2011	2012	2013	2014	2015e
Inward remittance flows[a]	**539**	**590**	**633**	**573**	**658**	**755**	**706**	**724**	**725**	**720**
of which										
Compensation of employees	520	573	623	560	642	750	700	718	719	—
Personal transfers	19	16	10	13	16	5	5	5	5	—
Outward remittance flows	**1,853**	**2,520**	**2,672**	**2,549**	**2,267**	**2,194**	**1,996**	**1,958**	**1,960**	—
of which										
Compensation of employees	1,278	1,619	1,576	1,101	978	953	942	927	928	—
Personal transfers	575	902	1,096	1,448	1,289	1,241	1,054	1,031	1,031	—

a. Net FDI inflows US$49.96 billion in 2013.

Isle of Man

Population (thousands, 2013)	87.1
Population growth (avg. annual %, 2005–14)	0.9
Population density (people per sq km, 2014)	152.9
Labor force, total	–
Unemployment rate (% of labor force)	–
Urban population (% of pop., 2014)	52.1
Surface area (thousands of sq km, 2014)	0.6
GNI, Atlas method (current US$ billions, 2007)	4.0
GNI per capita, Atlas method (current US$, 2007)	48,300.0
GDP growth (avg. annual %, 2003–06)	6.6
Poverty headcount ratio at national poverty line (% of pop.)	–
Age dependency ratio (% of working-age pop.)	–
Account at a formal financial institution (% age 15+)	–
Mobile cellular subscriptions (per 100 people)	–
Internet users (per 100 people)	–

Migration

EMIGRATION

- Stock of emigrants, 2013: **0.9 thousands**
- Stock of emigrants as percentage of population, 2013: **1.0 percent**
- Top destination countries, 2013: Australia, Greece, Romania, the Netherlands, France, Bermuda, the Russian Federation, the Slovak Republic, República Bolivariana de Venezuela, the Plurinational State of Bolivia
- Tertiary-educated as a percentage of total emigrants in OECD countries, 2011: Not available
- Tertiary-educated women as a percentage of total women emigrants in OECD countries, 2011: Not available
- Number of refugees, 2014: Not available
- Second generation diaspora in Australia, Europe, and the United States, 2012: Not available

IMMIGRATION

- Stock of immigrants, 2013: **44.7 thousands**
- Stock of immigrants as percentage of population, 2013: **51.7 percent**
- Top source countries, 2013: the United Kingdom, Ireland, South Africa, Australia, the United States, the Channel Islands, Canada, New Zealand
- Women as percentage of immigrants, 2013: **50.4 percent**
- Number of refugees, 2014: Not available

Remittances

US$ millions	2006	2007	2008	2009	2010	2011	2012	2013	2014	2015e
Inward remittance flows	–	–	–	–	–	–	–	–	–	–
of which										
Compensation of employees	–	–	–	–	–	–	–	–	–	–
Personal transfers	–	–	–	–	–	–	–	–	–	–
Outward remittance flows	–	–	–	–	–	–	–	–	–	–
of which										
Compensation of employees	–	–	–	–	–	–	–	–	–	–
Personal transfers	–	–	–	–	–	–	–	–	–	–

Israel

HIGH INCOME OECD

Population (millions, 2014)	8.2
Population growth (avg. annual %, 2005–14)	1.9
Population density (people per sq km, 2014)	379.6
Labor force (millions, 2014)	3.7
Unemployment rate (% of labor force, 2014)	6.1
Urban population (% of pop., 2014)	92.1
Surface area (thousands of sq km, 2014)	22.1
GNI, Atlas method (current US$ billions, 2014)	290.2
GNI per capita, Atlas method (current US$, 2014)	35,320.0
GDP growth (avg. annual %, 2011–14)	3.4
Poverty headcount ratio at national poverty line (% of pop.)	
Age dependency ratio (% of working-age pop., 2014)	63.4
Account at a formal financial institution (% age 15+, 2014)	90.0
Mobile cellular subscriptions (per 100 people, 2014)	121.5
Internet users (per 100 people, 2014)	71.4

Migration

EMIGRATION

- Stock of emigrants, 2013: **367.3 thousands**
- Stock of emigrants as percentage of population, 2013: **4.6 percent**
- Top destination countries, 2013: the United States, the West Bank and Gaza, Germany, Canada, the United Kingdom, Australia, France, the Netherlands, Italy, Turkey
- Tertiary-educated as a percentage of total emigrants in OECD countries, 2011: **42.8 percent**
- Tertiary-educated women as a percentage of total women emigrants in OECD countries, 2011: **44.2 percent**
- Number of refugees, 2014: **952**
- Second generation diaspora in Australia, Europe, and the United States, 2012: **144.3 thousands**

IMMIGRATION

- Stock of immigrants, 2013: **2,049.1 thousands**
- Stock of immigrants as percentage of population, 2013: **25.4 percent**
- Top source countries, 2013: Morocco, Ukraine, the Russian Federation, Romania, Ethiopia, the United States, Iraq, Poland, the Islamic Republic of Iran, Algeria
- Women as percentage of immigrants, 2013: **54.6 percent**
- Number of refugees, 2014: **39,678**

Remittances

US$ millions	2006	2007	2008	2009	2010	2011	2012	2013	2014	2015e
Inward remittance flows[a]	**489**	**580**	**628**	**507**	**572**	**595**	**685**	**765**	**859**	**863**
of which										
Compensation of employees	489	580	628	507	572	595	685	765	859	–
Personal transfers	–	–	–	–	–	–	–	–	–	–
Outward remittance flows	**2,335**	**2,798**	**3,636**	**3,421**	**3,727**	**4,344**	**4,326**	**5,039**	**5,155**	–
of which										
Compensation of employees	2,335	2,798	3,636	3,421	3,727	4,344	4,326	5,039	5,155	–
Personal transfers	–	–	–	–	–	–	–	–	–	–

a. Net FDI inflows US$12.45 billion in 2013.

Italy

Population (millions, 2014)	61.3
Population growth (avg. annual %, 2005–14)	0.6
Population density (people per sq km, 2014)	208.5
Labor force (millions, 2014)	26.0
Unemployment rate (% of labor force, 2014)	12.5
Urban population (% of pop., 2014)	68.8
Surface area (thousands of sq km, 2014)	301.3
GNI, Atlas method (current US$ billions, 2014)	2,102.2
GNI per capita, Atlas method (current US$, 2014)	34,270.0
GDP growth (avg. annual %, 2011–14)	-1.1
Poverty headcount ratio at national poverty line (% of pop.)	—
Age dependency ratio (% of working-age pop., 2014)	55.8
Account at a formal financial institution (% age 15+, 2014)	87.3
Mobile cellular subscriptions (per 100 people, 2014)	154.2
Internet users (per 100 people, 2014)	62.0

Migration

EMIGRATION

- Stock of emigrants, 2013: **2,928.8 thousands**
- Stock of emigrants as percentage of population, 2013: **4.9 percent**
- Top destination countries, 2013: Germany, the United States, France, Canada, Switzerland, Australia, Argentina, the United Kingdom, Belgium, Spain
- Tertiary-educated as a percentage of total emigrants in OECD countries, 2011: **17.9 percent**
- Tertiary-educated women as a percentage of total women emigrants in OECD countries, 2011: **16.2 percent**
- Number of refugees, 2014: **58**
- Second generation diaspora in Australia, Europe, and the United States, 2012: **3,260.8 thousands**

IMMIGRATION

- Stock of immigrants, 2013: **5,766.2 thousands**
- Stock of immigrants as percentage of population, 2013: **9.6 percent**
- Top source countries, 2013: Romania, Albania, Morocco, Germany, Ukraine, Switzerland, China, Moldova, France, the Philippines
- Women as percentage of immigrants, 2013: **53.5 percent**
- Number of refugees, 2014: **93,662**

Remittances

US$ millions	2006	2007	2008	2009	2010	2011	2012	2013	2014	2015e
Inward remittance flows[a]	**2,556**	**3,063**	**7,355**	**7,036**	**7,977**	**8,726**	**9,169**	**9,328**	**9,982**	**9,872**
of which										
Compensation of employees	2,244	2,717	4,919	4,646	5,774	6,360	6,701	6,652	7,256	—
Personal transfers	312	346	2,436	2,389	2,204	2,366	2,468	2,676	2,726	—
Outward remittance flows	**8,352**	**11,182**	**14,445**	**14,390**	**12,886**	**14,501**	**11,826**	**11,629**	**11,154**	—
of which										
Compensation of employees	2,649	2,860	3,695	3,437	2,866	2,726	1,975	2,685	2,508	—
Personal transfers	5,703	8,322	10,750	10,953	10,020	11,775	9,851	8,944	8,646	—

a. Net FDI inflows US$19.53 billion in 2013.

Jamaica

Population (millions, 2014)	2.7
Population growth (avg. annual %, 2005–14)	0.3
Population density (people per sq km, 2014)	251.3
Labor force (millions, 2014)	1.3
Unemployment rate (% of labor force, 2014)	13.2
Urban population (% of pop., 2014)	54.6
Surface area (thousands of sq km, 2014)	11.0
GNI, Atlas method (current US$ billions, 2014)	14.0
GNI per capita, Atlas method (current US$, 2014)	5,150.0
GDP growth (avg. annual %, 2011–14)	0.6
Poverty headcount ratio at national poverty line (% of pop., 2012)	19.9
Age dependency ratio (% of working-age pop., 2014)	49.5
Account at a formal financial institution (% age 15+, 2014)	78.3
Mobile cellular subscriptions (per 100 people, 2014)	102.9
Internet users (per 100 people, 2014)	40.5

Migration

EMIGRATION

- Stock of emigrants, 2013: **1,097.6 thousands**
- Stock of emigrants as percentage of population, 2013: **40.4 percent**
- Top destination countries, 2013: the United States, the United Kingdom, Canada, the Cayman Islands, The Bahamas, Antigua and Barbuda, Sint Maarten (Dutch part), Germany, Bermuda, Curaçao
- Tertiary-educated as a percentage of total emigrants in OECD countries, 2011: **30.4 percent**
- Tertiary-educated women as a percentage of total women emigrants in OECD countries, 2011: **34.7 percent**
- Number of refugees, 2014: **1,682**
- Second generation diaspora in Australia, Europe, and the United States, 2012: **444.6 thousands**

IMMIGRATION

- Stock of immigrants, 2013: **34.9 thousands**
- Stock of immigrants as percentage of population, 2013: **1.3 percent**
- Top source countries, 2013: the United States, the United Kingdom, Trinidad and Tobago, Cuba, Canada, India, The Bahamas, Barbados, St. Lucia, Guatemala
- Women as percentage of immigrants, 2013: **48.1 percent**
- Number of refugees, 2014: **18**

Remittances

US$ millions	2006	2007	2008	2009	2010	2011	2012	2013	2014	2015e
Inward remittance flows[a]	1,924	2,122	2,157	1,889	2,026	2,106	2,167	2,172	2,269	2,320
of which										
Compensation of employees	154	158	135	99	120	81	124	107	112	–
Personal transfers	1,769	1,964	2,021	1,790	1,906	2,025	2,042	2,065	2,157	–
Outward remittance flows	358	396	365	269	279	305	334	297	271	–
of which										
Compensation of employees	58	93	51	32	31	44	66	57	44	–
Personal transfers	300	303	313	237	248	261	267	241	227	–

a. Net FDI inflows US$0.59 billion, net ODA received US$0.07 billion in 2013.

Japan

Population (millions, 2014)	127.1
Population growth (avg. annual %, 2005–14)	0.0
Population density (people per sq km, 2014)	348.7
Labor force (millions, 2014)	65.3
Unemployment rate (% of labor force, 2014)	3.7
Urban population (% of pop., 2014)	93.0
Surface area (thousands of sq km, 2014)	378.0
GNI, Atlas method (current US$ billions, 2014)	5,339.1
GNI per capita, Atlas method (current US$, 2014)	42,000.0
GDP growth (avg. annual %, 2011–14)	0.7
Poverty headcount ratio at national poverty line (% of pop.)	–
Age dependency ratio (% of working-age pop., 2014)	63.0
Account at a formal financial institution (% age 15+, 2014)	96.6
Mobile cellular subscriptions (per 100 people, 2014)	120.2
Internet users (per 100 people, 2014)	90.6

Migration

EMIGRATION

- Stock of emigrants, 2013: **1,012.9 thousands**
- Stock of emigrants as percentage of population, 2013: **0.8 percent**
- Top destination countries, 2013: the United States, Brunei Darussalam, Thailand, China, Australia, Brazil, the United Kingdom, Canada, the Republic of Korea, Germany
- Tertiary-educated as a percentage of total emigrants in OECD countries, 2011: **49.0 percent**
- Tertiary-educated women as a percentage of total women emigrants in OECD countries, 2011: **49.3 percent**
- Number of refugees, 2014: **257**
- Second generation diaspora in Australia, Europe, and the United States, 2012: **340.7 thousands**

IMMIGRATION

- Stock of immigrants, 2013: **2,437.3 thousands**
- Stock of immigrants as percentage of population, 2013: **1.9 percent**
- Top source countries, 2013: the Republic of Korea, China, Brazil, the Philippines, Peru, the United States, Thailand, Vietnam, Indonesia, India
- Women as percentage of immigrants, 2013: **55.3 percent**
- Number of refugees, 2014: **2,552**

Remittances

US$ millions	2006	2007	2008	2009	2010	2011	2012	2013	2014	2015e
Inward remittance flows[a]	1,177	1,384	1,732	1,595	1,684	2,132	2,540	2,364	3,733	4,509
of which										
Compensation of employees	151	123	177	171	175	190	212	124	181	–
Personal transfers	1,026	1,261	1,556	1,423	1,510	1,942	2,327	2,240	3,552	–
Outward remittance flows	3,332	3,639	4,548	3,932	4,366	4,536	4,043	2,872	4,215	–
of which										
Compensation of employees	180	184	201	209	226	265	279	172	219	–
Personal transfers	3,152	3,456	4,347	3,723	4,140	4,271	3,763	2,700	3,996	–

a. Net FDI inflows US$7.41 billion in 2013.

Jordan

Population (millions, 2014)	6.6
Population growth (avg. annual %, 2005–14)	2.2
Population density (people per sq km, 2014)	74.4
Labor force (millions, 2014)	1.8
Unemployment rate (% of labor force, 2014)	11.1
Urban population (% of pop., 2014)	83.4
Surface area (thousands of sq km, 2014)	89.3
GNI, Atlas method (current US$ billions, 2014)	34.1
GNI per capita, Atlas method (current US$, 2014)	5,160.0
GDP growth (avg. annual %, 2011–14)	2.8
Poverty headcount ratio at national poverty line (% of pop., 2010)	14.4
Age dependency ratio (% of working-age pop., 2014)	65.6
Account at a formal financial institution (% age 15+, 2014)	24.6
Mobile cellular subscriptions (per 100 people, 2014)	147.8
Internet users (per 100 people, 2014)	44.0

Migration

EMIGRATION

- Stock of emigrants, 2013: **782.0 thousands**
- Stock of emigrants as percentage of population, 2013: **12.1 percent**
- Top destination countries, 2013: Saudi Arabia, the United Arab Emirates, the United States, the West Bank and Gaza, Kuwait, Qatar, Libya, Germany, Bahrain, Indonesia
- Tertiary-educated as a percentage of total emigrants in OECD countries, 2011: **41.1 percent**
- Tertiary-educated women as a percentage of total women emigrants in OECD countries, 2011: **37.9 percent**
- Number of refugees, 2014: **1,679**
- Second generation diaspora in Australia, Europe, and the United States, 2012: **51.0 thousands**

IMMIGRATION

- Stock of immigrants, 2013: **3,592.8 thousands**
- Stock of immigrants as percentage of population, 2013: **55.6 percent**
- Top source countries, 2013: the West Bank and Gaza, the Syrian Arab Republic, Iraq, the Arab Republic of Egypt, Sri Lanka, Bangladesh, Indonesia, China, India, Saudi Arabia
- Women as percentage of immigrants, 2013: **47.9 percent**
- Number of refugees, 2014: **2,771,477**

Remittances

US$ millions	2006	2007	2008	2009	2010	2011	2012	2013	2014	2015e
Inward remittance flows[a]	2,794	3,326	3,510	3,465	3,517	3,368	3,490	3,643	3,701	3,776
of which										
Compensation of employees	280	333	351	347	352	337	349	364	–	–
Personal transfers	2,514	2,994	3,159	3,119	3,165	3,031	3,141	3,278	–	–
Outward remittance flows	402	479	472	502	495	439	460	457	–	–
of which										
Compensation of employees	47	57	56	59	58	52	54	54	–	–
Personal transfers	354	423	416	443	436	388	405	403	–	–

a. Net FDI inflows US$1.75 billion, net ODA received US$1.41 billion in 2013.

Kazakhstan

Population (millions, 2014)	17.3
Population growth (avg. annual %, 2005–14)	1.4
Population density (people per sq km, 2014)	6.4
Labor force (millions, 2014)	9.3
Unemployment rate (% of labor force, 2014)	4.1
Urban population (% of pop., 2014)	53.3
Surface area (thousands of sq km, 2014)	2,724.9
GNI, Atlas method (current US$ billions, 2014)	204.8
GNI per capita, Atlas method (current US$, 2014)	11,850.0
GDP growth (avg. annual %, 2011–14)	5.7
Poverty headcount ratio at national poverty line (% of pop., 2013)	2.9
Age dependency ratio (% of working-age pop., 2014)	48.9
Account at a formal financial institution (% age 15+, 2014)	53.9
Mobile cellular subscriptions (per 100 people, 2014)	168.6
Internet users (per 100 people, 2014)	54.9

Migration

EMIGRATION

- Stock of emigrants, 2013: **3,827.0 thousands**
- Stock of emigrants as percentage of population, 2013: **22.5 percent**
- Top destination countries, 2013: the Russian Federation, Germany, Ukraine, Uzbekistan, Belarus, the United States, Azerbaijan, Moldova, the Kyrgyz Republic, Turkmenistan
- Tertiary-educated as a percentage of total emigrants in OECD countries, 2011: **14.9 percent**
- Tertiary-educated women as a percentage of total women emigrants in OECD countries, 2011: **16.3 percent**
- Number of refugees, 2014: **2,187**
- Second generation diaspora in Australia, Europe, and the United States, 2012: **27.8 thousands**

IMMIGRATION

- Stock of immigrants, 2013: **3,476.2 thousands**
- Stock of immigrants as percentage of population, 2013: **20.4 percent**
- Top source countries, 2013: the Russian Federation, Uzbekistan, Ukraine, the Democratic Republic of Korea, Germany, Turkey, Belarus, Azerbaijan, Tajikistan, Poland
- Women as percentage of immigrants, 2013: **50.7 percent**
- Number of refugees, 2014: **628**

Remittances

US$ millions	2006	2007	2008	2009	2010	2011	2012	2013	2014	2015e
Inward remittance flows[a]	**84**	**143**	**126**	**198**	**226**	**180**	**178**	**207**	**229**	**182**
of which										
Compensation of employees	11	11	5	5	5	4	4	4	4	–
Personal transfers	73	132	120	193	221	176	174	203	225	–
Outward remittance flows	**2,958**	**4,212**	**3,462**	**2,934**	**3,006**	**3,409**	**3,809**	**3,804**	**3,558**	**–**
of which										
Compensation of employees	959	1,214	1,457	1,310	1,411	1,734	1,932	1,808	1,797	–
Personal transfers	2,000	2,998	2,004	1,624	1,595	1,675	1,877	1,996	1,761	–

a. Net FDI inflows US$9.95 billion, net ODA received US$0.09 billion in 2013.

Kenya

MIDDLE INCOME

Population (millions, 2014)	44.9
Population growth (avg. annual %, 2005–14)	2.6
Population density (people per sq km, 2014)	78.8
Labor force (millions, 2014)	17.5
Unemployment rate (% of labor force, 2014)	9.2
Urban population (% of pop., 2014)	25.2
Surface area (thousands of sq km, 2014)	580.4
GNI, Atlas method (current US$ billions, 2014)	58.1
GNI per capita, Atlas method (current US$, 2014)	1,290.0
GDP growth (avg. annual %, 2011–14)	5.4
Poverty headcount ratio at national poverty line (% of pop., 2005)	45.9
Age dependency ratio (% of working-age pop., 2014)	81.4
Account at a formal financial institution (% age 15+, 2014)	55.2
Mobile cellular subscriptions (per 100 people, 2014)	73.8
Internet users (per 100 people, 2014)	43.4

Migration

EMIGRATION

- Stock of emigrants, 2013: **475.5 thousands**
- Stock of emigrants as percentage of population, 2013: **1.1 percent**
- Top destination countries, 2013: the United Kingdom, the United States, Tanzania, Uganda, Canada, South Africa, Australia, Germany, South Sudan, Switzerland
- Tertiary-educated as a percentage of total emigrants in OECD countries, 2011: **42.7 percent**
- Tertiary-educated women as a percentage of total women emigrants in OECD countries, 2011: **40.2 percent**
- Number of refugees, 2014: **8,529**
- Second generation diaspora in Australia, Europe, and the United States, 2012: **124.1 thousands**

IMMIGRATION

- Stock of immigrants, 2013: **892.7 thousands**
- Stock of immigrants as percentage of population, 2013: **2.0 percent**
- Top source countries, 2013: Somalia, Tanzania, Uganda, Sudan, India, Ethiopia, South Sudan, the United Kingdom, Cameroon, the Democratic Republic of Congo
- Women as percentage of immigrants, 2013: **44.9 percent**
- Number of refugees, 2014: **551,336**

Remittances

US$ millions	2006	2007	2008	2009	2010	2011	2012	2013	2014	2015e
Inward remittance flows[a]	570	645	667	631	686	934	1,211	1,304	1,441	1,565
of which										
Compensation of employees	–	–	–	–	–	–	–	–	–	–
Personal transfers	570	645	667	631	686	934	1,211	1,304	1,441	–
Outward remittance flows	25	16	64	61	19	26	15	16	171	–
of which										
Compensation of employees	–	–	–	–	–	–	–	–	–	–
Personal transfers	25	16	64	61	19	26	15	16	171	–

a. Net FDI inflows US$0.37 billion, net ODA received US$3.24 billion in 2013.

Kiribati

Population (thousands, 2013)	110.5
Population growth (avg. annual %, 2005–14)	2.0
Population density (people per sq km, 2014)	136.4
Labor force, total	–
Unemployment rate (% of labor force)	–
Urban population (% of pop., 2014)	44.2
Surface area (thousands of sq km, 2014)	0.8
GNI, Atlas method (current US$ billions, 2014)	0.3
GNI per capita, Atlas method (current US$, 2014)	2,950.0
GDP growth (avg. annual %, 2011–14)	3.1
Poverty headcount ratio at national poverty line (% of pop.)	–
Age dependency ratio (% of working-age pop., 2014)	63.0
Account at a formal financial institution (% age 15+)	–
Mobile cellular subscriptions (per 100 people, 2014)	17.4
Internet users (per 100 people, 2014)	12.3

Migration

EMIGRATION

- Stock of emigrants, 2013: **5.4 thousands**
- Stock of emigrants as percentage of population, 2013: **4.9 percent**
- Top destination countries, 2013: the United States, New Zealand, Australia, the Marshall Islands, Brazil, Tuvalu, Vanuatu, Samoa, France, Switzerland
- Tertiary-educated as a percentage of total emigrants in OECD countries, 2011: **17.5 percent**
- Tertiary-educated women as a percentage of total women emigrants in OECD countries, 2011: **16.8 percent**
- Number of refugees, 2014: Not available
- Second generation diaspora in Australia, Europe, and the United States, 2012: Not available

IMMIGRATION

- Stock of immigrants, 2013: **4.2 thousands**
- Stock of immigrants as percentage of population, 2013: **3.9 percent**
- Top source countries, 2013: Tuvalu, Fiji, the United States, Australia, New Zealand, the United Kingdom
- Women as percentage of immigrants, 2013: **51.9 percent**
- Number of refugees, 2014: Not available

Remittances

US$ millions	2006	2007	2008	2009	2010	2011	2012	2013	2014	2015e
Inward remittance flows[a]	12	13	13	13	15	16	17	17	16	16
of which										
Compensation of employees	9	10	10	10	11	12	12	12	11	–
Personal transfers	3	3	3	3	4	5	5	5	5	–
Outward remittance flows	0	1	1	1	1	1	1	1	1	–
of which										
Compensation of employees	–	–	–	–	–	–	–	–	–	–
Personal transfers	0	1	1	1	1	1	1	1	1	–

a. Net FDI inflows US$0.00 billion, net ODA received US$0.06 billion in 2013.

Korea, Democratic Republic of

Population (millions, 2014)	25.0
Population growth (avg. annual %, 2005–14)	0.6
Population density (people per sq km, 2014)	207.8
Labor force (millions, 2014)	15.3
Unemployment rate (% of labor force, 2014)	4.1
Urban population (% of pop., 2014)	60.7
Surface area (thousands of sq km, 2014)	120.5
GNI, Atlas method (current US$ billions)	–
GNI per capita, Atlas method (current US$)	–
GDP growth (avg. annual %)	–
Poverty headcount ratio at national poverty line (% of pop.)	–
Age dependency ratio (% of working-age pop., 2014)	44.9
Account at a formal financial institution (% age 15+)	–
Mobile cellular subscriptions (per 100 people, 2014)	11.2
Internet users (per 100 people, 2014)	–

Migration

EMIGRATION

- Stock of emigrants, 2013: **223.7 thousands**
- Stock of emigrants as percentage of population, 2013: **0.9 percent**
- Top destination countries, 2013: Kazakhstan, Armenia, Uzbekistan, the Russian Federation, the Philippines, Argentina, China, Azerbaijan, Austria, Germany
- Tertiary-educated as a percentage of total emigrants in OECD countries, 2011: Not available
- Tertiary-educated women as a percentage of total women emigrants in OECD countries, 2011: Not available
- Number of refugees, 2014: **1,270**
- Second generation diaspora in Australia, Europe, and the United States, 2012: Not available

IMMIGRATION

- Stock of immigrants, 2013: **46.8 thousands**
- Stock of immigrants as percentage of population, 2013: **0.2 percent**
- Top source countries, 2013: China, the Republic of Korea, the Philippines, Brazil, Indonesia, the United States, Vietnam, Thailand, Peru, India
- Women as percentage of immigrants, 2013: **50.4 percent**
- Number of refugees, 2014: Not available

Remittances

US$ millions	2006	2007	2008	2009	2010	2011	2012	2013	2014	2015e
Inward remittance flows[a]	–	–	–	–	–	–	–	–	–	–
of which										
Compensation of employees	–	–	–	–	–	–	–	–	–	–
Personal transfers	–	–	–	–	–	–	–	–	–	–
Outward remittance flows	–	–	–	–	–	–	–	–	–	–
of which										
Compensation of employees	–	–	–	–	–	–	–	–	–	–
Personal transfers	–	–	–	–	–	–	–	–	–	–

a. Net FDI inflows US$0.23 billion, net ODA received US$0.11 billion in 2013.

Korea, Republic of

	HIGH INCOME OECD
Population (millions, 2014)	50.4
Population growth (avg. annual %, 2005–14)	0.5
Population density (people per sq km, 2014)	517.3
Labor force (millions, 2014)	26.4
Unemployment rate (% of labor force, 2014)	3.5
Urban population (% of pop., 2014)	82.4
Surface area (thousands of sq km, 2014)	100.3
GNI, Atlas method (current US$ billions, 2014)	1,365.8
GNI per capita, Atlas method (current US$, 2014)	27,090.0
GDP growth (avg. annual %, 2011–14)	3.0
Poverty headcount ratio at national poverty line (% of pop.)	—
Age dependency ratio (% of working-age pop., 2014)	37.0
Account at a formal financial institution (% age 15+, 2014)	94.4
Mobile cellular subscriptions (per 100 people, 2014)	115.5
Internet users (per 100 people, 2014)	84.3

Migration

EMIGRATION

- Stock of emigrants, 2013: **2,604.9 thousands**
- Stock of emigrants as percentage of population, 2013: **5.2 percent**
- Top destination countries, 2013: the United States, Japan, China, Canada, Australia, Germany, Indonesia, New Zealand, the United Kingdom, France
- Tertiary-educated as a percentage of total emigrants in OECD countries, 2011: Not available
- Tertiary-educated women as a percentage of total women emigrants in OECD countries, 2011: Not available
- Number of refugees, 2014: **468**
- Second generation diaspora in Australia, Europe, and the United States, 2012: **44.8 thousands**

IMMIGRATION

- Stock of immigrants, 2013: **1,232.2 thousands**
- Stock of immigrants as percentage of population, 2013: **2.5 percent**
- Top source countries, 2013: China, Vietnam, the United States, the Philippines, Thailand, Indonesia, Mongolia, Uzbekistan, Japan, Sri Lanka
- Women as percentage of immigrants, 2013: **44.1 percent**
- Number of refugees, 2014: **1,149**

Remittances

US$ millions	2006	2007	2008	2009	2010	2011	2012	2013	2014	2015e
Inward remittance flows[a]	4,826	5,130	6,952	5,982	5,836	6,582	6,571	6,455	6,481	6,589
of which										
Compensation of employees	685	692	745	594	711	751	711	721	805	—
Personal transfers	4,141	4,438	6,208	5,388	5,125	5,831	5,860	5,734	5,677	—
Outward remittance flows	7,215	7,723	7,545	7,153	9,123	9,586	9,380	8,991	9,549	—
of which										
Compensation of employees	141	186	556	647	1,078	1,183	1,150	1,169	1,219	—
Personal transfers	7,074	7,537	6,990	6,505	8,045	8,403	8,230	7,822	8,331	—

a. Net FDI inflows US$12.77 billion in 2013.

Kosovo

	MIDDLE INCOME
Population (millions, 2014)	1.8
Population growth (avg. annual %, 2005–14)	0.7
Population density (people per sq km, 2014)	167.5
Labor force, total	–
Unemployment rate (% of labor force)	–
Urban population (% of pop.)	–
Surface area (thousands of sq km, 2014)	10.9
GNI, Atlas method (current US$ billions, 2014)	7.3
GNI per capita, Atlas method (current US$, 2014)	3,990.0
GDP growth (avg. annual %, 2011–14)	3.0
Poverty headcount ratio at national poverty line (% of pop., 2011)	29.7
Age dependency ratio (% of working-age pop., 2010)	51.9
Account at a formal financial institution (% age 15+, 2014)	47.8
Mobile cellular subscriptions (per 100 people)	–
Internet users (per 100 people)	–

Migration

EMIGRATION

- Stock of emigrants, 2013: **550.0 thousands**
- Stock of emigrants as percentage of population, 2013: **30.3 percent**
- Top destination countries, 2013: Germany, Switzerland, Italy, Slovenia, Austria, the United States, France, Sweden, the United Kingdom, Belgium
- Tertiary-educated as a percentage of total emigrants in OECD countries, 2011: **5.2 percent**
- Tertiary-educated women as a percentage of total women emigrants in OECD countries, 2011: **4.3 percent**
- Number of refugees, 2014: Not available
- Second generation diaspora in Australia, Europe, and the United States, 2012: Not available

IMMIGRATION

- Stock of immigrants, 2013: Not available
- Stock of immigrants as percentage of population, 2013: Not available
- Top source countries, 2013: Not available
- Women as percentage of immigrants, 2013: Not available
- Number of refugees, 2014: Not available

Remittances

US$ millions	2006	2007	2008	2009	2010	2011	2012	2013	2014	2015e
Inward remittance flows[a]	**771**	**919**	**1,042**	**1,055**	**997**	**1,122**	**1,059**	**1,122**	**1,192**	**1,152**
of which										
Compensation of employees	185	213	258	236	234	308	283	297	274	–
Personal transfers	586	706	784	819	763	814	776	825	918	–
Outward remittance flows	**120**	**96**	**127**	**156**	**127**	**151**	**118**	**97**	**100**	**–**
of which										
Compensation of employees	1	1	1	1	6	18	7	6	8	–
Personal transfers	119	95	125	154	121	133	111	91	92	–

a. Net FDI inflows US$0.34 billion, net ODA received US$0.53 billion in 2013.

Kuwait

Population (millions, 2014)	3.8
Population growth (avg. annual %, 2005–14)	5.5
Population density (people per sq km, 2014)	210.6
Labor force (millions, 2014)	2.0
Unemployment rate (% of labor force, 2014)	3.0
Urban population (% of pop., 2014)	98.3
Surface area (thousands of sq km, 2014)	17.8
GNI, Atlas method (current US$ billions, 2014)	185.0
GNI per capita, Atlas method (current US$, 2014)	49,300.0
GDP growth (avg. annual %, 2011–14)	3.9
Poverty headcount ratio at national poverty line (% of pop.)	–
Age dependency ratio (% of working-age pop., 2014)	32.3
Account at a formal financial institution (% age 15+, 2014)	72.9
Mobile cellular subscriptions (per 100 people, 2014)	218.4
Internet users (per 100 people, 2014)	78.7

Migration

EMIGRATION

- Stock of emigrants, 2013: **322.8 thousands**
- Stock of emigrants as percentage of population, 2013: **9.0 percent**
- Top destination countries, 2013: Saudi Arabia, the United Arab Emirates, the United States, the West Bank and Gaza, the United Kingdom, Canada, Qatar, Libya, India, Bahrain
- Tertiary-educated as a percentage of total emigrants in OECD countries, 2011: **48.8 percent**
- Tertiary-educated women as a percentage of total women emigrants in OECD countries, 2011: **48.6 percent**
- Number of refugees, 2014: **982**
- Second generation diaspora in Australia, Europe, and the United States, 2012: **9.3 thousands**

IMMIGRATION

- Stock of immigrants, 2013: **2,592.8 thousands**
- Stock of immigrants as percentage of population, 2013: **72.1 percent**
- Top source countries, 2013: India, the Arab Republic of Egypt, Bangladesh, Pakistan, the Philippines, the Syrian Arab Republic, Indonesia, Nepal, the Republic of Yemen, the Islamic Republic of Iran
- Women as percentage of immigrants, 2013: **30.6 percent**
- Number of refugees, 2014: **606**

Remittances

US$ millions	2006	2007	2008	2009	2010	2011	2012	2013	2014	2015e
Inward remittance flows[a]	–	–	–	–	5	6	3	4	4	4
of which										
Compensation of employees	–	–	–	–	5	6	3	4	4	–
Personal transfers	–	–	–	–	–	–	–	–	–	–
Outward remittance flows	3,183	9,764	10,323	11,749	11,864	13,012	15,459	17,711	18,129	–
of which										
Compensation of employees	–	–	–	100	142	162	139	132	179	–
Personal transfers	3,183	9,764	10,323	11,649	11,722	12,851	15,320	17,580	17,950	–

a. Net FDI inflows US$1.43 billion in 2013.

Kyrgyz Republic

MIDDLE INCOME

Population (millions, 2014)	5.8
Population growth (avg. annual %, 2005–14)	1.3
Population density (people per sq km, 2014)	30.4
Labor force (millions, 2014)	2.7
Unemployment rate (% of labor force, 2014)	8.1
Urban population (% of pop., 2014)	35.6
Surface area (thousands of sq km, 2014)	199.9
GNI, Atlas method (current US$ billions, 2014)	7.3
GNI per capita, Atlas method (current US$, 2014)	1,250.0
GDP growth (avg. annual %, 2011–14)	5.1
Poverty headcount ratio at national poverty line (% of pop., 2013)	37.0
Age dependency ratio (% of working-age pop., 2014)	54.5
Account at a formal financial institution (% age 15+, 2014)	18.5
Mobile cellular subscriptions (per 100 people, 2014)	134.5
Internet users (per 100 people, 2014)	28.3

Migration

EMIGRATION

- Stock of emigrants, 2013: **738.3 thousands**
- Stock of emigrants as percentage of population, 2013: **12.9 percent**
- Top destination countries, 2013: the Russian Federation, Germany, Ukraine, Uzbekistan, Tajikistan, Kazakhstan, Belarus, Turkey, the United States, Azerbaijan
- Tertiary-educated as a percentage of total emigrants in OECD countries, 2011: **46.6 percent**
- Tertiary-educated women as a percentage of total women emigrants in OECD countries, 2011: **52.9 percent**
- Number of refugees, 2014: **2,410**
- Second generation diaspora in Australia, Europe, and the United States, 2012: **0.5 thousands**

IMMIGRATION

- Stock of immigrants, 2013: **227.0 thousands**
- Stock of immigrants as percentage of population, 2013: **4.0 percent**
- Top source countries, 2013: the Russian Federation, Ukraine, Kazakhstan, Belarus, Uzbekistan, Azerbaijan, Georgia, Poland, Moldova, Lithuania
- Women as percentage of immigrants, 2013: **54.7 percent**
- Number of refugees, 2014: **479**

Remittances

US$ millions	2006	2007	2008	2009	2010	2011	2012	2013	2014	2015e
Inward remittance flows[a]	473	704	1,223	982	1,266	1,709	2,031	2,278	2,243	1,740
of which										
Compensation of employees	–	–	–	–	–	–	–	–	–	–
Personal transfers	473	704	1,223	982	1,266	1,709	2,031	2,278	2,243	–
Outward remittance flows	68	90	101	107	168	228	286	390	455	–
of which										
Compensation of employees	24	21	24	26	32	29	29	22	24	–
Personal transfers	44	70	76	82	135	198	257	368	431	–

a. Net FDI inflows US$0.76 billion, net ODA received US$0.54 billion in 2013.

Lao People's Democratic Republic

MIDDLE INCOME

Population (millions, 2014)	6.7
Population growth (avg. annual %, 2005–14)	1.7
Population density (people per sq km, 2014)	29.0
Labor force (millions, 2014)	3.4
Unemployment rate (% of labor force, 2014)	1.4
Urban population (% of pop., 2014)	37.6
Surface area (thousands of sq km, 2014)	236.8
GNI, Atlas method (current US$ billions, 2014)	11.1
GNI per capita, Atlas method (current US$, 2014)	1,660.0
GDP growth (avg. annual %, 2011–14)	8.0
Poverty headcount ratio at national poverty line (% of pop., 2012)	23.2
Age dependency ratio (% of working-age pop., 2014)	63.6
Account at a formal financial institution (% age 15+)	–
Mobile cellular subscriptions (per 100 people, 2014)	67.0
Internet users (per 100 people, 2014)	14.3

Migration

EMIGRATION

- Stock of emigrants, 2013: **1,294.2 thousands**
- Stock of emigrants as percentage of population, 2013: **19.7 percent**
- Top destination countries, 2013: Thailand, the United States, Bangladesh, France, Canada, Australia, Vietnam, China, Germany, Switzerland
- Tertiary-educated as a percentage of total emigrants in OECD countries, 2011: **19.5 percent**
- Tertiary-educated women as a percentage of total women emigrants in OECD countries, 2011: **17.6 percent**
- Number of refugees, 2014: **7,471**
- Second generation diaspora in Australia, Europe, and the United States, 2012: **203.5 thousands**

IMMIGRATION

- Stock of immigrants, 2013: **21.8 thousands**
- Stock of immigrants as percentage of population, 2013: **0.3 percent**
- Top source countries, 2013: Vietnam, China, Thailand, Cambodia, Myanmar, Australia
- Women as percentage of immigrants, 2013: **45.7 percent**
- Number of refugees, 2014: Not available

Remittances

US$ millions	2006	2007	2008	2009	2010	2011	2012	2013	2014	2015e
Inward remittance flows[a]	4	6	18	38	42	110	59	60	60	68
of which										
Compensation of employees	4	6	12	28	35	30	42	56	–	–
Personal transfers	–	–	6	10	7	80	17	3	–	–
Outward remittance flows	5	6	9	22	19	76	70	69	–	–
of which										
Compensation of employees	5	6	6	8	14	34	64	67	–	–
Personal transfers	–	–	4	14	6	41	6	2	–	–

a. Net FDI inflows US$0.43 billion, net ODA received US$0.42 billion in 2013.

Latvia

Population (millions, 2014)	2.0
Population growth (avg. annual %, 2005–14)	-1.3
Population density (people per sq km, 2014)	32.0
Labor force (millions, 2014)	1.0
Unemployment rate (% of labor force, 2014)	10.0
Urban population (% of pop., 2014)	67.4
Surface area (thousands of sq km, 2014)	64.5
GNI, Atlas method (current US$ billions, 2014)	30.4
GNI per capita, Atlas method (current US$, 2014)	15,280.0
GDP growth (avg. annual %, 2011–14)	3.9
Poverty headcount ratio at national poverty line (% of pop., 2012)	19.4
Age dependency ratio (% of working-age pop., 2014)	51.3
Account at a formal financial institution (% age 15+, 2014)	90.2
Mobile cellular subscriptions (per 100 people, 2014)	124.2
Internet users (per 100 people, 2014)	75.8

Migration

EMIGRATION

- Stock of emigrants, 2013: **342.3 thousands**
- Stock of emigrants as percentage of population, 2013: **17.0 percent**
- Top destination countries, 2013: the Russian Federation, the United Kingdom, the United States, Ukraine, Ireland, Germany, Lithuania, Belarus, Norway, Canada
- Tertiary-educated as a percentage of total emigrants in OECD countries, 2011: **38.0 percent**
- Tertiary-educated women as a percentage of total women emigrants in OECD countries, 2011: **40.0 percent**
- Number of refugees, 2014: **206**
- Second generation diaspora in Australia, Europe, and the United States, 2012: **46.3 thousands**

IMMIGRATION

- Stock of immigrants, 2013: **323.6 thousands**
- Stock of immigrants as percentage of population, 2013: **16.1 percent**
- Top source countries, 2013: the Russian Federation, Belarus, Ukraine, Lithuania, Kazakhstan, Estonia, Germany, Azerbaijan, Uzbekistan, Moldova
- Women as percentage of immigrants, 2013: **61.2 percent**
- Number of refugees, 2014: **163**

Remittances

US$ millions	2006	2007	2008	2009	2010	2011	2012	2013	2014	2015e
Inward remittance flows[a]	**1,646**	**1,812**	**1,920**	**1,585**	**1,258**	**1,505**	**1,499**	**1,605**	**1,774**	**1,651**
of which										
Compensation of employees	480	551	599	588	612	697	730	762	953	–
Personal transfers	1,166	1,261	1,322	997	645	808	769	842	821	–
Outward remittance flows	**892**	**1,118**	**913**	**673**	**443**	**559**	**569**	**608**	**615**	**–**
of which										
Compensation of employees	25	41	56	43	44	47	68	70	66	–
Personal transfers	867	1,076	857	630	399	512	501	537	549	–

a. Net FDI inflows US$0.99 billion in 2013.

Lebanon

MIDDLE INCOME

Population (millions, 2014)	4.5
Population growth (avg. annual %, 2005–14)	1.6
Population density (people per sq km, 2014)	444.5
Labor force (millions, 2014)	1.7
Unemployment rate (% of labor force, 2014)	6.4
Urban population (% of pop., 2014)	87.7
Surface area (thousands of sq km, 2014)	10.5
GNI, Atlas method (current US$ billions, 2014)	45.6
GNI per capita, Atlas method (current US$, 2014)	10,030.0
GDP growth (avg. annual %, 2011–14)	1.8
Poverty headcount ratio at national poverty line (% of pop., 2004)	28.6
Age dependency ratio (% of working-age pop., 2014)	47.5
Account at a formal financial institution (% age 15+, 2014)	46.9
Mobile cellular subscriptions (per 100 people, 2014)	88.3
Internet users (per 100 people, 2014)	74.7

Migration

EMIGRATION

- Stock of emigrants, 2013: **810.9 thousands**
- Stock of emigrants as percentage of population, 2013: **18.0 percent**
- Top destination countries, 2013: Saudi Arabia, the United States, Australia, Germany, Canada, France, Sweden, the United Arab Emirates, the United Kingdom, Denmark
- Tertiary-educated as a percentage of total emigrants in OECD countries, 2011: **37.8 percent**
- Tertiary-educated women as a percentage of total women emigrants in OECD countries, 2011: **34.2 percent**
- Number of refugees, 2014: **4,246**
- Second generation diaspora in Australia, Europe, and the United States, 2012: **148.2 thousands**

IMMIGRATION

- Stock of immigrants, 2013: **1,586.7 thousands**
- Stock of immigrants as percentage of population, 2013: **35.3 percent**
- Top source countries, 2013: the Syrian Arab Republic, the West Bank and Gaza, Iraq, the Arab Republic of Egypt, Sri Lanka, Bangladesh, Indonesia, China, India, Saudi Arabia
- Women as percentage of immigrants, 2013: **45.3 percent**
- Number of refugees, 2014: **1,606,693**

Remittances

US$ millions	2006	2007	2008	2009	2010	2011	2012	2013	2014	2015e
Inward remittance flows[a]	**5,202**	**5,769**	**7,181**	**7,558**	**6,914**	**6,913**	**6,671**	**8,085**	**7,404**	**7,456**
of which										
Compensation of employees	579	747	1,405	1,173	545	557	544	967	957	–
Personal transfers	4,623	5,022	5,775	6,385	6,369	6,356	6,127	7,118	6,447	–
Outward remittance flows	**3,445**	**2,962**	**4,366**	**5,749**	**4,390**	**4,227**	**4,698**	**5,352**	**5,604**	–
of which										
Compensation of employees	661	597	790	1,034	544	519	634	671	857	–
Personal transfers	2,784	2,365	3,576	4,715	3,847	3,708	4,064	4,680	4,747	–

a. Net FDI inflows US$2.88 billion, net ODA received US$0.63 billion in 2013.

Lesotho

Population (millions, 2014)	2.1
Population growth (avg. annual %, 2005–14)	1.0
Population density (people per sq km, 2014)	69.5
Labor force (thousands, 2013)	889.2
Unemployment rate (% of labor force, 2014)	26.2
Urban population (% of pop., 2014)	26.8
Surface area (thousands of sq km, 2014)	30.4
GNI, Atlas method (current US$ billions, 2014)	2.8
GNI per capita, Atlas method (current US$, 2014)	1,330.0
GDP growth (avg. annual %, 2011–14)	4.3
Poverty headcount ratio at national poverty line (% of pop., 2010)	57.1
Age dependency ratio (% of working-age pop., 2014)	68.0
Account at a formal financial institution (% age 15+)	–
Mobile cellular subscriptions (per 100 people, 2014)	101.9
Internet users (per 100 people, 2014)	11.0

Migration

EMIGRATION

- Stock of emigrants, 2013: **324.0 thousands**
- Stock of emigrants as percentage of population, 2013: **15.6 percent**
- Top destination countries, 2013: South Africa, Mozambique, Botswana, the United States, Malaysia, Tanzania, Swaziland, the Netherlands, Australia, Kenya
- Tertiary-educated as a percentage of total emigrants in OECD countries, 2011: **52.3 percent**
- Tertiary-educated women as a percentage of total women emigrants in OECD countries, 2011: **55.9 percent**
- Number of refugees, 2014: **11**
- Second generation diaspora in Australia, Europe, and the United States, 2012: Not available

IMMIGRATION

- Stock of immigrants, 2013: **3.1 thousands**
- Stock of immigrants as percentage of population, 2013: **0.1 percent**
- Top source countries, 2013: South Africa, Zimbabwe, the United States, Zambia, Pakistan, India, Uganda, Mozambique, Malawi, Swaziland
- Women as percentage of immigrants, 2013: **35.4 percent**
- Number of refugees, 2014: **38**

Remittances

US$ millions	2006	2007	2008	2009	2010	2011	2012	2013	2014	2015e
Inward remittance flows[a]	**614**	**638**	**576**	**548**	**610**	**649**	**555**	**463**	**380**	**386**
of which										
Compensation of employees	608	632	570	543	604	643	549	458	376	–
Personal transfers	6	6	6	5	6	6	5	5	4	–
Outward remittance flows	–	–	–	–	–	–	–	–	–	–
of which										
Compensation of employees	–	–	–	–	–	–	–	–	–	–
Personal transfers	–	–	–	–	–	–	–	–	–	–

a. Net FDI inflows US$0.05 billion, net ODA received US$0.32 billion in 2013.

Liberia

	LOW INCOME
Population (millions, 2014)	4.4
Population growth (avg. annual %, 2005–14)	3.2
Population density (people per sq km, 2014)	45.6
Labor force (millions, 2014)	1.6
Unemployment rate (% of labor force, 2014)	3.8
Urban population (% of pop., 2014)	49.3
Surface area (thousands of sq km, 2014)	111.4
GNI, Atlas method (current US$ billions, 2014)	1.6
GNI per capita, Atlas method (current US$, 2014)	370.0
GDP growth (avg. annual %, 2011–14)	6.3
Poverty headcount ratio at national poverty line (% of pop., 2007)	63.8
Age dependency ratio (% of working-age pop., 2014)	83.9
Account at a formal financial institution (% age 15+)	—
Mobile cellular subscriptions (per 100 people, 2014)	73.4
Internet users (per 100 people, 2014)	5.4

Migration

EMIGRATION

- Stock of emigrants, 2013: **370.5 thousands**
- Stock of emigrants as percentage of population, 2013: **8.6 percent**
- Top destination countries, 2013: Guinea, Côte d'Ivoire, the United States, Sierra Leone, Ghana, Nigeria, Australia, Germany, Italy, the Netherlands
- Tertiary-educated as a percentage of total emigrants in OECD countries, 2011: **28.3 percent**
- Tertiary-educated women as a percentage of total women emigrants in OECD countries, 2011: **24.3 percent**
- Number of refugees, 2014: **13,509**
- Second generation diaspora in Australia, Europe, and the United States, 2012: **21.6 thousands**

IMMIGRATION

- Stock of immigrants, 2013: **225.5 thousands**
- Stock of immigrants as percentage of population, 2013: **5.3 percent**
- Top source countries, 2013: Côte d'Ivoire, Guinea, Sierra Leone, Ghana, Nigeria, Mali, Lebanon, India, The Gambia, the United States
- Women as percentage of immigrants, 2013: **46.9 percent**
- Number of refugees, 2014: **38,572**

Remittances

US$ millions	2006	2007	2008	2009	2010	2011	2012	2013	2014	2015e
Inward remittance flows[a]	79	62	58	25	31	360	516	383	495	603
of which										
Compensation of employees	18	20	22	18	31	102	7	9	20	–
Personal transfers	60	42	36	7	0	258	509	375	475	–
Outward remittance flows	0	0	0	1	1	1	471	435	366	–
of which										
Compensation of employees	0	0	0	1	1	1	103	111	50	–
Personal transfers	–	–	–	–	–	–	369	324	317	–

a. Net FDI inflows US$0.70 billion, net ODA received US$0.53 billion in 2013.

Libya

	MIDDLE INCOME
Population (millions, 2014)	6.3
Population growth (avg. annual %, 2005–14)	0.9
Population density (people per sq km, 2014)	3.6
Labor force (millions, 2014)	2.3
Unemployment rate (% of labor force, 2014)	19.2
Urban population (% of pop., 2014)	78.4
Surface area (thousands of sq km, 2014)	1,759.5
GNI, Atlas method (current US$ billions, 2014)	49.0
GNI per capita, Atlas method (current US$, 2014)	7,820.0
GDP growth (avg. annual %, 2011–14)	1.2
Poverty headcount ratio at national poverty line (% of pop.)	–
Age dependency ratio (% of working-age pop., 2014)	51.8
Account at a formal financial institution (% age 15+)	–
Mobile cellular subscriptions (per 100 people, 2014)	161.1
Internet users (per 100 people, 2014)	17.8

Migration

EMIGRATION

- Stock of emigrants, 2013: **146.8 thousands**
- Stock of emigrants as percentage of population, 2013: **2.3 percent**
- Top destination countries, 2013: Italy, the United Kingdom, Israel, Vietnam, the Arab Republic of Egypt, Algeria, Turkey, Côte d'Ivoire, Canada, Germany
- Tertiary-educated as a percentage of total emigrants in OECD countries, 2011: **29.6 percent**
- Tertiary-educated women as a percentage of total women emigrants in OECD countries, 2011: **25.1 percent**
- Number of refugees, 2014: **4,158**
- Second generation diaspora in Australia, Europe, and the United States, 2012: **32.8 thousands**

IMMIGRATION

- Stock of immigrants, 2013: **756.0 thousands**
- Stock of immigrants as percentage of population, 2013: **12.1 percent**
- Top source countries, 2013: the West Bank and Gaza, Somalia, Iraq, Saudi Arabia, the Syrian Arab Republic, the Republic of Yemen, the Arab Republic of Egypt, Jordan, Sudan, Indonesia
- Women as percentage of immigrants, 2013: **34.1 percent**
- Number of refugees, 2014: **27,954**

Remittances

US$ millions	2006	2007	2008	2009	2010	2011	2012	2013	2014	2015e
Inward remittance flows[a]	16	–	–	–	–	–	–	–	–	–
of which Compensation of employees	10	–	–	–	–	–	–	–	–	–
Personal transfers	6	–	–	–	–	–	–	–	–	–
Outward remittance flows	945	762	964	1,361	1,609	650	1,971	3,199	–	–
of which Compensation of employees	65	–	–	–	–	–	–	–	–	–
Personal transfers	880	762	964	1,361	1,609	650	1,971	3,199	–	–

a. Net FDI inflows US$0.70 billion, net ODA received US$0.13 billion in 2013.

Liechtenstein

Population (thousands, 2013)	37.3
Population growth (avg. annual %, 2005–14)	0.8
Population density (people per sq km, 2014)	233.0
Labor force, total	–
Unemployment rate (% of labor force)	–
Urban population (% of pop., 2014)	14.3
Surface area (thousands of sq km, 2014)	0.2
GNI, Atlas method (current US$ billions, 2009)	4.2
GNI per capita, Atlas method (current US$, 2009)	115,530.0
GDP growth (avg. annual %, 2005–08)	3.2
Poverty headcount ratio at national poverty line (% of pop.)	–
Age dependency ratio (% of working-age pop.)	–
Account at a formal financial institution (% age 15+)	–
Mobile cellular subscriptions (per 100 people, 2014)	104.3
Internet users (per 100 people, 2014)	95.2

Migration

EMIGRATION

- Stock of emigrants, 2013: **4.0 thousands**
- Stock of emigrants as percentage of population, 2013: **10.9 percent**
- Top destination countries, 2013: Switzerland, Austria, Germany, Portugal, Italy, Spain, Kenya, Canada, the United States, Ukraine
- Tertiary-educated as a percentage of total emigrants in OECD countries, 2011: **6.6 percent**
- Tertiary-educated women as a percentage of total women emigrants in OECD countries, 2011: **4.1 percent**
- Number of refugees, 2014: Not available
- Second generation diaspora in Australia, Europe, and the United States, 2012: Not available

IMMIGRATION

- Stock of immigrants, 2013: **12.2 thousands**
- Stock of immigrants as percentage of population, 2013: **33.0 percent**
- Top source countries, 2013: Switzerland, Austria, Germany, Italy, Turkey, Portugal, Spain, Serbia, Bosnia and Herzegovina, the Former Yugoslav Republic of Macedonia
- Women as percentage of immigrants, 2013: **49.5 percent**
- Number of refugees, 2014: **97**

Remittances

US$ millions	2006	2007	2008	2009	2010	2011	2012	2013	2014	2015e
Inward remittance flows	–	–	–	–	–	–	–	–	–	–
of which										
Compensation of employees	–	–	–	–	–	–	–	–	–	–
Personal transfers	–	–	–	–	–	–	–	–	–	–
Outward remittance flows	–	–	–	–	–	–	–	–	–	–
of which										
Compensation of employees	–	–	–	–	–	–	–	–	–	–
Personal transfers	–	–	–	–	–	–	–	–	–	–

Lithuania

Population (millions, 2014)	2.9
Population growth (avg. annual %, 2005–14)	-1.4
Population density (people per sq km, 2014)	46.7
Labor force (millions, 2014)	1.5
Unemployment rate (% of labor force, 2014)	11.3
Urban population (% of pop., 2014)	66.5
Surface area (thousands of sq km, 2014)	65.3
GNI, Atlas method (current US$ billions, 2014)	45.2
GNI per capita, Atlas method (current US$, 2014)	15,430.0
GDP growth (avg. annual %, 2011–14)	4.1
Poverty headcount ratio at national poverty line (% of pop., 2012)	20.6
Age dependency ratio (% of working-age pop., 2014)	49.4
Account at a formal financial institution (% age 15+, 2014)	77.9
Mobile cellular subscriptions (per 100 people, 2014)	147.0
Internet users (per 100 people, 2014)	72.1

Migration

EMIGRATION

- Stock of emigrants, 2013: **588.9 thousands**
- Stock of emigrants as percentage of population, **2013: 19.9 percent**
- Top destination countries, 2013: the United Kingdom, the Russian Federation, Poland, the United States, Germany, Ireland, Norway, Ukraine, Latvia, Spain
- Tertiary-educated as a percentage of total emigrants in OECD countries, 2011: **33.7 percent**
- Tertiary-educated women as a percentage of total women emigrants in OECD countries, 2011: **36.0 percent**
- Number of refugees, 2014: **177**
- Second generation diaspora in Australia, Europe, and the United States, 2012: **218.2 thousands**

IMMIGRATION

- Stock of immigrants, 2013: **221.5 thousands**
- Stock of immigrants as percentage of population, 2013: **7.5 percent**
- Top source countries, 2013: the Russian Federation, Belarus, Ukraine, Latvia, Kazakhstan, Poland, the United Kingdom, Germany, Uzbekistan, Azerbaijan
- Women as percentage of immigrants, 2013: **57.8 percent**
- Number of refugees, 2014: **972**

Remittances

US$ millions	2006	2007	2008	2009	2010	2011	2012	2013	2014	2015e
Inward remittance flows[a]	994	1,433	1,565	1,239	1,673	1,954	1,508	2,060	2,113	2,029
of which										
Compensation of employees	248	256	303	257	378	353	185	225	156	–
Personal transfers	746	1,178	1,262	982	1,295	1,601	1,323	1,835	1,956	–
Outward remittance flows	426	567	652	679	552	1,026	1,135	852	905	–
of which										
Compensation of employees	51	85	116	187	96	110	136	148	161	–
Personal transfers	375	482	537	492	456	916	999	704	744	–

a. Net FDI inflows US$0.71 billion in 2013.

Luxembourg

Population (thousands, 2013)	556.1
Population growth (avg. annual %, 2005-14)	1.9
Population density (people per sq km, 2014)	214.7
Labor force (thousands, 2013)	266.0
Unemployment rate (% of labor force, 2014)	6.1
Urban population (% of pop., 2014)	89.9
Surface area (thousands of sq km, 2014)	2.6
GNI, Atlas method (current US$ billions, 2014)	42.3
GNI per capita, Atlas method (current US$, 2014)	75,990.0
GDP growth (avg. annual %, 2011-14)	2.5
Poverty headcount ratio at national poverty line (% of pop.)	—
Age dependency ratio (% of working-age pop., 2014)	44.1
Account at a formal financial institution (% age 15+, 2014)	96.2
Mobile cellular subscriptions (per 100 people, 2014)	148.4
Internet users (per 100 people, 2014)	94.7

Migration

EMIGRATION

- Stock of emigrants, 2013: **66.0 thousands**
- Stock of emigrants as percentage of population, 2013: **12.1 percent**
- Top destination countries, 2013: Germany, France, Belgium, Italy, Portugal, the United States, Switzerland, Spain, the Netherlands, Austria
- Tertiary-educated as a percentage of total emigrants in OECD countries, 2011: **25.4 percent**
- Tertiary-educated women as a percentage of total women emigrants in OECD countries, 2011: **24.9 percent**
- Number of refugees, 2014: Not available
- Second generation diaspora in Australia, Europe, and the United States, 2012: **19.3 thousands**

IMMIGRATION

- Stock of immigrants, 2013: **229.4 thousands**
- Stock of immigrants as percentage of population, 2013: **42.2 percent**
- Top source countries, 2013: Portugal, France, Italy, Belgium, Germany, Montenegro, Serbia, the United Kingdom, the Netherlands, Spain
- Women as percentage of immigrants, 2013: **49.5 percent**
- Number of refugees, 2014: **1,046**

Remittances

US$ millions	2006	2007	2008	2009	2010	2011	2012	2013	2014	2015e
Inward remittance flows[a]	1,347	1,473	1,630	1,657	1,653	1,773	1,673	1,838	1,784	1,692
of which										
Compensation of employees	1,312	1,447	1,595	1,630	1,625	1,742	1,644	1,718	1,751	—
Personal transfers	35	26	35	27	28	30	29	120	33	—
Outward remittance flows	7,561	9,370	11,006	10,725	10,645	11,720	11,269	12,262	12,700	—
of which										
Compensation of employees	7,463	9,247	10,867	10,604	10,523	11,582	11,125	12,113	12,548	—
Personal transfers	98	124	139	121	121	139	144	149	152	—

a. Net FDI inflows US$23.25 billion in 2013.

Macao SAR, China

Population (thousands, 2013)	577.9
Population growth (avg. annual %, 2005–14)	2.3
Population density (people per sq km, 2014)	19,073.1
Labor force (thousands, 2013)	360.8
Unemployment rate (% of labor force, 2014)	1.5
Urban population (% of pop., 2014)	100.0
Surface area (thousands of sq km, 2014)	0.0
GNI, Atlas method (current US$ billions, 2014)	44.1
GNI per capita, Atlas method (current US$, 2014)	76,270.0
GDP growth (avg. annual %, 2011–14)	10.2
Poverty headcount ratio at national poverty line (% of pop.)	–
Age dependency ratio (% of working-age pop., 2014)	27.1
Account at a formal financial institution (% age 15+)	–
Mobile cellular subscriptions (per 100 people, 2014)	322.6
Internet users (per 100 people, 2014)	69.8

Migration

EMIGRATION

- Stock of emigrants, 2013: **136.8 thousands**
- Stock of emigrants as percentage of population, 2013: **24.1 percent**
- Top destination countries, 2013: Hong Kong SAR, China, China, Singapore, the United States, Canada, Australia, Portugal, Norway, France, Colombia
- Tertiary-educated as a percentage of total emigrants in OECD countries, 2011: Not available
- Tertiary-educated women as a percentage of total women emigrants in OECD countries, 2011: Not available
- Number of refugees, 2014: Not available
- Second generation diaspora in Australia, Europe, and the United States, 2012: Not available

IMMIGRATION

- Stock of immigrants, 2013: **333.3 thousands**
- Stock of immigrants as percentage of population, 2013: **58.7 percent**
- Top source countries, 2013: China, Hong Kong SAR, China, the Philippines, Portugal, Thailand
- Women as percentage of immigrants, 2013: **51.4 percent**
- Number of refugees, 2014: Not available

Remittances

US$ millions	2006	2007	2008	2009	2010	2011	2012	2013	2014	2015e
Inward remittance flows[a]	**55**	**54**	**52**	**48**	**47**	**48**	**47**	**49**	**49**	**51**
of which										
Compensation of employees	–	–	–	–	–	–	–	–	–	–
Personal transfers	55	54	52	48	47	48	47	49	–	–
Outward remittance flows	**476**	**823**	**936**	**667**	**539**	**654**	**853**	**1,060**	**1,123**	**–**
of which										
Compensation of employees	151	168	196	121	94	115	185	145	208	–
Personal transfers	326	655	741	545	446	538	669	915	915	–

a. Net FDI inflows US$3.74 billion in 2013.

Macedonia, Former Yugoslav Republic of

Population (millions, 2014)	2.1
Population growth (avg. annual %, 2005–14)	0.2
Population density (people per sq km, 2014)	82.3
Labor force (thousands, 2013)	952.7
Unemployment rate (% of labor force, 2014)	27.9
Urban population (% of pop., 2014)	57.0
Surface area (thousands of sq km, 2014)	25.7
GNI, Atlas method (current US$ billions, 2014)	10.7
GNI per capita, Atlas method (current US$, 2014)	5,150.0
GDP growth (avg. annual %, 2011–14)	2.1
Poverty headcount ratio at national poverty line (% of pop., 2010)	27.1
Age dependency ratio (% of working-age pop., 2014)	41.2
Account at a formal financial institution (% age 15+, 2014)	71.8
Mobile cellular subscriptions (per 100 people, 2014)	109.1
Internet users (per 100 people, 2014)	68.1

Migration

EMIGRATION

- Stock of emigrants, 2013: **626.3 thousands**
- Stock of emigrants as percentage of population, 2013: **30.2 percent**
- Top destination countries, 2013: Germany, the United States, Turkey, Italy, Switzerland, Australia, Serbia, Austria, Croatia, Slovenia
- Tertiary-educated as a percentage of total emigrants in OECD countries, 2011: **8.9 percent**
- Tertiary-educated women as a percentage of total women emigrants in OECD countries, 2011: **8.9 percent**
- Number of refugees, 2014: **1,746**
- Second generation diaspora in Australia, Europe, and the United States, 2012: Not available

IMMIGRATION

- Stock of immigrants, 2013: **139.8 thousands**
- Stock of immigrants as percentage of population, 2013: **6.7 percent**
- Top source countries, 2013: Turkey, Albania, Serbia, Montenegro, Bosnia and Herzegovina, the Arab Republic of Egypt, Croatia, Bulgaria, Slovenia, Greece
- Women as percentage of immigrants, 2013: **58.4 percent**
- Number of refugees, 2014: **880**

Remittances

US$ millions	2006	2007	2008	2009	2010	2011	2012	2013	2014	2015e
Inward remittance flows[a]	**267**	**345**	**407**	**381**	**388**	**434**	**394**	**376**	**367**	**365**
of which										
Compensation of employees	69	106	140	121	128	162	140	122	96	–
Personal transfers	198	239	266	260	260	272	254	254	270	–
Outward remittance flows	**18**	**25**	**33**	**26**	**23**	**25**	**24**	**24**	**24**	–
of which										
Compensation of employees	2	3	5	4	3	4	4	6	6	–
Personal transfers	16	22	28	22	19	21	20	19	18	–

a. Net FDI inflows US$0.40 billion, net ODA received US$0.25 billion in 2013.

Madagascar

Population (millions, 2014)	23.6
Population growth (avg. annual %, 2005–14)	2.8
Population density (people per sq km, 2014)	40.5
Labor force (millions, 2014)	12.1
Unemployment rate (% of labor force, 2014)	3.6
Urban population (% of pop., 2014)	34.5
Surface area (thousands of sq km, 2014)	587.3
GNI, Atlas method (current US$ billions, 2014)	10.4
GNI per capita, Atlas method (current US$, 2014)	440.0
GDP growth (avg. annual %, 2011–14)	2.5
Poverty headcount ratio at national poverty line (% of pop., 2010)	75.3
Age dependency ratio (% of working-age pop., 2014)	81.4
Account at a formal financial institution (% age 15+, 2014)	5.7
Mobile cellular subscriptions (per 100 people, 2014)	38.2
Internet users (per 100 people, 2014)	3.7

Migration

EMIGRATION

- Stock of emigrants, 2013: **166.9 thousands**
- Stock of emigrants as percentage of population, 2013: **0.7 percent**
- Top destination countries, 2013: France, Comoros, Canada, Italy, Switzerland, the United States, Mauritius, Germany, Seychelles, Botswana
- Tertiary-educated as a percentage of total emigrants in OECD countries, 2011: **30.1 percent**
- Tertiary-educated women as a percentage of total women emigrants in OECD countries, 2011: **27.8 percent**
- Number of refugees, 2014: **264**
- Second generation diaspora in Australia, Europe, and the United States, 2012: **42.3 thousands**

IMMIGRATION

- Stock of immigrants, 2013: **34.3 thousands**
- Stock of immigrants as percentage of population, 2013: **0.1 percent**
- Top source countries, 2013: France, Comoros, India, Algeria, China, Pakistan, Mauritius, Germany, Italy, the United States
- Women as percentage of immigrants, 2013: **44.6 percent**
- Number of refugees, 2014: **6**

Remittances

US$ millions	2006	2007	2008	2009	2010	2011	2012	2013	2014	2015e
Inward remittance flows[a]	**175**	**301**	**375**	**338**	**547**	**398**	**397**	**427**	**427**	**427**
of which										
Compensation of employees	11	21	21	20	36	30	15	16	–	–
Personal transfers	164	280	354	317	512	368	382	411	–	–
Outward remittance flows	**17**	**19**	**23**	**30**	**35**	**46**	**54**	**50**	**–**	**–**
of which										
Compensation of employees	10	11	20	24	29	38	39	30	–	–
Personal transfers	8	9	3	6	6	8	15	21	–	–

a. Net FDI inflows US$0.57 billion, net ODA received US$0.50 billion in 2013.

Malawi

LOW INCOME

Population (millions, 2014)	16.7
Population growth (avg. annual %, 2005–14)	3.0
Population density (people per sq km, 2014)	177.1
Labor force (millions, 2014)	7.6
Unemployment rate (% of labor force, 2014)	7.5
Urban population (% of pop., 2014)	16.1
Surface area (thousands of sq km, 2014)	118.5
GNI, Atlas method (current US$ billions, 2014)	4.2
GNI per capita, Atlas method (current US$, 2014)	250.0
GDP growth (avg. annual %, 2011–14)	4.3
Poverty headcount ratio at national poverty line (% of pop., 2010)	50.7
Age dependency ratio (% of working-age pop., 2014)	95.2
Account at a formal financial institution (% age 15+, 2014)	16.1
Mobile cellular subscriptions (per 100 people, 2014)	30.5
Internet users (per 100 people, 2014)	5.8

Migration

EMIGRATION

- Stock of emigrants, 2013: **287.5 thousands**
- Stock of emigrants as percentage of population, 2013: **1.8 percent**
- Top destination countries, 2013: Zimbabwe, Mozambique, South Africa, the United Kingdom, Tanzania, Botswana, Zambia, the United States, Australia, Eritrea
- Tertiary-educated as a percentage of total emigrants in OECD countries, 2011: **42.6 percent**
- Tertiary-educated women as a percentage of total women emigrants in OECD countries, 2011: **38.9 percent**
- Number of refugees, 2014: **345**
- Second generation diaspora in Australia, Europe, and the United States, 2012: **8.9 thousands**

IMMIGRATION

- Stock of immigrants, 2013: **206.6 thousands**
- Stock of immigrants as percentage of population, 2013: **1.3 percent**
- Top source countries, 2013: Mozambique, Zambia, Zimbabwe, Tanzania, South Africa, Burundi, Rwanda, India, the Democratic Republic of Congo, the United Kingdom
- Women as percentage of immigrants, 2013: **52.4 percent**
- Number of refugees, 2014: **5,871**

Remittances

US$ millions	2006	2007	2008	2009	2010	2011	2012	2013	2014	2015e
Inward remittance flows[a]	15	21	17	17	22	25	28	28	28	29
of which										
Compensation of employees	0	0	0	1	1	1	1	–	–	–
Personal transfers	15	21	16	16	21	24	27	–	–	–
Outward remittance flows	7	10	10	13	15	17	18	–	–	–
of which										
Compensation of employees	7	7	6	7	7	7	7	–	–	–
Personal transfers	0	3	4	6	8	11	11	–	–	–

a. Net FDI inflows US$0.63 billion, net ODA received US$1.13 billion in 2013.

Malaysia

MIDDLE INCOME

Population (millions, 2014)	29.9
Population growth (avg. annual %, 2005–14)	1.7
Population density (people per sq km, 2014)	91.0
Labor force (millions, 2014)	13.3
Unemployment rate (% of labor force, 2014)	2.0
Urban population (% of pop., 2014)	74.0
Surface area (thousands of sq km, 2014)	330.8
GNI, Atlas method (current US$ billions, 2014)	332.5
GNI per capita, Atlas method (current US$, 2014)	11,120.0
GDP growth (avg. annual %, 2011–14)	5.4
Poverty headcount ratio at national poverty line (% of pop., 2012)	1.7
Age dependency ratio (% of working-age pop., 2014)	44.2
Account at a formal financial institution (% age 15+, 2014)	80.7
Mobile cellular subscriptions (per 100 people, 2014)	148.8
Internet users (per 100 people, 2014)	67.5

Migration

EMIGRATION

- Stock of emigrants, 2013: **1,683.1 thousands**
- Stock of emigrants as percentage of population, 2013: **5.7 percent**
- Top destination countries, 2013: Singapore, Bangladesh, Australia, the United States, the United Kingdom, Canada, New Zealand, Hong Kong SAR, China, India, China
- Tertiary-educated as a percentage of total emigrants in OECD countries, 2011: **54.9 percent**
- Tertiary-educated women as a percentage of total women emigrants in OECD countries, 2011: **54.7 percent**
- Number of refugees, 2014: **458**
- Second generation diaspora in Australia, Europe, and the United States, 2012: **56.9 thousands**

IMMIGRATION

- Stock of immigrants, 2013: **2,408.3 thousands**
- Stock of immigrants as percentage of population, 2013: **8.2 percent**
- Top source countries, 2013: Indonesia, the Philippines, Bangladesh, Thailand, Myanmar, Nepal, India, China, Singapore, Vietnam
- Women as percentage of immigrants, 2013: **42.5 percent**
- Number of refugees, 2014: **99,328**

Remittances

US$ millions	2006	2007	2008	2009	2010	2011	2012	2013	2014	2015e
Inward remittance flows[a]	**1,365**	**1,556**	**1,329**	**1,131**	**1,103**	**1,211**	**1,294**	**1,423**	**1,573**	**1,678**
of which Compensation of employees	1,365	1,556	1,329	1,131	1,103	1,211	1,294	1,423	1,573	–
Personal transfers	–	–	–	–	–	–	–	–	–	–
Outward remittance flows	**5,597**	**6,388**	**6,786**	**6,529**	**6,729**	**6,946**	**7,267**	**7,670**	**8,074**	–
of which Compensation of employees	1,449	1,738	1,547	1,554	1,753	1,971	2,292	2,695	3,099	–
Personal transfers	4,147	4,650	5,238	4,975	4,975	4,975	4,975	4,975	4,975	–

a. Net FDI inflows US$11.30 billion, net ODA received US$-0.12 billion in 2013.

Maldives

Population (thousands, 2013)	357.4
Population growth (avg. annual %, 2005–14)	1.8
Population density (people per sq km, 2014)	1,191.4
Labor force (thousands, 2013)	195.1
Unemployment rate (% of labor force, 2014)	11.6
Urban population (% of pop., 2014)	44.5
Surface area (thousands of sq km, 2014)	0.3
GNI, Atlas method (current US$ billions, 2014)	2.6
GNI per capita, Atlas method (current US$, 2014)	7,190.0
GDP growth (avg. annual %, 2011–14)	5.6
Poverty headcount ratio at national poverty line (% of pop.)	–
Age dependency ratio (% of working-age pop., 2014)	47.7
Account at a formal financial institution (% age 15+)	–
Mobile cellular subscriptions (per 100 people, 2014)	189.4
Internet users (per 100 people, 2014)	49.3

Migration

EMIGRATION

- Stock of emigrants, 2013: **1.3 thousands**
- Stock of emigrants as percentage of population, 2013: **0.4 percent**
- Top destination countries, 2013: Australia, India, the Arab Republic of Egypt, Switzerland, Greece, South Africa, the Russian Federation, Seychelles, Canada, Italy
- Tertiary-educated as a percentage of total emigrants in OECD countries, 2011: **38.1 percent**
- Tertiary-educated women as a percentage of total women emigrants in OECD countries, 2011: **40.5 percent**
- Number of refugees, 2014: **27**
- Second generation diaspora in Australia, Europe, and the United States, 2012: Not available

IMMIGRATION

- Stock of immigrants, 2013: **84.2 thousands**
- Stock of immigrants as percentage of population, 2013: **24.0 percent**
- Top source countries, 2013: Bangladesh, India, Sri Lanka, the Philippines, Italy, Germany, the United Kingdom, Pakistan, Thailand, Japan
- Women as percentage of immigrants, 2013: **44.6 percent**
- Number of refugees, 2014: Not available

Remittances

US$ millions	2006	2007	2008	2009	2010	2011	2012	2013	2014	2015e
Inward remittance flows[a]	3	8	6	5	3	3	3	3	3	4
of which										
Compensation of employees	3	8	6	5	3	3	3	3	3	–
Personal transfers	–	–	–	–	–	–	–	–	–	–
Outward remittance flows	84	189	219	190	189	240	260	266	324	–
of which										
Compensation of employees	0	0	0	0	0	1	1	1	1	–
Personal transfers	83	188	218	190	189	239	259	265	324	–

a. Net FDI inflows US$0.36 billion, net ODA received US$0.02 billion in 2013.

Mali

Population (millions, 2014)	17.1
Population growth (avg. annual %, 2005–14)	3.1
Population density (people per sq km, 2014)	14.0
Labor force (millions, 2014)	5.9
Unemployment rate (% of labor force, 2014)	8.1
Urban population (% of pop., 2014)	39.1
Surface area (thousands of sq km, 2014)	1,240.2
GNI, Atlas method (current US$ billions, 2014)	11.0
GNI per capita, Atlas method (current US$, 2014)	650.0
GDP growth (avg. annual %, 2011–14)	2.9
Poverty headcount ratio at national poverty line (% of pop., 2009)	43.6
Age dependency ratio (% of working-age pop., 2014)	100.4
Account at a formal financial institution (% age 15+, 2014)	13.3
Mobile cellular subscriptions (per 100 people, 2014)	149.0
Internet users (per 100 people, 2014)	7.0

Migration

EMIGRATION

- Stock of emigrants, 2013: **895.7 thousands**
- Stock of emigrants as percentage of population, 2013: **5.4 percent**
- Top destination countries, 2013: Côte d'Ivoire, Nigeria, France, Gabon, Niger, Burkina Faso, Mauritania, Senegal, the Republic of Congo, Spain
- Tertiary-educated as a percentage of total emigrants in OECD countries, 2011: **13.4 percent**
- Tertiary-educated women as a percentage of total women emigrants in OECD countries, 2011: **13.0 percent**
- Number of refugees, 2014: **139,224**
- Second generation diaspora in Australia, Europe, and the United States, 2012: **39.8 thousands**

IMMIGRATION

- Stock of immigrants, 2013: **195.6 thousands**
- Stock of immigrants as percentage of population, 2013: **1.2 percent**
- Top source countries, 2013: Côte d'Ivoire, Burkina Faso, Guinea, Mauritania, Senegal, Niger, Gabon, the Republic of Congo, Ghana, France
- Women as percentage of immigrants, 2013: **47.7 percent**
- Number of refugees, 2014: **15,188**

Remittances

US$ millions	2006	2007	2008	2009	2010	2011	2012	2013	2014	2015e
Inward remittance flows[a]	**212**	**344**	**431**	**454**	**473**	**784**	**827**	**895**	**895**	**895**
of which										
Compensation of employees	19	21	25	30	35	32	32	37	–	–
Personal transfers	193	323	406	424	437	752	795	857	–	–
Outward remittance flows	**57**	**83**	**105**	**167**	**176**	**129**	**111**	**134**	–	–
of which										
Compensation of employees	10	13	14	28	32	41	35	35	–	–
Personal transfers	47	69	91	139	144	87	76	99	–	–

a. Net FDI inflows US$0.31 billion, net ODA received US$1.39 billion in 2013.

Malta

Population (thousands, 2013)	427.4
Population growth (avg. annual %, 2005–14)	0.6
Population density (people per sq km, 2014)	1,335.6
Labor force (thousands, 2013)	189.1
Unemployment rate (% of labor force, 2014)	5.9
Urban population (% of pop., 2014)	95.3
Surface area (thousands of sq km, 2014)	0.3
GNI, Atlas method (current US$ billions, 2014)	8.9
GNI per capita, Atlas method (current US$, 2014)	21,000.0
GDP growth (avg. annual %, 2011–14)	2.1
Poverty headcount ratio at national poverty line (% of pop.)	–
Age dependency ratio (% of working-age pop., 2014)	50.2
Account at a formal financial institution (% age 15+, 2014)	96.3
Mobile cellular subscriptions (per 100 people, 2014)	127.0
Internet users (per 100 people, 2014)	73.2

Migration

EMIGRATION

- Stock of emigrants, 2013: **109.9 thousands**
- Stock of emigrants as percentage of population, 2013: **26.0 percent**
- Top destination countries, 2013: Australia, the United Kingdom, the United States, Canada, Italy, Germany, Belgium, France, Kenya, Ireland
- Tertiary-educated as a percentage of total emigrants in OECD countries, 2011: **19.6 percent**
- Tertiary-educated women as a percentage of total women emigrants in OECD countries, 2011: **18.2 percent**
- Number of refugees, 2014: Not available
- Second generation diaspora in Australia, Europe, and the United States, 2012: Not available

IMMIGRATION

- Stock of immigrants, 2013: **34.5 thousands**
- Stock of immigrants as percentage of population, 2013: **8.1 percent**
- Top source countries, 2013: the United Kingdom, Australia, Canada, Italy, the United States, Germany, Libya, the Russian Federation, Serbia, the Arab Republic of Egypt
- Women as percentage of immigrants, 2013: **49.5 percent**
- Number of refugees, 2014: **6,055**

Remittances

US$ millions	2006	2007	2008	2009	2010	2011	2012	2013	2014	2015e
Inward remittance flows[a]	**36**	**50**	**264**	**260**	**230**	**227**	**200**	**201**	**196**	**198**
of which										
Compensation of employees	35	49	53	53	36	37	33	33	31	–
Personal transfers	0	0	211	207	194	190	166	168	165	–
Outward remittance flows	**43**	**49**	**1,320**	**1,861**	**1,612**	**1,127**	**1,080**	**1,047**	**1,018**	**–**
of which										
Compensation of employees	39	45	48	42	41	34	39	32	24	–
Personal transfers	4	4	1,273	1,819	1,571	1,093	1,041	1,015	994	–

a. Net FDI inflows US$0.39 billion in 2013.

Marshall Islands

MIDDLE INCOME

Population (thousands, 2013)	52.9
Population growth (avg. annual %, 2005–14)	0.2
Population density (people per sq km, 2014)	293.9
Labor force, total	–
Unemployment rate (% of labor force)	–
Urban population (% of pop., 2014)	72.4
Surface area (thousands of sq km, 2014)	0.2
GNI, Atlas method (current US$ billions, 2014)	0.2
GNI per capita, Atlas method (current US$, 2014)	4,390.0
GDP growth (avg. annual %, 2011–14)	1.1
Poverty headcount ratio at national poverty line (% of pop.)	–
Age dependency ratio (% of working-age pop.)	–
Account at a formal financial institution (% age 15+)	–
Mobile cellular subscriptions (per 100 people, 2014)	29.4
Internet users (per 100 people, 2014)	16.8

Migration

EMIGRATION

- Stock of emigrants, 2013: **9.8 thousands**
- Stock of emigrants as percentage of population, 2013: **18.5 percent**
- Top destination countries, 2013: the United States, Guam, the Federated States of Micronesia, the Northern Mariana Islands, Palau, Australia, the Philippines, Greece, Italy, the Netherlands
- Tertiary-educated as a percentage of total emigrants in OECD countries, 2011: **10.5 percent**
- Tertiary-educated women as a percentage of total women emigrants in OECD countries, 2011: **9.8 percent**
- Number of refugees, 2014: Not available
- Second generation diaspora in Australia, Europe, and the United States, 2012: Not available

IMMIGRATION

- Stock of immigrants, 2013: **2.1 thousands**
- Stock of immigrants as percentage of population, 2013: **4.0 percent**
- Top source countries, 2013: the Philippines, the United States, China, Kiribati, the Federated States of Micronesia, Tuvalu, Palau, Japan, Fiji, Solomon Islands
- Women as percentage of immigrants, 2013: **35.6 percent**
- Number of refugees, 2014: Not available

Remittances

US$ millions	2006	2007	2008	2009	2010	2011	2012	2013	2014	2015e
Inward remittance flows[a]	**26**	**25**	**23**	**24**	**22**	**22**	**23**	**25**	**26**	**27**
of which										
Compensation of employees	23	22	20	20	19	19	18	19	19	–
Personal transfers	3	3	3	4	3	3	5	6	7	–
Outward remittance flows	**4**	**4**	**4**	**4**	**8**	**9**	**23**	**24**	**24**	–
of which										
Compensation of employees	0	0	0	0	3	4	11	9	7	–
Personal transfers	3	4	4	4	5	6	12	15	17	–

a. Net FDI inflows US$0.03 billion, net ODA received US$0.09 billion in 2013.

Mauritania

Population (millions, 2014)	4.0
Population growth (avg. annual %, 2005–14)	2.6
Population density (people per sq km, 2014)	3.9
Labor force (millions, 2014)	1.3
Unemployment rate (% of labor force, 2014)	31.0
Urban population (% of pop., 2014)	59.3
Surface area (thousands of sq km, 2014)	1,030.7
GNI, Atlas method (current US$ billions, 2014)	5.0
GNI per capita, Atlas method (current US$, 2014)	1,270.0
GDP growth (avg. annual %, 2011–14)	5.6
Poverty headcount ratio at national poverty line (% of pop., 2008)	42.0
Age dependency ratio (% of working-age pop., 2014)	76.8
Account at a formal financial institution (% age 15+, 2014)	20.4
Mobile cellular subscriptions (per 100 people, 2014)	94.2
Internet users (per 100 people, 2014)	10.7

Migration

EMIGRATION

- Stock of emigrants, 2013: **136.3 thousands**
- Stock of emigrants as percentage of population, 2013: **3.5 percent**
- Top destination countries, 2013: Senegal, Nigeria, France, Mali, Spain, Côte d'Ivoire, The Gambia, the Republic of Congo, Belgium, Italy
- Tertiary-educated as a percentage of total emigrants in OECD countries, 2011: **16.6 percent**
- Tertiary-educated women as a percentage of total women emigrants in OECD countries, 2011: **13.4 percent**
- Number of refugees, 2014: **34,079**
- Second generation diaspora in Australia, Europe, and the United States, 2012: Not available

IMMIGRATION

- Stock of immigrants, 2013: **102.6 thousands**
- Stock of immigrants as percentage of population, 2013: **2.6 percent**
- Top source countries, 2013: Senegal, Mali, Guinea, Algeria, France, Guinea-Bissau, Benin, Cameroon, Morocco, Saudi Arabia
- Women as percentage of immigrants, 2013: **40.0 percent**
- Number of refugees, 2014: **75,619**

Remittances

US$ millions	2006	2007	2008	2009	2010	2011	2012	2013	2014	2015e
Inward remittance flows[a]	–	–	–	–	–	–	–	–	–	–
of which										
Compensation of employees	–	–	–	–	–	–	–	–	–	–
Personal transfers	–	–	–	–	–	–	–	–	–	–
Outward remittance flows	–	–	–	–	–	–	240	255	188	–
of which										
Compensation of employees	–	–	–	–	–	–	240	255	188	–
Personal transfers	–	–	–	–	–	–	–	–	–	–

a. Net FDI inflows US$1.13 billion, net ODA received US$0.29 billion in 2013.

Mauritius

	MIDDLE INCOME
Population (millions, 2014)	1.3
Population growth (avg. annual %, 2005-14)	0.3
Population density (people per sq km, 2014)	621.1
Labor force (thousands, 2013)	592.3
Unemployment rate (% of labor force, 2014)	7.7
Urban population (% of pop., 2014)	39.8
Surface area (thousands of sq km, 2014)	2.0
GNI, Atlas method (current US$ billions, 2014)	12.1
GNI per capita, Atlas method (current US$, 2014)	9,630.0
GDP growth (avg. annual %, 2011-14)	3.5
Poverty headcount ratio at national poverty line (% of pop.)	–
Age dependency ratio (% of working-age pop., 2014)	40.8
Account at a formal financial institution (% age 15+, 2014)	82.2
Mobile cellular subscriptions (per 100 people, 2014)	132.2
Internet users (per 100 people, 2014)	41.4

Migration

EMIGRATION

- Stock of emigrants, 2013: **172.2 thousands**
- Stock of emigrants as percentage of population, 2013: **13.7 percent**
- Top destination countries, 2013: the United Kingdom, France, Australia, Canada, Italy, South Africa, the United States, Switzerland, Ireland, Botswana
- Tertiary-educated as a percentage of total emigrants in OECD countries, 2011: **32.7 percent**
- Tertiary-educated women as a percentage of total women emigrants in OECD countries, 2011: **28.0 percent**
- Number of refugees, 2014: **76**
- Second generation diaspora in Australia, Europe, and the United States, 2012: **62.8 thousands**

IMMIGRATION

- Stock of immigrants, 2013: **45.0 thousands**
- Stock of immigrants as percentage of population, 2013: **3.6 percent**
- Top source countries, 2013: China, India, France, Madagascar, the United Kingdom, South Africa, Germany, Italy, Seychelles, Australia
- Women as percentage of immigrants, 2013: **61.0 percent**
- Number of refugees, 2014: Not available

Remittances

US$ millions	2006	2007	2008	2009	2010	2011	2012	2013	2014	2015e
Inward remittance flows[a]	**215**	**215**	**215**	**211**	**226**	**249**	**249**	**249**	**249**	**249**
of which										
Compensation of employees	1	1	1	1	1	1	1	1	1	–
Personal transfers	–	–	–	–	–	–	–	–	–	–
Outward remittance flows	**10**	**10**	**13**	**10**	**8**	**9**	**8**	**8**	**9**	–
of which										
Compensation of employees	10	10	13	10	8	9	8	8	9	–
Personal transfers	–	–	–	–	–	–	–	–	–	–

a. Net FDI inflows US$0.26 billion, net ODA received US$0.15 billion in 2013.

Mexico

	MIDDLE INCOME
Population (millions, 2014)	125.4
Population growth (avg. annual %, 2005–14)	1.5
Population density (people per sq km, 2014)	64.5
Labor force (millions, 2014)	55.6
Unemployment rate (% of labor force, 2014)	4.9
Urban population (% of pop., 2014)	79.0
Surface area (thousands of sq km, 2014)	1,964.4
GNI, Atlas method (current US$ billions, 2014)	1,237.5
GNI per capita, Atlas method (current US$, 2014)	9,870.0
GDP growth (avg. annual %, 2011–14)	2.9
Poverty headcount ratio at national poverty line (% of pop., 2012)	52.3
Age dependency ratio (% of working-age pop., 2014)	52.4
Account at a formal financial institution (% age 15+, 2014)	38.7
Mobile cellular subscriptions (per 100 people, 2014)	82.5
Internet users (per 100 people, 2014)	44.4

Migration

EMIGRATION

- Stock of emigrants, 2013: **13,220.3 thousands**
- Stock of emigrants as percentage of population, 2013: **10.7 percent**
- Top destination countries, 2013: the United States, Canada, Spain, Guatemala, France, Argentina, the United Kingdom, Germany, the Plurinational State of Bolivia, Italy
- Tertiary-educated as a percentage of total emigrants in OECD countries, 2011: **7.3 percent**
- Tertiary-educated women as a percentage of total women emigrants in OECD countries, 2011: **8.2 percent**
- Number of refugees, 2014: **10,637**
- Second generation diaspora in Australia, Europe, and the United States, 2012: **8,279.0 thousands**

IMMIGRATION

- Stock of immigrants, 2013: **1,103.5 thousands**
- Stock of immigrants as percentage of population, 2013: **0.9 percent**
- Top source countries, 2013: the United States, Guatemala, Spain, Colombia, Argentina, Cuba, Honduras, República Bolivariana de Venezuela, El Salvador, Canada
- Women as percentage of immigrants, 2013: **49.2 percent**
- Number of refugees, 2014: **1,785**

Remittances

US$ millions	2006	2007	2008	2009	2010	2011	2012	2013	2014	2015e
Inward remittance flows[a]	26,543	26,880	26,041	22,076	22,080	23,588	23,366	23,433	24,462	25,949
of which										
Compensation of employees	976	821	897	769	776	786	928	1,130	815	–
Personal transfers	25,567	26,059	25,145	21,306	21,304	22,803	22,438	22,303	23,647	–
Outward remittance flows	–	–	–	–	–	–	–	867	1,002	–
of which										
Compensation of employees	–	–	–	–	–	–	–	–	–	–
Personal transfers	–	–	–	–	–	–	–	867	1,002	–

a. Net FDI inflows US$44.89 billion, net ODA received US$0.56 billion in 2013.

Micronesia, Federated States of

	MIDDLE INCOME
Population (thousands, 2013)	104.0
Population growth (avg. annual %, 2005–14)	-0.2
Population density (people per sq km, 2014)	148.6
Labor force, total	—
Unemployment rate (% of labor force)	—
Urban population (% of pop., 2014)	22.4
Surface area (thousands of sq km, 2014)	0.7
GNI, Atlas method (current US$ billions, 2014)	0.3
GNI per capita, Atlas method (current US$, 2014)	3,200.0
GDP growth (avg. annual %, 2011–14)	-1.1
Poverty headcount ratio at national poverty line (% of pop.)	—
Age dependency ratio (% of working-age pop., 2014)	63.3
Account at a formal financial institution (% age 15+)	—
Mobile cellular subscriptions (per 100 people, 2014)	30.3
Internet users (per 100 people, 2014)	29.6

Migration

EMIGRATION

- Stock of emigrants, 2013: **29.3 thousands**
- Stock of emigrants as percentage of population, 2013: **28.3 percent**
- Top destination countries, 2013: the United States, Guam, the Northern Mariana Islands, Palau, the Marshall Islands, Canada, Australia, Vanuatu, Kenya, the Slovak Republic
- Tertiary-educated as a percentage of total emigrants in OECD countries, 2011: **12.0 percent**
- Tertiary-educated women as a percentage of total women emigrants in OECD countries, 2011: **10.5 percent**
- Number of refugees, 2014: Not available
- Second generation diaspora in Australia, Europe, and the United States, 2012: Not available

IMMIGRATION

- Stock of immigrants, 2013: **2.6 thousands**
- Stock of immigrants as percentage of population, 2013: **2.5 percent**
- Top source countries, 2013: the Philippines, the United States, China, Guam, the Marshall Islands, the Northern Mariana Islands, Palau, Japan, Australia, New Zealand
- Women as percentage of immigrants, 2013: **45.5 percent**
- Number of refugees, 2014: Not available

Remittances

US$ millions	2006	2007	2008	2009	2010	2011	2012	2013	2014	2015e
Inward remittance flows[a]	—	—	—	17	18	19	21	22	22	23
of which										
Compensation of employees	—	—	—	0	1	1	1	1	—	—
Personal transfers	—	—	—	17	17	19	20	21	—	—
Outward remittance flows	—	—	—	15	17	17	18	16	—	—
of which										
Compensation of employees	—	—	—	2	3	3	3	2	—	—
Personal transfers	—	—	—	13	14	14	15	14	—	—

a. Net FDI inflows US$0.00 billion, net ODA received US$0.14 billion in 2013.

Moldova

Population (millions, 2014)	3.6
Population growth (avg. annual %, 2005–14)	-0.1
Population density (people per sq km, 2014)	123.8
Labor force (millions, 2014)	1.2
Unemployment rate (% of labor force, 2014)	3.4
Urban population (% of pop., 2014)	44.9
Surface area (thousands of sq km, 2014)	33.9
GNI, Atlas method (current US$ billions, 2014)	9.1
GNI per capita, Atlas method (current US$, 2014)	2,560.0
GDP growth (avg. annual %, 2011–14)	4.9
Poverty headcount ratio at national poverty line (% of pop., 2013)	12.7
Age dependency ratio (% of working-age pop., 2014)	34.6
Account at a formal financial institution (% age 15+, 2014)	17.8
Mobile cellular subscriptions (per 100 people, 2014)	108.0
Internet users (per 100 people, 2014)	46.6

Migration

EMIGRATION

- Stock of emigrants, 2013: **859.4 thousands**
- Stock of emigrants as percentage of population, 2013: **24.2 percent**
- Top destination countries, 2013: the Russian Federation, Ukraine, Italy, Romania, the United States, Germany, Portugal, Uzbekistan, Spain, Israel
- Tertiary-educated as a percentage of total emigrants in OECD countries, 2011: **30.8 percent**
- Tertiary-educated women as a percentage of total women emigrants in OECD countries, 2011: **31.9 percent**
- Number of refugees, 2014: **2,224**
- Second generation diaspora in Australia, Europe, and the United States, 2012: **10.1 thousands**

IMMIGRATION

- Stock of immigrants, 2013: **391.5 thousands**
- Stock of immigrants as percentage of population, 2013: **11.0 percent**
- Top source countries, 2013: the Russian Federation, Ukraine, Belarus, Kazakhstan, Uzbekistan, Poland, Azerbaijan, Lithuania, Latvia, Georgia
- Women as percentage of immigrants, 2013: **53.0 percent**
- Number of refugees, 2014: **293**

Remittances

US$ millions	2006	2007	2008	2009	2010	2011	2012	2013	2014	2015e
Inward remittance flows[a]	1,176	1,491	1,888	1,199	1,351	1,600	1,987	2,192	2,084	1,842
of which Compensation of employees	573	649	842	563	743	899	1,010	1,118	1,068	–
Personal transfers	603	842	1,046	635	608	701	977	1,074	1,015	–
Outward remittance flows	57	72	92	74	79	51	96	106	147	–
of which Compensation of employees	50	56	79	66	59	36	53	56	73	–
Personal transfers	6	16	13	8	19	15	44	50	74	–

a. Net FDI inflows US$0.29 billion, net ODA received US$0.37 billion in 2013.

Monaco

Population (thousands, 2013)	37.6
Population growth (avg. annual %, 2005–14)	1.2
Population density (people per sq km, 2014)	18,811.5
Labor force, total	–
Unemployment rate (% of labor force)	–
Urban population (% of pop., 2014)	100.0
Surface area (thousands of sq km, 2014)	0.0
GNI, Atlas method (current US$ billions, 2008)	6.7
GNI per capita, Atlas method (current US$, 2008)	186,710.0
GDP growth (avg. annual %, 2004–07)	7.9
Poverty headcount ratio at national poverty line (% of pop.)	–
Age dependency ratio (% of working-age pop.)	–
Account at a formal financial institution (% age 15+)	–
Mobile cellular subscriptions (per 100 people, 2014)	88.5
Internet users (per 100 people, 2014)	92.4

Migration

EMIGRATION

- Stock of emigrants, 2013: **53.0 thousands**
- Stock of emigrants as percentage of population, 2013: **141.2 percent**
- Top destination countries, 2013: France, Greece, Italy, the United States, Libya, Switzerland, Brazil, Canada, the Arab Republic of Egypt, Australia
- Tertiary-educated as a percentage of total emigrants in OECD countries, 2011: **20.3 percent**
- Tertiary-educated women as a percentage of total women emigrants in OECD countries, 2011: **21.5 percent**
- Number of refugees, 2014: Not available
- Second generation diaspora in Australia, Europe, and the United States, 2012: Not available

IMMIGRATION

- Stock of immigrants, 2013: **24.3 thousands**
- Stock of immigrants as percentage of population, 2013: **64.7 percent**
- Top source countries, 2013: France, Italy, the United Kingdom, Switzerland, Germany, Belgium, Portugal, the Netherlands, the United States, Morocco
- Women as percentage of immigrants, 2013: **50.6 percent**
- Number of refugees, 2014: **33**

Remittances

US$ millions	2006	2007	2008	2009	2010	2011	2012	2013	2014	2015e
Inward remittance flows	–	–	–	–	–	–	–	–	–	–
of which										
Compensation of employees	–	–	–	–	–	–	–	–	–	–
Personal transfers	–	–	–	–	–	–	–	–	–	–
Outward remittance flows	–	–	–	–	–	–	–	–	–	–
of which										
Compensation of employees	–	–	–	–	–	–	–	–	–	–
Personal transfers	–	–	–	–	–	–	–	–	–	–

Mongolia

Population (millions, 2014)	2.9
Population growth (avg. annual %, 2005–14)	1.5
Population density (people per sq km, 2014)	1.9
Labor force (millions, 2014)	1.3
Unemployment rate (% of labor force, 2014)	4.8
Urban population (% of pop., 2014)	71.2
Surface area (thousands of sq km, 2014)	1,564.1
GNI, Atlas method (current US$ billions, 2014)	12.5
GNI per capita, Atlas method (current US$, 2014)	4,280.0
GDP growth (avg. annual %, 2011–14)	12.3
Poverty headcount ratio at national poverty line (% of pop., 2012)	27.4
Age dependency ratio (% of working-age pop., 2014)	46.8
Account at a formal financial institution (% age 15+, 2014)	91.8
Mobile cellular subscriptions (per 100 people, 2014)	105.1
Internet users (per 100 people, 2014)	27.0

Migration

EMIGRATION

- Stock of emigrants, 2013: **74.8 thousands**
- Stock of emigrants as percentage of population, 2013: **2.6 percent**
- Top destination countries, 2013: the Republic of Korea, the Russian Federation, the Czech Republic, China, Ukraine, Sweden, Austria, Hungary, France, Australia
- Tertiary-educated as a percentage of total emigrants in OECD countries, 2011: **36.0 percent**
- Tertiary-educated women as a percentage of total women emigrants in OECD countries, 2011: **39.9 percent**
- Number of refugees, 2014: **2,125**
- Second generation diaspora in Australia, Europe, and the United States, 2012: Not available

IMMIGRATION

- Stock of immigrants, 2013: **17.2 thousands**
- Stock of immigrants as percentage of population, 2013: **0.6 percent**
- Top source countries, 2013: China, the Russian Federation, the Republic of Korea, the United States, the Democratic Republic of Korea, Japan, Vietnam, Australia, Turkey, Kazakhstan
- Women as percentage of immigrants, 2013: **26.8 percent**
- Number of refugees, 2014: Not available

Remittances

US$ millions	2006	2007	2008	2009	2010	2011	2012	2013	2014	2015e
Inward remittance flows[a]	181	178	225	200	266	279	320	256	255	249
of which										
Compensation of employees	2	4	6	8	18	30	34	46	54	–
Personal transfers	180	174	218	192	248	249	286	210	201	–
Outward remittance flows	77	90	172	83	169	336	523	424	337	–
of which										
Compensation of employees	–	–	23	12	51	146	278	236	166	–
Personal transfers	77	90	149	71	119	191	245	188	171	–

a. Net FDI inflows US$2.15 billion, net ODA received US$0.43 billion in 2013.

Montenegro

Population (thousands, 2013)	621.8
Population growth (avg. annual %, 2005–14)	0.1
Population density (people per sq km, 2014)	46.2
Labor force (thousands, 2013)	251.7
Unemployment rate (% of labor force, 2014)	19.1
Urban population (% of pop., 2014)	63.8
Surface area (thousands of sq km, 2014)	13.8
GNI, Atlas method (current US$ billions, 2014)	4.5
GNI per capita, Atlas method (current US$, 2014)	7,320.0
GDP growth (avg. annual %, 2011–14)	1.5
Poverty headcount ratio at national poverty line (% of pop., 2013)	8.6
Age dependency ratio (% of working-age pop., 2014)	47.5
Account at a formal financial institution (% age 15+, 2014)	59.8
Mobile cellular subscriptions (per 100 people, 2014)	163.0
Internet users (per 100 people, 2014)	61.0

Migration

EMIGRATION

- Stock of emigrants, 2013: **281.8 thousands**
- Stock of emigrants as percentage of population, 2013: **45.4 percent**
- Top destination countries, 2013: Serbia, Turkey, Croatia, Germany, the United States, Austria, Luxembourg, the Former Yugoslav Republic of Macedonia, Albania, Italy
- Tertiary-educated as a percentage of total emigrants in OECD countries, 2011: **17.4 percent**
- Tertiary-educated women as a percentage of total women emigrants in OECD countries, 2011: **19.3 percent**
- Number of refugees, 2014: **593**
- Second generation diaspora in Australia, Europe, and the United States, 2012: Not available

IMMIGRATION

- Stock of immigrants, 2013: **50.7 thousands**
- Stock of immigrants as percentage of population, 2013: **8.2 percent**
- Top source countries, 2013: Albania, Serbia, Bosnia and Herzegovina, Croatia, the Former Yugoslav Republic of Macedonia, Slovenia, Hungary, the Russian Federation, the Arab Republic of Egypt, Greece
- Women as percentage of immigrants, 2013: **60.9 percent**
- Number of refugees, 2014: **6,455**

Remittances

US$ millions	2006	2007	2008	2009	2010	2011	2012	2013	2014	2015e
Inward remittance flows[a]	—	196	298	303	301	343	333	423	431	431
of which										
Compensation of employees	—	110	208	217	211	250	240	263	280	—
Personal transfers	—	87	90	86	90	94	92	160	151	—
Outward remittance flows	—	27	27	26	28	35	42	65	74	—
of which										
Compensation of employees	—	7	8	8	11	16	17	17	23	—
Personal transfers	—	20	20	17	16	19	26	49	52	—

a. Net FDI inflows US$0.45 billion, net ODA received US$0.13 billion in 2013.

Morocco

Population (millions, 2014)	33.9
Population growth (avg. annual %, 2005–14)	1.2
Population density (people per sq km, 2014)	76.0
Labor force (millions, 2014)	12.5
Unemployment rate (% of labor force, 2014)	10.2
Urban population (% of pop., 2014)	59.7
Surface area (thousands of sq km, 2014)	446.6
GNI, Atlas method (current US$ billions, 2014)	105.8
GNI per capita, Atlas method (current US$, 2014)	3,070.0
GDP growth (avg. annual %, 2011–14)	3.8
Poverty headcount ratio at national poverty line (% of pop., 2007)	8.9
Age dependency ratio (% of working-age pop., 2014)	50.2
Account at a formal financial institution (% age 15+)	–
Mobile cellular subscriptions (per 100 people, 2014)	131.7
Internet users (per 100 people, 2014)	56.8

Migration

EMIGRATION

- Stock of emigrants, 2013: **3,040.3 thousands**
- Stock of emigrants as percentage of population, 2013: **9.1 percent**
- Top destination countries, 2013: France, Spain, Italy, Belgium, the Netherlands, Israel, Germany, the United States, Canada, the United Kingdom
- Tertiary-educated as a percentage of total emigrants in OECD countries, 2011: **15.7 percent**
- Tertiary-educated women as a percentage of total women emigrants in OECD countries, 2011: **14.6 percent**
- Number of refugees, 2014: **1,501**
- Second generation diaspora in Australia, Europe, and the United States, 2012: **904.4 thousands**

IMMIGRATION

- Stock of immigrants, 2013: **50.8 thousands**
- Stock of immigrants as percentage of population, 2013: **0.2 percent**
- Top source countries, 2013: Algeria, France, South Sudan, Italy, Libya, the Syrian Arab Republic, Sudan, Saudi Arabia, the Republic of Yemen, Jordan
- Women as percentage of immigrants, 2013: **47.7 percent**
- Number of refugees, 2014: **1,200**

Remittances

US$ millions	2006	2007	2008	2009	2010	2011	2012	2013	2014	2015e
Inward remittance flows[a]	5,451	6,730	6,894	6,269	6,423	7,256	6,508	6,882	7,053	6,679
of which										
Compensation of employees	–	–	–	–	–	–	–	–	–	–
Personal transfers	5,451	6,730	6,894	6,269	6,423	7,256	6,508	6,882	–	–
Outward remittance flows	38	49	54	60	62	71	64	63	–	–
of which										
Compensation of employees	–	–	–	–	–	–	–	–	–	–
Personal transfers	38	49	54	60	62	71	64	63	–	–

a. Net FDI inflows US$3.36 billion, net ODA received US$1.97 billion in 2013.

Mozambique

Population (millions, 2014)	27.2
Population growth (avg. annual %, 2005–14)	2.8
Population density (people per sq km, 2014)	34.6
Labor force (millions, 2014)	12.5
Unemployment rate (% of labor force, 2014)	22.6
Urban population (% of pop., 2014)	31.9
Surface area (thousands of sq km, 2014)	799.4
GNI, Atlas method (current US$ billions, 2014)	16.4
GNI per capita, Atlas method (current US$, 2014)	600.0
GDP growth (avg. annual %, 2011–14)	7.2
Poverty headcount ratio at national poverty line (% of pop., 2008)	54.7
Age dependency ratio (% of working-age pop., 2014)	95.5
Account at a formal financial institution (% age 15+)	–
Mobile cellular subscriptions (per 100 people, 2014)	69.7
Internet users (per 100 people, 2014)	5.9

Migration

EMIGRATION

- Stock of emigrants, 2013: **727.4 thousands**
- Stock of emigrants as percentage of population, 2013: **2.7 percent**
- Top destination countries, 2013: South Africa, Zimbabwe, Portugal, Malawi, Tanzania, Swaziland, the United Kingdom, the United States, Brazil, Kenya
- Tertiary-educated as a percentage of total emigrants in OECD countries, 2011: **32.3 percent**
- Tertiary-educated women as a percentage of total women emigrants in OECD countries, 2011: **33.8 percent**
- Number of refugees, 2014: **45**
- Second generation diaspora in Australia, Europe, and the United States, 2012: **18.6 thousands**

IMMIGRATION

- Stock of immigrants, 2013: **218.8 thousands**
- Stock of immigrants as percentage of population, 2013: **0.8 percent**
- Top source countries, 2013: Malawi, Zimbabwe, South Africa, Lesotho, Tanzania, Cabo Verde, Zambia, Portugal, India, the Democratic Republic of Congo
- Women as percentage of immigrants, 2013: **38.6 percent**
- Number of refugees, 2014: **4,524**

Remittances

US$ millions	2006	2007	2008	2009	2010	2011	2012	2013	2014	2015e
Inward remittance flows[a]	**80**	**99**	**116**	**111**	**116**	**130**	**174**	**152**	**155**	**156**
of which										
Compensation of employees	64	68	82	80	82	97	72	70	53	–
Personal transfers	16	31	34	31	33	33	102	82	103	–
Outward remittance flows	**26**	**45**	**57**	**66**	**54**	**41**	**96**	**100**	**194**	**–**
of which										
Compensation of employees	14	19	19	25	20	9	26	15	70	–
Personal transfers	12	26	38	41	33	33	70	85	124	–

a. Net FDI inflows US$6.70 billion, net ODA received US$2.31 billion in 2013.

Myanmar

Population (millions, 2014)	53.4
Population growth (avg. annual %, 2005–14)	0.7
Population density (people per sq km, 2014)	81.8
Labor force (millions, 2014)	30.2
Unemployment rate (% of labor force, 2014)	3.3
Urban population (% of pop., 2014)	33.6
Surface area (thousands of sq km, 2014)	676.6
GNI, Atlas method (current US$ billions, 2014)	68.1
GNI per capita, Atlas method (current US$, 2014)	1,270.0
GDP growth (avg. annual %, 2011–14)	8.4
Poverty headcount ratio at national poverty line (% of pop.)	–
Age dependency ratio (% of working-age pop., 2014)	49.9
Account at a formal financial institution (% age 15+, 2014)	22.6
Mobile cellular subscriptions (per 100 people, 2014)	49.5
Internet users (per 100 people, 2014)	2.1

Migration

EMIGRATION

- Stock of emigrants, 2013: **3,139.6 thousands**
- Stock of emigrants as percentage of population, 2013: **5.9 percent**
- Top destination countries, 2013: Thailand, Saudi Arabia, Bangladesh, the United States, Pakistan, Malaysia, India, China, Australia, Vietnam
- Tertiary-educated as a percentage of total emigrants in OECD countries, 2011: **31.4 percent**
- Tertiary-educated women as a percentage of total women emigrants in OECD countries, 2011: **31.0 percent**
- Number of refugees, 2014: **478,976**
- Second generation diaspora in Australia, Europe, and the United States, 2012: **41.6 thousands**

IMMIGRATION

- Stock of immigrants, 2013: **103.1 thousands**
- Stock of immigrants as percentage of population, 2013: **0.2 percent**
- Top source countries, 2013: China, India, Pakistan, Bangladesh
- Women as percentage of immigrants, 2013: **46.8 percent**
- Number of refugees, 2014: Not available

Remittances

US$ millions	2006	2007	2008	2009	2010	2011	2012	2013	2014	2015e
Inward remittance flows[a]	**115**	**81**	**55**	**54**	**115**	**127**	**275**	**1,644**	**3,103**	**3,478**
of which										
Compensation of employees	50	81	55	54	115	127	275	229	118	–
Personal transfers	65	–	–	–	–	–	–	1,414	2,984	–
Outward remittance flows	**31**	**–**	**–**	**–**	**–**	**–**	**–**	**419**	**773**	**–**
of which										
Compensation of employees	–	–	–	–	–	–	–	–	–	–
Personal transfers	31	–	–	–	–	–	–	419	773	–

a. Net FDI inflows US$2.25 billion, net ODA received US$3.93 billion in 2013.

Namibia

Population (millions, 2014)	2.4
Population growth (avg. annual %, 2005–14)	1.8
Population density (people per sq km, 2014)	2.9
Labor force (thousands, 2013)	901.9
Unemployment rate (% of labor force, 2014)	18.6
Urban population (% of pop., 2014)	45.7
Surface area (thousands of sq km, 2014)	824.3
GNI, Atlas method (current US$ billions, 2014)	13.5
GNI per capita, Atlas method (current US$, 2014)	5,630.0
GDP growth (avg. annual %, 2011–14)	5.6
Poverty headcount ratio at national poverty line (% of pop., 2009)	28.7
Age dependency ratio (% of working-age pop., 2014)	67.8
Account at a formal financial institution (% age 15+, 2014)	58.1
Mobile cellular subscriptions (per 100 people, 2014)	113.8
Internet users (per 100 people, 2014)	14.8

Migration

EMIGRATION

- Stock of emigrants, 2013: **138.6 thousands**
- Stock of emigrants as percentage of population, 2013: **5.9 percent**
- Top destination countries, 2013: South Africa, Tanzania, Botswana, Australia, the United States, Angola, Canada, Switzerland, the Netherlands, Austria
- Tertiary-educated as a percentage of total emigrants in OECD countries, 2011: **42.3 percent**
- Tertiary-educated women as a percentage of total women emigrants in OECD countries, 2011: **41.5 percent**
- Number of refugees, 2014: **1,235**
- Second generation diaspora in Australia, Europe, and the United States, 2012: **0.6 thousands**

IMMIGRATION

- Stock of immigrants, 2013: **65.4 thousands**
- Stock of immigrants as percentage of population, 2013: **2.8 percent**
- Top source countries, 2013: Angola, Zambia, South Africa, Zimbabwe, Botswana
- Women as percentage of immigrants, 2013: **40.6 percent**
- Number of refugees, 2014: **1,755**

Remittances

US$ millions	2006	2007	2008	2009	2010	2011	2012	2013	2014	2015e
Inward remittance flows[a]	**16**	**16**	**14**	**13**	**15**	**15**	**13**	**11**	**10**	**10**
of which										
Compensation of employees	10	9	8	8	9	9	8	7	6	–
Personal transfers	7	6	5	5	6	6	5	5	4	–
Outward remittance flows	**20**	**16**	**42**	**15**	**28**	**27**	**18**	**16**	**12**	**–**
of which										
Compensation of employees	16	12	39	12	24	23	15	13	9	–
Personal transfers	4	4	3	3	4	4	3	3	2	–

a. Net FDI inflows US$-0.56 billion, net ODA received US$0.26 billion in 2013.

Nepal

Population (millions, 2014)	28.2
Population growth (avg. annual %, 2005–14)	1.1
Population density (people per sq km, 2014)	196.5
Labor force (millions, 2014)	15.6
Unemployment rate (% of labor force, 2014)	2.7
Urban population (% of pop., 2014)	18.2
Surface area (thousands of sq km, 2014)	147.2
GNI, Atlas method (current US$ billions, 2014)	20.6
GNI per capita, Atlas method (current US$, 2014)	730.0
GDP growth (avg. annual %, 2011–14)	4.4
Poverty headcount ratio at national poverty line (% of pop., 2010)	25.2
Age dependency ratio (% of working-age pop., 2014)	63.7
Account at a formal financial institution (% age 15+, 2014)	33.8
Mobile cellular subscriptions (per 100 people, 2014)	82.5
Internet users (per 100 people, 2014)	15.4

Migration

EMIGRATION

- Stock of emigrants, 2013: **1,986.2 thousands**
- Stock of emigrants as percentage of population, 2013: **7.1 percent**
- Top destination countries, 2013: India, Saudi Arabia, Qatar, the United Arab Emirates, the United States, Malaysia, Kuwait, the United Kingdom, Bangladesh, Australia
- Tertiary-educated as a percentage of total emigrants in OECD countries, 2011: **39.1 percent**
- Tertiary-educated women as a percentage of total women emigrants in OECD countries, 2011: **35.6 percent**
- Number of refugees, 2014: **8,532**
- Second generation diaspora in Australia, Europe, and the United States, 2012: **5.7 thousands**

IMMIGRATION

- Stock of immigrants, 2013: **971.2 thousands**
- Stock of immigrants as percentage of population, 2013: **3.5 percent**
- Top source countries, 2013: India, Bhutan, China, Pakistan, Bangladesh, Sri Lanka
- Women as percentage of immigrants, 2013: **68.3 percent**
- Number of refugees, 2014: **38,480**

Remittances

US$ millions	2006	2007	2008	2009	2010	2011	2012	2013	2014	2015e
Inward remittance flows[a]	1,453	1,734	2,727	2,983	3,464	4,217	4,793	5,589	5,770	6,594
of which										
Compensation of employees	80	87	146	127	132	206	160	185	207	–
Personal transfers	1,373	1,647	2,581	2,856	3,332	4,010	4,633	5,403	5,562	–
Outward remittance flows	79	4	5	12	32	39	50	28	9	–
of which										
Compensation of employees	10	4	5	12	32	39	50	28	9	–
Personal transfers	69	–	–	–	–	–	–	–	–	–

a. Net FDI inflows US$0.07 billion, net ODA received US$0.87 billion in 2013.

Netherlands, The

	HIGH INCOME OECD
Population (millions, 2014)	16.9
Population growth (avg. annual %, 2005–14)	0.3
Population density (people per sq km, 2014)	500.6
Labor force (millions, 2014)	9.0
Unemployment rate (% of labor force, 2014)	6.9
Urban population (% of pop., 2014)	89.9
Surface area (thousands of sq km, 2014)	41.5
GNI, Atlas method (current US$ billions, 2014)	874.6
GNI per capita, Atlas method (current US$, 2014)	51,890.0
GDP growth (avg. annual %, 2011–14)	0.3
Poverty headcount ratio at national poverty line (% of pop.)	–
Age dependency ratio (% of working-age pop., 2014)	52.5
Account at a formal financial institution (% age 15+, 2014)	99.3
Mobile cellular subscriptions (per 100 people, 2014)	116.4
Internet users (per 100 people, 2014)	93.2

Migration

EMIGRATION

- Stock of emigrants, 2013: **1,008.7 thousands**
- Stock of emigrants as percentage of population, 2013: **6.0 percent**
- Top destination countries, 2013: Germany, Canada, Belgium, Australia, the United States, the United Kingdom, Spain, France, Turkey, Switzerland
- Tertiary-educated as a percentage of total emigrants in OECD countries, 2011: **34.4 percent**
- Tertiary-educated women as a percentage of total women emigrants in OECD countries, 2011: **30.3 percent**
- Number of refugees, 2014: **63**
- Second generation diaspora in Australia, Europe, and the United States, 2012: **411.3 thousands**

IMMIGRATION

- Stock of immigrants, 2013: **1,964.9 thousands**
- Stock of immigrants as percentage of population, 2013: **11.7 percent**
- Top source countries, 2013: Turkey, Suriname, Morocco, Indonesia, Germany, Poland, Curaçao, China, Serbia, Belgium
- Women as percentage of immigrants, 2013: **52.2 percent**
- Number of refugees, 2014: **82,433**

Remittances

US$ millions	2006	2007	2008	2009	2010	2011	2012	2013	2014	2015e
Inward remittance flows[a]	1,552	1,630	1,649	1,712	1,720	1,788	1,641	1,619	1,540	1,517
of which										
Compensation of employees	1,241	1,318	1,384	1,461	1,455	1,509	1,384	1,348	1,259	–
Personal transfers	311	312	265	251	265	278	257	271	282	–
Outward remittance flows	6,076	10,086	12,696	11,662	9,398	10,246	9,576	9,807	9,945	–
of which										
Compensation of employees	4,314	8,003	10,393	9,585	7,324	8,115	7,545	7,570	7,485	–
Personal transfers	1,763	2,083	2,303	2,077	2,074	2,131	2,031	2,236	2,461	–

a. Net FDI inflows US$309.71 billion in 2013.

New Caledonia

Population (thousands, 2013)	266.0
Population growth (avg. annual %, 2005–14)	1.5
Population density (people per sq km, 2014)	14.6
Labor force (thousands, 2013)	117.0
Unemployment rate (% of labor force)	–
Urban population (% of pop., 2014)	69.7
Surface area (thousands of sq km, 2014)	18.6
GNI, Atlas method (current US$ billions, 2000)	3.0
GNI per capita, Atlas method (current US$, 2000)	14,020.0
GDP growth (avg. annual %)	–
Poverty headcount ratio at national poverty line (% of pop.)	–
Age dependency ratio (% of working-age pop., 2014)	48.1
Account at a formal financial institution (% age 15+)	–
Mobile cellular subscriptions (per 100 people, 2014)	93.6
Internet users (per 100 people, 2014)	70.0

Migration

EMIGRATION

- Stock of emigrants, 2013: **6.4 thousands**
- Stock of emigrants as percentage of population, 2013: **2.4 percent**
- Top destination countries, 2013: French Polynesia, Australia, the United States, Vanuatu, Argentina, Canada, Ukraine, Colombia, the Netherlands, Norway
- Tertiary-educated as a percentage of total emigrants in OECD countries, 2011: Not available
- Tertiary-educated women as a percentage of total women emigrants in OECD countries, 2011: Not available
- Number of refugees, 2014: Not available
- Second generation diaspora in Australia, Europe, and the United States, 2012: Not available

IMMIGRATION

- Stock of immigrants, 2013: **63.0 thousands**
- Stock of immigrants as percentage of population, 2013: **24.1 percent**
- Top source countries, 2013: France, Vanuatu, Indonesia, Tunisia, the Lao People's Democratic Republic, Algeria, Vietnam, Cambodia, Morocco, French Polynesia
- Women as percentage of immigrants, 2013: **46.2 percent**
- Number of refugees, 2014: Not available

Remittances

US$ millions	2006	2007	2008	2009	2010	2011	2012	2013	2014	2015e
Inward remittance flows[a]	**537**	**491**	**544**	**509**	**492**	**594**	**498**	**558**	**558**	**565**
of which										
Compensation of employees	533	488	538	504	487	588	493	553	–	–
Personal transfers	4	3	6	6	5	6	5	5	–	–
Outward remittance flows	**50**	**56**	**68**	**92**	**83**	**87**	**68**	**45**	**–**	**–**
of which										
Compensation of employees	32	37	50	78	73	77	59	38	–	–
Personal transfers	18	18	18	15	10	10	9	8	–	–

a. Net FDI inflows US$2.21 billion in 2013.

New Zealand

Population (millions, 2014)	4.5
Population growth (avg. annual %, 2005–14)	1.0
Population density (people per sq km, 2014)	17.1
Labor force (millions, 2014)	2.4
Unemployment rate (% of labor force, 2014)	5.6
Urban population (% of pop., 2014)	86.3
Surface area (thousands of sq km, 2014)	267.7
GNI, Atlas method (current US$ billions, 2011)	139.8
GNI per capita, Atlas method (current US$, 2011)	31,890.0
GDP growth (avg. annual %, 2011–14)	2.3
Poverty headcount ratio at national poverty line (% of pop.)	–
Age dependency ratio (% of working-age pop., 2014)	53.2
Account at a formal financial institution (% age 15+, 2014)	99.5
Mobile cellular subscriptions (per 100 people, 2014)	112.1
Internet users (per 100 people, 2014)	85.5

Migration

EMIGRATION

- Stock of emigrants, 2013: **763.7 thousands**
- Stock of emigrants as percentage of population, 2013: **17.2 percent**
- Top destination countries, 2013: Australia, the United Kingdom, the United States, Brunei Darussalam, Canada, Malaysia, Japan, Samoa, the Netherlands, China
- Tertiary-educated as a percentage of total emigrants in OECD countries, 2011: **28.6 percent**
- Tertiary-educated women as a percentage of total women emigrants in OECD countries, 2011: **31.4 percent**
- Number of refugees, 2014: **14**
- Second generation diaspora in Australia, Europe, and the United States, 2012: **137.3 thousands**

IMMIGRATION

- Stock of immigrants, 2013: **1,261.2 thousands**
- Stock of immigrants as percentage of population, 2013: **28.4 percent**
- Top source countries, 2013: the United Kingdom, China, India, Australia, South Africa, Fiji, Samoa, the Philippines, the Republic of Korea, Tonga
- Women as percentage of immigrants, 2013: **53.2 percent**
- Number of refugees, 2014: **1,277**

Remittances

US$ millions	2006	2007	2008	2009	2010	2011	2012	2013	2014	2015e
Inward remittance flows[a]	**335**	**384**	**421**	**331**	**371**	**455**	**462**	**459**	**462**	**468**
of which										
Compensation of employees	–	–	–	–	–	–	–	–	–	–
Personal transfers	335	384	421	331	371	455	462	459	462	–
Outward remittance flows	**552**	**623**	**624**	**524**	**534**	**610**	**662**	**708**	**713**	**–**
of which										
Compensation of employees	53	66	93	82	93	119	123	144	139	–
Personal transfers	499	557	532	443	441	491	538	564	574	–

a. Net FDI inflows US$-0.51 billion in 2013.

Nicaragua

	MIDDLE INCOME
Population (millions, 2014)	6.0
Population growth (avg. annual %, 2005–14)	1.2
Population density (people per sq km, 2014)	50.0
Labor force (millions, 2014)	2.7
Unemployment rate (% of labor force, 2014)	5.3
Urban population (% of pop., 2014)	58.5
Surface area (thousands of sq km, 2014)	130.4
GNI, Atlas method (current US$ billions, 2014)	11.3
GNI per capita, Atlas method (current US$, 2014)	1,870.0
GDP growth (avg. annual %, 2011–14)	5.1
Poverty headcount ratio at national poverty line (% of pop., 2009)	42.5
Age dependency ratio (% of working-age pop., 2014)	55.0
Account at a formal financial institution (% age 15+, 2014)	18.9
Mobile cellular subscriptions (per 100 people, 2014)	114.6
Internet users (per 100 people, 2014)	17.6

Migration

EMIGRATION

- Stock of emigrants, 2013: **633.1 thousands**
- Stock of emigrants as percentage of population, 2013: **10.6 percent**
- Top destination countries, 2013: Costa Rica, the United States, Spain, Panama, Canada, Guatemala, El Salvador, Honduras, Mexico, República Bolivariana de Venezuela
- Tertiary-educated as a percentage of total emigrants in OECD countries, 2011: **24.3 percent**
- Tertiary-educated women as a percentage of total women emigrants in OECD countries, 2011: **24.8 percent**
- Number of refugees, 2014: **1,575**
- Second generation diaspora in Australia, Europe, and the United States, 2012: **169.0 thousands**

IMMIGRATION

- Stock of immigrants, 2013: **41.5 thousands**
- Stock of immigrants as percentage of population, 2013: **0.7 percent**
- Top source countries, 2013: Honduras, Costa Rica, the United States, El Salvador, Guatemala, Cuba, Mexico, Spain, Colombia, Panama
- Women as percentage of immigrants, 2013: **48.2 percent**
- Number of refugees, 2014: **273**

Remittances

US$ millions	2006	2007	2008	2009	2010	2011	2012	2013	2014	2015e
Inward remittance flows[a]	698	740	820	770	825	914	1,016	1,081	1,140	1,195
of which										
Compensation of employees	–	–	2	2	2	2	2	4	4	–
Personal transfers	698	740	818	768	823	912	1,014	1,078	1,136	–
Outward remittance flows	–	–	1	1	1	1	2	1	1	–
of which										
Compensation of employees	–	–	1	1	1	1	2	1	1	–
Personal transfers	–	–	–	–	–	–	–	–	–	–

a. Net FDI inflows US$0.82 billion, net ODA received US$0.50 billion in 2013.

Niger

LOW INCOME

Population (millions, 2014)	19.1
Population growth (avg. annual %, 2005–14)	3.9
Population density (people per sq km, 2014)	15.1
Labor force (millions, 2014)	6.1
Unemployment rate (% of labor force, 2014)	5.1
Urban population (% of pop., 2014)	18.5
Surface area (thousands of sq km, 2014)	1,267.0
GNI, Atlas method (current US$ billions, 2014)	7.8
GNI per capita, Atlas method (current US$, 2014)	410.0
GDP growth (avg. annual %, 2011–14)	6.4
Poverty headcount ratio at national poverty line (% of pop., 2011)	48.9
Age dependency ratio (% of working-age pop., 2014)	112.7
Account at a formal financial institution (% age 15+, 2014)	3.5
Mobile cellular subscriptions (per 100 people, 2014)	44.4
Internet users (per 100 people, 2014)	2.0

Migration

EMIGRATION

- Stock of emigrants, 2013: **290.3 thousands**
- Stock of emigrants as percentage of population, 2013: **1.6 percent**
- Top destination countries, 2013: Nigeria, Benin, Côte d'Ivoire, Cameroon, Togo, Burkina Faso, Ghana, Mali, France, Chad
- Tertiary-educated as a percentage of total emigrants in OECD countries, 2011: **35.9 percent**
- Tertiary-educated women as a percentage of total women emigrants in OECD countries, 2011: **37.4 percent**
- Number of refugees, 2014: **712**
- Second generation diaspora in Australia, Europe, and the United States, 2012: **8.5 thousands**

IMMIGRATION

- Stock of immigrants, 2013: **132.3 thousands**
- Stock of immigrants as percentage of population, 2013: **0.7 percent**
- Top source countries, 2013: Mali, Nigeria, Burkina Faso, Benin, Togo, Ghana, Côte d'Ivoire, Senegal, Chad, South Sudan
- Women as percentage of immigrants, 2013: **52.7 percent**
- Number of refugees, 2014: **77,821**

Remittances

US$ millions	2006	2007	2008	2009	2010	2011	2012	2013	2014	2015e
Inward remittance flows[a]	78	79	94	102	134	166	152	146	146	146
of which										
Compensation of employees	29	37	41	41	48	74	63	60	–	–
Personal transfers	49	43	53	60	87	92	89	86	–	–
Outward remittance flows	29	18	22	25	72	112	91	91	–	–
of which										
Compensation of employees	2	6	7	9	16	48	37	39	–	–
Personal transfers	27	12	15	16	56	63	54	53	–	–

a. Net FDI inflows US$0.72 billion, net ODA received US$0.77 billion in 2013.

Nigeria

Population (millions, 2014)	177.5
Population growth (avg. annual %, 2005–14)	2.7
Population density (people per sq km, 2014)	194.9
Labor force (millions, 2014)	55.8
Unemployment rate (% of labor force, 2014)	7.5
Urban population (% of pop., 2014)	46.9
Surface area (thousands of sq km, 2014)	923.8
GNI, Atlas method (current US$ billions, 2014)	526.5
GNI per capita, Atlas method (current US$, 2014)	2,970.0
GDP growth (avg. annual %, 2011–14)	5.2
Poverty headcount ratio at national poverty line (% of pop., 2009)	46.0
Age dependency ratio (% of working-age pop., 2014)	88.0
Account at a formal financial institution (% age 15+, 2014)	44.2
Mobile cellular subscriptions (per 100 people, 2014)	77.8
Internet users (per 100 people, 2014)	42.7

Migration

EMIGRATION

- Stock of emigrants, 2013: **1,117.9 thousands**
- Stock of emigrants as percentage of population, 2013: **0.6 percent**
- Top destination countries, 2013: the United States, the United Kingdom, Cameroon, Ghana, Italy, Côte d'Ivoire, Benin, Spain, Germany, Gabon
- Tertiary-educated as a percentage of total emigrants in OECD countries, 2011: **51.2 percent**
- Tertiary-educated women as a percentage of total women emigrants in OECD countries, 2011: **47.4 percent**
- Number of refugees, 2014: **90,865**
- Second generation diaspora in Australia, Europe, and the United States, 2012: **158.0 thousands**

IMMIGRATION

- Stock of immigrants, 2013: **1,233.6 thousands**
- Stock of immigrants as percentage of population, 2013: **0.7 percent**
- Top source countries, 2013: Benin, Ghana, Mali, Togo, Niger, Chad, Cameroon, Mauritania, Liberia, the Arab Republic of Egypt
- Women as percentage of immigrants, 2013: **46.3 percent**
- Number of refugees, 2014: **1,217**

Remittances

US$ millions	2006	2007	2008	2009	2010	2011	2012	2013	2014	2015e
Inward remittance flows[a]	**16,932**	**18,011**	**19,206**	**18,368**	**19,745**	**20,617**	**20,543**	**20,797**	**20,829**	**20,771**
of which										
Compensation of employees	192	218	127	138	167	180	180	190	198	–
Personal transfers	16,740	17,793	19,079	18,230	19,578	20,436	20,362	20,607	20,631	–
Outward remittance flows	**102**	**54**	**58**	**47**	**47**	**76**	**39**	**50**	**58**	**–**
of which										
Compensation of employees	66	28	35	19	19	43	15	23	21	–
Personal transfers	35	26	23	28	29	32	24	27	37	–

a. Net FDI inflows US$5.56 billion, net ODA received US$2.53 billion in 2013.

Northern Mariana Islands

Population (thousands, 2013)	54.5
Population growth (avg. annual %, 2005–14)	-1.9
Population density (people per sq km, 2014)	118.6
Labor force, total	–
Unemployment rate (% of labor force)	–
Urban population (% of pop., 2014)	89.3
Surface area (thousands of sq km, 2014)	0.5
GNI, Atlas method (current US$ billions)	–
GNI per capita, Atlas method (current US$)	–
GDP growth (avg. annual %)	–
Poverty headcount ratio at national poverty line (% of pop.)	–
Age dependency ratio (% of working-age pop.)	–
Account at a formal financial institution (% age 15+)	–
Mobile cellular subscriptions (per 100 people, 2004)	31.0
Internet users (per 100 people)	–

Migration

EMIGRATION

- Stock of emigrants, 2013: **10.0 thousands**
- Stock of emigrants as percentage of population, 2013: **18.6 percent**
- Top destination countries, 2013: the United States, Guam, the Federated States of Micronesia, Palau, the Russian Federation, Greece, South Africa, Chile, Turkey, Australia
- Tertiary-educated as a percentage of total emigrants in OECD countries, 2011: **30.2 percent**
- Tertiary-educated women as a percentage of total women emigrants in OECD countries, 2011: **30.3 percent**
- Number of refugees, 2014: Not available
- Second generation diaspora in Australia, Europe, and the United States, 2012: Not available

IMMIGRATION

- Stock of immigrants, 2013: **24.2 thousands**
- Stock of immigrants as percentage of population, 2013: **44.8 percent**
- Top source countries, 2013: the Philippines, China, the Republic of Korea, the United States, the Federated States of Micronesia, Puerto Rico, Guam, Palau, Japan, Bangladesh
- Women as percentage of immigrants, 2013: **49.5 percent**
- Number of refugees, 2014: Not available

Remittances

US$ millions	2006	2007	2008	2009	2010	2011	2012	2013	2014	2015e
Inward remittance flows[a]	–	–	–	–	–	–	–	–	–	–
of which										
Compensation of employees	–	–	–	–	–	–	–	–	–	–
Personal transfers	–	–	–	–	–	–	–	–	–	–
Outward remittance flows	–	–	–	–	–	–	–	–	–	–
of which										
Compensation of employees	–	–	–	–	–	–	–	–	–	–
Personal transfers	–	–	–	–	–	–	–	–	–	–

a. Net FDI inflows US$0.01 billion in 2013.

Norway

	HIGH INCOME OECD
Population (millions, 2014)	5.1
Population growth (avg. annual %, 2005–14)	1.1
Population density (people per sq km, 2014)	14.1
Labor force (millions, 2014)	2.7
Unemployment rate (% of labor force, 2014)	3.4
Urban population (% of pop., 2014)	80.2
Surface area (thousands of sq km, 2014)	385.2
GNI, Atlas method (current US$ billions, 2014)	532.3
GNI per capita, Atlas method (current US$, 2014)	103,630.0
GDP growth (avg. annual %, 2011–14)	1.7
Poverty headcount ratio at national poverty line (% of pop.)	–
Age dependency ratio (% of working-age pop., 2014)	51.8
Account at a formal financial institution (% age 15+, 2014)	100.0
Mobile cellular subscriptions (per 100 people, 2014)	116.5
Internet users (per 100 people, 2014)	96.3

Migration

EMIGRATION

- Stock of emigrants, 2013: **204.3 thousands**
- Stock of emigrants as percentage of population, 2013: **4.0 percent**
- Top destination countries, 2013: Sweden, the United States, Denmark, Spain, the United Kingdom, Bangladesh, Germany, Canada, Turkey, Australia
- Tertiary-educated as a percentage of total emigrants in OECD countries, 2011: **34.4 percent**
- Tertiary-educated women as a percentage of total women emigrants in OECD countries, 2011: **32.0 percent**
- Number of refugees, 2014: Not available
- Second generation diaspora in Australia, Europe, and the United States, 2012: **183.2 thousands**

IMMIGRATION

- Stock of immigrants, 2013: **692.0 thousands**
- Stock of immigrants as percentage of population, 2013: **13.6 percent**
- Top source countries, 2013: Poland, Sweden, Lithuania, Germany, Somalia, Denmark, Iraq, the Philippines, Pakistan, the United Kingdom
- Women as percentage of immigrants, 2013: **47.7 percent**
- Number of refugees, 2014: **46,980**

Remittances

US$ millions	2006	2007	2008	2009	2010	2011	2012	2013	2014	2015e
Inward remittance flows[a]	**529**	**617**	**685**	**631**	**680**	**765**	**767**	**791**	**761**	**766**
of which										
Compensation of employees	529	617	685	631	680	765	767	791	761	–
Personal transfers	–	–	–	–	–	–	–	–	–	–
Outward remittance flows	**2,597**	**3,577**	**4,750**	**4,174**	**4,118**	**4,427**	**5,100**	**5,779**	**5,822**	**–**
of which										
Compensation of employees	2,597	3,577	4,750	4,174	4,118	4,427	5,100	5,779	5,822	–
Personal transfers	–	–	–	–	–	–	–	–	–	–

a. Net FDI inflows US$1.00 billion in 2013.

Oman

Population (millions, 2014)	4.2
Population growth (avg. annual %, 2005–14)	5.5
Population density (people per sq km, 2014)	13.7
Labor force (millions, 2014)	2.2
Unemployment rate (% of labor force, 2014)	7.2
Urban population (% of pop., 2014)	77.2
Surface area (thousands of sq km, 2014)	309.5
GNI, Atlas method (current US$ billions, 2014)	65.9
GNI per capita, Atlas method (current US$, 2014)	16,870.0
GDP growth (avg. annual %, 2011–14)	3.2
Poverty headcount ratio at national poverty line (% of pop.)	–
Age dependency ratio (% of working-age pop., 2014)	31.0
Account at a formal financial institution (% age 15+)	–
Mobile cellular subscriptions (per 100 people, 2014)	157.8
Internet users (per 100 people, 2014)	70.2

Migration

EMIGRATION

- Stock of emigrants, 2013: **24.0 thousands**
- Stock of emigrants as percentage of population, 2013: **0.6 percent**
- Top destination countries, 2013: the West Bank and Gaza, the United Kingdom, Libya, Australia, the United States, Canada, the Arab Republic of Egypt, Jordan, the Netherlands, the Philippines
- Tertiary-educated as a percentage of total emigrants in OECD countries, 2011: **32.6 percent**
- Tertiary-educated women as a percentage of total women emigrants in OECD countries, 2011: **31.7 percent**
- Number of refugees, 2014: **20**
- Second generation diaspora in Australia, Europe, and the United States, 2012: Not available

IMMIGRATION

- Stock of immigrants, 2013: **1,112.0 thousands†**
- Stock of immigrants as percentage of population, 2013: **28.5 percent**
- Top source countries, 2013: India, Bangladesh, Pakistan, the Arab Republic of Egypt, Indonesia, the Philippines, Sri Lanka, Jordan, the United Arab Emirates, Sudan
- Women as percentage of immigrants, 2013: **19.0 percent**
- Number of refugees, 2014: **150**

Remittances

US$ millions	2006	2007	2008	2009	2010	2011	2012	2013	2014	2015e
Inward remittance flows[a]	**39**	**39**	**39**	**39**	**39**	**39**	**39**	**39**	**39**	**39**
of which										
Compensation of employees	39	39	39	39	39	39	39	39	39	–
Personal transfers	–	–	–	–	–	–	–	–	–	–
Outward remittance flows	**2,788**	**3,670**	**5,181**	**5,316**	**5,704**	**7,215**	**8,087**	**9,104**	**10,301**	–
of which										
Compensation of employees	–	–	–	–	–	–	–	–	–	–
Personal transfers	2,788	3,670	5,181	5,316	5,704	7,215	8,087	9,104	10,301	–

a. Net FDI inflows US$1.63 billion in 2013.
†According to De Bel-Air (2015), the stock of immigrants in Oman is 1,849,412, mainly from India, Bangladesh, and Pakistan, which represents 87 percent of the workforce in 2013.

Pakistan

	MIDDLE INCOME
Population (millions, 2014)	185.0
Population growth (avg. annual %, 2005–14)	2.1
Population density (people per sq km, 2014)	240.0
Labor force (millions, 2014)	65.4
Unemployment rate (% of labor force, 2014)	5.2
Urban population (% of pop., 2014)	38.3
Surface area (thousands of sq km, 2014)	796.1
GNI, Atlas method (current US$ billions, 2014)	258.3
GNI per capita, Atlas method (current US$, 2014)	1,400.0
GDP growth (avg. annual %, 2011–14)	3.8
Poverty headcount ratio at national poverty line (% of pop., 2005)	22.3
Age dependency ratio (% of working-age pop., 2014)	65.8
Account at a formal financial institution (% age 15+, 2014)	8.7
Mobile cellular subscriptions (per 100 people, 2014)	73.3
Internet users (per 100 people, 2014)	13.8

Migration

EMIGRATION

- Stock of emigrants, 2013: **6,170.4 thousands**
- Stock of emigrants as percentage of population, 2013: **3.4 percent**
- Top destination countries, 2013: Saudi Arabia, the United Arab Emirates, India, the United Kingdom, the United States, Kuwait, Canada, Singapore, Oman, Qatar
- Tertiary-educated as a percentage of total emigrants in OECD countries, 2011: **36.1 percent**
- Tertiary-educated women as a percentage of total women emigrants in OECD countries, 2011: **33.3 percent**
- Number of refugees, 2014: **335,866**
- Second generation diaspora in Australia, Europe, and the United States, 2012: **410.5 thousands**

IMMIGRATION

- Stock of immigrants, 2013: **4,080.8 thousands**
- Stock of immigrants as percentage of population, 2013: **2.3 percent**
- Top source countries, 2013: Afghanistan, India, Bangladesh, Myanmar, Somalia, Iraq, the Islamic Republic of Iran, Algeria
- Women as percentage of immigrants, 2013: **43.5 percent**
- Number of refugees, 2014: **1,505,516**

Remittances

US$ millions	2006	2007	2008	2009	2010	2011	2012	2013	2014	2015e
Inward remittance flows[a]	5,121	5,998	7,039	8,717	9,690	12,263	14,007	14,629	17,066	19,609
of which										
Compensation of employees	8	6	14	16	23	28	29	32	39	–
Personal transfers	5,113	5,992	7,025	8,701	9,667	12,235	13,978	14,597	17,027	–
Outward remittance flows	3	2	–	8	9	28	34	16	16	–
of which										
Compensation of employees	2	–	–	8	9	2	10	2	1	–
Personal transfers	1	2	–	–	–	26	24	14	15	–

a. Net FDI inflows US$1.33 billion, net ODA received US$2.17 billion in 2013.

Migration and Remittances Factbook 2016

Palau

Population (thousands, 2013)	21.1
Population growth (avg. annual %, 2005–14)	0.6
Population density (people per sq km, 2014)	45.9
Labor force, total	–
Unemployment rate (% of labor force)	–
Urban population (% of pop., 2014)	86.5
Surface area (thousands of sq km, 2014)	0.5
GNI, Atlas method (current US$ billions, 2014)	0.2
GNI per capita, Atlas method (current US$, 2014)	11,110.0
GDP growth (avg. annual %, 2011–14)	4.7
Poverty headcount ratio at national poverty line (% of pop.)	–
Age dependency ratio (% of working-age pop.)	–
Account at a formal financial institution (% age 15+)	–
Mobile cellular subscriptions (per 100 people, 2014)	90.6
Internet users (per 100 people, 2004)	27.0

Migration

EMIGRATION

- Stock of emigrants, 2013: **5.6 thousands**
- Stock of emigrants as percentage of population, 2013: **26.7 percent**
- Top destination countries, 2013: the United States, Guam, the Northern Mariana Islands, Vietnam, the Federated States of Micronesia, the Marshall Islands, the Philippines, Canada, Australia, Brazil
- Tertiary-educated as a percentage of total emigrants in OECD countries, 2011: **28.9 percent**
- Tertiary-educated women as a percentage of total women emigrants in OECD countries, 2011: **29.2 percent**
- Number of refugees, 2014: Not available
- Second generation diaspora in Australia, Europe, and the United States, 2012: Not available

IMMIGRATION

- Stock of immigrants, 2013: **5.6 thousands**
- Stock of immigrants as percentage of population, 2013: **26.7 percent**
- Top source countries, 2013: the Philippines, China, the Federated States of Micronesia, the United States, Guam, Japan, the Northern Mariana Islands, the Republic of Korea, the Marshall Islands
- Women as percentage of immigrants, 2013: **39.3 percent**
- Number of refugees, 2014: Not available

Remittances

US$ millions	2006	2007	2008	2009	2010	2011	2012	2013	2014	2015e
Inward remittance flows[a]	2	2	2	2	2	2	2	2	2	2
of which										
Compensation of employees	0	0	0	0	0	0	0	0	0	–
Personal transfers	1	1	1	1	1	2	2	2	2	–
Outward remittance flows	11	11	10	9	9	9	10	10	10	–
of which										
Compensation of employees	–	–	–	–	–	–	–	–	–	–
Personal transfers	11	11	10	9	9	9	10	10	10	–

a. Net FDI inflows US$0.02 billion, net ODA received US$0.04 billion in 2013.

Panama

Population (millions, 2014)	3.9
Population growth (avg. annual %, 2005–14)	1.7
Population density (people per sq km, 2014)	52.0
Labor force (millions, 2014)	1.8
Unemployment rate (% of labor force, 2014)	4.3
Urban population (% of pop., 2014)	66.3
Surface area (thousands of sq km, 2014)	75.4
GNI, Atlas method (current US$ billions, 2014)	43.1
GNI per capita, Atlas method (current US$, 2014)	11,130.0
GDP growth (avg. annual %, 2011–14)	8.9
Poverty headcount ratio at national poverty line (% of pop., 2013)	25.8
Age dependency ratio (% of working-age pop., 2014)	53.7
Account at a formal financial institution (% age 15+, 2014)	43.4
Mobile cellular subscriptions (per 100 people, 2014)	158.1
Internet users (per 100 people, 2014)	44.9

Migration

EMIGRATION

- Stock of emigrants, 2013: **143.7 thousands**
- Stock of emigrants as percentage of population, 2013: **3.8 percent**
- Top destination countries, 2013: the United States, Costa Rica, Spain, Canada, Mexico, Colombia, Puerto Rico, Ecuador, Italy, the Dominican Republic
- Tertiary-educated as a percentage of total emigrants in OECD countries, 2011: **35.8 percent**
- Tertiary-educated women as a percentage of total women emigrants in OECD countries, 2011: **35.6 percent**
- Number of refugees, 2014: **83**
- Second generation diaspora in Australia, Europe, and the United States, 2012: **93.0 thousands**

IMMIGRATION

- Stock of immigrants, 2013: **158.4 thousands**
- Stock of immigrants as percentage of population, 2013: **4.2 percent**
- Top source countries, 2013: Colombia, China, the United States, Nicaragua, República Bolivariana de Venezuela, the Dominican Republic, Costa Rica, Mexico, India, Peru
- Women as percentage of immigrants, 2013: **49.2 percent**
- Number of refugees, 2014: **17,221**

Remittances

US$ millions	2006	2007	2008	2009	2010	2011	2012	2013	2014	2015e
Inward remittance flows[a]	**157**	**180**	**245**	**337**	**410**	**368**	**411**	**452**	**760**	**779**
of which										
Compensation of employees	8	7	9	9	10	24	30	28	108	–
Personal transfers	149	173	236	328	400	345	381	424	652	–
Outward remittance flows	**121**	**151**	**258**	**450**	**486**	**464**	**564**	**644**	**818**	–
of which										
Compensation of employees	–	–	–	–	–	–	–	–	6	–
Personal transfers	121	151	258	450	486	464	564	644	812	–

a. Net FDI inflows US$5.05 billion, net ODA received US$0.01 billion in 2013.

Migration and Remittances Factbook 2016

Papua New Guinea

Population (millions, 2014)	7.5
Population growth (avg. annual %, 2005–14)	2.3
Population density (people per sq km, 2014)	16.5
Labor force (millions, 2014)	3.4
Unemployment rate (% of labor force, 2014)	2.5
Urban population (% of pop., 2014)	13.0
Surface area (thousands of sq km, 2014)	462.8
GNI, Atlas method (current US$ billions, 2014)	16.7
GNI per capita, Atlas method (current US$, 2014)	2,240.0
GDP growth (avg. annual %, 2011–14)	8.2
Poverty headcount ratio at national poverty line (% of pop., 2009)	39.9
Age dependency ratio (% of working-age pop., 2014)	68.1
Account at a formal financial institution (% age 15+)	–
Mobile cellular subscriptions (per 100 people, 2014)	44.9
Internet users (per 100 people, 2014)	9.4

Migration

EMIGRATION

- Stock of emigrants, 2013: **39.0 thousands**
- Stock of emigrants as percentage of population, 2013: **0.5 percent**
- Top destination countries, 2013: Australia, the United States, New Zealand, Canada, Switzerland, the Netherlands, China, Italy, Vanuatu, France
- Tertiary-educated as a percentage of total emigrants in OECD countries, 2011: **37.1 percent**
- Tertiary-educated women as a percentage of total women emigrants in OECD countries, 2011: **37.8 percent**
- Number of refugees, 2014: **285**
- Second generation diaspora in Australia, Europe, and the United States, 2012: **4.9 thousands**

IMMIGRATION

- Stock of immigrants, 2013: **25.4 thousands**
- Stock of immigrants as percentage of population, 2013: **0.3 percent**
- Top source countries, 2013: Indonesia, Australia, the United States, the Philippines, New Zealand, the United Kingdom, Ireland, Malaysia, India, Sri Lanka
- Women as percentage of immigrants, 2013: **36.6 percent**
- Number of refugees, 2014: **9,503**

Remittances

US$ millions	2006	2007	2008	2009	2010	2011	2012	2013	2014	2015e
Inward remittance flows[a]	4	8	7	5	3	17	14	14	10	22
of which										
Compensation of employees	1	2	2	3	3	10	12	13	9	–
Personal transfers	3	5	5	2	1	7	2	0	1	–
Outward remittance flows	159	284	321	315	394	552	512	483	−55	–
of which										
Compensation of employees	61	150	119	135	168	240	186	200	175	–
Personal transfers	97	134	202	181	226	312	326	284	−230	–

a. Net FDI inflows US$0.02 billion, net ODA received US$0.66 billion in 2013.

Paraguay

Population (millions, 2014)	6.6
Population growth (avg. annual %, 2005–14)	1.4
Population density (people per sq km, 2014)	16.5
Labor force (millions, 2014)	3.2
Unemployment rate (% of labor force, 2014)	4.5
Urban population (% of pop., 2014)	59.4
Surface area (thousands of sq km, 2014)	406.8
GNI, Atlas method (current US$ billions, 2014)	28.8
GNI per capita, Atlas method (current US$, 2014)	4,400.0
GDP growth (avg. annual %, 2011–14)	5.5
Poverty headcount ratio at national poverty line (% of pop., 2013)	23.8
Age dependency ratio (% of working-age pop., 2014)	57.3
Account at a formal financial institution (% age 15+)	–
Mobile cellular subscriptions (per 100 people, 2014)	105.6
Internet users (per 100 people, 2014)	43.0

Migration

EMIGRATION

- Stock of emigrants, 2013: **958.9 thousands**
- Stock of emigrants as percentage of population, 2013: **14.8 percent**
- Top destination countries, 2013: Argentina, Spain, Brazil, the United States, Canada, the Plurinational State of Bolivia, Italy, Uruguay, Chile, Germany
- Tertiary-educated as a percentage of total emigrants in OECD countries, 2011: **15.3 percent**
- Tertiary-educated women as a percentage of total women emigrants in OECD countries, 2011: **15.6 percent**
- Number of refugees, 2014: **87**
- Second generation diaspora in Australia, Europe, and the United States, 2012: **21.6 thousands**

IMMIGRATION

- Stock of immigrants, 2013: **185.8 thousands**
- Stock of immigrants as percentage of population, 2013: **2.9 percent**
- Top source countries, 2013: Brazil, Argentina, Uruguay, the Republic of Korea, Chile, Japan, the United States, Germany, Mexico, Peru
- Women as percentage of immigrants, 2013: **47.5 percent**
- Number of refugees, 2014: **149**

Remittances

US$ millions	2006	2007	2008	2009	2010	2011	2012	2013	2014	2015e
Inward remittance flows[a]	336	341	363	377	410	541	634	623	507	524
of which										
Compensation of employees	–	–	–	–	–	–	–	–	–	–
Personal transfers	336	341	363	377	410	541	634	623	507	–
Outward remittance flows	–	–	–	–	–	–	–	–	–	–
of which										
Compensation of employees	–	–	–	–	–	–	–	–	–	–
Personal transfers	–	–	–	–	–	–	–	–	–	–

a. Net FDI inflows US$0.07 billion, net ODA received US$0.13 billion in 2013.

Peru

	MIDDLE INCOME
Population (millions, 2014)	31.0
Population growth (avg. annual %, 2005–14)	1.3
Population density (people per sq km, 2014)	24.2
Labor force (millions, 2014)	17.0
Unemployment rate (% of labor force, 2014)	4.2
Urban population (% of pop., 2014)	78.3
Surface area (thousands of sq km, 2014)	1,285.2
GNI, Atlas method (current US$ billions, 2014)	196.9
GNI per capita, Atlas method (current US$, 2014)	6,360.0
GDP growth (avg. annual %, 2011–14)	5.1
Poverty headcount ratio at national poverty line (% of pop., 2013)	23.9
Age dependency ratio (% of working-age pop., 2014)	53.5
Account at a formal financial institution (% age 15+, 2014)	29.0
Mobile cellular subscriptions (per 100 people, 2014)	102.9
Internet users (per 100 people, 2014)	40.2

Migration

EMIGRATION

- Stock of emigrants, 2013: **1,454.4 thousands**
- Stock of emigrants as percentage of population, 2013: **4.8 percent**
- Top destination countries, 2013: the United States, Argentina, Spain, Chile, Italy, Japan, República Bolivariana de Venezuela, Canada, China, Ecuador
- Tertiary-educated as a percentage of total emigrants in OECD countries, 2011: **27.8 percent**
- Tertiary-educated women as a percentage of total women emigrants in OECD countries, 2011: **27.8 percent**
- Number of refugees, 2014: **4,323**
- Second generation diaspora in Australia, Europe, and the United States, 2012: **162.4 thousands**

IMMIGRATION

- Stock of immigrants, 2013: **104.9 thousands**
- Stock of immigrants as percentage of population, 2013: **0.3 percent**
- Top source countries, 2013: Argentina, the United States, Chile, Colombia, the Plurinational State of Bolivia, Spain, Brazil, China, Ecuador, Japan
- Women as percentage of immigrants, 2013: **49.0 percent**
- Number of refugees, 2014: **1,250**

Remittances

US$ millions	2006	2007	2008	2009	2010	2011	2012	2013	2014	2015e
Inward remittance flows[a]	1,837	2,131	2,444	2,409	2,534	2,697	2,788	2,707	2,639	2,654
of which										
Compensation of employees	–	–	–	–	–	–	–	–	–	–
Personal transfers	1,837	2,131	2,444	2,409	2,534	2,697	2,788	2,707	2,639	–
Outward remittance flows	–	–	–	–	–	–	–	–	–	–
of which										
Compensation of employees	–	–	–	–	–	–	–	–	–	–
Personal transfers	–	–	–	–	–	–	–	–	–	–

a. Net FDI inflows US$9.30 billion, net ODA received US$0.37 billion in 2013.

Philippines, The

Population (millions, 2014)	99.1
Population growth (avg. annual %, 2005–14)	1.6
Population density (people per sq km, 2014)	332.5
Labor force (millions, 2014)	43.8
Unemployment rate (% of labor force, 2014)	7.1
Urban population (% of pop., 2014)	44.5
Surface area (thousands of sq km, 2014)	300.0
GNI, Atlas method (current US$ billions, 2014)	347.5
GNI per capita, Atlas method (current US$, 2014)	3,500.0
GDP growth (avg. annual %, 2011–14)	5.9
Poverty headcount ratio at national poverty line (% of pop., 2012)	25.2
Age dependency ratio (% of working-age pop., 2014)	58.0
Account at a formal financial institution (% age 15+, 2014)	28.1
Mobile cellular subscriptions (per 100 people, 2014)	111.2
Internet users (per 100 people, 2014)	39.7

Migration

EMIGRATION

- Stock of emigrants, 2013: **6,001.7 thousands**
- Stock of emigrants as percentage of population, 2013: **6.2 percent**
- Top destination countries, 2013: the United States, the United Arab Emirates, Saudi Arabia, Canada, Malaysia, Japan, Australia, Qatar, Kuwait, Italy
- Tertiary-educated as a percentage of total emigrants in OECD countries, 2011: **48.6 percent**
- Tertiary-educated women as a percentage of total women emigrants in OECD countries, 2011: **50.8 percent**
- Number of refugees, 2014: **653**
- Second generation diaspora in Australia, Europe, and the United States, 2012: **946.1 thousands**

IMMIGRATION

- Stock of immigrants, 2013: **213.2 thousands**
- Stock of immigrants as percentage of population, 2013: **0.2 percent**
- Top source countries, 2013: China, the United States, Japan, India, the Republic of Korea, the Democratic Republic of Korea, Canada, the United Kingdom, Australia, Germany
- Women as percentage of immigrants, 2013: **48.2 percent**
- Number of refugees, 2014: **193**

Remittances

US$ millions	2006	2007	2008	2009	2010	2011	2012	2013	2014	2015e
Inward										
remittance flows[a]	15,496	16,437	18,851	19,960	21,557	23,054	24,610	26,717	28,403	29,791
of which										
Compensation										
of employees	2,773	3,034	4,100	4,591	5,141	5,853	6,524	7,039	7,516	–
Personal transfers	12,723	13,403	14,751	15,369	16,415	17,201	18,086	19,678	20,888	–
Outward										
remittance flows	63	66	117	94	109	135	152	210	183	–
of which										
Compensation										
of employees	45	45	58	58	82	104	107	165	133	–
Personal transfers	19	21	59	36	27	31	45	46	50	–

a. Net FDI inflows US$3.74 billion, net ODA received US$0.19 billion in 2013.

Poland

Population (millions, 2014)	38.0
Population growth (avg. annual %, 2005–14)	0.0
Population density (people per sq km, 2014)	124.1
Labor force (millions, 2014)	18.3
Unemployment rate (% of labor force, 2014)	9.2
Urban population (% of pop., 2014)	60.6
Surface area (thousands of sq km, 2014)	312.7
GNI, Atlas method (current US$ billions, 2014)	520.1
GNI per capita, Atlas method (current US$, 2014)	13,690.0
GDP growth (avg. annual %, 2011–14)	2.8
Poverty headcount ratio at national poverty line (% of pop., 2012)	17.3
Age dependency ratio (% of working-age pop., 2014)	42.7
Account at a formal financial institution (% age 15+, 2014)	77.9
Mobile cellular subscriptions (per 100 people, 2014)	156.4
Internet users (per 100 people, 2014)	66.6

Migration

EMIGRATION

- Stock of emigrants, 2013: **3,883.0 thousands**
- Stock of emigrants as percentage of population, 2013: **10.2 percent**
- Top destination countries, 2013: Germany, the United Kingdom, the United States, Canada, Ukraine, Italy, Ireland, France, the Netherlands, Sweden
- Tertiary-educated as a percentage of total emigrants in OECD countries, 2011: **29.3 percent**
- Tertiary-educated women as a percentage of total women emigrants in OECD countries, 2011: **30.8 percent**
- Number of refugees, 2014: **1,291**
- Second generation diaspora in Australia, Europe, and the United States, 2012: **1,237.0 thousands**

IMMIGRATION

- Stock of immigrants, 2013: **663.8 thousands**
- Stock of immigrants as percentage of population, 2013: **1.7 percent**
- Top source countries, 2013: Ukraine, Germany, Belarus, Lithuania, the Russian Federation, the United Kingdom, France, the United States, Italy, Ireland
- Women as percentage of immigrants, 2013: **58.8 percent**
- Number of refugees, 2014: **15,695**

Remittances

US$ millions	2006	2007	2008	2009	2010	2011	2012	2013	2014	2015e
Inward remittance flows[a]	8,486	10,468	10,408	8,094	7,659	7,712	6,989	7,400	7,409	7,223
of which										
Compensation of employees	5,531	6,226	5,708	4,442	3,962	3,825	3,497	3,684	3,740	–
Personal transfers	2,955	4,242	4,700	3,652	3,697	3,887	3,492	3,716	3,669	–
Outward remittance flows	820	1,208	1,741	1,378	1,306	1,395	1,521	1,557	2,185	–
of which										
Compensation of employees	796	1,177	1,690	1,332	1,212	1,303	1,345	1,367	1,965	–
Personal transfers	24	31	51	46	94	92	176	190	220	–

a. Net FDI inflows US$0.80 billion in 2013.

Portugal

Population (millions, 2014)	10.4
Population growth (avg. annual %, 2005–14)	-0.1
Population density (people per sq km, 2014)	113.5
Labor force (millions, 2014)	5.4
Unemployment rate (% of labor force, 2014)	14.2
Urban population (% of pop., 2014)	62.9
Surface area (thousands of sq km, 2014)	92.2
GNI, Atlas method (current US$ billions, 2014)	222.1
GNI per capita, Atlas method (current US$, 2014)	21,360.0
GDP growth (avg. annual %, 2011–14)	-1.5
Poverty headcount ratio at national poverty line (% of pop.)	—
Age dependency ratio (% of working-age pop., 2014)	52.9
Account at a formal financial institution (% age 15+, 2014)	87.4
Mobile cellular subscriptions (per 100 people, 2014)	111.8
Internet users (per 100 people, 2014)	64.6

Migration

EMIGRATION

- Stock of emigrants, 2013: **2,028.6 thousands**
- Stock of emigrants as percentage of population, 2013: **19.4 percent**
- Top destination countries, 2013: France, Switzerland, the United States, Canada, Germany, Brazil, Spain, the United Kingdom, Luxembourg, South Africa
- Tertiary-educated as a percentage of total emigrants in OECD countries, 2011: **10.6 percent**
- Tertiary-educated women as a percentage of total women emigrants in OECD countries, 2011: **11.3 percent**
- Number of refugees, 2014: **25**
- Second generation diaspora in Australia, Europe, and the United States, 2012: **787.7 thousands**

IMMIGRATION

- Stock of immigrants, 2013: **893.8 thousands**
- Stock of immigrants as percentage of population, 2013: **8.5 percent**
- Top source countries, 2013: Angola, Brazil, France, Mozambique, Cabo Verde, Ukraine, Guinea-Bissau, Germany, República Bolivariana de Venezuela, Romania
- Women as percentage of immigrants, 2013: **53.3 percent**
- Number of refugees, 2014: **634**

Remittances

US$ millions	2006	2007	2008	2009	2010	2011	2012	2013	2014	2015e
Inward remittance flows[a]	**3,485**	**4,162**	**4,288**	**3,788**	**3,726**	**3,922**	**3,991**	**4,455**	**4,433**	**4,300**
of which										
Compensation of employees	440	610	641	598	517	539	461	446	424	—
Personal transfers	3,045	3,551	3,647	3,190	3,209	3,382	3,530	4,009	4,009	—
Outward remittance flows	**1,211**	**1,128**	**1,235**	**1,299**	**1,258**	**1,443**	**1,175**	**1,231**	**1,180**	**—**
of which										
Compensation of employees	445	346	388	518	506	627	499	493	442	—
Personal transfers	766	783	847	781	752	815	675	739	739	—

a. Net FDI inflows US$10.87 billion in 2013.

Puerto Rico

HIGH INCOME NON-OECD

Population (millions, 2014)	3.5
Population growth (avg. annual %, 2005–14)	-0.8
Population density (people per sq km, 2014)	400.0
Labor force (millions, 2014)	1.2
Unemployment rate (% of labor force, 2014)	14.3
Urban population (% of pop., 2014)	93.6
Surface area (thousands of sq km, 2014)	8.9
GNI, Atlas method (current US$ billions, 2014)	69.4
GNI per capita, Atlas method (current US$, 2014)	19,310.0
GDP growth (avg. annual %, 2011–14)	-1.5
Poverty headcount ratio at national poverty line (% of pop.)	—
Age dependency ratio (% of working-age pop., 2014)	50.1
Account at a formal financial institution (% age 15+, 2014)	69.7
Mobile cellular subscriptions (per 100 people, 2014)	87.1
Internet users (per 100 people, 2014)	78.8

Migration

EMIGRATION

- Stock of emigrants, 2013: **1,712.3 thousands**
- Stock of emigrants as percentage of population, 2013: **47.6 percent**
- Top destination countries, 2013: the United States, the Dominican Republic, the Virgin Islands (U.S.), Haiti, Mexico, the Northern Mariana Islands, Ecuador, Panama, Colombia, Canada
- Tertiary-educated as a percentage of total emigrants in OECD countries, 2011: **18.2 percent**
- Tertiary-educated women as a percentage of total women emigrants in OECD countries, 2011: **19.8 percent**
- Number of refugees, 2014: Not available
- Second generation diaspora in Australia, Europe, and the United States, 2012: Not available

IMMIGRATION

- Stock of immigrants, 2013: **319.4 thousands**
- Stock of immigrants as percentage of population, 2013: **8.9 percent**
- Top source countries, 2013: the United States, the Dominican Republic, Cuba, Colombia, República Bolivariana de Venezuela, Mexico, Spain, Dominica, Panama, Argentina
- Women as percentage of immigrants, 2013: **53.4 percent**
- Number of refugees, 2014: Not available

Remittances

US$ millions	2006	2007	2008	2009	2010	2011	2012	2013	2014	2015e
Inward **remittance flows**	–	–	–	–	–	–	–	–	–	–
of which										
Compensation of employees	–	–	–	–	–	–	–	–	–	–
Personal transfers	–	–	–	–	–	–	–	–	–	–
Outward **remittance flows**	–	–	–	–	–	–	–	–	–	–
of which										
Compensation of employees	–	–	–	–	–	–	–	–	–	–
Personal transfers	–	–	–	–	–	–	–	–	–	–

Qatar

	HIGH INCOME NON-OECD
Population (millions, 2014)	2.2
Population growth (avg. annual %, 2005–14)	10.9
Population density (people per sq km, 2014)	187.1
Labor force (millions, 2014)	1.6
Unemployment rate (% of labor force, 2014)	0.3
Urban population (% of pop., 2014)	99.2
Surface area (thousands of sq km, 2014)	11.6
GNI, Atlas method (current US$ billions, 2014)	200.3
GNI per capita, Atlas method (current US$, 2014)	92,200.0
GDP growth (avg. annual %, 2011–14)	6.7
Poverty headcount ratio at national poverty line (% of pop.)	–
Age dependency ratio (% of working-age pop., 2014)	19.6
Account at a formal financial institution (% age 15+)	–
Mobile cellular subscriptions (per 100 people, 2014)	145.8
Internet users (per 100 people, 2014)	91.5

Migration

EMIGRATION

- Stock of emigrants, 2013: **19.9 thousands**
- Stock of emigrants as percentage of population, 2013: **0.9 percent**
- Top destination countries, 2013: the West Bank and Gaza, the United States, Canada, Libya, the United Arab Emirates, Australia, the Arab Republic of Egypt, Algeria, Kuwait, Oman
- Tertiary-educated as a percentage of total emigrants in OECD countries, 2011: **40.7 percent**
- Tertiary-educated women as a percentage of total women emigrants in OECD countries, 2011: **39.5 percent**
- Number of refugees, 2014: **18**
- Second generation diaspora in Australia, Europe, and the United States, 2012: Not available

IMMIGRATION

- Stock of immigrants, 2013: **1,908.5 thousands**
- Stock of immigrants as percentage of population, 2013: **90.8 percent**
- Top source countries, 2013: India, Nepal, the Philippines, the Arab Republic of Egypt, Bangladesh, Sri Lanka, Pakistan, Sudan, the Republic of Yemen, Indonesia
- Women as percentage of immigrants, 2013: **21.9 percent**
- Number of refugees, 2014: **132**

Remittances

US$ millions	2006	2007	2008	2009	2010	2011	2012	2013	2014	2015e
Inward remittance flows[a]	–	–	–	–	–	574	803	574	499	503
of which										
Compensation of employees	–	–	–	–	–	–	–	–	–	–
Personal transfers	–	–	–	–	–	574	803	574	499	–
Outward remittance flows	3,690	4,483	5,380	7,105	8,141	10,445	10,413	11,281	11,230	–
of which										
Compensation of employees	–	–	–	–	–	131	130	141	140	–
Personal transfers	3,690	4,483	5,380	7,105	8,141	10,314	10,283	11,140	11,090	–

a. Net FDI inflows US$–0.84 billion in 2013.

Romania

Population (millions, 2014)	19.9
Population growth (avg. annual %, 2005–14)	-0.7
Population density (people per sq km, 2014)	86.6
Labor force (millions, 2014)	9.5
Unemployment rate (% of labor force, 2014)	7.0
Urban population (% of pop., 2014)	54.4
Surface area (thousands of sq km, 2014)	238.4
GNI, Atlas method (current US$ billions, 2014)	189.5
GNI per capita, Atlas method (current US$, 2014)	9,520.0
GDP growth (avg. annual %, 2011–14)	2.0
Poverty headcount ratio at national poverty line (% of pop., 2012)	22.4
Age dependency ratio (% of working-age pop., 2014)	48.2
Account at a formal financial institution (% age 15+, 2014)	60.8
Mobile cellular subscriptions (per 100 people, 2014)	105.9
Internet users (per 100 people, 2014)	54.1

Migration

EMIGRATION

- Stock of emigrants, 2013: **3,430.5 thousands**
- Stock of emigrants as percentage of population, 2013: **17.2 percent**
- Top destination countries, 2013: Italy, Spain, Germany, Hungary, the United States, Israel, the United Kingdom, Canada, Austria, France
- Tertiary-educated as a percentage of total emigrants in OECD countries, 2011: **19.5 percent**
- Tertiary-educated women as a percentage of total women emigrants in OECD countries, 2011: **20.0 percent**
- Number of refugees, 2014: **1,910**
- Second generation diaspora in Australia, Europe, and the United States, 2012: **229.6 thousands**

IMMIGRATION

- Stock of immigrants, 2013: **198.8 thousands**
- Stock of immigrants as percentage of population, 2013: **1.0 percent**
- Top source countries, 2013: Moldova, Italy, Bulgaria, Spain, Ukraine, Hungary, the Syrian Arab Republic, the Russian Federation, Greece, the United Kingdom
- Women as percentage of immigrants, 2013: **49.8 percent**
- Number of refugees, 2014: **2,136**

Remittances

US$ millions	2006	2007	2008	2009	2010	2011	2012	2013	2014	2015e
Inward remittance flows[a]	6,673	8,461	9,285	4,881	3,879	3,889	3,674	3,519	3,381	3,230
of which										
Compensation of employees	1,165	1,626	1,705	683	641	695	734	734	723	–
Personal transfers	5,509	6,835	7,580	4,198	3,238	3,194	2,940	2,785	2,658	–
Outward remittance flows	49	344	651	299	359	363	339	547	638	–
of which										
Compensation of employees	42	55	169	63	88	128	116	90	80	–
Personal transfers	6	289	482	236	271	235	223	457	558	–

a. Net FDI inflows US$3.85 billion in 2013.

Russian Federation

Population (millions, 2014)	143.8
Population growth (avg. annual %, 2005–14)	0.0
Population density (people per sq km, 2014)	8.8
Labor force (millions, 2014)	76.8
Unemployment rate (% of labor force, 2014)	5.1
Urban population (% of pop., 2014)	73.9
Surface area (thousands of sq km, 2014)	17,098.3
GNI, Atlas method (current US$ billions, 2014)	1,930.6
GNI per capita, Atlas method (current US$, 2014)	13,220.0
GDP growth (avg. annual %, 2011–14)	2.4
Poverty headcount ratio at national poverty line (% of pop., 2013)	10.8
Age dependency ratio (% of working-age pop., 2014)	42.0
Account at a formal financial institution (% age 15+, 2014)	67.4
Mobile cellular subscriptions (per 100 people, 2014)	155.1
Internet users (per 100 people, 2014)	70.5

Migration

EMIGRATION

- Stock of emigrants, 2013: **10,910.5 thousands**
- Stock of emigrants as percentage of population, 2013: **7.6 percent**
- Top destination countries, 2013: Ukraine, Kazakhstan, Germany, Belarus, Uzbekistan, the United States, Tajikistan, Moldova, Azerbaijan, Latvia
- Tertiary-educated as a percentage of total emigrants in OECD countries, 2011: **35.8 percent**
- Tertiary-educated women as a percentage of total women emigrants in OECD countries, 2011: **39.3 percent**
- Number of refugees, 2014: **72,752**
- Second generation diaspora in Australia, Europe, and the United States, 2012: **893.5 thousands**

IMMIGRATION

- Stock of immigrants, 2013: **11,048.1 thousands**
- Stock of immigrants as percentage of population, 2013: **7.7 percent**
- Top source countries, 2013: Ukraine, Kazakhstan, Uzbekistan, Azerbaijan, Belarus, the Kyrgyz Republic, Armenia, Tajikistan, Georgia, Moldova
- Women as percentage of immigrants, 2013: **50.9 percent**
- Number of refugees, 2014: **235,717**

Remittances

US$ millions	2006	2007	2008	2009	2010	2011	2012	2013	2014	2015e
Inward remittance flows[a]	3,820	4,666	5,737	5,105	5,250	6,103	5,788	6,751	7,777	7,870
of which										
Compensation of employees	1,899	2,613	3,792	3,326	3,619	3,871	3,884	4,256	4,139	–
Personal transfers	1,921	2,054	1,945	1,779	1,631	2,232	1,903	2,495	3,637	–
Outward remittance flows	12,104	19,881	29,719	21,148	21,454	26,010	31,648	37,217	32,640	–
of which										
Compensation of employees	6,067	9,931	18,149	12,193	12,131	13,393	15,715	17,426	14,213	–
Personal transfers	6,038	9,950	11,570	8,954	9,323	12,618	15,933	19,791	18,427	–

a. Net FDI inflows US$69.22 billion in 2013.

Rwanda

Population (millions, 2014)	11.3
Population growth (avg. annual %, 2005–14)	2.5
Population density (people per sq km, 2014)	459.7
Labor force (millions, 2014)	5.7
Unemployment rate (% of labor force, 2014)	0.6
Urban population (% of pop., 2014)	27.8
Surface area (thousands of sq km, 2014)	26.3
GNI, Atlas method (current US$ billions, 2014)	7.9
GNI per capita, Atlas method (current US$, 2014)	700.0
GDP growth (avg. annual %, 2011–14)	7.1
Poverty headcount ratio at national poverty line (% of pop., 2010)	44.9
Age dependency ratio (% of working-age pop., 2014)	79.1
Account at a formal financial institution (% age 15+, 2014)	38.1
Mobile cellular subscriptions (per 100 people, 2014)	64.0
Internet users (per 100 people, 2014)	10.6

Migration

EMIGRATION

- Stock of emigrants, 2013: **345.8 thousands**
- Stock of emigrants as percentage of population, 2013: **3.1 percent**
- Top destination countries, 2013: the Democratic Republic of Congo, Uganda, Burundi, Tanzania, the Republic of Congo, France, Zambia, Malawi, Canada, Belgium
- Tertiary-educated as a percentage of total emigrants in OECD countries, 2011: **33.9 percent**
- Tertiary-educated women as a percentage of total women emigrants in OECD countries, 2011: **31.7 percent**
- Number of refugees, 2014: **79,374**
- Second generation diaspora in Australia, Europe, and the United States, 2012: **3.7 thousands**

IMMIGRATION

- Stock of immigrants, 2013: **452.4 thousands**
- Stock of immigrants as percentage of population, 2013: **4.1 percent**
- Top source countries, 2013: the Democratic Republic of Congo, Uganda, Burundi, Tanzania, Kenya, Belgium, India, France, Germany, the United Kingdom
- Women as percentage of immigrants, 2013: **52.3 percent**
- Number of refugees, 2014: **73,812**

Remittances

US$ millions	2006	2007	2008	2009	2010	2011	2012	2013	2014	2015e
Inward remittance flows[a]	29	121	68	93	106	174	182	123	128	130
of which										
Compensation of employees	4	23	4	4	8	8	7	8	9	–
Personal transfers	25	99	63	88	98	166	175	115	119	–
Outward remittance flows	55	77	70	71	76	103	107	53	126	–
of which										
Compensation of employees	38	48	38	36	43	47	50	6	71	–
Personal transfers	17	29	32	35	33	56	57	47	55	–

a. Net FDI inflows US$0.26 billion, net ODA received US$1.08 billion in 2013.

Samoa

Population (thousands, 2013)	191.8
Population growth (avg. annual %, 2005–14)	0.7
Population density (people per sq km, 2014)	67.8
Labor force (thousands, 2013)	49.9
Unemployment rate (% of labor force)	–
Urban population (% of pop., 2014)	19.3
Surface area (thousands of sq km, 2014)	2.8
GNI, Atlas method (current US$ billions, 2014)	0.8
GNI per capita, Atlas method (current US$, 2014)	4,060.0
GDP growth (avg. annual %, 2011–14)	1.4
Poverty headcount ratio at national poverty line (% of pop.)	–
Age dependency ratio (% of working-age pop., 2014)	74.5
Account at a formal financial institution (% age 15+)	–
Mobile cellular subscriptions (per 100 people, 2014)	55.5
Internet users (per 100 people, 2014)	21.2

Migration

EMIGRATION

- Stock of emigrants, 2013: **114.6 thousands**
- Stock of emigrants as percentage of population, 2013: **60.2 percent**
- Top destination countries, 2013: New Zealand, American Samoa, Australia, the United States, Tonga, Canada, Italy, Ireland, Sweden, the Netherlands
- Tertiary-educated as a percentage of total emigrants in OECD countries, 2011: **9.9 percent**
- Tertiary-educated women as a percentage of total women emigrants in OECD countries, 2011: **11.0 percent**
- Number of refugees, 2014: Not available
- Second generation diaspora in Australia, Europe, and the United States, 2012: Not available

IMMIGRATION

- Stock of immigrants, 2013: **10.5 thousands**
- Stock of immigrants as percentage of population, 2013: **5.5 percent**
- Top source countries, 2013: New Zealand, American Samoa, Australia, the United States, Fiji, Tonga, Tuvalu, China, Japan, Papua New Guinea
- Women as percentage of immigrants, 2013: **49.4 percent**
- Number of refugees, 2014: Not available

Remittances

US$ millions	2006	2007	2008	2009	2010	2011	2012	2013	2014	2015e
Inward remittance flows[a]	87	97	109	119	139	160	178	165	141	171
of which										
Compensation of employees	1	1	1	0	0	0	2	13	11	–
Personal transfers	86	96	108	119	138	159	175	152	129	–
Outward remittance flows	21	10	9	8	9	12	11	18	12	–
of which										
Compensation of employees	8	2	1	2	1	1	1	8	5	–
Personal transfers	13	8	7	7	8	11	10	10	7	–

a. Net FDI inflows US$0.02 billion, net ODA received US$0.12 billion in 2013.

San Marino

Population (thousands, 2013)	31.6
Population growth (avg. annual %, 2005–14)	0.9
Population density (people per sq km, 2014)	526.6
Labor force, total	–
Unemployment rate (% of labor force)	–
Urban population (% of pop., 2014)	94.2
Surface area (thousands of sq km, 2014)	0.1
GNI, Atlas method (current US$ billions, 2008)	1.6
GNI per capita, Atlas method (current US$, 2008)	52,140.0
GDP growth (avg. annual %, 2004-07)	2.9
Poverty headcount ratio at national poverty line (% of pop.)	–
Age dependency ratio (% of working-age pop.)	–
Account at a formal financial institution (% age 15+)	–
Mobile cellular subscriptions (per 100 people, 2014)	118.8
Internet users (per 100 people, 2011)	49.6

Migration

EMIGRATION

- Stock of emigrants, 2013: **3.4 thousands**
- Stock of emigrants as percentage of population, 2013: **11.0 percent**
- Top destination countries, 2013: Italy, the United States, France, Ukraine, the Russian Federation, Brazil, Argentina, Canada, Switzerland, Australia
- Tertiary-educated as a percentage of total emigrants in OECD countries, 2011: **18.2 percent**
- Tertiary-educated women as a percentage of total women emigrants in OECD countries, 2011: **16.4 percent**
- Number of refugees, 2014: Not available
- Second generation diaspora in Australia, Europe, and the United States, 2012: Not available

IMMIGRATION

- Stock of immigrants, 2013: **4.9 thousands**
- Stock of immigrants as percentage of population, 2013: **15.5 percent**
- Top source countries, 2013: Italy, Romania, Argentina, Ukraine, the Russian Federation, Albania, Poland, Brazil, France, Cuba
- Women as percentage of immigrants, 2013: **44.5 percent**
- Number of refugees, 2014: Not available

Remittances

US$ millions	2006	2007	2008	2009	2010	2011	2012	2013	2014	2015e
Inward remittance flows	–	–	–	–	–	–	–	–	–	–
of which										
Compensation of employees	–	–	–	–	–	–	–	–	–	–
Personal transfers	–	–	–	–	–	–	–	–	–	–
Outward remittance flows	–	–	–	–	–	–	–	–	–	–
of which										
Compensation of employees	–	–	–	–	–	–	–	–	–	–
Personal transfers	–	–	–	–	–	–	–	–	–	–

São Tomé and Príncipe

	MIDDLE INCOME
Population (thousands, 2013)	186.3
Population growth (avg. annual %, 2005–14)	2.2
Population density (people per sq km, 2014)	194.1
Labor force (thousands, 2013)	65.4
Unemployment rate (% of labor force)	–
Urban population (% of pop., 2014)	64.5
Surface area (thousands of sq km, 2014)	1.0
GNI, Atlas method (current US$ billions, 2014)	0.3
GNI per capita, Atlas method (current US$, 2014)	1,670.0
GDP growth (avg. annual %, 2011–14)	4.5
Poverty headcount ratio at national poverty line (% of pop., 2009)	61.7
Age dependency ratio (% of working-age pop., 2014)	85.3
Account at a formal financial institution (% age 15+)	–
Mobile cellular subscriptions (per 100 people, 2014)	64.9
Internet users (per 100 people, 2014)	24.4

Migration

EMIGRATION

- Stock of emigrants, 2013: **36.1 thousands**
- Stock of emigrants as percentage of population, 2013: **19.8 percent**
- Top destination countries, 2013: Portugal, Angola, Gabon, Cabo Verde, Equatorial Guinea, France, the Netherlands, the United States, Italy, Brazil
- Tertiary-educated as a percentage of total emigrants in OECD countries, 2011: **10.6 percent**
- Tertiary-educated women as a percentage of total women emigrants in OECD countries, 2011: **10.4 percent**
- Number of refugees, 2014: **19**
- Second generation diaspora in Australia, Europe, and the United States, 2012: Not available

IMMIGRATION

- Stock of immigrants, 2013: **6.3 thousands**
- Stock of immigrants as percentage of population, 2013: **3.5 percent**
- Top source countries, 2013: Angola, South Sudan, the Democratic Republic of Congo, Rwanda, Sudan, Chad, Nigeria, Central African Republic, Cameroon, Equatorial Guinea
- Women as percentage of immigrants, 2013: **45.9 percent**
- Number of refugees, 2014: Not available

Remittances

US$ millions	2006	2007	2008	2009	2010	2011	2012	2013	2014	2015e
Inward remittance flows[a]	2	2	3	2	6	7	6	27	27	27
of which										
Compensation of employees	–	–	–	–	–	–	–	1	2	–
Personal transfers	2	2	3	2	6	7	6	26	25	–
Outward remittance flows	1	1	0	1	1	1	1	1	1	–
of which										
Compensation of employees	1	1	0	1	1	1	1	1	1	–
Personal transfers	–	–	–	–	–	–	–	–	–	–

a. Net FDI inflows US$0.01 billion, net ODA received US$0.05 billion in 2013.

Saudi Arabia

Population (millions, 2014)	30.9
Population growth (avg. annual %, 2005–14)	2.5
Population density (people per sq km, 2014)	14.4
Labor force (millions, 2014)	12.1
Unemployment rate (% of labor force, 2014)	5.6
Urban population (% of pop., 2014)	82.9
Surface area (thousands of sq km, 2014)	2,149.7
GNI, Atlas method (current US$ billions, 2014)	759.3
GNI per capita, Atlas method (current US$, 2014)	25,140.0
GDP growth (avg. annual %, 2011–14)	5.4
Poverty headcount ratio at national poverty line (% of pop.)	–
Age dependency ratio (% of working-age pop., 2014)	46.2
Account at a formal financial institution (% age 15+, 2014)	69.4
Mobile cellular subscriptions (per 100 people, 2014)	179.6
Internet users (per 100 people, 2014)	63.7

Migration

EMIGRATION

- Stock of emigrants, 2013: **291.7 thousands**
- Stock of emigrants as percentage of population, 2013: **1.0 percent**
- Top destination countries, 2013: the United States, the United Kingdom, Libya, the West Bank and Gaza, Canada, the Arab Republic of Egypt, Australia, Algeria, the United Arab Emirates, Turkey
- Tertiary-educated as a percentage of total emigrants in OECD countries, 2011: **40.2 percent**
- Tertiary-educated women as a percentage of total women emigrants in OECD countries, 2011: **40.2 percent**
- Number of refugees, 2014: **601**
- Second generation diaspora in Australia, Europe, and the United States, 2012: **13.7 thousands**

IMMIGRATION

- Stock of immigrants, 2013: **14,600.5 thousands†**
- Stock of immigrants as percentage of population, 2013: **48.3 percent**
- Top source countries, 2013: India, Bangladesh, Indonesia, Pakistan, the Arab Republic of Egypt, the Syrian Arab Republic, the Republic of Yemen, the Philippines, Myanmar, Sri Lanka
- Women as percentage of immigrants, 2013: **29.3 percent**
- Number of refugees, 2014: **554**

Remittances

US$ millions	2006	2007	2008	2009	2010	2011	2012	2013	2014	2015e
Inward										
remittance flowsª	106	124	216	214	236	244	246	269	269	274
of which										
Compensation										
of employees	106	124	216	214	236	244	246	269	269	–
Personal transfers	–	–	–	–	–	–	–	–	–	–
Outward										
remittance flows	15,964	16,447	21,696	26,470	27,069	28,475	29,493	34,984	36,924	–
of which										
Compensation										
of employees	665	701	751	782	890	879	870	913	926	–
Personal transfers	15,299	15,746	20,945	25,688	26,179	27,596	28,623	34,071	35,999	–

a. Net FDI inflows US$8.86 billion in 2013.
†The figures for Saudi Arabia are based on estimates compiled by Gulf Labour Markets and Migration (GLMM), Demographic and Economic Module of the GLMM Database, Migration Policy Centre, European University Institute, Florence. The numbers presented in the report reflect the stock of migrants before the regularization campaigns.

Senegal

Population (millions, 2014)	14.7
Population growth (avg. annual %, 2005–14)	2.9
Population density (people per sq km, 2014)	76.2
Labor force (millions, 2014)	6.3
Unemployment rate (% of labor force, 2014)	10.0
Urban population (% of pop., 2014)	43.4
Surface area (thousands of sq km, 2014)	196.7
GNI, Atlas method (current US$ billions, 2014)	15.4
GNI per capita, Atlas method (current US$, 2014)	1,050.0
GDP growth (avg. annual %, 2011–14)	3.6
Poverty headcount ratio at national poverty line (% of pop., 2010)	46.7
Age dependency ratio (% of working-age pop., 2014)	87.8
Account at a formal financial institution (% age 15+, 2014)	11.9
Mobile cellular subscriptions (per 100 people, 2014)	98.8
Internet users (per 100 people, 2014)	17.7

Migration

EMIGRATION

- Stock of emigrants, 2013: **540.4 thousands**
- Stock of emigrants as percentage of population, 2013: **3.8 percent**
- Top destination countries, 2013: France, The Gambia, Italy, Spain, Mauritania, Gabon, Côte d'Ivoire, the United States, Mali, the Republic of Congo
- Tertiary-educated as a percentage of total emigrants in OECD countries, 2011: **19.3 percent**
- Tertiary-educated women as a percentage of total women emigrants in OECD countries, 2011: **21.8 percent**
- Number of refugees, 2014: **23,090**
- Second generation diaspora in Australia, Europe, and the United States, 2012: **64.2 thousands**

IMMIGRATION

- Stock of immigrants, 2013: **209.4 thousands**
- Stock of immigrants as percentage of population, 2013: **1.5 percent**
- Top source countries, 2013: Mauritania, Guinea, Mali, Guinea-Bissau, Sierra Leone, France, The Gambia, Algeria, Morocco, Benin
- Women as percentage of immigrants, 2013: **51.1 percent**
- Number of refugees, 2014: **14,267**

Remittances

US$ millions	2006	2007	2008	2009	2010	2011	2012	2013	2014	2015e
Inward remittance flows[a]	925	1,192	1,476	1,350	1,478	1,614	1,614	1,614	1,614	1,614
of which										
Compensation of employees	75	85	98	97	94	102	–	–	–	–
Personal transfers	851	1,107	1,378	1,254	1,384	1,512	–	–	–	–
Outward remittance flows	96	143	144	174	216	209	–	–	–	–
of which										
Compensation of employees	10	13	14	15	17	18	–	–	–	–
Personal transfers	87	130	130	159	200	191	–	–	–	–

a. Net FDI inflows US$0.31 billion, net ODA received US$0.98 billion in 2013.

Serbia

	MIDDLE INCOME
Population (millions, 2014)	7.1
Population growth (avg. annual %, 2005–14)	-0.5
Population density (people per sq km, 2014)	81.5
Labor force (millions, 2014)	3.1
Unemployment rate (% of labor force, 2014)	22.2
Urban population (% of pop., 2014)	55.5
Surface area (thousands of sq km, 2014)	88.4
GNI, Atlas method (current US$ billions, 2014)	41.5
GNI per capita, Atlas method (current US$, 2014)	5,820.0
GDP growth (avg. annual %, 2011–14)	0.3
Poverty headcount ratio at national poverty line (% of pop., 2011)	24.6
Age dependency ratio (% of working-age pop., 2014)	49.5
Account at a formal financial institution (% age 15+, 2014)	83.1
Mobile cellular subscriptions (per 100 people, 2014)	122.1
Internet users (per 100 people, 2014)	53.5

Migration

EMIGRATION

- Stock of emigrants, 2013: **1,292.9 thousands**
- Stock of emigrants as percentage of population, 2013: **18.0 percent**
- Top destination countries, 2013: Germany, Austria, Switzerland, Croatia, the United States, Turkey, France, Italy, the Netherlands, Australia
- Tertiary-educated as a percentage of total emigrants in OECD countries, 2011: **14.7 percent**
- Tertiary-educated women as a percentage of total women emigrants in OECD countries, 2011: **14.6 percent**
- Number of refugees, 2014: **46,090**
- Second generation diaspora in Australia, Europe, and the United States, 2012: **273.2 thousands**

IMMIGRATION

- Stock of immigrants, 2013: **770.5 thousands**
- Stock of immigrants as percentage of population, 2013: **10.8 percent**
- Top source countries, 2013: Bosnia and Herzegovina, Croatia, Montenegro, the Former Yugoslav Republic of Macedonia, Germany, Slovenia, Romania, Austria, France, the Russian Federation
- Women as percentage of immigrants, 2013: **56.8 percent**
- Number of refugees, 2014: **43,739**

Remittances

US$ millions	2006	2007	2008	2009	2010	2011	2012	2013	2014	2015e
Inward remittance flows[a]	—	**3,765**	**3,544**	**4,648**	**4,118**	**3,960**	**3,549**	**4,025**	**3,696**	**3,632**
of which										
Compensation of employees	—	145	191	184	164	187	211	234	237	—
Personal transfers	—	3,620	3,354	4,464	3,954	3,773	3,338	3,792	3,459	—
Outward remittance flows	—	**129**	**180**	**153**	**155**	**204**	**218**	**255**	**267**	—
of which										
Compensation of employees	—	15	24	20	19	29	40	49	53	—
Personal transfers	—	114	156	133	136	175	178	206	214	—

a. Net FDI inflows US$2.06 billion, net ODA received US$0.78 billion in 2013.

Seychelles

Population (thousands, 2013)	91.5
Population growth (avg. annual %, 2005-14)	1.0
Population density (people per sq km, 2014)	201.2
Labor force, total	−
Unemployment rate (% of labor force)	−
Urban population (% of pop., 2014)	53.6
Surface area (thousands of sq km, 2014)	0.5
GNI, Atlas method (current US$ billions, 2014)	1.3
GNI per capita, Atlas method (current US$, 2014)	14,100.0
GDP growth (avg. annual %, 2011-14)	6.0
Poverty headcount ratio at national poverty line (% of pop., 2006)	37.8
Age dependency ratio (% of working-age pop., 2014)	43.0
Account at a formal financial institution (% age 15+)	−
Mobile cellular subscriptions (per 100 people, 2014)	162.2
Internet users (per 100 people, 2014)	54.3

Migration

EMIGRATION

- Stock of emigrants, 2013: **9.6 thousands**
- Stock of emigrants as percentage of population, 2013: **10.6 percent**
- Top destination countries, 2013: Australia, the United States, Italy, Canada, South Africa, France, Kenya, Botswana, Switzerland, Mauritius
- Tertiary-educated as a percentage of total emigrants in OECD countries, 2011: **26.5 percent**
- Tertiary-educated women as a percentage of total women emigrants in OECD countries, 2011: **26.4 percent**
- Number of refugees, 2014: **18**
- Second generation diaspora in Australia, Europe, and the United States, 2012: Not available

IMMIGRATION

- Stock of immigrants, 2013: **12.1 thousands**
- Stock of immigrants as percentage of population, 2013: **13.4 percent**
- Top source countries, 2013: India, Madagascar, the Philippines, Sri Lanka, Mauritius, China, Kenya, the United Kingdom, South Africa, France
- Women as percentage of immigrants, 2013: **30.4 percent**
- Number of refugees, 2014: Not available

Remittances

US$ millions	2006	2007	2008	2009	2010	2011	2012	2013	2014	2015e
Inward remittance flows[a]	13	5	3	16	17	25	18	13	15	15
of which										
Compensation of employees	0	1	1	1	1	1	1	1	1	−
Personal transfers	13	4	2	15	16	24	17	12	14	−
Outward remittance flows	17	52	51	62	41	50	57	61	58	−
of which										
Compensation of employees	8	5	7	9	3	3	10	12	8	−
Personal transfers	10	47	44	54	38	47	47	50	49	−

a. Net FDI inflows US$0.06 billion, net ODA received US$0.03 billion in 2013.

Sierra Leone

Population (millions, 2014)	6.3
Population growth (avg. annual %, 2005–14)	2.6
Population density (people per sq km, 2014)	87.5
Labor force (millions, 2014)	2.4
Unemployment rate (% of labor force, 2014)	3.3
Urban population (% of pop., 2014)	39.6
Surface area (thousands of sq km, 2014)	72.3
GNI, Atlas method (current US$ billions, 2014)	4.4
GNI per capita, Atlas method (current US$, 2014)	700.0
GDP growth (avg. annual %, 2011–14)	11.3
Poverty headcount ratio at national poverty line (% of pop., 2011)	52.9
Age dependency ratio (% of working-age pop., 2014)	82.9
Account at a formal financial institution (% age 15+, 2014)	14.1
Mobile cellular subscriptions (per 100 people, 2014)	76.7
Internet users (per 100 people, 2014)	2.1

Migration

EMIGRATION

- Stock of emigrants, 2013: **336.0 thousands**
- Stock of emigrants as percentage of population, 2013: **5.4 percent**
- Top destination countries, 2013: Guinea, the United States, the United Kingdom, Liberia, Senegal, Germany, the Netherlands, Australia, Nigeria, Canada
- Tertiary-educated as a percentage of total emigrants in OECD countries, 2011: **33.7 percent**
- Tertiary-educated women as a percentage of total women emigrants in OECD countries, 2011: **31.9 percent**
- Number of refugees, 2014: **4,947**
- Second generation diaspora in Australia, Europe, and the United States, 2012: **4.7 thousands**

IMMIGRATION

- Stock of immigrants, 2013: **96.4 thousands**
- Stock of immigrants as percentage of population, 2013: **1.6 percent**
- Top source countries, 2013: Guinea, Liberia, The Gambia, Nigeria, Ghana, Lebanon, Mali, Senegal, India, Côte d'Ivoire
- Women as percentage of immigrants, 2013: **46.2 percent**
- Number of refugees, 2014: **1,371**

Remittances

US$ millions	2006	2007	2008	2009	2010	2011	2012	2013	2014	2015e
Inward remittance flows[a]	**16**	**42**	**23**	**36**	**44**	**59**	**61**	**68**	**68**	**72**
of which										
Compensation of employees	4	2	2	3	3	3	4	5	–	–
Personal transfers	12	40	20	33	42	56	57	63	–	–
Outward remittance flows	**4**	**4**	**3**	**3**	**11**	**21**	**20**	**9**	**–**	**–**
of which										
Compensation of employees	2	3	1	2	2	2	3	4	–	–
Personal transfers	2	1	2	2	9	18	18	5	–	–

a. Net FDI inflows US$0.38 billion, net ODA received US$0.44 billion in 2013.

Singapore

Population (millions, 2014)	5.5
Population growth (avg. annual %, 2005–14)	2.7
Population density (people per sq km, 2014)	7,736.5
Labor force (millions, 2014)	3.1
Unemployment rate (% of labor force, 2014)	3.0
Urban population (% of pop., 2014)	100.0
Surface area (thousands of sq km, 2014)	0.7
GNI, Atlas method (current US$ billions, 2014)	301.6
GNI per capita, Atlas method (current US$, 2014)	55,150.0
GDP growth (avg. annual %, 2011–14)	4.2
Poverty headcount ratio at national poverty line (% of pop.)	–
Age dependency ratio (% of working-age pop., 2014)	36.9
Account at a formal financial institution (% age 15+, 2014)	96.4
Mobile cellular subscriptions (per 100 people, 2014)	158.1
Internet users (per 100 people, 2014)	82.0

Migration

EMIGRATION

- Stock of emigrants, 2013: **282.2 thousands**
- Stock of emigrants as percentage of population, 2013: **5.2 percent**
- Top destination countries, 2013: Australia, Malaysia, the United Kingdom, the United States, Indonesia, China, Canada, Hong Kong SAR, China, Bangladesh, New Zealand
- Tertiary-educated as a percentage of total emigrants in OECD countries, 2011: **48.4 percent**
- Tertiary-educated women as a percentage of total women emigrants in OECD countries, 2011: **48.3 percent**
- Number of refugees, 2014: **55**
- Second generation diaspora in Australia, Europe, and the United States, 2012: **47.0 thousands**

IMMIGRATION

- Stock of immigrants, 2013: **2,323.3 thousands**
- Stock of immigrants as percentage of population, 2013: **43.0 percent**
- Top source countries, 2013: Malaysia, China, Indonesia, India, Pakistan, Bangladesh, Hong Kong SAR, China, Macao SAR, China, Thailand, the United States
- Women as percentage of immigrants, 2013: **55.8 percent**
- Number of refugees, 2014: Not available

Remittances

US$ millions	2006	2007	2008	2009	2010	2011	2012	2013	2014	2015e
Inward remittance flows[a]	–	–	–	–	–	–	–	–	–	–
of which										
Compensation of employees	–	–	–	–	–	–	–	–	–	–
Personal transfers	–	–	–	–	–	–	–	–	–	–
Outward remittance flows	–	–	–	–	–	–	–	–	–	–
of which										
Compensation of employees	–	–	–	–	–	–	–	–	–	–
Personal transfers	–	–	–	–	–	–	–	–	–	–

a. Net FDI inflows US$64.79 billion in 2013.

224   *Migration and Remittances Factbook 2016*

Sint Maarten (Dutch part)

Population (thousands, 2013)	37.7
Population growth (avg. annual %, 2005–14)	0.6
Population density (people per sq km, 2014)	1,107.8
Labor force, total	—
Unemployment rate (% of labor force)	—
Urban population (% of pop., 2014)	100.0
Surface area (thousands of sq km, 2014)	0.0
GNI, Atlas method (current US$ billions)	—
GNI per capita, Atlas method (current US$)	—
GDP growth (avg. annual %)	—
Poverty headcount ratio at national poverty line (% of pop.)	—
Age dependency ratio (% of working-age pop.)	—
Account at a formal financial institution (% age 15+)	—
Mobile cellular subscriptions (per 100 people)	—
Internet users (per 100 people)	—

Migration

EMIGRATION

- Stock of emigrants, 2013: **21.8 thousands**
- Stock of emigrants as percentage of population, 2013: **59.6 percent**
- Top destination countries, 2013: the Netherlands, South Africa, the United States, Curaçao, Aruba, the Virgin Islands (U.S.), República Bolivariana de Venezuela, Canada, St. Kitts and Nevis, Australia
- Tertiary-educated as a percentage of total emigrants in OECD countries, 2011: Not available
- Tertiary-educated women as a percentage of total women emigrants in OECD countries, 2011: Not available
- Number of refugees, 2014: Not available
- Second generation diaspora in Australia, Europe, and the United States, 2012: Not available

IMMIGRATION

- Stock of immigrants, 2013: **27.0 thousands**
- Stock of immigrants as percentage of population, 2013: **73.8 percent**
- Top source countries, 2013: the Dominican Republic, Haiti, Jamaica, Guyana, Dominica, Curaçao, Aruba, St. Kitts and Nevis, India, Cuba
- Women as percentage of immigrants, 2013: **51.8 percent**
- Number of refugees, 2014: Not available

Remittances

US$ millions	2006	2007	2008	2009	2010	2011	2012	2013	2014	2015e
Inward remittance flows[a]	—	—	—	—	—	54	56	73	62	62
of which										
Compensation of employees	—	—	—	—	—	11	12	22	13	—
Personal transfers	—	—	—	—	—	43	43	51	49	—
Outward remittance flows	—	—	—	—	—	105	108	108	114	—
of which										
Compensation of employees	—	—	—	—	—	38	40	41	48	—
Personal transfers	—	—	—	—	—	68	68	67	66	—

a. Net FDI inflows US$0.05 billion in 2013.

Slovak Republic

Population (millions, 2014)	5.4
Population growth (avg. annual %, 2005–14)	0.1
Population density (people per sq km, 2014)	112.7
Labor force (millions, 2014)	2.7
Unemployment rate (% of labor force, 2014)	13.3
Urban population (% of pop., 2014)	53.8
Surface area (thousands of sq km, 2014)	49.0
GNI, Atlas method (current US$ billions, 2014)	96.2
GNI per capita, Atlas method (current US$, 2014)	17,750.0
GDP growth (avg. annual %, 2011–14)	2.1
Poverty headcount ratio at national poverty line (% of pop., 2012)	12.8
Age dependency ratio (% of working-age pop., 2014)	39.9
Account at a formal financial institution (% age 15+, 2014)	77.2
Mobile cellular subscriptions (per 100 people, 2014)	116.9
Internet users (per 100 people, 2014)	80.0

Migration

EMIGRATION

- Stock of emigrants, 2013: **592.3 thousands**
- Stock of emigrants as percentage of population, 2013: **10.9 percent**
- Top destination countries, 2013: the Czech Republic, Germany, the United Kingdom, Austria, the United States, Hungary, Canada, Switzerland, Ireland, Italy
- Tertiary-educated as a percentage of total emigrants in OECD countries, 2011: **21.9 percent**
- Tertiary-educated women as a percentage of total women emigrants in OECD countries, 2011: **22.0 percent**
- Number of refugees, 2014: **311**
- Second generation diaspora in Australia, Europe, and the United States, 2012: **289.1 thousands**

IMMIGRATION

- Stock of immigrants, 2013: **158.1 thousands**
- Stock of immigrants as percentage of population, 2013: **2.9 percent**
- Top source countries, 2013: the Czech Republic, Hungary, Ukraine, Romania, the United Kingdom, Poland, Germany, Austria, the Russian Federation, France
- Women as percentage of immigrants, 2013: **53.3 percent**
- Number of refugees, 2014: **771**

Remittances

US$ millions	2006	2007	2008	2009	2010	2011	2012	2013	2014	2015e
Inward remittance flows[a]	1,088	1,483	1,973	1,671	1,591	1,753	1,928	2,072	2,395	2,367
of which										
Compensation of employees	1,088	1,483	1,973	1,671	1,591	1,753	1,928	2,072	2,121	–
Personal transfers	–	–	–	–	–	–	–	–	274	–
Outward remittance flows	48	73	144	138	70	70	154	175	225	–
of which										
Compensation of employees	48	73	144	138	70	70	154	175	191	–
Personal transfers	–	–	–	–	–	–	–	–	34	–

a. Net FDI inflows US$1.00 billion in 2013.

Slovenia

Population (millions, 2014)	2.1
Population growth (avg. annual %, 2005–14)	0.3
Population density (people per sq km, 2014)	102.4
Labor force (millions, 2014)	1.0
Unemployment rate (% of labor force, 2014)	9.5
Urban population (% of pop., 2014)	49.7
Surface area (thousands of sq km, 2014)	20.3
GNI, Atlas method (current US$ billions, 2014)	48.6
GNI per capita, Atlas method (current US$, 2014)	23,580.0
GDP growth (avg. annual %, 2011–14)	0.0
Poverty headcount ratio at national poverty line (% of pop., 2012)	14.5
Age dependency ratio (% of working-age pop., 2014)	47.5
Account at a formal financial institution (% age 15+, 2014)	97.2
Mobile cellular subscriptions (per 100 people, 2014)	112.1
Internet users (per 100 people, 2014)	71.6

Migration

EMIGRATION

- Stock of emigrants, 2013: **171.3 thousands**
- Stock of emigrants as percentage of population, 2013: **8.3 percent**
- Top destination countries, 2013: Croatia, Germany, Austria, Serbia, Canada, the United States, Australia, Switzerland, Italy, France
- Tertiary-educated as a percentage of total emigrants in OECD countries, 2011: **17.7 percent**
- Tertiary-educated women as a percentage of total women emigrants in OECD countries, 2011: **16.1 percent**
- Number of refugees, 2014: **25**
- Second generation diaspora in Australia, Europe, and the United States, 2012: **91.0 thousands**

IMMIGRATION

- Stock of immigrants, 2013: **365.6 thousands**
- Stock of immigrants as percentage of population, 2013: **17.7 percent**
- Top source countries, 2013: Bosnia and Herzegovina, Croatia, Serbia, Kosovo, the Former Yugoslav Republic of Macedonia, Germany, Italy, Austria, Argentina, Switzerland
- Women as percentage of immigrants, 2013: **39.4 percent**
- Number of refugees, 2014: **231**

Remittances

US$ millions	2006	2007	2008	2009	2010	2011	2012	2013	2014	2015e
Inward remittance flows[a]	**279**	**320**	**380**	**329**	**347**	**489**	**645**	**694**	**757**	**737**
of which										
Compensation of employees	274	315	347	298	317	455	608	653	718	–
Personal transfers	6	5	33	31	30	34	36	42	40	–
Outward remittance flows	**140**	**248**	**380**	**246**	**196**	**198**	**186**	**203**	**215**	**–**
of which										
Compensation of employees	139	247	340	161	118	130	126	140	158	–
Personal transfers	1	1	40	85	78	68	60	63	57	–

a. Net FDI inflows US$0.10 billion in 2013.

Solomon Islands

Population (thousands, 2013)	572.2
Population growth (avg. annual %, 2005–14)	2.2
Population density (people per sq km, 2014)	20.4
Labor force (thousands, 2013)	228.0
Unemployment rate (% of labor force, 2014)	3.9
Urban population (% of pop., 2014)	21.9
Surface area (thousands of sq km, 2014)	28.9
GNI, Atlas method (current US$ billions, 2014)	1.0
GNI per capita, Atlas method (current US$, 2014)	1,830.0
GDP growth (avg. annual %, 2011–14)	5.5
Poverty headcount ratio at national poverty line (% of pop., 2005)	22.7
Age dependency ratio (% of working-age pop., 2014)	76.0
Account at a formal financial institution (% age 15+)	–
Mobile cellular subscriptions (per 100 people, 2014)	65.8
Internet users (per 100 people, 2014)	9.0

Migration

EMIGRATION

- Stock of emigrants, 2013: **3.0 thousands**
- Stock of emigrants as percentage of population, 2013: **0.5 percent**
- Top destination countries, 2013: Australia, Papua New Guinea, Vanuatu, the United States, Ukraine, Canada, Switzerland, the Russian Federation, the Marshall Islands, the Netherlands
- Tertiary-educated as a percentage of total emigrants in OECD countries, 2011: **35.3 percent**
- Tertiary-educated women as a percentage of total women emigrants in OECD countries, 2011: **32.8 percent**
- Number of refugees, 2014: **70**
- Second generation diaspora in Australia, Europe, and the United States, 2012: Not available

IMMIGRATION

- Stock of immigrants, 2013: **7.9 thousands**
- Stock of immigrants as percentage of population, 2013: **1.4 percent**
- Top source countries, 2013: France, Indonesia, Australia, Vanuatu, French Polynesia, New Zealand, India, Bangladesh, Pakistan, the United Kingdom
- Women as percentage of immigrants, 2013: **43.9 percent**
- Number of refugees, 2014: Not available

Remittances

US$ millions	2006	2007	2008	2009	2010	2011	2012	2013	2014	2015e
Inward remittance flows[a]	**11**	**13**	**9**	**13**	**14**	**17**	**21**	**21**	**16**	**17**
of which										
Compensation of employees	2	2	2	2	3	4	5	5	6	–
Personal transfers	9	11	8	10	11	13	16	15	10	–
Outward remittance flows	**11**	**12**	**14**	**39**	**62**	**67**	**47**	**45**	**46**	**–**
of which										
Compensation of employees	2	4	3	4	3	5	6	8	11	–
Personal transfers	9	8	11	35	58	62	41	37	35	–

a. Net FDI inflows US$0.05 billion, net ODA received US$0.29 billion in 2013.

Somalia

	LOW INCOME
Population (millions, 2014)	10.5
Population growth (avg. annual %, 2005–14)	2.4
Population density (people per sq km, 2014)	16.8
Labor force (millions, 2014)	3.1
Unemployment rate (% of labor force, 2014)	6.9
Urban population (% of pop., 2014)	39.1
Surface area (thousands of sq km, 2014)	637.7
GNI, Atlas method (current US$ billions)	–
GNI per capita, Atlas method (current US$)	–
GDP growth (avg. annual %)	–
Poverty headcount ratio at national poverty line (% of pop.)	–
Age dependency ratio (% of working-age pop., 2014)	98.9
Account at a formal financial institution (% age 15+, 2014)	7.9
Mobile cellular subscriptions (per 100 people, 2014)	50.9
Internet users (per 100 people, 2014)	1.6

Migration

EMIGRATION

- Stock of emigrants, 2013: **1,920.9 thousands**
- Stock of emigrants as percentage of population, 2013: **18.7 percent**
- Top destination countries, 2013: Kenya, Ethiopia, the Republic of Yemen, Libya, Djibouti, the United States, the United Kingdom, Sweden, the Arab Republic of Egypt, Saudi Arabia
- Tertiary-educated as a percentage of total emigrants in OECD countries, 2011: **13.8 percent**
- Tertiary-educated women as a percentage of total women emigrants in OECD countries, 2011: **11.1 percent**
- Number of refugees, 2014: **1,106,019**
- Second generation diaspora in Australia, Europe, and the United States, 2012: Not available

IMMIGRATION

- Stock of immigrants, 2013: **24.6 thousands**
- Stock of immigrants as percentage of population, 2013: **0.2 percent**
- Top source countries, 2013: Ethiopia, Eritrea, the Republic of Yemen, Bangladesh, the Democratic Republic of Congo, South Sudan, Uganda
- Women as percentage of immigrants, 2013: **45.8 percent**
- Number of refugees, 2014: **2,717**

Remittances

US$ millions	2006	2007	2008	2009	2010	2011	2012	2013	2014	2015e
Inward remittance flows[a]	–	–	–	–	–	–	–	–	–	–
of which										
Compensation of employees	–	–	–	–	–	–	–	–	–	–
Personal transfers	–	–	–	–	–	–	–	–	–	–
Outward remittance flows	–	–	–	–	–	–	–	–	–	–
of which										
Compensation of employees	–	–	–	–	–	–	–	–	–	–
Personal transfers	–	–	–	–	–	–	–	–	–	–

a. Net FDI inflows US$0.11 billion, net ODA received US$0.99 billion in 2013.

South Africa

Population (millions, 2014)	54.0
Population growth (avg. annual %, 2005–14)	1.4
Population density (people per sq km, 2014)	44.5
Labor force (millions, 2014)	20.0
Unemployment rate (% of labor force, 2014)	25.1
Urban population (% of pop., 2014)	64.3
Surface area (thousands of sq km, 2014)	1,219.1
GNI, Atlas method (current US$ billions, 2014)	367.2
GNI per capita, Atlas method (current US$, 2014)	6,800.0
GDP growth (avg. annual %, 2011–14)	2.3
Poverty headcount ratio at national poverty line (% of pop., 2010)	53.8
Age dependency ratio (% of working-age pop., 2014)	52.8
Account at a formal financial institution (% age 15+, 2014)	68.8
Mobile cellular subscriptions (per 100 people, 2014)	149.7
Internet users (per 100 people, 2014)	49.0

Migration

EMIGRATION

- Stock of emigrants, 2013: **806.3 thousands**
- Stock of emigrants as percentage of population, 2013: **1.5 percent**
- Top destination countries, 2013: the United Kingdom, Australia, the United States, New Zealand, Canada, Botswana, the Netherlands, Chile, Israel, Zimbabwe
- Tertiary-educated as a percentage of total emigrants in OECD countries, 2011: **47.9 percent**
- Tertiary-educated women as a percentage of total women emigrants in OECD countries, 2011: **47.9 percent**
- Number of refugees, 2014: **392**
- Second generation diaspora in Australia, Europe, and the United States, 2012: **89.8 thousands**

IMMIGRATION

- Stock of immigrants, 2013: **2,685.2 thousands**
- Stock of immigrants as percentage of population, 2013: **5.1 percent**
- Top source countries, 2013: Zimbabwe, Mozambique, Lesotho, the United Kingdom, Namibia, Swaziland, Malawi, Zambia, Portugal, Botswana
- Women as percentage of immigrants, 2013: **42.5 percent**
- Number of refugees, 2014: **112,112**

Remittances

US$ millions	2006	2007	2008	2009	2010	2011	2012	2013	2014	2015e
Inward remittance flows[a]	692	792	784	862	1,070	1,158	1,085	971	913	1,003
of which										
Compensation of employees	692	792	784	862	1,070	1,158	1,085	971	913	–
Personal transfers	–	–	–	–	–	–	–	–	–	–
Outward remittance flows	1,055	1,173	1,119	1,144	1,353	1,423	1,320	1,182	1,094	–
of which										
Compensation of employees	1,055	1,173	1,119	1,144	1,353	1,423	1,320	1,182	1,094	–
Personal transfers	–	–	–	–	–	–	–	–	–	–

a. Net FDI inflows US$8.23 billion, net ODA received US$1.29 billion in 2013.

South Sudan

LOW INCOME

Population (millions, 2014)	11.9
Population growth (avg. annual %, 2005–14)	4.3
Population density (people per sq km)	–
Labor force, total	–
Unemployment rate (% of labor force)	–
Urban population (% of pop., 2014)	18.6
Surface area (thousands of sq km, 2014)	644.3
GNI, Atlas method (current US$ billions, 2014)	11.6
GNI per capita, Atlas method (current US$, 2014)	970.0
GDP growth (avg. annual %, 2011–14)	-8.6
Poverty headcount ratio at national poverty line (% of pop., 2009)	50.6
Age dependency ratio (% of working-age pop., 2014)	84.7
Account at a formal financial institution (% age 15+)	–
Mobile cellular subscriptions (per 100 people, 2014)	24.5
Internet users (per 100 people, 2014)	15.9

Migration

EMIGRATION

- Stock of emigrants, 2013: **759.1 thousands**
- Stock of emigrants as percentage of population, 2013: **6.6 percent**
- Top destination countries, 2013: Chad, Ethiopia, Uganda, Sudan, Saudi Arabia, the United States, the United Arab Emirates, Australia, Kenya, Canada
- Tertiary-educated as a percentage of total emigrants in OECD countries, 2011: **15.1 percent**
- Tertiary-educated women as a percentage of total women emigrants in OECD countries, 2011: **6.2 percent**
- Number of refugees, 2014: **616,191**
- Second generation diaspora in Australia, Europe, and the United States, 2012: Not available

IMMIGRATION

- Stock of immigrants, 2013: **629.6 thousands**
- Stock of immigrants as percentage of population, 2013: **5.5 percent**
- Top source countries, 2013: Sudan, Uganda, the Democratic Republic of Congo, Ethiopia, Kenya, Chad, the Arab Republic of Egypt, Central African Republic, Nigeria, Eritrea
- Women as percentage of immigrants, 2013: **40.3 percent**
- Number of refugees, 2014: **248,152**

Remittances

US$ millions	2006	2007	2008	2009	2010	2011	2012	2013	2014	2015e
Inward remittance flows[a]	–	–	–	–	–	–	–	–	–	–
of which										
Compensation of employees	–	–	–	–	–	–	–	–	–	–
Personal transfers	–	–	–	–	–	–	–	–	–	–
Outward remittance flows	–	–	–	–	–	–	–	–	–	–
of which										
Compensation of employees	–	–	–	–	–	–	–	–	–	–
Personal transfers	–	–	–	–	–	–	–	–	–	–

a. Net FDI inflows US$-0.08 billion, net ODA received US$1.45 billion in 2013.

Spain

Population (millions, 2014)	46.4
Population growth (avg. annual %, 2005–14)	0.8
Population density (people per sq km, 2014)	92.8
Labor force (millions, 2014)	23.3
Unemployment rate (% of labor force, 2014)	24.7
Urban population (% of pop., 2014)	79.4
Surface area (thousands of sq km, 2014)	505.9
GNI, Atlas method (current US$ billions, 2014)	1,366.0
GNI per capita, Atlas method (current US$, 2014)	29,440.0
GDP growth (avg. annual %, 2011–14)	-1.0
Poverty headcount ratio at national poverty line (% of pop.)	–
Age dependency ratio (% of working-age pop., 2014)	50.0
Account at a formal financial institution (% age 15+, 2014)	97.6
Mobile cellular subscriptions (per 100 people, 2014)	107.8
Internet users (per 100 people, 2014)	76.2

Migration

EMIGRATION

- Stock of emigrants, 2013: **1,231.0 thousands**
- Stock of emigrants as percentage of population, 2013: **2.6 percent**
- Top destination countries, 2013: France, Germany, the United States, Argentina, the United Kingdom, Switzerland, República Bolivariana de Venezuela, Belgium, Brazil, Italy
- Tertiary-educated as a percentage of total emigrants in OECD countries, 2011: **27.8 percent**
- Tertiary-educated women as a percentage of total women emigrants in OECD countries, 2011: **27.7 percent**
- Number of refugees, 2014: **50**
- Second generation diaspora in Australia, Europe, and the United States, 2012: **873.3 thousands**

IMMIGRATION

- Stock of immigrants, 2013: **6,618.0 thousands**
- Stock of immigrants as percentage of population, 2013: **14.2 percent**
- Top source countries, 2013: Romania, Morocco, Ecuador, the United Kingdom, Colombia, Argentina, Germany, France, Peru, the Plurinational State of Bolivia
- Women as percentage of immigrants, 2013: **50.9 percent**
- Number of refugees, 2014: **5,737**

Remittances

US$ millions	2006	2007	2008	2009	2010	2011	2012	2013	2014	2015e
Inward										
remittance flows[a]	7,352	8,963	9,742	8,583	8,687	9,655	9,715	10,649	10,750	10,517
of which										
Compensation										
of employees	1,281	1,677	1,840	1,523	1,575	1,693	2,084	3,019	3,119	–
Personal transfers	6,071	7,287	7,901	7,060	7,111	7,962	7,631	7,631	7,631	–
Outward										
remittance flows	9,682	12,508	12,450	10,630	9,958	10,558	8,841	8,794	8,825	–
of which										
Compensation										
of employees	794	897	749	557	434	456	379	332	363	–
Personal transfers	8,888	11,610	11,701	10,074	9,524	10,102	8,462	8,462	8,462	–

a. Net FDI inflows US$45.10 billion in 2013.

Sri Lanka

MIDDLE INCOME

Population (millions, 2014)	20.6
Population growth (avg. annual %, 2005–14)	1.0
Population density (people per sq km, 2014)	329.1
Labor force (millions, 2014)	8.5
Unemployment rate (% of labor force, 2014)	4.6
Urban population (% of pop., 2014)	18.3
Surface area (thousands of sq km, 2014)	65.6
GNI, Atlas method (current US$ billions, 2014)	71.4
GNI per capita, Atlas method (current US$, 2014)	3,460.0
GDP growth (avg. annual %, 2011–14)	6.4
Poverty headcount ratio at national poverty line (% of pop., 2012)	6.7
Age dependency ratio (% of working-age pop., 2014)	50.8
Account at a formal financial institution (% age 15+, 2014)	82.7
Mobile cellular subscriptions (per 100 people, 2014)	103.2
Internet users (per 100 people, 2014)	25.8

Migration

EMIGRATION

- Stock of emigrants, 2013: **1,780.1 thousands**
- Stock of emigrants as percentage of population, 2013: **8.7 percent**
- Top destination countries, 2013: Saudi Arabia, India, the United Arab Emirates, the United Kingdom, Canada, Qatar, Australia, Italy, Germany, the United States
- Tertiary-educated as a percentage of total emigrants in OECD countries, 2011: **35.0 percent**
- Tertiary-educated women as a percentage of total women emigrants in OECD countries, 2011: **33.6 percent**
- Number of refugees, 2014: **121,957**
- Second generation diaspora in Australia, Europe, and the United States, 2012: **40.5 thousands**

IMMIGRATION

- Stock of immigrants, 2013: **325.0 thousands**
- Stock of immigrants as percentage of population, 2013: **1.6 percent**
- Top source countries, 2013: India, Australia, France, the United Kingdom, China, Pakistan, Sweden, Malaysia, Germany, the United States
- Women as percentage of immigrants, 2013: **49.8 percent**
- Number of refugees, 2014: **498**

Remittances

US$ millions	2006	2007	2008	2009	2010	2011	2012	2013	2014	2015e
Inward remittance flows[a]	**2,167**	**2,507**	**2,925**	**3,337**	**4,123**	**5,153**	**6,000**	**6,422**	**7,036**	**7,189**
of which										
Compensation of employees	6	6	7	7	7	8	14	15	19	–
Personal transfers	2,161	2,502	2,918	3,330	4,116	5,145	5,985	6,407	7,018	–
Outward remittance flows	**274**	**305**	**373**	**420**	**526**	**581**	**680**	**854**	**887**	**–**
of which										
Compensation of employees	17	17	20	17	18	19	34	66	68	–
Personal transfers	258	288	353	403	508	562	646	788	819	–

a. Net FDI inflows US$0.93 billion, net ODA received US$0.42 billion in 2013.

St. Kitts and Nevis

HIGH INCOME NON-OECD

Population (thousands, 2013)	54.9
Population growth (avg. annual %, 2005–14)	1.3
Population density (people per sq km, 2014)	211.3
Labor force, total	–
Unemployment rate (% of labor force)	–
Urban population (% of pop., 2014)	32.0
Surface area (thousands of sq km, 2014)	0.3
GNI, Atlas method (current US$ billions, 2014)	0.8
GNI per capita, Atlas method (current US$, 2014)	14,920.0
GDP growth (avg. annual %, 2011–14)	3.3
Poverty headcount ratio at national poverty line (% of pop.)	–
Age dependency ratio (% of working-age pop.)	–
Account at a formal financial institution (% age 15+)	–
Mobile cellular subscriptions (per 100 people, 2014)	139.8
Internet users (per 100 people, 2014)	65.4

Migration

EMIGRATION

- Stock of emigrants, 2013: **29.1 thousands**
- Stock of emigrants as percentage of population, 2013: **53.5 percent**
- Top destination countries, 2013: the United States, the Virgin Islands (U.S.), Canada, Sint Maarten (Dutch part), Antigua and Barbuda, Curaçao, Jamaica, the Dominican Republic, Bermuda, the Netherlands
- Tertiary-educated as a percentage of total emigrants in OECD countries, 2011: **33.0 percent**
- Tertiary-educated women as a percentage of total women emigrants in OECD countries, 2011: **37.0 percent**
- Number of refugees, 2014: **15**
- Second generation diaspora in Australia, Europe, and the United States, 2012: Not available

IMMIGRATION

- Stock of immigrants, 2013: **5.7 thousands**
- Stock of immigrants as percentage of population, 2013: **10.4 percent**
- Top source countries, 2013: the United States, Guyana, the Dominican Republic, the Virgin Islands (U.S.), the United Kingdom, Antigua and Barbuda, Jamaica, Dominica, Trinidad and Tobago, St. Vincent and the Grenadines
- Women as percentage of immigrants, 2013: **45.0 percent**
- Number of refugees, 2014: Not available

Remittances

US$ millions	2006	2007	2008	2009	2010	2011	2012	2013	2014	2015e
Inward remittance flows[a]	33	36	40	39	47	45	51	52	52	52
of which										
Compensation of employees	0	0	0	0	0	0	0	0	–	–
Personal transfers	33	36	40	39	47	44	51	51	–	–
Outward remittance flows	5	6	6	6	6	6	6	7	–	–
of which										
Compensation of employees	1	1	1	1	1	0	0	0	–	–
Personal transfers	4	5	5	5	5	6	6	6	–	–

a. Net FDI inflows US$0.11 billion, net ODA received US$0.03 billion in 2013.

Migration and Remittances Factbook 2016

St. Lucia

Population (thousands, 2013)	183.6
Population growth (avg. annual %, 2005–14)	1.2
Population density (people per sq km, 2014)	301.1
Labor force (thousands, 2013)	97.3
Unemployment rate (% of labor force)	–
Urban population (% of pop., 2014)	18.5
Surface area (thousands of sq km, 2014)	0.6
GNI, Atlas method (current US$ billions, 2014)	1.3
GNI per capita, Atlas method (current US$, 2014)	7,260.0
GDP growth (avg. annual %, 2011–14)	0.1
Poverty headcount ratio at national poverty line (% of pop.)	–
Age dependency ratio (% of working-age pop., 2014)	48.0
Account at a formal financial institution (% age 15+)	–
Mobile cellular subscriptions (per 100 people, 2014)	102.6
Internet users (per 100 people, 2014)	51.0

Migration

EMIGRATION

- Stock of emigrants, 2013: **56.5 thousands**
- Stock of emigrants as percentage of population, 2013: **31.0 percent**
- Top destination countries, 2013: the United States, the United Kingdom, France, Canada, Barbados, the Virgin Islands (U.S.), Antigua and Barbuda, Trinidad and Tobago, Jamaica, Sint Maarten (Dutch part)
- Tertiary-educated as a percentage of total emigrants in OECD countries, 2011: **23.1 percent**
- Tertiary-educated women as a percentage of total women emigrants in OECD countries, 2011: **24.3 percent**
- Number of refugees, 2014: **921**
- Second generation diaspora in Australia, Europe, and the United States, 2012: Not available

IMMIGRATION

- Stock of immigrants, 2013: **12.2 thousands**
- Stock of immigrants as percentage of population, 2013: **6.7 percent**
- Top source countries, 2013: Guyana, the United Kingdom, Trinidad and Tobago, Barbados, the United States, St. Vincent and the Grenadines, Canada, Dominica, Jamaica, Grenada
- Women as percentage of immigrants, 2013: **50.1 percent**
- Number of refugees, 2014: Not available

Remittances

US$ millions	2006	2007	2008	2009	2010	2011	2012	2013	2014	2015e
Inward remittance flows[a]	28	29	29	28	29	29	30	30	30	30
of which										
Compensation of employees	0	0	0	0	0	0	0	0	–	–
Personal transfers	28	28	29	28	29	29	29	30	–	–
Outward remittance flows	3	3	3	3	3	3	3	3	–	–
of which										
Compensation of employees	–	–	–	–	–	–	–	–	–	–
Personal transfers	3	3	3	3	3	3	3	3	–	–

a. Net FDI inflows US$0.08 billion, net ODA received US$0.02 billion in 2013.

St. Martin (French part)

Population (thousands, 2013)	31.5
Population growth (avg. annual %, 2005–14)	1.4
Population density (people per sq km, 2014)	579.6
Labor force, total	–
Unemployment rate (% of labor force)	–
Urban population (% of pop.)	–
Surface area (thousands of sq km, 2014)	0.1
GNI, Atlas method (current US$ billions)	–
GNI per capita, Atlas method (current US$)	–
GDP growth (avg. annual %)	–
Poverty headcount ratio at national poverty line (% of pop.)	–
Age dependency ratio (% of working-age pop.)	–
Account at a formal financial institution (% age 15+)	–
Mobile cellular subscriptions (per 100 people)	–
Internet users (per 100 people)	–

Migration

EMIGRATION

- Stock of emigrants, 2013: **0.0 thousands**
- Stock of emigrants as percentage of population, 2013: **0.0 percent**
- Top destination countries, 2013: Aruba
- Tertiary-educated as a percentage of total emigrants in OECD countries, 2011: Not available
- Tertiary-educated women as a percentage of total women emigrants in OECD countries, 2011: Not available
- Number of refugees, 2014: Not available
- Second generation diaspora in Australia, Europe, and the United States, 2012: Not available

IMMIGRATION

- Stock of immigrants, 2013: Not available
- Stock of immigrants as percentage of population, 2013: Not available
- Top source countries, 2013: Not available
- Women as percentage of immigrants, 2013: Not available
- Number of refugees, 2014: Not available

Remittances

US$ millions	2006	2007	2008	2009	2010	2011	2012	2013	2014	2015e
Inward remittance flows	–	–	–	–	–	–	–	–	–	–
of which										
Compensation of employees	–	–	–	–	–	–	–	–	–	–
Personal transfers	–	–	–	–	–	–	–	–	–	–
Outward remittance flows	–	–	–	–	–	–	–	–	–	–
of which										
Compensation of employees	–	–	–	–	–	–	–	–	–	–
Personal transfers	–	–	–	–	–	–	–	–	–	–

St. Vincent and the Grenadines

Population (thousands, 2013)	109.4
Population growth (avg. annual %, 2005–14)	0.1
Population density (people per sq km, 2014)	280.4
Labor force (thousands, 2013)	55.0
Unemployment rate (% of labor force)	–
Urban population (% of pop., 2014)	50.2
Surface area (thousands of sq km, 2014)	0.4
GNI, Atlas method (current US$ billions, 2014)	0.7
GNI per capita, Atlas method (current US$, 2014)	6,610.0
GDP growth (avg. annual %, 2011–14)	0.8
Poverty headcount ratio at national poverty line (% of pop.)	–
Age dependency ratio (% of working-age pop., 2014)	47.1
Account at a formal financial institution (% age 15+)	–
Mobile cellular subscriptions (per 100 people, 2014)	105.2
Internet users (per 100 people, 2014)	56.5

Migration

EMIGRATION

- Stock of emigrants, 2013: **60.6 thousands**
- Stock of emigrants as percentage of population, 2013: **55.4 percent**
- Top destination countries, 2013: the United States, Canada, the United Kingdom, Trinidad and Tobago, Barbados, Antigua and Barbuda, the Virgin Islands (U.S.), Grenada, St. Lucia, Guyana
- Tertiary-educated as a percentage of total emigrants in OECD countries, 2011: **27.5 percent**
- Tertiary-educated women as a percentage of total women emigrants in OECD countries, 2011: **30.6 percent**
- Number of refugees, 2014: **1,736**
- Second generation diaspora in Australia, Europe, and the United States, 2012: Not available

IMMIGRATION

- Stock of immigrants, 2013: **10.3 thousands**
- Stock of immigrants as percentage of population, 2013: **9.4 percent**
- Top source countries, 2013: Trinidad and Tobago, Guyana, the United Kingdom, the United States, Barbados, Canada, St. Lucia, Jamaica, Dominica, Antigua and Barbuda
- Women as percentage of immigrants, 2013: **50.7 percent**
- Number of refugees, 2014: Not available

Remittances

US$ millions	2006	2007	2008	2009	2010	2011	2012	2013	2014	2015e
Inward remittance flows[a]	**26**	**29**	**27**	**29**	**29**	**29**	**31**	**32**	**32**	**32**
of which										
Compensation of employees	4	6	4	7	6	6	8	8	–	–
Personal transfers	22	22	23	22	23	23	23	24	–	–
Outward remittance flows	**5**	**6**	**5**	**5**	**6**	**6**	**6**	**6**	**–**	**–**
of which										
Compensation of employees	1	1	0	0	0	0	1	1	–	–
Personal transfers	5	5	5	5	5	5	6	6	–	–

a. Net FDI inflows US$0.13 billion, net ODA received US$0.01 billion in 2013.

Sudan

	MIDDLE INCOME
Population (millions, 2014)	39.4
Population growth (avg. annual %, 2005–14)	2.3
Population density (people per sq km, 2014)	21.6
Labor force (millions, 2014)	12.5
Unemployment rate (% of labor force, 2014)	14.8
Urban population (% of pop., 2014)	33.6
Surface area (thousands of sq km, 2014)	1,879.4
GNI, Atlas method (current US$ billions, 2014)	67.3
GNI per capita, Atlas method (current US$, 2014)	1,710.0
GDP growth (avg. annual %, 2011–14)	0.6
Poverty headcount ratio at national poverty line (% of pop., 2009)	46.5
Age dependency ratio (% of working-age pop., 2014)	79.0
Account at a formal financial institution (% age 15+, 2014)	15.3
Mobile cellular subscriptions (per 100 people, 2014)	72.2
Internet users (per 100 people, 2014)	24.6

Migration

EMIGRATION

- Stock of emigrants, 2013: **1,508.3 thousands**
- Stock of emigrants as percentage of population, 2013: **3.9 percent**
- Top destination countries, 2013: Saudi Arabia, South Sudan, the United Arab Emirates, Chad, Qatar, Kuwait, Kenya, Ethiopia, the Republic of Yemen, Uganda
- Tertiary-educated as a percentage of total emigrants in OECD countries, 2011: **31.7 percent**
- Tertiary-educated women as a percentage of total women emigrants in OECD countries, 2011: **28.9 percent**
- Number of refugees, 2014: **665,908**
- Second generation diaspora in Australia, Europe, and the United States, 2012: **17.8 thousands**

IMMIGRATION

- Stock of immigrants, 2013: **446.7 thousands**
- Stock of immigrants as percentage of population, 2013: **1.2 percent**
- Top source countries, 2013: Eritrea, South Sudan, Chad, Ethiopia, Nigeria, Central African Republic, the Arab Republic of Egypt, Kenya, Libya, India
- Women as percentage of immigrants, 2013: **49.2 percent**
- Number of refugees, 2014: **277,818**

Remittances

US$ millions	2006	2007	2008	2009	2010	2011	2012	2013	2014	2015e
Inward remittance flows[a]	**801**	**1,000**	**1,591**	**1,394**	**1,100**	**442**	**401**	**424**	**507**	**513**
of which										
Compensation of employees	2	2	3	29	129	4	0	0	29	–
Personal transfers	799	997	1,588	1,365	971	438	401	424	478	–
Outward remittance flows	**2**	**2**	**2**	**0**	**1**	**2**	**8**	**64**	**36**	**–**
of which										
Compensation of employees	2	2	2	0	1	2	8	64	36	–
Personal transfers	–	–	–	–	–	–	–	–	–	–

a. Net FDI inflows US$1.69 billion, net ODA received US$1.16 billion in 2013.

Suriname

	MIDDLE INCOME
Population (thousands, 2013)	538.2
Population growth (avg. annual %, 2005-14)	1.0
Population density (people per sq km, 2014)	3.5
Labor force (thousands, 2013)	213.8
Unemployment rate (% of labor force, 2014)	5.6
Urban population (% of pop., 2014)	66.1
Surface area (thousands of sq km, 2014)	163.8
GNI, Atlas method (current US$ billions, 2014)	5.4
GNI per capita, Atlas method (current US$, 2014)	9,950.0
GDP growth (avg. annual %, 2011-14)	3.3
Poverty headcount ratio at national poverty line (% of pop.)	–
Age dependency ratio (% of working-age pop., 2014)	51.3
Account at a formal financial institution (% age 15+)	–
Mobile cellular subscriptions (per 100 people, 2014)	170.6
Internet users (per 100 people, 2014)	40.1

Migration

EMIGRATION

- Stock of emigrants, 2013: **263.3 thousands**
- Stock of emigrants as percentage of population, 2013: **49.4 percent**
- Top destination countries, 2013: the Netherlands, France, the United States, Guyana, Curaçao, Aruba, Canada, Sint Maarten (Dutch part), Brazil, the Dominican Republic
- Tertiary-educated as a percentage of total emigrants in OECD countries, 2011: **17.2 percent**
- Tertiary-educated women as a percentage of total women emigrants in OECD countries, 2011: **17.6 percent**
- Number of refugees, 2014: **17**
- Second generation diaspora in Australia, Europe, and the United States, 2012: Not available

IMMIGRATION

- Stock of immigrants, 2013: **41.7 thousands**
- Stock of immigrants as percentage of population, 2013: **7.8 percent**
- Top source countries, 2013: Guyana, the Netherlands, Brazil, China, France, Haiti, the United States
- Women as percentage of immigrants, 2013: **45.3 percent**
- Number of refugees, 2014: Not available

Remittances

US$ millions	2006	2007	2008	2009	2010	2011	2012	2013	2014	2015e
Inward remittance flows[a]	2	3	2	5	4	7	8	8	10	9
of which										
Compensation of employees	2	2	2	4	4	4	1	1	1	–
Personal transfers	0	0	0	1	1	4	7	7	9	–
Outward remittance flows	4	6	8	5	1	3	12	19	21	–
of which										
Compensation of employees	3	4	7	4	0	1	11	15	15	–
Personal transfers	2	2	2	1	1	2	2	4	6	–

a. Net FDI inflows US$0.14 billion, net ODA received US$0.03 billion in 2013.

Swaziland

Population (millions, 2014)	1.3
Population growth (avg. annual %, 2005–14)	1.5
Population density (people per sq km, 2014)	73.8
Labor force (thousands, 2013)	457.0
Unemployment rate (% of labor force, 2014)	22.3
Urban population (% of pop., 2014)	21.3
Surface area (thousands of sq km, 2014)	17.4
GNI, Atlas method (current US$ billions, 2014)	4.5
GNI per capita, Atlas method (current US$, 2014)	3,550.0
GDP growth (avg. annual %, 2011–14)	2.4
Poverty headcount ratio at national poverty line (% of pop., 2009)	63.0
Age dependency ratio (% of working-age pop., 2014)	69.9
Account at a formal financial institution (% age 15+)	–
Mobile cellular subscriptions (per 100 people, 2014)	72.3
Internet users (per 100 people, 2014)	27.1

Migration

EMIGRATION

- Stock of emigrants, 2013: **97.8 thousands**
- Stock of emigrants as percentage of population, 2013: **7.8 percent**
- Top destination countries, 2013: South Africa, Greece, Tanzania, Botswana, Portugal, Australia, Canada, Switzerland, the Netherlands, Kenya
- Tertiary-educated as a percentage of total emigrants in OECD countries, 2011: **48.0 percent**
- Tertiary-educated women as a percentage of total women emigrants in OECD countries, 2011: **50.0 percent**
- Number of refugees, 2014: **151**
- Second generation diaspora in Australia, Europe, and the United States, 2012: Not available

IMMIGRATION

- Stock of immigrants, 2013: **25.5 thousands**
- Stock of immigrants as percentage of population, 2013: **2.0 percent**
- Top source countries, 2013: South Africa, Mozambique, the United States, Lesotho, Burundi, the Democratic Republic of Congo, Rwanda, Angola, Somalia, the Republic of Congo
- Women as percentage of immigrants, 2013: **45.5 percent**
- Number of refugees, 2014: **496**

Remittances

US$ millions	2006	2007	2008	2009	2010	2011	2012	2013	2014	2015e
Inward remittance flows[a]	96	95	90	93	55	38	31	30	24	25
of which										
Compensation of employees	94	94	87	91	53	36	28	26	20	–
Personal transfers	1	1	3	2	2	2	3	4	5	–
Outward remittance flows	17	8	6	11	12	12	27	9	7	–
of which										
Compensation of employees	15	7	5	10	11	11	8	8	5	–
Personal transfers	1	1	2	1	1	2	19	1	2	–

a. Net FDI inflows US$0.03 billion, net ODA received US$0.12 billion in 2013.

Sweden

Population (millions, 2014)	9.7
Population growth (avg. annual %, 2005–14)	0.7
Population density (people per sq km, 2014)	23.8
Labor force (millions, 2014)	5.1
Unemployment rate (% of labor force, 2014)	8.0
Urban population (% of pop., 2014)	85.7
Surface area (thousands of sq km, 2014)	447.4
GNI, Atlas method (current US$ billions, 2014)	596.9
GNI per capita, Atlas method (current US$, 2014)	61,610.0
GDP growth (avg. annual %, 2011–14)	1.5
Poverty headcount ratio at national poverty line (% of pop.)	–
Age dependency ratio (% of working-age pop., 2014)	58.0
Account at a formal financial institution (% age 15+, 2014)	99.7
Mobile cellular subscriptions (per 100 people, 2014)	127.8
Internet users (per 100 people, 2014)	92.5

Migration

EMIGRATION

- Stock of emigrants, 2013: **352.0 thousands**
- Stock of emigrants as percentage of population, 2013: **3.7 percent**
- Top destination countries, 2013: the United States, Norway, Finland, the United Kingdom, Germany, Spain, Denmark, Australia, France, Switzerland
- Tertiary-educated as a percentage of total emigrants in OECD countries, 2011: **42.1 percent**
- Tertiary-educated women as a percentage of total women emigrants in OECD countries, 2011: **44.6 percent**
- Number of refugees, 2014: **8**
- Second generation diaspora in Australia, Europe, and the United States, 2012: **149.0 thousands**

IMMIGRATION

- Stock of immigrants, 2013: **1,453.6 thousands**
- Stock of immigrants as percentage of population, 2013: **15.1 percent**
- Top source countries, 2013: Finland, Iraq, Poland, the Islamic Republic of Iran, Bosnia and Herzegovina, Somalia, Germany, Turkey, Denmark, Norway
- Women as percentage of immigrants, 2013: **50.7 percent**
- Number of refugees, 2014: **142,152**

Remittances

US$ millions	2006	2007	2008	2009	2010	2011	2012	2013	2014	2015e
Inward remittance flows[a]	**597**	**774**	**825**	**715**	**762**	**4,175**	**4,070**	**4,466**	**4,442**	**4,377**
of which										
Compensation of employees	375	532	568	501	535	3,921	3,828	3,960	3,979	–
Personal transfers	222	242	257	214	227	255	242	506	464	–
Outward remittance flows	**585**	**885**	**915**	**822**	**820**	**1,070**	**1,045**	**1,518**	**1,427**	**–**
of which										
Compensation of employees	559	857	886	797	793	1,040	1,016	1,096	1,041	–
Personal transfers	26	28	29	25	26	29	28	422	386	–

a. Net FDI inflows US$0.42 billion in 2013.

Switzerland

Population (millions, 2014)	8.2
Population growth (avg. annual %, 2005–14)	1.0
Population density (people per sq km, 2014)	207.3
Labor force (millions, 2014)	4.8
Unemployment rate (% of labor force, 2014)	4.5
Urban population (% of pop., 2014)	73.8
Surface area (thousands of sq km, 2014)	41.3
GNI, Atlas method (current US$ billions, 2014)	712.8
GNI per capita, Atlas method (current US$, 2014)	88,120.0
GDP growth (avg. annual %, 2011–14)	1.6
Poverty headcount ratio at national poverty line (% of pop.)	–
Age dependency ratio (% of working-age pop., 2014)	48.4
Account at a formal financial institution (% age 15+, 2014)	98.0
Mobile cellular subscriptions (per 100 people, 2014)	140.5
Internet users (per 100 people, 2014)	87.0

Migration

EMIGRATION

- Stock of emigrants, 2013: **650.0 thousands**
- Stock of emigrants as percentage of population, 2013: **8.0 percent**
- Top destination countries, 2013: Italy, France, Spain, Germany, the United States, Canada, the United Kingdom, Portugal, Australia, Austria
- Tertiary-educated as a percentage of total emigrants in OECD countries, 2011: **26.9 percent**
- Tertiary-educated women as a percentage of total women emigrants in OECD countries, 2011: **27.3 percent**
- Number of refugees, 2014: **11**
- Second generation diaspora in Australia, Europe, and the United States, 2012: **233.5 thousands**

IMMIGRATION

- Stock of immigrants, 2013: **2,480.9 thousands†**
- Stock of immigrants as percentage of population, 2013: **30.7 percent**
- Top source countries, 2013: Germany, Italy, Portugal, France, Kosovo, Serbia, Turkey, Austria, Spain, the Former Yugoslav Republic of Macedonia
- Women as percentage of immigrants, 2013: **48.1 percent**
- Number of refugees, 2014: **62,566**

Remittances

US$ millions	2006	2007	2008	2009	2010	2011	2012	2013	2014	2015e
Inward remittance flows[a]	1,795	1,796	2,215	2,342	2,495	2,617	2,417	2,438	2,349	2,258
of which										
Compensation of employees	1,795	1,796	2,215	2,342	2,495	2,617	2,417	2,438	2,349	–
Personal transfers	–	–	–	–	–	–	–	–	–	–
Outward remittance flows	10,705	12,248	14,459	14,906	16,878	21,588	21,966	23,289	24,693	–
of which										
Compensation of employees	10,705	12,248	14,459	14,906	16,878	21,588	21,966	23,289	24,693	–
Personal transfers	–	–	–	–	–	–	–	–	–	–

a. Net FDI inflows US$-22.72 billion in 2013.
†Data from the 2013 Statistique de la population et des ménages (STATPOP) supplemented with new data on Kosovo's migrant from national sources (145,882).

Syrian Arab Republic

Population (millions, 2014)	22.2
Population growth (avg. annual %, 2005–14)	2.3
Population density (people per sq km, 2014)	120.7
Labor force (millions, 2014)	6.1
Unemployment rate (% of labor force, 2014)	10.8
Urban population (% of pop., 2014)	57.3
Surface area (thousands of sq km, 2014)	185.2
GNI, Atlas method (current US$ billions, 2007)	36.2
GNI per capita, Atlas method (current US$, 2007)	1,860.0
GDP growth (avg. annual %, 2003–06)	5.9
Poverty headcount ratio at national poverty line (% of pop., 2007)	35.2
Age dependency ratio (% of working-age pop., 2014)	68.8
Account at a formal financial institution (% age 15+)	–
Mobile cellular subscriptions (per 100 people, 2014)	70.9
Internet users (per 100 people, 2014)	28.1

Migration

EMIGRATION

- Stock of emigrants, 2013: **3,971.5 thousands**
- Stock of emigrants as percentage of population, 2013: **18.2 percent**
- Top destination countries, 2013: Saudi Arabia, Lebanon, Jordan, Turkey, Iraq, Kuwait, the Arab Republic of Egypt, the United States, the United Arab Emirates, Germany
- Tertiary-educated as a percentage of total emigrants in OECD countries, 2011: **34.2 percent**
- Tertiary-educated women as a percentage of total women emigrants in OECD countries, 2011: **28.0 percent**
- Number of refugees, 2014: **3,883,554**
- Second generation diaspora in Australia, Europe, and the United States, 2012: **54.8 thousands**

IMMIGRATION

- Stock of immigrants, 2013: **1,394.2 thousands**†
- Stock of immigrants as percentage of population, 2013: **6.4 percent**
- Top source countries, 2013: Iraq, the West Bank and Gaza, Somalia, Afghanistan, Sudan, South Sudan
- Women as percentage of immigrants, 2013: **48.9 percent**
- Number of refugees, 2014: **677,746**

Remittances

US$ millions	2006	2007	2008	2009	2010	2011	2012	2013	2014	2015e
Inward remittance flowsᵃ	795	1,030	1,325	1,350	1,623	–	–	–	–	–
of which										
Compensation of employees	25	30	75	150	200	–	–	–	–	–
Personal transfers	770	1,000	1,250	1,200	1,423	–	–	–	–	–
Outward remittance flows	235	250	210	211	530	–	–	–	–	–
of which										
Compensation of employees	75	80	30	31	36	–	–	–	–	–
Personal transfers	160	170	180	180	494	–	–	–	–	–

a. Net ODA received US$3.63 billion in 2013.
†According to UNRWA, the country hosts 517,255 refugees from the West Bank and Gaza (as of January 2014).

Tajikistan

Population (millions, 2014)	8.3
Population growth (avg. annual %, 2005–14)	2.2
Population density (people per sq km, 2014)	59.3
Labor force (millions, 2014)	3.7
Unemployment rate (% of labor force, 2014)	10.9
Urban population (% of pop., 2014)	26.7
Surface area (thousands of sq km, 2014)	142.6
GNI, Atlas method (current US$ billions, 2014)	8.9
GNI per capita, Atlas method (current US$, 2014)	1,080.0
GDP growth (avg. annual %, 2011–14)	7.2
Poverty headcount ratio at national poverty line (% of pop., 2009)	47.2
Age dependency ratio (% of working-age pop., 2014)	61.2
Account at a formal financial institution (% age 15+, 2014)	11.5
Mobile cellular subscriptions (per 100 people, 2014)	95.1
Internet users (per 100 people, 2014)	17.5

Migration

EMIGRATION

- Stock of emigrants, 2013: **607.8 thousands**
- Stock of emigrants as percentage of population, 2013: **7.5 percent**
- Top destination countries, 2013: the Russian Federation, Kazakhstan, Ukraine, Afghanistan, Germany, Uzbekistan, Belarus, the United States, Azerbaijan, Moldova
- Tertiary-educated as a percentage of total emigrants in OECD countries, 2011: **45.9 percent**
- Tertiary-educated women as a percentage of total women emigrants in OECD countries, 2011: **52.9 percent**
- Number of refugees, 2014: **690**
- Second generation diaspora in Australia, Europe, and the United States, 2012: **0.7 thousands**

IMMIGRATION

- Stock of immigrants, 2013: **275.7 thousands**
- Stock of immigrants as percentage of population, 2013: **3.4 percent**
- Top source countries, 2013: the Russian Federation, the Kyrgyz Republic, Afghanistan, Uzbekistan, Ukraine, the Islamic Republic of Iran, Moldova, Kazakhstan, Turkey, Belarus
- Women as percentage of immigrants, 2013: **56.9 percent**
- Number of refugees, 2014: **2,017**

Remittances

US$ millions	2006	2007	2008	2009	2010	2011	2012	2013	2014	2015e
Inward remittance flows[a]	1,019	1,691	2,544	1,748	2,306	3,060	3,626	4,219	3,854	2,962
of which										
Compensation of employees	4	5	7	6	10	21	21	43	34	–
Personal transfers	1,015	1,685	2,537	1,742	2,296	3,039	3,604	4,175	3,819	–
Outward remittance flows	395	184	199	124	231	201	263	240	206	–
of which										
Compensation of employees	2	4	5	4	6	6	14	19	12	–
Personal transfers	393	180	194	120	225	195	249	221	194	–

a. Net FDI inflows US$-0.05 billion, net ODA received US$0.38 billion in 2013.

Tanzania

LOW INCOME

Population (millions, 2014)	51.8
Population growth (avg. annual %, 2005–14)	3.1
Population density (people per sq km, 2014)	58.5
Labor force (millions, 2014)	25.3
Unemployment rate (% of labor force, 2014)	3.1
Urban population (% of pop., 2014)	30.9
Surface area (thousands of sq km, 2014)	947.3
GNI, Atlas method (current US$ billions, 2014)	46.4
GNI per capita, Atlas method (current US$, 2014)	920.0
GDP growth (avg. annual %, 2011–14)	6.8
Poverty headcount ratio at national poverty line (% of pop., 2011)	28.2
Age dependency ratio (% of working-age pop., 2014)	93.9
Account at a formal financial institution (% age 15+, 2014)	19.0
Mobile cellular subscriptions (per 100 people, 2014)	62.8
Internet users (per 100 people, 2014)	4.9

Migration

EMIGRATION

- Stock of emigrants, 2013: **250.1 thousands**
- Stock of emigrants as percentage of population, 2013: **0.5 percent**
- Top destination countries, 2013: Rwanda, Kenya, the United Kingdom, Uganda, Burundi, Canada, the United States, South Africa, Malawi, Mozambique
- Tertiary-educated as a percentage of total emigrants in OECD countries, 2011: **46.1 percent**
- Tertiary-educated women as a percentage of total women emigrants in OECD countries, 2011: **41.4 percent**
- Number of refugees, 2014: **827**
- Second generation diaspora in Australia, Europe, and the United States, 2012: **17.6 thousands**

IMMIGRATION

- Stock of immigrants, 2013: **652.9 thousands**
- Stock of immigrants as percentage of population, 2013: **1.3 percent**
- Top source countries, 2013: Burundi, the Democratic Republic of Congo, Kenya, India, Rwanda, China, the United Kingdom, Uganda, Mozambique, the United States
- Women as percentage of immigrants, 2013: **47.6 percent**
- Number of refugees, 2014: **88,492**

Remittances

US$ millions	2006	2007	2008	2009	2010	2011	2012	2013	2014	2015e
Inward remittance flows[a]	15	25	37	40	344	410	390	382	389	401
of which										
Compensation of employees	6	6	9	11	12	24	21	30	32	–
Personal transfers	9	19	28	28	332	385	369	352	358	–
Outward remittance flows	30	39	48	47	123	133	162	130	98	–
of which										
Compensation of employees	23	29	28	40	44	41	57	68	49	–
Personal transfers	6	10	20	7	79	93	105	62	49	–

a. Net FDI inflows US$2.09 billion, net ODA received US$3.43 billion in 2013.

Thailand

MIDDLE INCOME

Population (millions, 2014)	67.7
Population growth (avg. annual %, 2005–14)	0.3
Population density (people per sq km, 2014)	132.6
Labor force (millions, 2014)	40.1
Unemployment rate (% of labor force, 2014)	0.9
Urban population (% of pop., 2014)	49.2
Surface area (thousands of sq km, 2014)	513.1
GNI, Atlas method (current US$ billions, 2014)	391.7
GNI per capita, Atlas method (current US$, 2014)	5,780.0
GDP growth (avg. annual %, 2011–14)	3.0
Poverty headcount ratio at national poverty line (% of pop., 2012)	12.6
Age dependency ratio (% of working-age pop., 2014)	39.0
Account at a formal financial institution (% age 15+, 2014)	78.1
Mobile cellular subscriptions (per 100 people, 2014)	144.4
Internet users (per 100 people, 2014)	34.9

Migration

EMIGRATION

- Stock of emigrants, 2013: **1,007.3 thousands**
- Stock of emigrants as percentage of population, 2013: **1.5 percent**
- Top destination countries, 2013: the United States, Germany, Malaysia, Australia, Japan, the United Kingdom, Sweden, the Republic of Korea, Cambodia, Brunei Darussalam
- Tertiary-educated as a percentage of total emigrants in OECD countries, 2011: **28.9 percent**
- Tertiary-educated women as a percentage of total women emigrants in OECD countries, 2011: **28.6 percent**
- Number of refugees, 2014: **225**
- Second generation diaspora in Australia, Europe, and the United States, 2012: **106.4 thousands**

IMMIGRATION

- Stock of immigrants, 2013: **4,490.9 thousands**
- Stock of immigrants as percentage of population, 2013: **6.7 percent**
- Top source countries, 2013: Myanmar, the Lao People's Democratic Republic, Cambodia, China, the United Kingdom, Japan, India, the United States, Germany, France
- Women as percentage of immigrants, 2013: **46.8 percent**
- Number of refugees, 2014: **130,207**

Remittances

US$ millions	2006	2007	2008	2009	2010	2011	2012	2013	2014	2015e
Inward remittance flows[a]	**1,333**	**1,635**	**1,898**	**2,776**	**3,580**	**4,554**	**4,713**	**5,690**	**5,655**	**5,703**
of which										
Compensation of employees	–	–	–	837	1,278	1,738	1,877	1,866	1,864	–
Personal transfers	1,333	1,635	1,898	1,939	2,302	2,816	2,836	3,824	3,792	–
Outward remittance flows	**–**	**–**	**–**	**2,558**	**2,397**	**2,631**	**2,683**	**3,136**	**3,118**	**–**
of which										
Compensation of employees	–	–	–	1,506	1,323	1,408	1,458	1,647	1,658	–
Personal transfers	–	–	–	1,052	1,074	1,223	1,225	1,488	1,460	–

a. Net FDI inflows US$15.82 billion, net ODA received US$-0.02 billion in 2013.

Timor-Leste

Population (millions, 2014)	1.2
Population growth (avg. annual %, 2005–14)	2.3
Population density (people per sq km, 2014)	81.5
Labor force (thousands, 2013)	264.4
Unemployment rate (% of labor force, 2014)	4.7
Urban population (% of pop., 2014)	32.1
Surface area (thousands of sq km, 2014)	14.9
GNI, Atlas method (current US$ billions, 2014)	3.2
GNI per capita, Atlas method (current US$, 2014)	2,680.0
GDP growth (avg. annual %, 2011–14)	6.4
Poverty headcount ratio at national poverty line (% of pop., 2007)	49.9
Age dependency ratio (% of working-age pop., 2014)	91.5
Account at a formal financial institution (% age 15+)	–
Mobile cellular subscriptions (per 100 people, 2014)	58.7
Internet users (per 100 people, 2014)	1.1

Migration

EMIGRATION

- Stock of emigrants, 2013: **33.4 thousands**
- Stock of emigrants as percentage of population, 2013: **2.8 percent**
- Top destination countries, 2013: Indonesia, Australia, Portugal, Vietnam, the Philippines, Brazil, Kenya, Italy, Norway, Canada
- Tertiary-educated as a percentage of total emigrants in OECD countries, 2011: **18.6 percent**
- Tertiary-educated women as a percentage of total women emigrants in OECD countries, 2011: **19.2 percent**
- Number of refugees, 2014: **8**
- Second generation diaspora in Australia, Europe, and the United States, 2012: Not available

IMMIGRATION

- Stock of immigrants, 2013: **11.6 thousands**
- Stock of immigrants as percentage of population, 2013: **1.0 percent**
- Top source countries, 2013: Indonesia, China, the Philippines, Australia, Portugal, Pakistan, Vietnam, Brazil, New Zealand, Malaysia
- Women as percentage of immigrants, 2013: **41.2 percent**
- Number of refugees, 2014: Not available

Remittances

US$ millions	2006	2007	2008	2009	2010	2011	2012	2013	2014	2015e
Inward remittance flows[a]	4	10	18	113	137	137	120	34	44	45
of which										
Compensation of employees	3	10	12	107	125	120	97	4	4	–
Personal transfers	0	0	5	6	12	17	23	29	39	–
Outward remittance flows	1	3	16	86	103	105	107	8	28	–
of which										
Compensation of employees	0	0	2	1	2	1	1	2	4	–
Personal transfers	0	3	14	84	102	103	106	6	24	–

a. Net FDI inflows US$0.06 billion, net ODA received US$0.26 billion in 2013.

Togo

Population (millions, 2014)	7.1
Population growth (avg. annual %, 2005-14)	2.7
Population density (people per sq km, 2014)	130.8
Labor force (millions, 2014)	3.3
Unemployment rate (% of labor force, 2014)	6.9
Urban population (% of pop., 2014)	39.5
Surface area (thousands of sq km, 2014)	56.8
GNI, Atlas method (current US$ billions, 2014)	4.0
GNI per capita, Atlas method (current US$, 2014)	570.0
GDP growth (avg. annual %, 2011-14)	5.4
Poverty headcount ratio at national poverty line (% of pop., 2011)	58.7
Age dependency ratio (% of working-age pop., 2014)	82.4
Account at a formal financial institution (% age 15+, 2014)	17.6
Mobile cellular subscriptions (per 100 people, 2014)	69.0
Internet users (per 100 people, 2014)	5.7

Migration

EMIGRATION

- Stock of emigrants, 2013: **461.1 thousands**
- Stock of emigrants as percentage of population, 2013: **6.7 percent**
- Top destination countries, 2013: Ghana, Nigeria, Côte d'Ivoire, Benin, France, Gabon, Burkina Faso, Germany, Niger, Italy
- Tertiary-educated as a percentage of total emigrants in OECD countries, 2011: **31.4 percent**
- Tertiary-educated women as a percentage of total women emigrants in OECD countries, 2011: **24.5 percent**
- Number of refugees, 2014: **9,229**
- Second generation diaspora in Australia, Europe, and the United States, 2012: **7.8 thousands**

IMMIGRATION

- Stock of immigrants, 2013: **202.5 thousands**
- Stock of immigrants as percentage of population, 2013: **2.9 percent**
- Top source countries, 2013: Benin, Ghana, Nigeria, Niger, Côte d'Ivoire, France, Mali, Rwanda, Lebanon, Germany
- Women as percentage of immigrants, 2013: **50.3 percent**
- Number of refugees, 2014: **21,768**

Remittances

US$ millions	2006	2007	2008	2009	2010	2011	2012	2013	2014	2015e
Inward remittance flows[a]	**232**	**284**	**337**	**335**	**337**	**244**	**345**	**397**	**397**	**397**
of which										
Compensation of employees	29	32	36	35	36	40	49	56	–	–
Personal transfers	203	252	301	300	301	204	295	342	–	–
Outward remittance flows	**39**	**47**	**58**	**72**	**63**	**92**	**153**	**178**	**–**	**–**
of which										
Compensation of employees	1	1	2	2	9	20	27	33	–	–
Personal transfers	38	46	56	70	54	72	126	145	–	–

a. Net FDI inflows US$0.20 billion, net ODA received US$0.22 billion in 2013.

Tonga

	MIDDLE INCOME
Population (thousands, 2013)	105.6
Population growth (avg. annual %, 2005–14)	0.5
Population density (people per sq km, 2014)	146.6
Labor force (thousands, 2013)	42.4
Unemployment rate (% of labor force)	–
Urban population (% of pop., 2014)	23.6
Surface area (thousands of sq km, 2014)	0.8
GNI, Atlas method (current US$ billions, 2014)	0.4
GNI per capita, Atlas method (current US$, 2014)	4,260.0
GDP growth (avg. annual %, 2011–14)	0.5
Poverty headcount ratio at national poverty line (% of pop.)	–
Age dependency ratio (% of working-age pop., 2014)	75.0
Account at a formal financial institution (% age 15+)	–
Mobile cellular subscriptions (per 100 people, 2014)	64.3
Internet users (per 100 people, 2014)	40.0

Migration

EMIGRATION

- Stock of emigrants, 2013: **56.3 thousands**
- Stock of emigrants as percentage of population, 2013: **53.6 percent**
- Top destination countries, 2013: New Zealand, the United States, Australia, American Samoa, Chile, Canada, Samoa, France, Sweden, Vanuatu
- Tertiary-educated as a percentage of total emigrants in OECD countries, 2011: **13.3 percent**
- Tertiary-educated women as a percentage of total women emigrants in OECD countries, 2011: **15.1 percent**
- Number of refugees, 2014: **19**
- Second generation diaspora in Australia, Europe, and the United States, 2012: **12.2 thousands**

IMMIGRATION

- Stock of immigrants, 2013: **5.4 thousands**
- Stock of immigrants as percentage of population, 2013: **5.2 percent**
- Top source countries, 2013: Fiji, Samoa, India, China, Japan
- Women as percentage of immigrants, 2013: **45.5 percent**
- Number of refugees, 2014: Not available

Remittances

US$ millions	2006	2007	2008	2009	2010	2011	2012	2013	2014	2015e
Inward remittance flows[a]	**79**	**101**	**94**	**72**	**77**	**79**	**118**	**121**	**121**	**122**
of which										
Compensation of employees	3	4	5	4	6	18	13	16	–	–
Personal transfers	75	97	89	68	71	61	105	105	–	–
Outward remittance flows	**12**	**11**	**12**	**9**	**6**	**5**	**7**	**5**	**–**	**–**
of which										
Compensation of employees	0	0	0	1	0	0	0	1	–	–
Personal transfers	12	11	12	8	6	5	7	5	–	–

a. Net FDI inflows US$0.01 billion, net ODA received US$0.08 billion in 2013.

Trinidad and Tobago

Population (millions, 2014)	1.4
Population growth (avg. annual %, 2005–14)	0.5
Population density (people per sq km, 2014)	264.0
Labor force (thousands, 2013)	686.7
Unemployment rate (% of labor force, 2014)	4.0
Urban population (% of pop., 2014)	8.6
Surface area (thousands of sq km, 2014)	5.1
GNI, Atlas method (current US$ billions, 2014)	27.2
GNI per capita, Atlas method (current US$, 2014)	20,070.0
GDP growth (avg. annual %, 2011–14)	1.0
Poverty headcount ratio at national poverty line (% of pop.)	–
Age dependency ratio (% of working-age pop., 2014)	42.7
Account at a formal financial institution (% age 15+)	–
Mobile cellular subscriptions (per 100 people, 2014)	147.3
Internet users (per 100 people, 2014)	65.1

Migration

EMIGRATION

- Stock of emigrants, 2013: **374.5 thousands**
- Stock of emigrants as percentage of population, 2013: **27.8 percent**
- Top destination countries, 2013: the United States, Canada, the United Kingdom, Jamaica, St. Vincent and the Grenadines, Grenada, Barbados, República Bolivariana de Venezuela, the Virgin Islands (U.S.), Australia
- Tertiary-educated as a percentage of total emigrants in OECD countries, 2011: **35.5 percent**
- Tertiary-educated women as a percentage of total women emigrants in OECD countries, 2011: **37.3 percent**
- Number of refugees, 2014: **371**
- Second generation diaspora in Australia, Europe, and the United States, 2012: **159.7 thousands**

IMMIGRATION

- Stock of immigrants, 2013: **32.5 thousands**
- Stock of immigrants as percentage of population, 2013: **2.4 percent**
- Top source countries, 2013: Grenada, St. Vincent and the Grenadines, Guyana, the United States, the United Kingdom, República Bolivariana de Venezuela, Barbados, St. Lucia, India
- Women as percentage of immigrants, 2013: **54.1 percent**
- Number of refugees, 2014: **66**

Remittances

US$ millions	2006	2007	2008	2009	2010	2011	2012	2013	2014	2015e
Inward remittance flows[a]	**91**	**109**	**95**	**109**	**91**	**126**	**126**	**126**	**126**	**129**
of which										
Compensation of employees	–	–	–	–	–	–	–	–	–	–
Personal transfers	91	109	95	109	91	126	–	–	–	–
Outward remittance flows	–	–	–	–	–	–	–	–	–	–
of which										
Compensation of employees	–	–	–	–	–	–	–	–	–	–
Personal transfers	–	–	–	–	–	–	–	–	–	–

a. Net FDI inflows US$1.99 billion in 2013.

Tunisia

Population (millions, 2014)	11.0
Population growth (avg. annual %, 2005–14)	1.0
Population density (people per sq km, 2014)	70.8
Labor force (millions, 2014)	4.0
Unemployment rate (% of labor force, 2014)	13.3
Urban population (% of pop., 2014)	66.6
Surface area (thousands of sq km, 2014)	163.6
GNI, Atlas method (current US$ billions, 2014)	46.5
GNI per capita, Atlas method (current US$, 2014)	4,230.0
GDP growth (avg. annual %, 2011–14)	1.9
Poverty headcount ratio at national poverty line (% of pop., 2010)	15.5
Age dependency ratio (% of working-age pop., 2014)	44.5
Account at a formal financial institution (% age 15+, 2014)	27.3
Mobile cellular subscriptions (per 100 people, 2014)	128.5
Internet users (per 100 people, 2014)	46.2

Migration

EMIGRATION

- Stock of emigrants, 2013: **670.9 thousands**
- Stock of emigrants as percentage of population, 2013: **6.2 percent**
- Top destination countries, 2013: France, Italy, Germany, Israel, Saudi Arabia, Switzerland, Canada, the United States, the United Kingdom, Belgium
- Tertiary-educated as a percentage of total emigrants in OECD countries, 2011: **19.9 percent**
- Tertiary-educated women as a percentage of total women emigrants in OECD countries, 2011: **18.5 percent**
- Number of refugees, 2014: **1,452**
- Second generation diaspora in Australia, Europe, and the United States, 2012: **383.6 thousands**

IMMIGRATION

- Stock of immigrants, 2013: **36.5 thousands**
- Stock of immigrants as percentage of population, 2013: **0.3 percent**
- Top source countries, 2013: Algeria, Morocco, France, Libya, Italy, Somalia, Sudan, Eritrea, Iraq, Ethiopia
- Women as percentage of immigrants, 2013: **49.2 percent**
- Number of refugees, 2014: **885**

Remittances

US$ millions	2006	2007	2008	2009	2010	2011	2012	2013	2014	2015e
Inward remittance flows[a]	1,510	1,716	1,977	1,964	2,063	2,004	2,266	2,291	2,347	2,347
of which										
Compensation of employees	206	269	252	238	338	345	354	383	385	–
Personal transfers	1,304	1,446	1,725	1,727	1,725	1,659	1,912	1,907	1,961	–
Outward remittance flows	16	15	16	13	13	19	18	20	28	–
of which										
Compensation of employees	10	8	10	6	7	6	9	9	11	–
Personal transfers	7	7	6	7	7	13	10	10	17	–

a. Net FDI inflows US$1.06 billion, net ODA received US$0.71 billion in 2013.

Turkey

Population (millions, 2014)	75.9
Population growth (avg. annual %, 2005–14)	1.3
Population density (people per sq km, 2014)	98.7
Labor force (millions, 2014)	27.8
Unemployment rate (% of labor force, 2014)	9.2
Urban population (% of pop., 2014)	72.9
Surface area (thousands of sq km, 2014)	783.6
GNI, Atlas method (current US$ billions, 2014)	822.4
GNI per capita, Atlas method (current US$, 2014)	10,830.0
GDP growth (avg. annual %, 2011–14)	4.5
Poverty headcount ratio at national poverty line (% of pop., 2012)	2.3
Age dependency ratio (% of working-age pop., 2014)	50.0
Account at a formal financial institution (% age 15+, 2014)	56.5
Mobile cellular subscriptions (per 100 people, 2014)	94.8
Internet users (per 100 people, 2014)	51.0

Migration

EMIGRATION

- Stock of emigrants, 2013: **3,110.1 thousands**
- Stock of emigrants as percentage of population, 2013: **4.1 percent**
- Top destination countries, 2013: Germany, France, the Netherlands, Austria, the United States, Saudi Arabia, Belgium, Kazakhstan, Switzerland, the United Kingdom
- Tertiary-educated as a percentage of total emigrants in OECD countries, 2011: **8.9 percent**
- Tertiary-educated women as a percentage of total women emigrants in OECD countries, 2011: **7.0 percent**
- Number of refugees, 2014: **63,940**
- Second generation diaspora in Australia, Europe, and the United States, 2012: **1,196.2 thousands**

IMMIGRATION

- Stock of immigrants, 2013: **2,504.5 thousands**
- Stock of immigrants as percentage of population, 2013: **3.3 percent**
- Top source countries, 2013: Bulgaria, the Syrian Arab Republic, Germany, Serbia, Greece, the Former Yugoslav Republic of Macedonia, Montenegro, the Netherlands, Romania, the Russian Federation
- Women as percentage of immigrants, 2013: **48.4 percent**
- Number of refugees, 2014: **1,587,345**

Remittances

US$ millions	2006	2007	2008	2009	2010	2011	2012	2013	2014	2015e
Inward remittance flows[a]	**1,146**	**1,248**	**1,658**	**1,165**	**1,100**	**1,210**	**1,153**	**1,135**	**1,128**	**1,085**
of which										
Compensation of employees	35	39	45	36	45	42	40	42	36	–
Personal transfers	1,111	1,209	1,613	1,129	1,055	1,168	1,113	1,093	1,092	–
Outward remittance flows	**107**	**106**	**111**	**141**	**168**	**205**	**255**	**330**	**918**	**–**
of which										
Compensation of employees	107	106	111	141	168	205	255	330	918	–
Personal transfers	–	–	–	–	–	–	–	–	–	–

a. Net FDI inflows US$12.46 billion, net ODA received US$2.74 billion in 2013.

Turkmenistan

Population (millions, 2014)	5.3
Population growth (avg. annual %, 2005–14)	1.2
Population density (people per sq km, 2014)	11.3
Labor force (millions, 2014)	2.3
Unemployment rate (% of labor force, 2014)	10.5
Urban population (% of pop., 2014)	49.7
Surface area (thousands of sq km, 2014)	488.1
GNI, Atlas method (current US$ billions, 2014)	42.5
GNI per capita, Atlas method (current US$, 2014)	8,020.0
GDP growth (avg. annual %, 2011–14)	11.6
Poverty headcount ratio at national poverty line (% of pop.)	–
Age dependency ratio (% of working-age pop., 2014)	48.2
Account at a formal financial institution (% age 15+, 2014)	1.8
Mobile cellular subscriptions (per 100 people, 2014)	135.8
Internet users (per 100 people, 2014)	12.2

Migration

EMIGRATION

- Stock of emigrants, 2013: **249.5 thousands**
- Stock of emigrants as percentage of population, 2013: **4.8 percent**
- Top destination countries, 2013: the Russian Federation, Ukraine, Uzbekistan, Germany, Belarus, Turkey, the Islamic Republic of Iran, Kazakhstan, Israel, Azerbaijan
- Tertiary-educated as a percentage of total emigrants in OECD countries, 2011: **35.4 percent**
- Tertiary-educated women as a percentage of total women emigrants in OECD countries, 2011: **37.4 percent**
- Number of refugees, 2014: **462**
- Second generation diaspora in Australia, Europe, and the United States, 2012: Not available

IMMIGRATION

- Stock of immigrants, 2013: **226.3 thousands**
- Stock of immigrants as percentage of population, 2013: **4.3 percent**
- Top source countries, 2013: the Russian Federation, Ukraine, Kazakhstan, Belarus, Uzbekistan, Azerbaijan, Georgia, Poland, Moldova, Lithuania
- Women as percentage of immigrants, 2013: **53.6 percent**
- Number of refugees, 2014: **34**

Remittances

US$ millions	2006	2007	2008	2009	2010	2011	2012	2013	2014	2015e
Inward remittance flows[a]	14	30	50	34	35	35	37	40	31	15
of which										
Compensation of employees	–	–	–	–	–	–	–	–	–	–
Personal transfers	–	–	–	–	–	–	–	–	–	–
Outward remittance flows	–	–	–	–	–	–	–	–	–	–
of which										
Compensation of employees	–	–	–	–	–	–	–	–	–	–
Personal transfers	–	–	–	–	–	–	–	–	–	–

a. Net FDI inflows US$3.08 billion, net ODA received US$0.04 billion in 2013.

Turks and Caicos Islands

Population (thousands, 2013)	33.7
Population growth (avg. annual %, 2005–14)	3.0
Population density (people per sq km, 2014)	35.5
Labor force, total	–
Unemployment rate (% of labor force)	–
Urban population (% of pop., 2014)	91.8
Surface area (thousands of sq km, 2014)	1.0
GNI, Atlas method (current US$ billions)	–
GNI per capita, Atlas method (current US$)	–
GDP growth (avg. annual %)	–
Poverty headcount ratio at national poverty line (% of pop.)	–
Age dependency ratio (% of working-age pop.)	–
Account at a formal financial institution (% age 15+)	–
Mobile cellular subscriptions (per 100 people)	–
Internet users (per 100 people)	–

Migration

EMIGRATION

- Stock of emigrants, 2013: **1.6 thousands**
- Stock of emigrants as percentage of population, 2013: **4.8 percent**
- Top destination countries, 2013: the United States, The Bahamas, Canada, Antigua and Barbuda, the Dominican Republic, Bermuda, Australia, France, Bulgaria, Chile
- Tertiary-educated as a percentage of total emigrants in OECD countries, 2011: **21.7 percent**
- Tertiary-educated women as a percentage of total women emigrants in OECD countries, 2011: **23.5 percent**
- Number of refugees, 2014: Not available
- Second generation diaspora in Australia, Europe, and the United States, 2012: Not available

IMMIGRATION

- Stock of immigrants, 2013: **11.4 thousands**
- Stock of immigrants as percentage of population, 2013: **34.3 percent**
- Top source countries, 2013: Haiti, the Dominican Republic, the United States, Canada, the United Kingdom, The Bahamas
- Women as percentage of immigrants, 2013: **48.3 percent**
- Number of refugees, 2014: Not available

Remittances

US$ millions	2006	2007	2008	2009	2010	2011	2012	2013	2014	2015e
Inward remittance flows	–	–	–	–	–	–	–	–	–	–
of which										
Compensation of employees	–	–	–	–	–	–	–	–	–	–
Personal transfers	–	–	–	–	–	–	–	–	–	–
Outward remittance flows	–	–	–	–	–	–	–	–	–	–
of which										
Compensation of employees	–	–	–	–	–	–	–	–	–	–
Personal transfers	–	–	–	–	–	–	–	–	–	–

Tuvalu

	MIDDLE INCOME
Population (thousands, 2013)	9.9
Population growth (avg. annual %, 2005–14)	0.3
Population density (people per sq km, 2014)	329.8
Labor force, total	–
Unemployment rate (% of labor force)	–
Urban population (% of pop., 2014)	58.8
Surface area (thousands of sq km, 2014)	0.0
GNI, Atlas method (current US$ billions, 2014)	0.1
GNI per capita, Atlas method (current US$, 2014)	5,720.0
GDP growth (avg. annual %, 2011–14)	3.0
Poverty headcount ratio at national poverty line (% of pop.)	–
Age dependency ratio (% of working-age pop.)	–
Account at a formal financial institution (% age 15+)	–
Mobile cellular subscriptions (per 100 people, 2014)	38.4
Internet users (per 100 people, 2014)	37.0

Migration

EMIGRATION

- Stock of emigrants, 2013: **3.9 thousands**
- Stock of emigrants as percentage of population, 2013: **39.3 percent**
- Top destination countries, 2013: New Zealand, Kiribati, the Russian Federation, Australia, the United States, Samoa, the Marshall Islands, Bulgaria, Austria, the Czech Republic
- Tertiary-educated as a percentage of total emigrants in OECD countries, 2011: **10.6 percent**
- Tertiary-educated women as a percentage of total women emigrants in OECD countries, 2011: **11.1 percent**
- Number of refugees, 2014: **15**
- Second generation diaspora in Australia, Europe, and the United States, 2012: Not available

IMMIGRATION

- Stock of immigrants, 2013: **0.1 thousands**
- Stock of immigrants as percentage of population, 2013: **1.5 percent**
- Top source countries, 2013: Fiji, Kiribati, the United States, Australia, the United Kingdom, Samoa, New Zealand, Solomon Islands
- Women as percentage of immigrants, 2013: **44.6 percent**
- Number of refugees, 2014: Not available

Remittances

US$ millions	2006	2007	2008	2009	2010	2011	2012	2013	2014	2015e
Inward remittance flows[a]	4	6	6	5	4	5	4	4	4	4
of which										
Compensation of employees	3	5	5	4	3	4	3	4	–	–
Personal transfers	1	1	1	1	0	0	0	0	–	–
Outward remittance flows	1	1	1	1	2	2	3	2	–	–
of which										
Compensation of employees	0	0	0	0	1	1	1	1	–	–
Personal transfers	1	1	1	1	1	2	2	1	–	–

a. Net FDI inflows US$0.00 billion, net ODA received US$0.03 billion in 2013.

Uganda

LOW INCOME

Population (millions, 2014)	37.8
Population growth (avg. annual %, 2005-14)	3.3
Population density (people per sq km, 2014)	188.4
Labor force (millions, 2014)	15.1
Unemployment rate (% of labor force, 2014)	3.8
Urban population (% of pop., 2014)	15.8
Surface area (thousands of sq km, 2014)	241.6
GNI, Atlas method (current US$ billions, 2014)	25.3
GNI per capita, Atlas method (current US$, 2014)	670.0
GDP growth (avg. annual %, 2011-14)	5.5
Poverty headcount ratio at national poverty line (% of pop., 2012)	19.5
Age dependency ratio (% of working-age pop., 2014)	103.4
Account at a formal financial institution (% age 15+, 2014)	27.8
Mobile cellular subscriptions (per 100 people, 2014)	52.4
Internet users (per 100 people, 2014)	17.7

Migration

EMIGRATION

- Stock of emigrants, 2013: **406.2 thousands**
- Stock of emigrants as percentage of population, 2013: **1.1 percent**
- Top destination countries, 2013: South Sudan, Rwanda, the United Kingdom, Kenya, the United States, Tanzania, Canada, South Africa, Sweden, Australia
- Tertiary-educated as a percentage of total emigrants in OECD countries, 2011: **47.1 percent**
- Tertiary-educated women as a percentage of total women emigrants in OECD countries, 2011: **43.9 percent**
- Number of refugees, 2014: **7,137**
- Second generation diaspora in Australia, Europe, and the United States, 2012: **42.6 thousands**

IMMIGRATION

- Stock of immigrants, 2013: **531.4 thousands**
- Stock of immigrants as percentage of population, 2013: **1.5 percent**
- Top source countries, 2013: the Democratic Republic of Congo, South Sudan, Rwanda, Kenya, Tanzania, Sudan, Burundi, Somalia, India, Eritrea
- Women as percentage of immigrants, 2013: **50.7 percent**
- Number of refugees, 2014: **385,498**

Remittances

US$ millions	2006	2007	2008	2009	2010	2011	2012	2013	2014	2015e
Inward remittance flows[a]	**411**	**452**	**724**	**781**	**771**	**816**	**913**	**941**	**887**	**908**
of which										
Compensation of employees	–	–	–	3	3	3	3	9	1	–
Personal transfers	411	452	724	778	768	813	910	932	886	–
Outward remittance flows	**206**	**236**	**381**	**483**	**332**	**402**	**329**	**371**	**289**	**–**
of which										
Compensation of employees	21	33	57	91	82	106	181	163	96	–
Personal transfers	185	203	324	392	250	295	148	208	193	–

a. Net FDI inflows US$1.10 billion, net ODA received US$1.69 billion in 2013.

Ukraine

Population (millions, 2014)	45.4
Population growth (avg. annual %, 2005–14)	-0.5
Population density (people per sq km, 2014)	78.3
Labor force (millions, 2014)	23.1
Unemployment rate (% of labor force, 2014)	7.7
Urban population (% of pop., 2014)	69.5
Surface area (thousands of sq km, 2014)	603.6
GNI, Atlas method (current US$ billions, 2014)	152.1
GNI per capita, Atlas method (current US$, 2014)	3,560.0
GDP growth (avg. annual %, 2011–14)	-0.4
Poverty headcount ratio at national poverty line (% of pop., 2013)	8.4
Age dependency ratio (% of working-age pop., 2014)	42.6
Account at a formal financial institution (% age 15+, 2014)	52.7
Mobile cellular subscriptions (per 100 people, 2014)	144.1
Internet users (per 100 people, 2014)	43.4

Migration

EMIGRATION

- Stock of emigrants, 2013: **5,583.9 thousands**
- Stock of emigrants as percentage of population, 2013: **12.3 percent**
- Top destination countries, 2013: the Russian Federation, the United States, Kazakhstan, Germany, Belarus, Poland, Italy, Uzbekistan, the Czech Republic, Israel
- Tertiary-educated as a percentage of total emigrants in OECD countries, 2011: **39.6 percent**
- Tertiary-educated women as a percentage of total women emigrants in OECD countries, 2011: **40.6 percent**
- Number of refugees, 2014: **237,618**
- Second generation diaspora in Australia, Europe, and the United States, 2012: **641.1 thousands**

IMMIGRATION

- Stock of immigrants, 2013: **5,417.7 thousands**
- Stock of immigrants as percentage of population, 2013: **11.9 percent**
- Top source countries, 2013: the Russian Federation, Belarus, Kazakhstan, Uzbekistan, Moldova, Poland, Azerbaijan, Georgia, Germany, Armenia
- Women as percentage of immigrants, 2013: **51.4 percent**
- Number of refugees, 2014: **3,176**

Remittances

US$ millions	2006	2007	2008	2009	2010	2011	2012	2013	2014	2015e
Inward remittance flows[a]	**3,102**	**5,290**	**6,782**	**5,941**	**6,535**	**7,822**	**8,449**	**9,667**	**7,354**	**6,217**
of which										
Compensation of employees	540	2,210	3,629	3,426	4,046	4,825	5,542	6,782	5,183	–
Personal transfers	2,562	3,080	3,153	2,515	2,489	2,997	2,907	2,885	2,171	–
Outward remittance flows	**255**	**353**	**714**	**613**	**703**	**849**	**1,003**	**1,716**	**1,702**	**–**
of which										
Compensation of employees	9	11	18	15	12	17	22	25	29	–
Personal transfers	246	342	696	598	691	832	981	1,691	1,673	–

a. Net FDI inflows US$4.51 billion, net ODA received US$0.80 billion in 2013.

United Arab Emirates

Population (millions, 2014)	9.1
Population growth (avg. annual %, 2005-14)	8.3
Population density (people per sq km, 2014)	108.7
Labor force (millions, 2014)	6.3
Unemployment rate (% of labor force, 2014)	3.6
Urban population (% of pop., 2014)	85.3
Surface area (thousands of sq km, 2014)	83.6
GNI, Atlas method (current US$ billions, 2014)	405.2
GNI per capita, Atlas method (current US$, 2014)	44,600.0
GDP growth (avg. annual %, 2011-14)	5.2
Poverty headcount ratio at national poverty line (% of pop.)	–
Age dependency ratio (% of working-age pop., 2014)	17.5
Account at a formal financial institution (% age 15+, 2014)	83.2
Mobile cellular subscriptions (per 100 people, 2014)	178.1
Internet users (per 100 people, 2014)	90.4

Migration

EMIGRATION

- Stock of emigrants, 2013: **153.7 thousands**
- Stock of emigrants as percentage of population, 2013: **1.7 percent**
- Top destination countries, 2013: Kuwait, France, Qatar, India, Canada, the West Bank and Gaza, the United States, the United Kingdom, Oman, Bahrain
- Tertiary-educated as a percentage of total emigrants in OECD countries, 2011: **31.4 percent**
- Tertiary-educated women as a percentage of total women emigrants in OECD countries, 2011: **34.6 percent**
- Number of refugees, 2014: **84**
- Second generation diaspora in Australia, Europe, and the United States, 2012: **1.4 thousands**

IMMIGRATION

- Stock of immigrants, 2013: **8,001.7 thousands**
- Stock of immigrants as percentage of population, 2013: **88.5 percent**
- Top source countries, 2013: India, Pakistan, Bangladesh, the Philippines, the Islamic Republic of Iran, Indonesia, the Arab Republic of Egypt, the Republic of Yemen, Nepal, Sudan
- Women as percentage of immigrants, 2013: **23.9 percent**
- Number of refugees, 2014: **409**

Remittances

US$ millions	2006	2007	2008	2009	2010	2011	2012	2013	2014	2015e
Inward remittance flows[a]	–	–	–	–	–	–	–	–	–	–
of which										
Compensation of employees	–	–	–	–	–	–	–	–	–	–
Personal transfers	–	–	–	–	–	–	–	–	–	–
Outward remittance flows	6,072	8,683	9,995	9,532	10,566	11,220	14,398	17,933	19,280	–
of which										
Compensation of employees	–	–	–	–	–	–	–	–	–	–
Personal transfers	6,072	8,683	9,995	9,532	10,566	11,220	14,398	17,933	19,280	–

a. Net FDI inflows US$10.49 billion in 2013.

United Kingdom

Population (millions, 2014)	64.5
Population growth (avg. annual %, 2005–14)	0.7
Population density (people per sq km, 2014)	266.6
Labor force (millions, 2014)	33.0
Unemployment rate (% of labor force, 2014)	6.3
Urban population (% of pop., 2014)	82.3
Surface area (thousands of sq km, 2014)	243.6
GNI, Atlas method (current US$ billions, 2014)	2,801.5
GNI per capita, Atlas method (current US$, 2014)	43,430.0
GDP growth (avg. annual %, 2011–14)	2.1
Poverty headcount ratio at national poverty line (% of pop.)	–
Age dependency ratio (% of working-age pop., 2014)	54.3
Account at a formal financial institution (% age 15+, 2014)	98.9
Mobile cellular subscriptions (per 100 people, 2014)	123.6
Internet users (per 100 people, 2014)	91.6

Migration

EMIGRATION

- Stock of emigrants, 2013: **5,151.1 thousands**
- Stock of emigrants as percentage of population, 2013: **8.0 percent**
- Top destination countries, 2013: Australia, the United States, Canada, Spain, South Africa, Ireland, New Zealand, Germany, Thailand, the Channel Islands
- Tertiary-educated as a percentage of total emigrants in OECD countries, 2011: **37.8 percent**
- Tertiary-educated women as a percentage of total women emigrants in OECD countries, 2011: **35.9 percent**
- Number of refugees, 2014: **132**
- Second generation diaspora in Australia, Europe, and the United States, 2012: **1,753.6 thousands**

IMMIGRATION

- Stock of immigrants, 2013: **7,838.8 thousands**
- Stock of immigrants as percentage of population, 2013: **12.2 percent**
- Top source countries, 2013: India, Poland, Pakistan, Ireland, Germany, Bangladesh, the United States, South Africa, Nigeria, China
- Women as percentage of immigrants, 2013: **51.5 percent**
- Number of refugees, 2014: **117,093**

Remittances

US$ millions	2006	2007	2008	2009	2010	2011	2012	2013	2014	2015e
Inward										
remittance flows[a]	**6,106**	**6,556**	**5,995**	**5,243**	**4,951**	**5,099**	**4,945**	**4,805**	**4,923**	**4,952**
of which										
Compensation										
of employees	1,730	1,971	1,940	1,830	1,696	1,796	1,776	1,712	1,769	–
Personal transfers	4,375	4,586	4,055	3,413	3,255	3,303	3,169	3,093	3,154	–
Outward										
remittance flows	**10,646**	**11,597**	**11,212**	**9,275**	**9,565**	**9,931**	**10,077**	**10,528**	**11,515**	–
of which										
Compensation										
of employees	3,501	3,440	3,255	2,245	2,299	2,073	2,010	2,222	2,495	–
Personal transfers	7,145	8,156	7,957	7,030	7,266	7,858	8,068	8,306	9,021	–

a. Net FDI inflows US$35.02 billion in 2013.

United States

Population (millions, 2014)	318.9
Population growth (avg. annual %, 2005–14)	0.9
Population density (people per sq km, 2014)	34.9
Labor force (millions, 2014)	161.0
Unemployment rate (% of labor force, 2014)	6.2
Urban population (% of pop., 2014)	81.4
Surface area (thousands of sq km, 2014)	9,831.5
GNI, Atlas method (current US$ billions, 2014)	17,601.1
GNI per capita, Atlas method (current US$, 2014)	55,200.0
GDP growth (avg. annual %, 2011–14)	2.1
Poverty headcount ratio at national poverty line (% of pop.)	–
Age dependency ratio (% of working-age pop., 2014)	50.3
Account at a formal financial institution (% age 15+, 2014)	93.6
Mobile cellular subscriptions (per 100 people, 2014)	98.4
Internet users (per 100 people, 2014)	87.4

Migration

EMIGRATION

- Stock of emigrants, 2013: **3,167.9 thousands**
- Stock of emigrants as percentage of population, 2013: **1.0 percent**
- Top destination countries, 2013: Mexico, Canada, the United Kingdom, Puerto Rico, Germany, Australia, Israel, the Republic of Korea, China, Italy
- Tertiary-educated as a percentage of total emigrants in OECD countries, 2011: **31.0 percent**
- Tertiary-educated women as a percentage of total women emigrants in OECD countries, 2011: **31.6 percent**
- Number of refugees, 2014: **4,965**
- Second generation diaspora in Australia, Europe, and the United States, 2012: **275.2 thousands**

IMMIGRATION

- Stock of immigrants, 2013: **46,136.4 thousands**
- Stock of immigrants as percentage of population, 2013: **14.6 percent**
- Top source countries, 2013: Mexico, China, India, the Philippines, Puerto Rico, Vietnam, El Salvador, Cuba, the Republic of Korea, the Dominican Republic
- Women as percentage of immigrants, 2013: **51.0 percent**
- Number of refugees, 2014: **267,174**

Remittances

US$ millions	2006	2007	2008	2009	2010	2011	2012	2013	2014	2015e
Inward remittance flows[a]	5,068	5,219	5,364	5,740	5,930	6,104	6,303	6,757	6,908	7,029
of which										
Compensation of employees	5,068	5,219	5,364	5,740	5,930	6,104	6,303	6,757	6,908	–
Personal transfers	–	–	–	–	–	–	–	–	–	–
Outward remittance flows	50,756	52,650	55,527	50,723	50,776	50,556	52,652	55,469	56,311	–
of which										
Compensation of employees	16,426	15,721	17,062	14,418	13,963	14,184	14,945	15,828	16,340	–
Personal transfers	34,330	36,929	38,465	36,305	36,813	36,372	37,707	39,641	39,971	–

a. Net FDI inflows US$287.16 billion in 2013.

Uruguay

Population (millions, 2014)	3.4
Population growth (avg. annual %, 2005–14)	0.3
Population density (people per sq km, 2014)	19.5
Labor force (millions, 2014)	1.8
Unemployment rate (% of labor force, 2014)	7.0
Urban population (% of pop., 2014)	95.2
Surface area (thousands of sq km, 2014)	176.2
GNI, Atlas method (current US$ billions, 2014)	55.9
GNI per capita, Atlas method (current US$, 2014)	16,350.0
GDP growth (avg. annual %, 2011–14)	4.3
Poverty headcount ratio at national poverty line (% of pop., 2013)	11.5
Age dependency ratio (% of working-age pop., 2014)	56.1
Account at a formal financial institution (% age 15+, 2014)	45.4
Mobile cellular subscriptions (per 100 people, 2014)	160.8
Internet users (per 100 people, 2014)	61.5

Migration

EMIGRATION

- Stock of emigrants, 2013: **340.4 thousands**
- Stock of emigrants as percentage of population, 2013: **10.0 percent**
- Top destination countries, 2013: Argentina, Spain, the United States, Brazil, Australia, Italy, Canada, Israel, República Bolivariana de Venezuela, Paraguay
- Tertiary-educated as a percentage of total emigrants in OECD countries, 2011: **21.6 percent**
- Tertiary-educated women as a percentage of total women emigrants in OECD countries, 2011: **22.4 percent**
- Number of refugees, 2014: **114**
- Second generation diaspora in Australia, Europe, and the United States, 2012: **38.9 thousands**

IMMIGRATION

- Stock of immigrants, 2013: **76.7 thousands**
- Stock of immigrants as percentage of population, 2013: **2.3 percent**
- Top source countries, 2013: Argentina, Brazil, Spain, Italy, the United States, Paraguay, Chile, Peru, Germany, República Bolivariana de Venezuela
- Women as percentage of immigrants, 2013: **51.3 percent**
- Number of refugees, 2014: **244**

Remittances

US$ millions	2006	2007	2008	2009	2010	2011	2012	2013	2014	2015e
Inward remittance flows[a]	89	96	108	101	125	129	122	123	122	123
of which										
Compensation of employees	–	–	–	–	–	–	–	–	–	–
Personal transfers	89	96	108	101	125	129	122	123	122	–
Outward remittance flows	3	4	5	6	7	7	10	11	10	–
of which										
Compensation of employees	–	–	–	–	–	–	–	–	–	–
Personal transfers	3	4	5	6	7	7	10	11	10	–

a. Net FDI inflows US$3.04 billion, net ODA received US$0.04 billion in 2013.

Uzbekistan

Population (millions, 2014)	30.8
Population growth (avg. annual %, 2005–14)	1.7
Population density (people per sq km, 2014)	72.3
Labor force (millions, 2014)	13.6
Unemployment rate (% of labor force, 2014)	10.6
Urban population (% of pop., 2014)	36.3
Surface area (thousands of sq km, 2014)	447.4
GNI, Atlas method (current US$ billions, 2014)	64.3
GNI per capita, Atlas method (current US$, 2014)	2,090.0
GDP growth (avg. annual %, 2011–14)	8.2
Poverty headcount ratio at national poverty line (% of pop., 2011)	16.0
Age dependency ratio (% of working-age pop., 2014)	49.6
Account at a formal financial institution (% age 15+)	40.7
Mobile cellular subscriptions (per 100 people, 2014)	73.8
Internet users (per 100 people, 2014)	43.5

Migration

EMIGRATION

- Stock of emigrants, 2013: **1,912.9 thousands**
- Stock of emigrants as percentage of population, 2013: **6.3 percent**
- Top destination countries, 2013: the Russian Federation, Kazakhstan, Ukraine, the United States, Germany, the Republic of Korea, Israel, Turkey, Belarus, Azerbaijan
- Tertiary-educated as a percentage of total emigrants in OECD countries, 2011: **44.5 percent**
- Tertiary-educated women as a percentage of total women emigrants in OECD countries, 2011: **48.5 percent**
- Number of refugees, 2014: **4,766**
- Second generation diaspora in Australia, Europe, and the United States, 2012: Not available

IMMIGRATION

- Stock of immigrants, 2013: **1,266.3 thousands**
- Stock of immigrants as percentage of population, 2013: **4.2 percent**
- Top source countries, 2013: the Russian Federation, Ukraine, Kazakhstan, Belarus, Azerbaijan, Georgia, Poland, Moldova, Lithuania, Armenia
- Women as percentage of immigrants, 2013: **53.6 percent**
- Number of refugees, 2014: **123**

Remittances

US$ millions	2006	2007	2008	2009	2010	2011	2012	2013	2014	2015e
Inward remittance flows[a]	898	1,693	3,007	2,071	2,858	4,276	5,693	6,689	5,653	2,525
of which										
Compensation of employees	–	–	–	–	–	–	–	–	–	–
Personal transfers	–	–	–	–	–	–	–	–	–	–
Outward remittance flows	–	–	–	–	–	–	–	–	–	–
of which										
Compensation of employees	–	–	–	–	–	–	–	–	–	–
Personal transfers	–	–	–	–	–	–	–	–	–	–

a. Net FDI inflows US$0.69 billion, net ODA received US$0.29 billion in 2013.

Vanuatu

Population (thousands, 2013)	258.9
Population growth (avg. annual %, 2005–14)	2.4
Population density (people per sq km, 2014)	21.2
Labor force (thousands, 2013)	115.7
Unemployment rate (% of labor force)	–
Urban population (% of pop., 2014)	25.8
Surface area (thousands of sq km, 2014)	12.2
GNI, Atlas method (current US$ billions, 2014)	0.8
GNI per capita, Atlas method (current US$, 2014)	3,160.0
GDP growth (avg. annual %, 2011–14)	1.8
Poverty headcount ratio at national poverty line (% of pop.)	–
Age dependency ratio (% of working-age pop., 2014)	69.2
Account at a formal financial institution (% age 15+)	–
Mobile cellular subscriptions (per 100 people, 2014)	60.4
Internet users (per 100 people, 2014)	18.8

Migration

EMIGRATION

- Stock of emigrants, 2013: **8.4 thousands**
- Stock of emigrants as percentage of population, 2013: **3.3 percent**
- Top destination countries, 2013: New Caledonia, Australia, France, Solomon Islands, French Polynesia, Colombia, the United States, Kenya, Switzerland, Italy
- Tertiary-educated as a percentage of total emigrants in OECD countries, 2011: **29.5 percent**
- Tertiary-educated women as a percentage of total women emigrants in OECD countries, 2011: **33.8 percent**
- Number of refugees, 2014: Not available
- Second generation diaspora in Australia, Europe, and the United States, 2012: Not available

IMMIGRATION

- Stock of immigrants, 2013: **3.7 thousands**
- Stock of immigrants as percentage of population, 2013: **1.5 percent**
- Top source countries, 2013: Australia, France, New Zealand, New Caledonia, Fiji, the United States, Solomon Islands, the United Kingdom, China, Papua New Guinea
- Women as percentage of immigrants, 2013: **42.4 percent**
- Number of refugees, 2014: Not available

Remittances

US$ millions	2006	2007	2008	2009	2010	2011	2012	2013	2014	2015e
Inward remittance flows[a]	5	6	9	11	12	22	22	24	24	24
of which										
Compensation of employees	5	4	9	11	12	22	22	23	–	–
Personal transfers	0	1	0	0	0	0	0	0	–	–
Outward remittance flows	3	3	3	3	3	4	2	2	–	–
of which										
Compensation of employees	3	2	2	2	3	3	2	2	–	–
Personal transfers	0	0	0	0	1	1	1	1	–	–

a. Net FDI inflows US$0.06 billion, net ODA received US$0.09 billion in 2013.

Venezuela, República Bolivariana de

Population (millions, 2014)	30.7
Population growth (avg. annual %, 2005–14)	1.5
Population density (people per sq km, 2014)	34.8
Labor force (millions, 2014)	14.3
Unemployment rate (% of labor force, 2014)	8.6
Urban population (% of pop., 2014)	88.9
Surface area (thousands of sq km, 2014)	912.1
GNI, Atlas method (current US$ billions, 2012)	373.3
GNI per capita, Atlas method (current US$, 2012)	12,500.0
GDP growth (avg. annual %, 2011–14)	1.8
Poverty headcount ratio at national poverty line (% of pop., 2012)	25.4
Age dependency ratio (% of working-age pop., 2014)	52.7
Account at a formal financial institution (% age 15+)	56.9
Mobile cellular subscriptions (per 100 people, 2014)	99.0
Internet users (per 100 people, 2014)	57.0

Migration

EMIGRATION

- Stock of emigrants, 2013: **655.4 thousands**
- Stock of emigrants as percentage of population, 2013: **2.2 percent**
- Top destination countries, 2013: the United States, Spain, Italy, Colombia, Portugal, the Dominican Republic, Ecuador, Canada, Mexico, Argentina
- Tertiary-educated as a percentage of total emigrants in OECD countries, 2011: **44.4 percent**
- Tertiary-educated women as a percentage of total women emigrants in OECD countries, 2011: **46.0 percent**
- Number of refugees, 2014: **7,989**
- Second generation diaspora in Australia, Europe, and the United States, 2012: **85.7 thousands**

IMMIGRATION

- Stock of immigrants, 2013: **1,171.3 thousands**
- Stock of immigrants as percentage of population, 2013: **3.9 percent**
- Top source countries, 2013: Colombia, Spain, Portugal, Italy, Peru, Ecuador, the Syrian Arab Republic, Chile, the Dominican Republic, China
- Women as percentage of immigrants, 2013: **58.5 percent**
- Number of refugees, 2014: **173,551**

Remittances

US$ millions	2006	2007	2008	2009	2010	2011	2012	2013	2014	2015e
Inward remittance flows[a]	165	151	137	131	143	138	118	120	111	111
of which										
Compensation of employees	20	20	20	22	22	20	23	24	–	–
Personal transfers	145	131	117	109	121	118	95	96	–	–
Outward remittance flows	257	662	842	581	805	782	899	1,117	–	–
of which										
Compensation of employees	32	27	28	31	42	42	43	48	–	–
Personal transfers	225	635	814	550	763	740	856	1,069	–	–

a. Net FDI inflows US$6.93 billion, net ODA received US$0.04 billion in 2013.

Vietnam

MIDDLE INCOME

Population (millions, 2014)	90.7
Population growth (avg. annual %, 2005–14)	1.1
Population density (people per sq km, 2014)	292.6
Labor force (millions, 2014)	54.2
Unemployment rate (% of labor force, 2014)	2.3
Urban population (% of pop., 2014)	33.0
Surface area (thousands of sq km, 2014)	331.0
GNI, Atlas method (current US$ billions, 2014)	171.9
GNI per capita, Atlas method (current US$, 2014)	1,890.0
GDP growth (avg. annual %, 2011–14)	5.7
Poverty headcount ratio at national poverty line (% of pop., 2012)	17.2
Age dependency ratio (% of working-age pop., 2014)	42.3
Account at a formal financial institution (% age 15+)	30.9
Mobile cellular subscriptions (per 100 people, 2014)	147.1
Internet users (per 100 people, 2014)	48.3

Migration

EMIGRATION

- Stock of emigrants, 2013: **2,592.2 thousands**
- Stock of emigrants as percentage of population, 2013: **2.9 percent**
- Top destination countries, 2013: the United States, Australia, Canada, Germany, France, the Republic of Korea, the Czech Republic, Japan, Cambodia, China
- Tertiary-educated as a percentage of total emigrants in OECD countries, 2011: **27.5 percent**
- Tertiary-educated women as a percentage of total women emigrants in OECD countries, 2011: **25.2 percent**
- Number of refugees, 2014: **313,392**
- Second generation diaspora in Australia, Europe, and the United States, 2012: **623.8 thousands**

IMMIGRATION

- Stock of immigrants, 2013: **68.3 thousands**
- Stock of immigrants as percentage of population, 2013: **0.1 percent**
- Top source countries, 2013: Libya, Myanmar, China, Indonesia, the Lao People's Democratic Republic, Cambodia, the United States, Nepal, India, the United Kingdom
- Women as percentage of immigrants, 2013: **42.0 percent**
- Number of refugees, 2014: Not available

Remittances

US$ millions	2006	2007	2008	2009	2010	2011	2012	2013	2014	2015e
Inward remittance flows[a]	3,800	6,180	6,805	6,020	8,260	8,600	10,000	11,000	12,000	12,248
of which										
Compensation of employees	–	–	–	–	–	–	–	–	–	–
Personal transfers	–	–	–	–	–	–	–	–	–	–
Outward remittance flows	–	–	–	–	–	–	–	–	–	–
of which										
Compensation of employees	–	–	–	–	–	–	–	–	–	–
Personal transfers	–	–	–	–	–	–	–	–	–	–

a. Net FDI inflows US$8.90 billion, net ODA received US$4.08 billion in 2013.

Virgin Islands (U.S.)

Population (thousands, 2013)	104.2
Population growth (avg. annual %, 2005–14)	-0.4
Population density (people per sq km, 2014)	297.6
Labor force (thousands, 2013)	51.5
Unemployment rate (% of labor force)	–
Urban population (% of pop., 2014)	95.2
Surface area (thousands of sq km, 2014)	0.4
GNI, Atlas method (current US$ billions)	–
GNI per capita, Atlas method (current US$)	–
GDP growth (avg. annual %)	–
Poverty headcount ratio at national poverty line (% of pop.)	–
Age dependency ratio (% of working-age pop., 2014)	59.4
Account at a formal financial institution (% age 15+)	–
Mobile cellular subscriptions (per 100 people, 2005)	74.5
Internet users (per 100 people, 2014)	50.1

Migration

EMIGRATION

- Stock of emigrants, 2013: **4.2 thousands**
- Stock of emigrants as percentage of population, 2013: **4.0 percent**
- Top destination countries, 2013: Grenada, Antigua and Barbuda, the Dominican Republic, Puerto Rico, St. Kitts and Nevis, Cabo Verde, Sint Maarten (Dutch part), Greece, Curaçao, St. Lucia
- Tertiary-educated as a percentage of total emigrants in OECD countries, 2011: **27.8 percent**
- Tertiary-educated women as a percentage of total women emigrants in OECD countries, 2011: **33.4 percent**
- Number of refugees, 2014: Not available
- Second generation diaspora in Australia, Europe, and the United States, 2012: Not available

IMMIGRATION

- Stock of immigrants, 2013: **63.3 thousands**
- Stock of immigrants as percentage of population, 2013: **60.4 percent**
- Top source countries, 2013: the United States, St. Kitts and Nevis, Dominica, the Dominican Republic, Antigua and Barbuda, Puerto Rico, St. Lucia, Trinidad and Tobago, Haiti, Grenada
- Women as percentage of immigrants, 2013: **53.0 percent**
- Number of refugees, 2014: Not available

Remittances

US$ millions	2006	2007	2008	2009	2010	2011	2012	2013	2014	2015e
Inward remittance flows —	–	–	–	–	–	–	–	–	–	–
of which										
Compensation of employees	–	–	–	–	–	–	–	–	–	–
Personal transfers	–	–	–	–	–	–	–	–	–	–
Outward remittance flows	–	–	–	–	–	–	–	–	–	–
of which										
Compensation of employees	–	–	–	–	–	–	–	–	–	–
Personal transfers	–	–	–	–	–	–	–	–	–	–

West Bank and Gaza

Population (millions, 2014)	4.3
Population growth (avg. annual %, 2005–14)	2.8
Population density (people per sq km, 2014)	713.4
Labor force (millions, 2014)	1.1
Unemployment rate (% of labor force, 2014)	26.2
Urban population (% of pop., 2014)	75.0
Surface area (thousands of sq km, 2014)	6.0
GNI, Atlas method (current US$ billions, 2014)	13.1
GNI per capita, Atlas method (current US$, 2014)	3,060.0
GDP growth (avg. annual %, 2011–14)	4.1
Poverty headcount ratio at national poverty line (% of pop., 2011)	25.8
Age dependency ratio (% of working-age pop., 2014)	77.0
Account at a formal financial institution (% age 15+)	24.2
Mobile cellular subscriptions (per 100 people, 2014)	72.1
Internet users (per 100 people, 2014)	53.7

Migration

EMIGRATION

- Stock of emigrants, 2013: **4,018.2 thousands**
- Stock of emigrants as percentage of population, 2013: **96.4 percent**
- Top destination countries, 2013: Jordan, Lebanon, Saudi Arabia, Libya, the Syrian Arab Republic, the Arab Republic of Egypt, Algeria, the United Arab Emirates, the United States, Iraq
- Tertiary-educated as a percentage of total emigrants in OECD countries, 2011: **39.9 percent**
- Tertiary-educated women as a percentage of total women emigrants in OECD countries, 2011: **33.4 percent**
- Number of refugees, 2014: **5,246,932**
- Second generation diaspora in Australia, Europe, and the United States, 2012: Not available

IMMIGRATION

- Stock of immigrants, 2013: **256.5 thousands**
- Stock of immigrants as percentage of population, 2013: **6.2 percent**
- Top source countries, 2013: Israel, Jordan, Saudi Arabia, the Arab Republic of Egypt, Kuwait, the United Arab Emirates, Qatar, Oman, Bahrain, the United States
- Women as percentage of immigrants, 2013: **55.6 percent**
- Number of refugees, 2014: **2,051,096**

Remittances

US$ millions	2006	2007	2008	2009	2010	2011	2012	2013	2014	2015e
Inward remittance flows[a]	**464**	**599**	**741**	**755**	**927**	**1,142**	**1,737**	**1,499**	**2,182**	**2,331**
of which										
Compensation of employees	310	385	498	487	578	737	823	1,141	1,298	–
Personal transfers	154	213	242	268	349	405	914	358	884	–
Outward remittance flows	**7**	**8**	**8**	**8**	**18**	**48**	**48**	**54**	**37**	**–**
of which										
Compensation of employees	1	1	1	1	1	1	1	1	1	–
Personal transfers	6	7	7	7	17	47	47	53	36	–

a. Net FDI inflows US$0.19 billion, net ODA received US$2.61 billion in 2013.

Yemen, Rep.

Population (millions, 2014)	26.2
Population growth (avg. annual %, 2005–14)	2.7
Population density (people per sq km, 2014)	49.6
Labor force (millions, 2014)	7.6
Unemployment rate (% of labor force, 2014)	17.4
Urban population (% of pop., 2014)	34.0
Surface area (thousands of sq km, 2014)	528.0
GNI, Atlas method (current US$ billions, 2014)	33.3
GNI per capita, Atlas method (current US$, 2014)	1,300.0
GDP growth (avg. annual %, 2011–14)	-1.1
Poverty headcount ratio at national poverty line (% of pop., 2005)	34.8
Age dependency ratio (% of working-age pop., 2014)	76.6
Account at a formal financial institution (% age 15+)	6.4
Mobile cellular subscriptions (per 100 people, 2014)	68.5
Internet users (per 100 people, 2014)	22.5

Migration

EMIGRATION

- Stock of emigrants, 2013: **1,268.9 thousands**
- Stock of emigrants as percentage of population, 2013: **5.0 percent**
- Top destination countries, 2013: Saudi Arabia, the United Arab Emirates, Kuwait, the United States, Qatar, Israel, Libya, Bahrain, the United Kingdom, the Arab Republic of Egypt
- Tertiary-educated as a percentage of total emigrants in OECD countries, 2011: **14.4 percent**
- Tertiary-educated women as a percentage of total women emigrants in OECD countries, 2011: **9.8 percent**
- Number of refugees, 2014: **2,580**
- Second generation diaspora in Australia, Europe, and the United States, 2012: **7.3 thousands**

IMMIGRATION

- Stock of immigrants, 2013: **314.7 thousands**
- Stock of immigrants as percentage of population, 2013: **1.2 percent**
- Top source countries, 2013: Somalia, Sudan, the Arab Republic of Egypt, Iraq, Ethiopia, the West Bank and Gaza, the Syrian Arab Republic, South Sudan, Eritrea, Vietnam
- Women as percentage of immigrants, 2013: **40.7 percent**
- Number of refugees, 2014: **257,632**

Remittances

US$ millions	2006	2007	2008	2009	2010	2011	2012	2013	2014	2015e
Inward remittance flows[a]	**1,283**	**1,322**	**1,411**	**1,160**	**1,526**	**1,404**	**3,351**	**3,343**	**3,351**	**3,435**
of which										
Compensation of employees	–	–	–	–	–	–	–	–	–	–
Personal transfers	1,283	1,322	1,411	1,160	1,526	1,404	3,351	3,343	3,351	–
Outward remittance flows	**120**	**319**	**337**	**337**	**338**	**333**	**338**	**333**	**335**	**–**
of which										
Compensation of employees	80	278	289	289	289	289	289	289	289	–
Personal transfers	41	41	48	48	50	45	49	45	47	–

a. Net FDI inflows US$-0.13 billion, net ODA received US$1.00 billion in 2013.

Zambia

Population (millions, 2014)	15.7
Population growth (avg. annual %, 2005–14)	2.9
Population density (people per sq km, 2014)	21.1
Labor force (millions, 2014)	6.7
Unemployment rate (% of labor force, 2014)	13.3
Urban population (% of pop., 2014)	40.5
Surface area (thousands of sq km, 2014)	752.6
GNI, Atlas method (current US$ billions, 2014)	26.4
GNI per capita, Atlas method (current US$, 2014)	1,680.0
GDP growth (avg. annual %, 2011–14)	6.4
Poverty headcount ratio at national poverty line (% of pop., 2010)	60.5
Age dependency ratio (% of working-age pop., 2014)	96.1
Account at a formal financial institution (% age 15+)	31.3
Mobile cellular subscriptions (per 100 people, 2014)	67.3
Internet users (per 100 people, 2014)	17.3

Migration

EMIGRATION

- Stock of emigrants, 2013: **231.2 thousands**
- Stock of emigrants as percentage of population, 2013: **1.5 percent**
- Top destination countries, 2013: South Africa, Malawi, the United Kingdom, Zimbabwe, Botswana, Tanzania, the United States, Namibia, Australia, Mozambique
- Tertiary-educated as a percentage of total emigrants in OECD countries, 2011: **53.5 percent**
- Tertiary-educated women as a percentage of total women emigrants in OECD countries, 2011: **52.6 percent**
- Number of refugees, 2014: **309**
- Second generation diaspora in Australia, Europe, and the United States, 2012: **3.7 thousands**

IMMIGRATION

- Stock of immigrants, 2013: **98.9 thousands**
- Stock of immigrants as percentage of population, 2013: **0.6 percent**
- Top source countries, 2013: Angola, the Democratic Republic of Congo, Rwanda, Zimbabwe, Malawi, Burundi, India, Tanzania, the Republic of Congo, South Africa
- Women as percentage of immigrants, 2013: **49.5 percent**
- Number of refugees, 2014: **25,561**

Remittances

US$ millions	2006	2007	2008	2009	2010	2011	2012	2013	2014	2015e
Inward remittance flows[a]	58	59	68	41	44	46	73	54	58	59
of which										
Compensation of employees	–	–	–	–	–	–	–	–	–	–
Personal transfers	58	59	68	41	44	46	73	54	58	–
Outward remittance flows	115	124	139	66	68	70	97	77	81	–
of which										
Compensation of employees	23	28	29	29	29	29	29	29	29	–
Personal transfers	93	96	110	37	39	42	68	48	52	–

a. Net FDI inflows US$2.10 billion, net ODA received US$1.14 billion in 2013.

Zimbabwe

Population (millions, 2014)	15.2
Population growth (avg. annual %, 2005–14)	1.7
Population density (people per sq km, 2014)	39.4
Labor force (millions, 2014)	7.7
Unemployment rate (% of labor force, 2014)	5.4
Urban population (% of pop., 2014)	32.5
Surface area (thousands of sq km, 2014)	390.8
GNI, Atlas method (current US$ billions, 2014)	12.8
GNI per capita, Atlas method (current US$, 2014)	840.0
GDP growth (avg. annual %, 2011–14)	7.7
Poverty headcount ratio at national poverty line (% of pop., 2011)	72.3
Age dependency ratio (% of working-age pop., 2014)	80.5
Account at a formal financial institution (% age 15+)	17.2
Mobile cellular subscriptions (per 100 people, 2014)	80.8
Internet users (per 100 people, 2014)	19.9

Migration

EMIGRATION

- Stock of emigrants, 2013: **973.2 thousands**
- Stock of emigrants as percentage of population, 2013: **6.5 percent**
- Top destination countries, 2013: South Africa, the United Kingdom, Malawi, Australia, Botswana, Mozambique, the United States, Canada, New Zealand, Zambia
- Tertiary-educated as a percentage of total emigrants in OECD countries, 2011: **44.0 percent**
- Tertiary-educated women as a percentage of total women emigrants in OECD countries, 2011: **44.9 percent**
- Number of refugees, 2014: **22,455**
- Second generation diaspora in Australia, Europe, and the United States, 2012: **23.5 thousands**

IMMIGRATION

- Stock of immigrants, 2013: **361.0 thousands**
- Stock of immigrants as percentage of population, 2013: **2.4 percent**
- Top source countries, 2013: Mozambique, Malawi, Zambia, the United Kingdom, South Africa, Botswana, the Democratic Republic of Congo, Rwanda, Burundi
- Women as percentage of immigrants, 2013: **43.0 percent**
- Number of refugees, 2014: **6,066**

Remittances

US$ millions	2006	2007	2008	2009	2010	2011	2012	2013	2014	2015e
Inward remittance flows[a]	–	–	–	–	–	–	–	–	–	–
of which										
Compensation of employees	–	–	–	–	–	–	–	–	–	–
Personal transfers	–	–	–	–	–	–	–	–	–	–
Outward remittance flows	–	–	–	–	–	–	–	–	–	–
of which										
Compensation of employees	–	–	–	–	–	–	–	–	–	–
Personal transfers	–	–	–	–	–	–	–	–	–	–

a. Net FDI inflows US$0.40 billion, net ODA received US$0.81 billion in 2013.

Glossary

World Development Indicators

Age dependency ratio is the ratio of dependents–people younger than 15 or older than 64—to the working-age population—those ages 15–64. Data are shown as the proportion of dependents per 100 working-age population. (Eurostat, United Nations Population Division, national statistical offices, Eurostat, United Nations Statistical Division, United States Census Bureau, and World Bank)

GDP growth is average annual growth in real gross domestic product at purchaser prices. GDP is the sum of gross value added by all resident producers in the economy plus any product taxes and minus any subsidies not included in the value of the products. It is calculated without deductions for depreciation of fabricated assets or for depletion and degradation of natural resources. (World Bank and Organisation for Economic Co-operation and Development)

GNI is gross national income. It is calculated as gross domestic product (GDP) plus net receipts of primary income (employee compensation and investment income) from abroad. GDP is the sum of value added by all resident producers plus any product taxes (less subsidies) not included in the valuation of output. (World Bank)

GNI per capita is gross national income (GNI) converted to U.S. dollars using the World Bank Atlas method divided by midyear population. GNI is the sum of value added by all resident producers plus any product taxes (less subsidies) not included in the valuation of output plus net receipts of primary income (compensation of employees and property income) from abroad.

GNI, calculated in national currency, is usually converted to U.S. dollars at official exchange rates for comparisons across economies. The World Bank Atlas method is used to smooth fluctuations in prices and exchange rates. It averages the exchange rate for a given year and the two preceding years, adjusted for differences in rates of inflation between the country and the Euro area, Japan, the United Kingdom, and the United States. (World Bank)

Internet users are individuals who have used the Internet (from any location) in the last 12 months. Internet can be used via a computer, mobile phone, personal digital assistant, games machine, digital TV, etc. (International Telecommunication Union)

Labor force comprises people ages 15 and older who meet the International Labour Organization definition of the economically active population: all people who supply labor for the production of goods and services during a specified period. It includes both the employed and the unemployed. (International Labour Organization, World Bank)

Mobile cellular subscriptions are subscriptions to a public mobile telephone service that provide access to the PSTN using cellular technology. The indicator includes (and is split into) the number of postpaid subscriptions, and the number of active prepaid accounts (i.e. that have been used during the last three months). The indicator applies to all mobile cellular subscriptions that offer voice communications. It excludes subscriptions via data cards or USB modems, subscriptions to public mobile data services, private trunked mobile radio, telepoint, radio paging, and telemetry services. (International Telecommunication Union)

Personal Remittances Received refers to personal transfers and compensation of employees. They comprise current transfers in cash or kind received by resident households from nonresident households and wages and salaries earned by nonresident workers or resident workers employed by nonresident entities. (International Monetary Fund and World Bank)

Population is the midyear estimate of all residents regardless of legal status citizenship, except for refugees not permanently settled in the country of asylum who are generally considered part of the population of their country of origin. (United Nations Population Division, national statistical offices, Eurostat, United Nations Statistical Division, United States Census Bureau, and World Bank)

Population density is the midyear population divided by land area. (World Bank, Food and Agriculture Organization)

Population growth is the average annual growth of midyear population. (World Bank)

Poverty headcount ratio is the percentage of the population living below the national poverty lines. National estimates are based on population-weighted subgroup estimates from household surveys. (World Bank)

Surface area is a country's total area, including areas under inland bodies of water and some coastal waterways. (Food and Agriculture Organization)

Unemployment rate refers to the share of the labor force that is without work but available for and seeking employment. (International Labour Organization)

Urban population refers to people living in urban areas as defined by national statistical offices. (United Nations, World Bank)

Financial Inclusion Database – Findex

Account at a formal financial institution denotes the percentage of respondents who report having an account (by themselves or together with someone else) at a bank or another type of financial institution in the past 12 months. (World Bank)

Other Data Sources

International Migrant Stock refer to the mid-year estimate of the number of people living in a country or area other than the one in which they were born or, in the absence of such data, the number of people of foreign citizenship. (United Nations, Department of Economic and Social Affairs, Population Division)

Refugee is someone who "owing to a well-founded fear of being persecuted for reasons of race, religion, nationality, membership of a particular social group or political opinion, is outside the country of his nationality, and is unable to, or owing to such fear, is unwilling to avail himself of the protection of that country," according to the 1951 Refugee Convention (UNHCR). The United Nations Relief and Works Agency defines a Palestine refugee as a person "whose normal place of residence was Mandatory Palestine between June 1946 and May 1948, who lost both their homes and means of livelihood as a result of the 1948 Arab-Israeli conflict." (UNRWA)

Second generation diaspora refers to the native-born children of immigrants for those children aged 15 years and over with at least one parent foreign-born living in an OECD country. In the United States, second generation refers to all persons born in the United States with one or both parents born outside the country. (OECD, and the United States Census Bureau)